The Development of Social Cognition and Communication

The Development of Social Cognition and Communication

Edited by

Bruce D. Homer
New York University

Catherine S. Tamis-LeMonda
New York University

2005

LAWRENCE ERLBAUM ASSOCIATES, PUBLISHERS
Mahwah, New Jersey London

Senior Editor: Lori Stone
Editorial Assistant: Rebecca Larsen
Cover Design: Kathryn Houghtaling Lacey
Textbook Production Manager: Paul Smolenski
Composition: LEA Book Production
Text and Cover Printer: Hamilton Printing Company

This book was typeset in 10/12 Palatino.
The heads were typeset in Futura.

Lawrence Erlbaum Associates, Inc., Publishers
10 Industrial Avenue
Mahwah, New Jersey 07430
www.erlbaum.com

Library of Congress Cataloging-in-Publication Data

The development of social cognition and communication / edited by Bruce D. Homer and Catherine S. Tamis-LeMonda
p. cm.
Based on a conference held in Oct. 2001 at New York University.
Includes bibliographical references and index.
ISBN 0-8058-4322-1 (casebound : alk. paper)
1. Child psychology—Congresses. 2. Cognition in children—Congresses. 3. Social perception in children—Congresses. 4. Children—Language—Congresses. 5. Philosophy of mind in children—Congresses. I. Homer, Bruce D. II. Tamis-LeMonda, Catherine S. (Catherine Susan), 1958–
BF721.D428 2005
155.4'13—dc22 2005040252
CIP

Books published by Lawrence Erlbaum Associates are printed on acid-free paper, and their bindings are chosen for strength and durability.

Printed in the United States of America
10 9 8 7 6 5 4 3 2 1

For Marc H. Bornstein,
mentor and friend.
—Catherine Tamis-Lemonda

To my daughter Talia,
for teaching me.
—Bruce Homer

Contents

II: Intentionality and Communication

III: Theory of Mind and Pedagogy

IV: Narrative and Autobiographical Memory

Preface

THE DEVELOPMENT OF SOCIAL COGNITION AND COMMUNICATION

Broadly construed, the study of developmental psychology has been dominated by two approaches. The first, founded on work by Piaget, has emphasized the role of cognitive processes that occur *within* the child, such as representation and knowledge construction. The second, building on the work of Vygotsky, has emphasized the role of external, social factors, such as dyadic engagements and the acquisition of cultural tools. Although Piaget recognized the importance of social experience in development and Vygotsky recognized the role of internal cognitive factors in development, with a few notable exceptions, followers of these two giants have focused almost exclusively on either the social or the cognitive aspects of development. Recent work in the field of developmental psychology has brought together these two theoretical traditions by assigning equal importance to the individual child and to the social environment in which the child is embedded. It is from this theoretical perspective that the contributors to this volume were asked to address the issue of the interconnectedness of social cognition and communication in early development.

The impetus for this book was a two-day conference held in October, 2001, at New York University. The conference brought together an international group of scholars with expertise from various sub-disciplines of developmental psychology. Each of the scholars was asked to prepare a paper addressing the interplay between communication and cognitive development during the first three years of life. The authors of this volume presented preliminary versions of their papers and engaged in lively discussions about the issues raised during their talks. As an outgrowth of these conversations, the participants of this conference reworked their papers in ways that built upon and complemented the thinking of one another, the result being the current collection of chapters contained in this book.

Each chapter in this volume examines a unique aspect of the interplay between children's cognitive development and their social interactions. The book is organized into four thematic sections, each of which is preceded by an integrative overview by the co-editors of this volume. The first section, *Language and Cognition*, presents three chapters that examine the function of language in young children's lives. The second section, *Intentionality and Communication*, presents five chapters that probe young children's understanding of intentions and their verbal and non-verbal communication. The third section, *Theory of Mind and Pedagogy*, presents three chapters that explore how developments in cognitive and communicative skills transform the ways in which children participate in the process of teaching and learning. The final section, *Narrative and Autobiographical Memory*, presents three chapters that examine the effects of a particularly important mode of communication (narrative) on young children's developing conception of themselves and their world. As a whole, this volume presents the most current research and theory on the interdependence of social cognition and communication in the early years of life.

This book was only possible due to the efforts and contributions of many people. In particular, the editors would like to express their thanks to the following organizations whose financial support made the conference and subsequent book possible: International Visitors Program of the Provost's Office of New York University, The Office of Program Development of the Steinhardt School of Education of New York University, The Dean of the Steinhardt School of Education of New York University, The National Science Foundation, and Lawrence Erlbaum Associates. We also thank Jerome Bruner for his enthusiastic participation in the Conference that formed the impetus for this work, and for his subsequent support and insightful comments during the preparation of this volume. Bruce D. Homer would like to thank his mentors, David R. Olson and Katherine Nelson, whose work and guidance have fostered his own interest in the relation between the cultural and the cognitive in development. Catherine S. Tamis-LeMonda expresses gratitude for the years of support offered by her mentor, colleague, and friend, Marc H. Bornstein, whose interest in the social and cultural contexts of language development and cognition served as the impetus for her own research in this area.

Foreword

David R. Olson
Ontario Institute for Studies in Education of the University of Toronto

As recently as a decade ago I could cite approvingly Richard Hughes suggestion in his classic *A high wind in Jamaica* (1928) that "You can no more think like a baby than you can think like a bee." Homer and Tamis-LeMonda's volume reports that considerable progress has been made both in understanding "what it feels like" to be a baby—by examining the expressions of emotion they respond to—and "how babies think"—by examining the range of thoughts and feelings they are willing to ascribe to themselves and others. The burden of the book is to demonstrate that the development of thinking and feeling is linked to the communicative routines and language that children share with others. The authors who contributed to this volume—a veritable who's who of leading researchers in the field—demonstrate in a variety of intriguing ways the dramatic congruity between the thoughts and feelings, plans and goals that infants recognize in themselves and those they can recognize and attribute to others. Cognitive development, in this important domain, is identical to social development.

The authors and editors succeed in making explicit the links between the communicative routines that parents engage in with their children and the intentional states that children recognize in themselves and others, in a sense, making good of Vygotsky's suggestion that the personal has its origins in the interpersonal. Stated too crudely this would reduce to the claim, long abandoned, that development is merely socialization. Rather as the studies in this volume demonstrate, the children are deeply involved in the construction of their own representational states, going through a series of attempts or "hypotheses" as to how to achieve a shared understanding of the beliefs, goals and intentions of themselves and others.

The process is one of "conscienceization" of bringing into consciousness, the processes and properties that are to be found in, that is implicit in, more primitive perception and action. The authors are in general agreement that the acquisition of language, and in some cases a meta-language, is important in distinguishing the thing from the representation of the thing and making the representation, itself, the object of the conceptual activity previously restricted to the thing itself. Such distancing provides the basis for all conceptual thought. Furthermore, the very categories for reflection are drawn both from the sensitivity of the infant to the recurrent patterns or structure in the environment and to the categories offered in the language of the adult. Hence, there is no contradiction in claiming both that the learner builds his or her cognitions out of their own resources and that the cognitions so constructed are social and shared with others.

A sign of the progress in the study of children's minds is the range of traditional topics from attachment theory to pedagogy that come to be seen in a new way through the prism of the social-cognitive theories discussed in this book. Thus, emotional development is seen in terms of the recognition of emotion in others (Walker-Andrews), the development of intentions in the recognition of intentions in others (Baldwin), and the acquisition of language in joint attention between infant and caretaker (Akhtar). The origins of planned action is traced to the representational powers of language (Jacques & Zelazo) and the shift from spontaneous actions into intentional ones is linked to the practice of framing them in discourse (Tamis-LeMonda & Adolph). Children's learning to use symbols is transformed into learning *about* symbols as objects in their own right (Homer & Nelson), patience and altruism come to be seen in terms of interpersonal understanding (Moore), and the study of children's memory takes on a new social dimension when construed in terms of social narratives (Brockmeier, Fivush & Haden).

Of equal interest is the way that the new understanding of children's minds has come to give new direction to the study of schooling and readiness for schooling. Schooling is in large part discourse about beliefs and the correct representations of those beliefs. Thus, concepts of mind play a crucial role for school readiness (Astington & Pelletier), as well as in children's (and teacher's) understanding of just what teaching and learning are (Frye & Ziv), and how alternative gestural representation interact with more verbal pedagogical ones in producing conceptual change (Goldin-Meadow). While an important part of culture is deliberately communicated in school contexts, even more is communicated indirectly through learning a natural language (Nelson) and consequently varies from culture to culture (Leichtman & Wang).

Collections of papers, even on a single topic, often lead authors to accentuate their differences and overlook their common intellectual commitments. Homer and Tamis-LeMonda have performed an admirable service in bringing together this collection of researchers, and in providing useful introductions and summaries to the sections of the volume as well as to the individual papers. While we may never know what, precisely, it feels like to be either a baby or a bee, neither are children's minds as opaque as they once seemed to be. As this volume shows, infants are superbly preadapted to the demands of the culture. Perhaps we should not be so surprised for culture is little more than that which children find easy to learn.

Part I

Language and Cognition

It is appropriate to begin a volume on the interconnectedness of communication and cognition in early child development with a section on language. Debate over the effects of language on cognition has a long history in a number of different fields, including linguistics, anthropology, philosophy and psychology. One extreme view (e.g., as expressed in the "strong" Sapir-Whorf Hypothesis) suggests that cognition is completely molded by language, and that we understand the world based on the way in which our culture's language dissects nature. Although anthropological and developmental research has not supported this strong view on the influence of language, there is a growing body of evidence to support a more moderate or "weak" version. In the moderate version, the focus is not so much on the structure of language per se, but rather on the socio-cultural uses of language. Many of the researchers and theorists who adopt this view have been influenced by Vygotsky's notion that language is a cultural tool that mediates human action, including thought. According to Vygotsky, "higher-order" cognitive functions are passed on to children from their culture through language.

The three chapters in this section all emphasize the importance of language in cognitive development by focusing on the ways in which language enables new modes of communication and cognition. All of the chapters characterize language acquisition as being more than just learning words, it is learning how to do things with language. In her chapter, Nelson provides an insightful overview of the role of language in children's cognitive development. She describes three main functions of language for children: language provides new "objects of contemplation," it provides a means of making cognitive processes social, and it provides children with access to knowledge accumulated by their culture. In the second chapter, Homer and Nelson review theory and research on children's acquisition of symbolic understanding. Homer and Nelson expand on the language functions raised in Nelson's opening chapter. They contend that language provides the social connection that is required for the use of symbols, provides a means of creating the "cognitive distance" required to view objects as symbols, and provides a means for parents to "scaffold" children's symbolic activities. In the final chapter of this section, Jacques and Zelazo examine the role of language in children's development of cognitive flexibility, which they define as the ability to consider multiple conflicting representations of a single event or object. The authors argue that language, particularly the use of labels, is fundamental to the development of cognitive flexibility in the preschool years.

THE FUNCTIONS OF LANGUAGE

In her chapter entitled, *Cognitive Functions of Language in Early Child Development*, Nelson points out that, despite whatever biological predisposition that may exist, learning language is a difficult and often frustrating process for young children. Nelson asks the deceptively simple question, why do children bother to learn language in the first place? She suggests that by understanding how language functions in children's lives, we can begin to understand the benefits that children derive from learning language.

Drawing on Dennett (1994), Nelson argues that language provides three main advantages for children. First, language creates a new set of "objects to contemplate," which includes abstract or imaginary concepts that cannot be derived solely from observation of the physical world. A second function of language is to allow thoughts and ideas to be expressed and contemplated by more than one person: By being able to express and debate ideas, cognition is no longer a solitary experience, but instead becomes a social activity. Finally, communicative exchanges enabled by language allow children access to the vast store of knowledge that has been accumulated by their culture. Because of language, we do not have to learn everything on our own, but instead we can take advantage of the experiences of others. Nelson concludes that the communicative and cognitive functions of language are inextricably intertwined, and more developmental research is needed on the role of language as a cultural tool of thought.

LANGUAGE AND SYMBOLIC UNDERSTANDING

In the second chapter, *Seeing Objects as Symbols and Symbols as Objects: Language and the Development of Dual Representation*, Homer and Nelson examine the role of language in children's development of symbolic understanding. They begin by noting that researchers have used the term *symbol* to refer to several different things, all of which fall under Peirce's (1955) category of *signs*. Peirce identified three different types of sign: *icons*, which rely on similarity for meaning; *indices*, which rely on temporal or spatial proximity for meaning; and *symbols*, which are arbitrary and rely on social convention for meaning. Homer and Nelson suggest that within any domain, children initially use iconic or indexical signs before they are able to use symbols. They support this claim by providing examples of the transition from iconic/indexical to symbolic sign use in the domains of language learning and literacy.

The authors extend this discussion to children's development of "dual representation," which entails understanding a sign as both a representation and an object. DeLoache (2000) has found dual representation to be difficult for children when signs are salient as objects. For example, when a model is used to represent a room, the model is a salient "toy" for children and consequently is difficult to see as a representation. Homer and Nelson argue that language facilitates children's ability to engage in dual representation in a number of ways. First, language provides the "cognitive distance" that allows symbols to be seen as objects. Second, language provides a means of making the social connection that is required for children to acquire their culture's symbol systems. Finally, language provides a means by which children's symbolic actions can be "scaffolded" by adults who either model or verbally direct children's symbolic activities. Homer and Nelson conclude by considering children's ability to dual-represent linguistic signs. They argue that in the same way that language facilitates the dual representation of physical signs, writing facilitates the dual representation of linguistic signs, thereby allowing language to become an "object of thought."

LANGUAGE AND COGNITIVE FLEXIBILITY

In the final chapter of this section entitled, *On the Possible Roots of Cognitive Flexibility*, Jacques and Zelazo examine how language, particularly labels, facilitate the emergence of cognitive flexibility. Cognitive flexibility, which is the ability to simultaneously hold conflicting representations of a single object or event, is a critical element of various cognitive achievements, including theory of mind and set shifting (an aspect of executive functions). The authors review literature on cognitive flexibility and suggest the importance of distinguishing between studies that use deductive measures of cognitive flexibility and those that use inductive measures. In deductive tasks, children are provided with all of the information that they need to solve the problem. For example, children are asked to sort cards with pictures that vary on two dimensions (e.g., color and shape). Before each trial, the children are told that they are playing the "color game" and that red cards go in one box whereas blue cards go in the other. After a certain period, there is a shift to the "shape game" in which children must stop sorting by color and instead sort by shape. Young children do not have the cognitive flexibility to make the shift between sorting by color to sorting by shape, even if they are told the "rules" of the shape game before each trial. In inductive tasks, children are required to make one or more inference about how to solve the problem. For example, in the *Flexible Item Selection Task* (FIST), children are shown a set of three cards with pictures that vary along three dimensions (e.g., color, shape and size). The children are asked to choose two cards that "go together." They are then asked to choose two cards that "go together in a different way." The children are not told explicitly what dimensions to use to group the cards, but instead they must induce the rules themselves.

Jacques and Zelazo provide a comprehensive review of the literature on children's cognitive flexibility as measured by these two types of tasks and find that children succeed on the deductive tasks at a younger age than they do on the inductive tasks. They argue that this difference is due in part to the fact that the inductive tasks provide children with labels (e.g., "color game," "red" and "blue") that facilitate children's performance. They support this claim by reviewing their own and other experiments' research on the effects of labels on cognitive flexibility using both inductive and deductive tasks. In general, the studies have found that in both types of tasks, labels significantly improved children's cognitive flexibility. Jacques and Zelazo provide a number of possible explanations for how language is affecting cognitive flexibility (e.g., by providing psychological distance, or by making the representations explicit), but they conclude that more research is needed to fully understand the function of language in the development of this important cognitive ability.

SUMMARY

The three chapters in this section provide an overview of the interconnectedness of developments in children's linguistic and cognitive abilities. The chapters focus on the functions of language for children and identify the ways in which children's linguistic developments enable new modes of cognition and communication. Developing the ability to represent the world with words and to communicate with others through language transforms children's ways of being in the world.

REFERENCES

DeLoache, J. S. (2000). Dual representation and young children's use of scale models. *Child Development, 71*(2), 329–338.

Dennett, D. (1994). Language and intelligence. In J. Khalfa (Ed.), *What is intelligence?* (pp. 161–178). Cambridge: Cambridge University Press.

Peirce, C. S. (1955). Logic as semiotic: The theory of signs. In J. Buchler (Ed.), *The philosophical writings of Peirce* (pp. 98–110). New York: Dover Books.

Chapter 1

Cognitive Functions of Language in Early Childhood

Katherine Nelson
City University of New York Graduate Center

Language learning is not necessarily fun; it is often frustrating. But most children persevere. Although language is in some way (that no one yet understands exactly or completely) biologically as well as culturally prepared, its acquisition nonetheless requires a long period of development, and considerable effort on the part of the child who is learning it, as well as on the part of those—mostly parents—in the teaching roles. Surely there must be a payoff for the child during this early period in order to sustain the effort. Therefore it is reasonable to ask what the child can do with language that he or she could not do without it. Why bother to learn? The assumption here is that language is not rewarding in and of itself but of what it makes possible on two fronts: communication and cognition.

The progress children make in learning language is of course a major focus of concern for parents and professionals in the early years of a child's life. How language is learned is also a major focus of research in linguistics, psycholinguistics, developmental psychology, sociolinguistics, cognitive science, and related fields. Much attention has been directed to questions of how much and what kind of special biological preparation or social tutoring is required in its learning. For example, studies of the acquisition of sound structure—prosody and phonology—have uncovered hitherto unsuspected capacities for discriminating language patterns in the first year of life, indicating special sensitivity to linguistic information (Jusczyk, 1997).

For all the attention to early language little has been directed to how language functions in the lives of young children and what benefits children derive from learning it. Moreover, for the hard questions of how children make sense of what they hear, researchers have mostly narrowed their attention to the first 10, 50 or 500 nouns that children produce during the second year, as though "language" consisted mainly of naming things. There are multiple theories and mountains of data competing for explanations of these developments but little light has been shed on how children use the forms they learn, or how these uses serve cognitive and communicative needs.

It would appear to a naïve observer scanning the educational and psychological literature that the main reason for a child to learn a first language is to later become literate, that is, to be able to learn to read that language when the child enters school. To set up this accomplishment parents and preschools are urged to talk to their young children and to read stories to them from the moment of birth or before. Largely neglected is what the child on the receiving end of this pre-literate concern and constant talk is doing with language between 1 and 5 years of age. Viewing the child as a language-*user* has the prospect of shedding light on both how language may serve the child's purposes and on the process of learning itself. The assumption here is that language function and language learning are intricately related in development.

Consider a claim from the philosopher and cognitive scientist Daniel Dennett commenting on the nature of human intelligence:

> The advent of language ... created a whole new class of objects-to-contemplate, verbally embodied surrogates that could be reviewed in any order at any pace. And this opened up a new dimension of self-improvement—all one had to do was to learn to savour one's own mistakes ... [other primates] never dispute over attributions, and ask for the grounds for each others' conclusions. No wonder their comprehension is so limited. Ours would be, too, if we had to generate it all on our own. (1994, pp. 177–178)

There are three claims made by Dennett in this passage. First, language creates new objects of contemplation that the individual may use in thinking, and thus in modifying behavior to solve problems. These surrogates may include abstractions that have no counterpart in the observable physical world, but play a part in folk and formal theorizing about the world; and they may be entirely imaginary, thereby opening up a world of fantasy. Second is the advantage of language as a social tool of thought, where explanations and theories can be challenged and tested. Finally, these advantages enlarge our knowledge because we do not have to do it all on our own; we can learn from others.

These are profound differences, that differentiate humans from other primates, and they also differentiate children from their former infant selves. The impact of language with respect to these differences is, I think, greatly underestimated in current developmental theories. Rather, there is a tendency among professionals as well as parents to take what children say as simply expressing what they *already* "know" or "think." Language then is taken as a communicative tool but not as a cognitive tool. It is seen as a mode of learning from others but not as a mode of thinking for oneself.

In this chapter I want to consider how children move toward the advantages that Dennett specifies as they move through the language learning process. I suspect that these advantages gradually dawn upon the child who begins with quite different interests. Therefore I think it important to question how the functions of language for the young child are related to issues of the forms learned, beginning with the acquisition of words and the concepts they impute, and continuing with cognitive functions of language as a representational system, both a cognitive tool and a medium for the communication of knowledge between speakers. The first section to follow considers the relation of words and concepts in the light of current theories about young children's learning of words.

WORDS AND CONCEPTS: THEORETICAL ISSUES

Classic Developmental Views of Language and Thought

Textbooks in developmental psychology tend to consider the relation between language and thought in terms of two classic but quite different developmental theories: those of Piaget and Vygotsky. Piaget (1962) viewed children's first words as revealing the nature of their nascent symbol constructions, which he saw as diffuse and idiosyncratic. He believed that individual symbols preceded the onset of the semiotic function at the end of the second year, when word meanings began to conform more closely to the referents of the language in use, but that it was not until school age that children acquired the logically based concepts that language was presumed to encode. Moreover, Piaget viewed children's language as primarily egocentric in function during the preschool years. In line with the assumption that early words expressed individually constructed meanings, conversations of 3- and 4-year-olds were seen as expressing personal meanings unadapted to an audience. Language for the young child, in this conception, serves to express unsocialized, individualistic meanings derived from preconceptual thought structures. Because Piaget believed that language expressed thought, and that it had no role in the formation of cognitive categories, his stance implied that one could analyze the child's thought by analyzing the child's speech. His early books on the child's conception of reality were based on this assumption, and provide rich examples of children's discussions of various topics revealing, in Piaget's view, startling differences in ontologies compared to the adult's (Piaget, 1929).

Vygotsky's view of the child's early language is usually posed as opposite to Piaget's. Yet Vygotsky also believed that the young child's concepts lacked the logical basis of adult concepts and that their words therefore had different meanings than the adults'. He proposed that children went through a series of stages in achieving more adult-like conceptual structures. But his main point was quite different from Piaget's. He viewed children's use of language as social and communicative from the outset, beginning on a different trajectory from the child's developing cognitive structures.

The classic disagreement between Vygotsky (1962) and Piaget (1926) on the question of the significance of egocentric or private speech reflects the major contrast between them. For Vygotsky the onset of private speech at about 4 years indicated the coming together of speech and cognition, which had previously been on separate tracks. At this point the child begins to use speech to direct action and thought, that is, for cognitive purposes of the self, eventually going underground to become "inner speech" or speech for thinking. Moreover, once language and thought come together Vygotsky's theory allows for the mediation of language in thought, that is, the development of preconcepts into adult-like concepts through the vehicle of language and its uses. This process follows the general external to internal scheme that Vygotsky put forth as a general genetic law of cultural development. "Any function in the child's cultural development appears twice on two planes … first it appears between people as an interpsychological category, and then within the child as an intrapsychological category" (cited by Wertsch, 1985, p. 60). The cultural development of "higher order" cognitive functions includes attention, memory, and concepts in Vygotsky's sense. It is important to note that this theory does not simply envision a transfer of concepts from one mind to another, but rather a transactional process whereby the child takes part in social interactions that involve higher levels of thought than he or she is presently capable of, and that through these social processes begins the separate internalization process of working through the higher level for his or her own cognitive functions.

These two classic positions on the relation of language and thought in development can be summarized as follows: For Piaget language expresses the individual child's thought but does not necessarily communicate to others and does not change the nature of thought. For Vygotsky early speech is primarily communicative but is not functionally connected to thought, whereas higher-order thought is mediated through interpersonal processes using symbolic language. Neither theorist gave much attention to how language might be learned, or how its learning might affect the younger child's thinking or communicative processes. More recent theorizing in the development of cognition and communication has generally followed in these pathways laid out more than 60 years ago. As the quotation from Dennett in the previous section suggests, there is a need for rethinking these pathways, and especially for considering the interactive processes that Vygotsky emphasized in relation to new issues of learning and using language in the early years.

Forming New "Objects-to-Contemplate": Are Concepts Prior to Words?

Most current conceptions of language and language development emphasize language as the expression of thought with little or no consideration of its possible role in the formulation of thought. This broadly held stance (similar to Piaget's position) may be viewed in terms of the different positions that theorists of widely varying perspectives have taken on the relation of word and concept. The standard literature in philosophy, cognitive and developmental psychology, and linguistics, contains many explicit statements of the position that concepts precede words in evolution and development. For example, Donald's (1991) position with respect to the evolution of cognition and language is stated thus: "The invention of symbols, including words, must have *followed* an advance in thought skills, and was an integral part of the evolution of [mental] model building" (p. 219). Similarly, Damasio (1999) in his book on consciousness states: "Of necessity, concepts precede words and sentences in both the evolution of the species and the daily experience of each and every one of us" (p. 184).

Scholars of child language concur on the developmental level, as seen in P. Bloom's insistence that language is "a tool for the communication of ideas. It is not a mechanism that gives rise to the capacity to generate and appreciate those ideas in the first place" (P. Bloom, 2000, p.

258). Lois Bloom (no relation) agrees: "Children learn language for acts of expression, in the effort to make known to others what their own thoughts and feelings are about" (L. Bloom, 2000, p. 22).

The import of these varying statements is that words are used to express meanings and have *no independent meaning* beyond that of the concepts they symbolize. It seems to follow automatically (as in P. Bloom's statement) that thought is independent of language. On the face of it this must be true; it is almost a tautology. This relation is represented in the classic semiotic triangle displaying the relation of word, object, and concept, shown in Fig. 1.1 (based on Ogden & Richards, 1923/1946).

Different disciplines may interpret the relationship in Fig. 1.1 in their own terms. In the case of the *linguistic interpretation* the relation of word and object is mediated through the concept. There is no real problem here if the concept is assumed somehow attached to the word in the semantic system. The question is how it becomes attached, and nativist theorists see the process as necessarily universal. Macnamara (1982) made this clear in his assumption that lexical concepts must be the same for all language users, and Fodor (1975) proposed the language of thought as the necessary basis for language on the grounds that we must all be biologically endowed with at least the basic lexical concepts in order to map them onto the language to be learned. Chomsky (1988) endorsed this claim for even such abstract social concepts as "persuade." Of course linguists do not have to take a nativist line; Saussure (1959/1915) and his structuralist successors initiated the ideas behind the semiotic triangle without the implication of the biological basis of lexical universals.

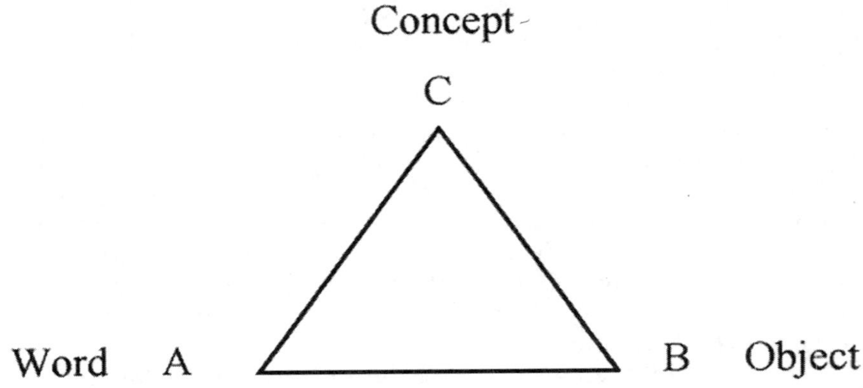

FIG. 1.1. The basic semiotic triangle (based on Ogden & Richards, 1923; reprinted from Nelson, 2002).

In the *evolutionary interpretation* of Fig. 1.1 humans must have had concepts that they wanted to communicate before they invented words to symbolize those concepts, as Donald, quoted earlier, states. This conjecture fits for words referring to objects, in that people might want to refer to, say, tigers in their absence. However, words such as kinship terms (e.g., *brother, mother, cousin*) depend themselves on symbolic relations. Is it likely that the people who invented language in the beginning all had the same concept of *brother* before inventing the word to express it? Did the concept include or exclude brother-in-law (which kind?), or adopted siblings? Language is rife with common words like these that, as anthropologists have documented, vary across cultures and even across different situations (see Lakoff 1987 for many examples, especially the concept of *mother*). As translators have assured us, there are few, if any, universal sets of concepts that are mapped onto words across all languages. Thus, although in the general evolutionary/historical/cultural sense, the statement that concepts precede words and not the reverse must be true, in any particular case it may not be so. Language uses often define or establish concepts and conceptual boundaries for the speakers in a community.

In the *developmental interpretation* of the claim it is asserted that children must have concepts in order to map words onto them to begin with. I endorse this version: indeed I staked out a claim of this kind (Nelson, 1973a, 1974). But in these works I also pointed out that children's concepts might be quite *different* from the adult's, and different in interesting ways, revealing something about children's preverbal thought (see Mandler, 2000; Nelson & Ware, 2002; see also Vygotsky, 1962). The problem of differences in concepts tends to be set aside in today's word learning literature as uninteresting or irrelevant, but I believe it is central to our understanding of the relation of words and concepts and to how children learn the meaning of words. Children are extremely clever at picking up words and figuring out what adults are referring to with them, and how words are used in certain contexts (Tomasello & Kruger, 1992). Yet aside from basic level object concepts this facility does not guarantee that children take the words of the adult language to refer to the same things (real world or imagined) as adults do, nor in any particular case to relate to the same concepts. Both Piaget and Vygotsky recognized this problem of meaning differences, but they drew different implications from it. Piaget believed that children needed to develop the logical structures that order concepts, while Vygotsky believed that children needed guidance in moving from spontaneous to scientific concepts.

The problem is that adults use words to communicate *their* concepts; the child's problem then is to match—or construct—a concept that *fits the context* of the adult's use. In ordinary communicative contexts the child may have available an unnamed concept—or an object or a picture of an object—that seems to fit the adult's use of a new word, or she may not. If not, the child's burden is to construct, on the basis of evidence from current context, ongoing discourse, and general background knowledge, a meaning that fits the adult's use. Of course such discourse is a two-person game, and parents generally attempt to clarify the child's understanding, if a confusion is evident. Parents are often quite good at guessing the child's meaning of a word, even when it is used in an anomalous way.

From this last perspective it can be seen that Fig. 1.1 is incomplete in considering only the abstract relation between object, word, and concept. When we recognize that language is necessarily based on *shared* conceptual meanings, the problem becomes more opaque. Unless it is assumed that child and adult see the world in the same way and have the same store of concepts to be named, the problem is one of aligning *different* concepts to the same words. Figure 1.2 represents an extended semiotic triangle that exemplifies this essentially social-cultural problem of meaning matching. To solve this problem, and to address the missing pieces of the previous interpretations, we need to consider the

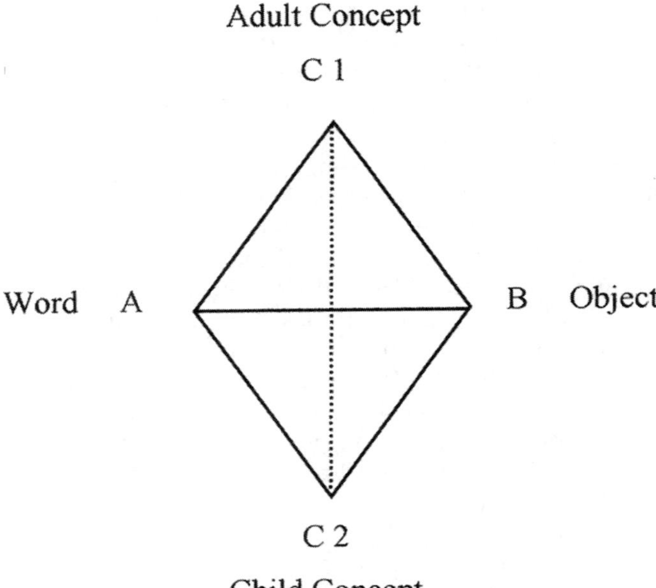

FIG. 1.2. The extended semiotic triangle showing relation between word and concepts of child and adult for establishing shared meaning. (Adapted from Figure 2.3, Nelson, 2002.)

broader context of learning words to express concepts. Lois Bloom (2000, p. 22) had this in mind in the completion of the quotation that was cited earlier: "Children learn language [to express their thoughts] ... and for acts of interpretation, in the effort to share the thoughts and feelings of other persons."

Words as Clues to Concepts

Quine's (1960) paradox of reference has played a major role in generating theories of word learning over the past 15 years, but reference is only part the problem, as illustrated in Fig. 1.2. Quine's emphasis on the ambiguity of reference, led to attempted developmental solutions (see Golinkoff et al., 2000, for examples), but these assume that the problem is only one of reference—that is, what object does the word point to in the real world? The problem, however, is more profound (as Quine's analysis actually implied): how does it happen that the child may project a concept from within his or her individual conceptual system that is the same as the conventional concept shared with adult language users based on their commonly held conceptual systems?

The most widely accepted answer to this question is based on the assumption that adults and children have the *same* conceptual systems, but children are not as practiced in applying theirs to words that are as yet unfamiliar to them. What they need to learn is rules of extension. I believe this assumption is deeply flawed. Given the differences between young language learning children and adults on the dimensions of perceptual perspective, experience in the world, breadth of general knowledge, social experience, among other matters, it seems obvious that children must be lacking in many varieties of conceptual knowledge that adults possess. To be sure, children may by the age of 2 years view everyday objects in much the same way that adults do, based on basic parameters of the three-dimensional world and the visual system tuned to it. On these grounds the vast amount of research documenting that children are disposed to extend novel names to novel objects on the basis of their shape, for example, is certainly convincing. However, it is extremely doubtful that these findings have any implications for how the meaning of words are acquired, in the sense of conventional shared concepts for words that are not common object names.

The evident gap between much of the data that is available in the psychological research on word learning and the general problems of meaning (e.g., Putnam, 1975) has several sources. One is the assumption in the psychological literature that the developing system of word meanings should be analyzed using the established categories of linguistic structure devised for the abstract "adult" system. Instead I think we can only reveal the categories and dimensions of the developing system on its own terms and not on the terms established for some finished form of that system. The key to the child's meaning can be found by taking an experiential perspective on how language fits into the infant's or young child's life at different points and with different degrees of mastery. In other words, as suggested earlier, functions of the child's language may reveal its forms and how they are being used and learned.

A major way in which standard analyses of early word learning have gone astray is through the long-standing assumption in child language studies that children begin to acquire words by learning nouns, that is, the names of things (Macnamara, 1982). Analysis of actual word learning data, however, indicates that common nouns (including names of things) are not the majority of words learned among the first 10 or 50, although they may be the most frequent *type*, if the categories are the grammatical ones of noun, verb, adjective, and "other" (for recent evidence and discussion see D'Odorico, Carubbi, Salerni, & Calvo, 2001). Two analytical practices have led to mischaracterizations of the data, and thus to fallible theories designed to explain the data. First, the term "noun" has several subcategories that do not refer to names of things, including proper nouns (names of individuals), and mass nouns (names of substances), as well as terms for places (e.g., *park*), types of people (e.g., *doctor*), events (e.g., *party*), and even abstract concepts (e.g., *heaven*) that are not names for things, that is, not labels of common objects. Children learn all of these kinds of words from the beginning of word learning (Nelson, Hampson, & Kessler Shaw, 1993). Thus, even when word counts show a majority of words to be nouns, these are not necessarily object labels.

A second analytic problem is that the very term *noun* applies to the role that words play in sentences, not to words standing alone. Many English words can fill two different "slots" as both noun and verb, for example the words *kiss* or *drink*, meaning the same action, but on one occasion used to say "give Daddy a kiss" and on another "kiss Daddy." When the word appears on a vocabulary checklist it is designated a verb, but the child may actually experience it used as a noun more frequently (Nelson, 1995). Traditional lexical categories state that nouns refer to "persons, places and things," but even with this broad semantic category description, many nouns lie outside its boundaries, and words that serve two roles with the same form, like *kiss* or *drink* remain ambiguous in their typology when used by a child as a single word utterance.

These reservations do not deny the claims that children may find it easier to learn to attach a label to a common object than to learn the appropriate application of an abstract term, or a verb. There is every reason, both theoretical and empirical to believe that they do (Fenson et al., 1994; Gentner, 1982). However, the strong bond between word and object that some theories project in support of the claim that children come to the word learning situation primed to expect that "words name whole objects" cannot be sustained. In place of the inappropriate (to the data) categorization of first words in terms of nouns and verbs, the actual ways in which children use words and conceptualize their experience, should be the aim (Nelson, 1973a, 1973b, 1974). Indeed, when words are classified according to categories of the child's interest, convergence on common conceptual domains of everyday experience (e.g., food, pets) is revealed (Nelson, 1973b). This is a much more difficult enterprise because it requires interpreting the intention of this child's use, taking a functional view of language for the child with the goal of eventually tracking how an earlier system becomes coordinated with that of the adult system. (For other analyses of child meanings and grammar from this perspective, see Braine, 1976; Halliday, 1975.)

In the end, however, children must conform to the conventional linguistic practices of the community, and fit or tune their concepts to the meanings that the community establishes for words and grammatical constructions. Clark (1983) addressed a related aspect of this general problem, that is, that the child comes to understand that there is a *conventional word* that maps onto concepts and thereafter abandons made up or idiosyncratic words. The problem posed by the double triangle (Fig. 1.2) is more opaque in that, whereas words and (concrete) referents are "viewable" in the external world, concepts are hidden mental objects. But the child must also come to understand that there is a *conventional concept* that the word expresses and thus must abandon prelinguistic or idiosyncratic or vague and incomplete concepts in relation to the words in use. This process can be seen in the way that children acquire meanings, as they fine-tune their original categories of the world to fit the adult's uses of their words.

For example, many children seem to start with a global category of 4-legged animals that they initially attach to the word *dog* and must then pare this to the single species we call dog. Or they generalize the word *dog* from their pet dog "Fido" to apply to all dogs. Thus children must become sensitive both to the language uses of the community and to the implied conceptual bases of language in order to be understood as well as to understand. That is, they must become adept at playing Wittgenstein's language games (Wittgenstein, 1953). A general Wittgensteinian approach to learning the meaning of words requires that the learner form concepts to fit the uses of words by speakers. In the child learner's case, the uses are initially those of parents, but eventually they must be extended to uses by all speakers of the community. The child cannot be provided with only a private meaning system, but must acquire one that will be used by all speakers of the language, more or less, to fit the sounds they utter.

This provision reverses for the naïve child learner's case the pervasive claim that concepts must precede words: in this case words necessarily come before concepts because *words pre-exist in the uses of the community*. Beyond the simple object cases moreover, words are absolutely essential for forming abstract concepts for all speakers. They take us beyond the apparent into the realm of sharing imagined realities. Furthermore, such imagined conceptions of reality tend to be culture specific (e.g., the concept of *heaven* or *jihad*).

The story thus far has brought out two critical points: first, words are expressed and understood as a reflection of the concepts that they symbolize. Second, concepts of individual speakers may vary, and words are not always a good match to what a speaker may want to express. In the beginning, a child's concepts may vary considerably from the conventional concept that the word of the language is presumed to symbolize. Moreover, the words that children acquire (in comprehension or production) are likely to be understood by them first in relation to their own concepts which may differ from the conventional ones. The problem then is to somehow adjust the concepts to fit the words. This is not done through definitions or ostensive labeling, but through exchange of uses of words, a process that rests on both social communicative functions of language and individual cognitive functions of language. These are thus two facets of the same process of the acquisition of meaning. What drives the process, however, may vary depending upon its phase, with communicative functions taking precedence at first, but with cognitive functional spin-offs. The next section examines this possibility.

LANGUAGE AS A TOOL OF THOUGHT

Implicit in the idea that meaning is learned from use is that children's understanding and knowledge of the world expands with their exposure to language, as they participate in conversations about aspects of the world that they have not yet and may never experience directly and personally, including aspects that are imaginary constructions of the culture at large (Harris, 2000). This is of course a powerful function of language in general, but it seems so obvious that it is rarely remarked on, much less studied. We need to understand, however, how it is that language serves to represent states of the world (and imagined unreal states as well) and to communicate these from one person to another using the words that both know. Learning words is only one step but a basic step toward becoming a participant in this process.

Words for Expanding the Knowledge Base

How does the learning of words affect the child's concepts and general knowledge base? One effect has already been noted, that of shaping or tuning concepts to fit words in use. This process was noted by Donald (1991) with regard to the first uses of language in human prehistory: "The use of the word reflects a process of sorting out the world into categories, of differentiating the things that may be named.... Previously fuzzy properties become sharper after symbolization" (p. 219). This way of framing the issue implies that preverbal concepts may be more diffuse than those that have been "appropriated" into the language. Sharing concepts and categories through language sharpens their edges at the same time that it may illuminate previously unrecognized relations to other concepts. The process of acquiring words to fit preverbal concepts and honing concepts to fit words must thereby massively affect the child's conceptual repertoire and may be expected to have significant cognitive consequences. One expected effect is that words may stabilize aspects of dynamic experience that otherwise appear fleeting and evanescent. Learning and using the word *dog* for example, may bring control over the concept or image of the dog that in the child's passing experience is too mobile to bring into sustained focus. In this sense, words perform functions similar to pictures or to the toy replicas that children engage with. Pictures, toys, and words are all symbolic forms that enable manipulable control over the symbolized entity.

Words thus symbolize aspects of the world that are dynamic and changing, as well as its static aspects, and in so doing they establish stability within the conceptual system. Because words are stable they can be called on mentally in order to reflect upon and manipulate aspects of representations in a way that is not possible for the real world thing or event. For example, Emily, a child whose bedtime monologues at 2 to 3 years have been analyzed, frequently repeated the words "Daddy coming," when she was 23 months old (Nelson, 1989). In another monologue from the same period Emily mused, "Daddy brings down basement washing," evoking the image of Daddy in another place or time. The Daddy who comes and goes can thus by means of language be manipulated in imagination as either arriving or being in another place, but retaining his identity and reality status.

Further, words can refer to entities that are not easily pictured, and that if they are represented in play, are played out over time. For example, events like lunch or "going to the doctor" may take on a stable constellation through reference in words. Children acquire such words to refer to activities in their very early vocabularies (Nelson et al., 1993). Emily verbalized her knowledge and concern in a monologue at age 2 about going to the doctor: "maybe the doctor take my jamas off." There is a great deal of evidence in this body of data from Emily's monologues (Nelson, 1989) that talking about everyday activities was a satisfying way of understanding her world. It is reasonable to believe that by talking about events in her life she was able to gain a measure of cognitive control over the dynamic and potentially destabilizing aspects of her world.

In addition to these advantages, words represent generality rather than specificity, and thus take a child beyond the specifics of particular things. Words apply to general categories, but more than this: they apply to the categories that are general across the people who use the language and over time, that is, they are shared conventional categories, not idiosyncratic ones. Inevitably, as already noted, words as they are used hone the child's concepts to the language being learned; the child's individual concepts become thereby socially shared concepts. Although the prelinguistic infant does form general, even global concepts as Mandler and McDonough (1993) have shown, these are not the concepts aligned with the words of the language. When the child's concepts are honed to fit the uses of related words they take on a new kind of generality, generality across kinds and across speakers. The disposition to generalize across instances of a verbal category is apparent in Emily's statement "Whenever you go to the airport have to take some luggage or you can't go." That is, "airport" → luggage. This kind of generalization reflects the process Vygotsky (1962) envisioned in terms of the interpsychological and intrapsychological phases. Here Emily is using the statement for herself, making general sense of the adult's statement that they have to take luggage to the airport.

Related to the previous point is the fact that by using language the child enters into a social/cultural world that extends beyond her own experience and beyond the family into the society at large. The words she learns and uses are used in the same conventional ways by all others who share the same cultural/linguistic world. The child's uses of words are constrained by the uses of these others; but by the same token, they take her into a "social network of minds". As Esther Goody (1997) put it: "Once a lexicon has been established a speaker hears the same word as does his listener [which] may [be] the crucial factor in escaping from the private worlds of thought into the shared social world of spoken language" (p. 391). But reciprocally, the child can begin to express her own individuality in this shared world by expressing her ideas and feelings in conventionally understood language. Or, as

Wittgenstein (1953) famously put it, to learn a language is to enter a form of life.

Representing Knowledge Offered by Others

On the basis of Dennett's (1994) claims I have postulated an increase in children's cognitive power through contemplation of "verbal surrogates" in absence of any objective counterparts. Additionally, one can expect a profound impact of knowledge about realities beyond the child's personal experience imparted through conversations with adults and peers. And, certainly we might expect an improvement in the child's own understanding through exchanging thoughts with others. By about 4 years of age children have in place a symbolic system of meanings in their native language in terms of basic grammar and a workable lexicon (Bloom & Lahey, 1978; Brown, 1973). Then language may be used to formulate new representations of the real or imagined world to be shared with other people, such as shared memories (Nelson & Fivush, 2004), imaginary play and stories (Harris, 2000), and those involved in "theory of mind" (Nelson, 2005). Recent work in the area of theory of mind has found, as would be expected, important effects of language competence on children's performance on standardized theory of mind tasks (Astington, 2001). Tellingly, individuals with deficits in language such as autistic disorder or childhood deafness typically perform poorly in theory of mind tasks, which require, as many theorists have claimed, meta-representational cognition. This representational (or meta-representational) function of language, internal to self or external for sharing with others, is what, in the end, language is all about. It enables the communication of knowledge, novel conceptualization, construction of narratives, and the proposal of theories.

Learning to represent states of affairs that differ from the here and now of immediate experience requires practice with other language users and the acquisition of complex linguistic structures necessary to represent complex aspects of dynamic events or abstract entities. When two or more persons are conversing the representation they are jointly constructing is external to each. Each contributes, but the conversation as such is outside the individual. It is thus necessary for the listener to transform what is verbally conveyed from language to nonverbal thought; this is what the child must become competent at. But this possibility must be a developmental achievement, making it possible for the individual to formulate a linguistic representation of a state of the world (real or imagined) internally (in the mind through private or inner speech) and to use that representation as an object to be remembered or to be subjected to further thought. There cannot be a linguistic representational cognitive system in place until the child has acquired sufficient language to "think in" language. This requirement is easily understood in terms of a second language, where as most learners know, it takes a great deal of learning and use before becoming capable of "thinking in" the second language. Many of us never achieve this for more than one language.

This consideration raises the question of how children operate with language before becoming capable of thinking in it. For example, when a parent reads a story to a child the representation is external to the child, it is on the page and in the voice of the parent. What then about the individual's representation, for example the child's representation of the story? How can we conceptualize this? There seem to be two possibilities:

- The heard words of the story make direct contact with the relevant concepts as they are encountered and directly set up a conceptual understanding.
- The heard words of the story are retained with their concepts and restructured into a story, using these or other words.

The first model assumes that the memory for the story is conceptual and that retelling the story requires newly accessing words from the child's existing repertoire that will re-represent the story. In this model language itself plays little role in the child's understanding mechanisms. Rather, language is simply a medium through which the ideas pass into memory and are later expressed when recall is required.

The second possibility assumes that the story memory is itself at least in part in words (either the original words or the child's substitutes) that in turn access the conceptual whole (constructed from the words) for the retelling. This model fits with the semiotic mediation assumption of Vygotsky's theory, with Wertsch's (1991) model of "voices in the mind," with the layered "hybrid" model of Donald's (1991) theory, and my own mediational representational model. The mediational model presented in Nelson (1996) emphasized that understanding extended text or discourse requires extensive practice with language in use for functions such as narrative, description, and explanation. The process involves retention of ongoing spoken language over extended time segments as each bit is related to the next, or held to be connected to something that comes later in the sequence. It assumes that actually retaining the words in working memory over time assists in this process of making temporal and causal connections. The mental representation in language provides support for the retention of the meaning of the story. However, the model also implies that becoming a good story understander rests on the experience of listening to stories and engaging in conversations that go beyond the here and now.

What we know about the development of story comprehension and narrative in the preschool years tends to support the language mediation model. Research on preschool language experiences in home and school demonstrates significant effects of both story reading and extended discourse on later literacy, vocabulary and related skills in a large sample of children from low income homes (Dickinson & Tabors, 2001). These effects imply the importance of practice in listening to linguistic representations in spoken language for understanding, but do not speak to the process involved. Observations of children's story listening suggest that they are focused on the specific words used in the story as they strive to understand what is being read to them. This is apparent in their frequent insistence on having a story read over and over (a common observation by parents, but see also Miller, Hoogstra, Mintz, Fung, & Williams, 1993), with the accompanying anticipation of the exact words, as well as the insistence that the reader not skip or misread any of the words but get them "right." Some preliterate children become so good at this practice that they "pretend read" whole books. An analysis of Emily's "reading" of a favorite book at naptime at the age of 2.5 indicated substantial memory for the words of the story but incomplete comprehension of the narrative or its overall meaning (Nelson, 1991). These observations suggest that the language used in the story, and in other extended discourse contexts, is critical to its memory and thus to the process of its interpretation. More systematic studies are very much needed in this area, however.

In a study of narrative production and understanding Henseler (Henseler, 2000) asked preschool children on one occasion to recount an experience of playing a narrative-based game and on another occasion to retell a story that they had heard read from a book only once. Children's own narrative recounting of the experienced event was skeletal and short, with few words for causal relations and no reference to mental concepts. In comparison, their retelling of the story was longer, and included more of the complex language, including causal terms and mental states, that were included in the story. In this study, receptive language competence was correlated more highly with measures of narrative and memory than expressive language, and the same has been found in other studies of memory (Walkenfeld, 2000), and story understanding (Fontaine, 2002). Although expressive language enables children to communicate their own ideas, these ideas may themselves be rather simple and short, as are the proto-narratives and explanations produced by most children younger than 5 years of age (Nelson, 1996). In contrast, using receptive language skills to comprehend the linguistic representations produced by others as stories, explanations, or descriptions of things not previously experienced, exposes the child to more complex language, more extended language, and more complex ideas and relations.

CONCLUSION: THE COGNITIVE FUNCTIONS OF LANGUAGE

Dennett's (1994) summary of the effects of the emergence of language on human cognitive powers quoted in the introduction to this chapter included the acquisition of new "objects-to-contemplate," that is, entities not in immediate concrete experience, as well as a new tool of thought for planning, problem solving, and evaluating solutions, and finally a valuable source of knowledge, the knowledge owned and contributed by others. This chapter has briefly considered these functions of language in the development of the child's knowledge and cognitive functions in the early years of life, beginning with the acquisition of first words. The function of words is at least in part to take the child beyond her own conceptions into conceptions that are partially shared with others. The move into narrative, description, and explanation made possible by the attainment of the 4-year-old level of language competence, receptive as well as expressive, goes beyond this. The effects of this level are truly profound, as profound as that claimed by evolutionary scholars with respect to the emergence of language in the human species.

For example, Damasio (1999) put it this way: "The glories of language lie ... in the ability to translate, ... thoughts into words and sentences, and words and sentences into thought; in the ability to classify knowledge rapidly and economically under the protective umbrella of a word; and in the ability to express imaginary constructions or distant abstractions with an efficient simple word" (p. 111). This brief summary implies, as my discussion throughout has aimed to do, that cognition and communication in language are intimately intertwined. Translating back and forth from one mind to another is what we do (or try to do) with language. In the process, knowledge is classified in ways that all can understand, and imaginary constructions and abstractions are put forth and shared.

A few years ago Hart and Risley (1995) published the results of their longitudinal study of the effects of language experience in the home on success in school among children of different social and economic classes. The differences between and within groups were extensive, and had important implications for later school success. Although the authors have been criticized for using numbers of words as indicators of the child's experience with language, the differences were impressive: The more words that were heard in the home during the preschool years, the better was performance in school. These findings are important for deciding how we deal with economic, cultural, and ethnic diversity among preschool and early school age children in establishing educational equity. Understanding what words and language generally contribute to children's cognitive growth can help us to appreciate on a deeper level what these differences mean and to design the kinds of practices that will equalize their opportunities to engage fully in educational experiences.

Still, as many who believe strongly in educational equity and diversity have insisted over the past 30 years (e.g. Labov, 1972), all children in all cultures do learn language and learn to use it in cognitive as well as communicative ways. Evidence is all around us in such forms as Hip Hop and other productions from "street language." What needs to be borne in mind is that although language makes many kinds of cognitive changes likely or necessary, such as acquiring the concepts encoded in the language used around children, not all such concepts are likely to be useful to children in school, whether in learning to read or in any other standard educational function, however useful they may be in the "street." Furthermore, they may not provide the kinds of experiences with representing in language both the real world of experience and the not-experienced or imaginary world that form the basis for learning in school, through both reading and oral presentations.

The basic language functions of establishing shared conceptual meanings and representations within a cultural community have important implications for understanding the process of how language gets into the mind and establishes conceptual systems that are not derived from observables in the real world. This process is relevant not only to education but also to understanding social and cultural deviance as well as conformity. For example, a concept like "jihad" has infected the minds of more than a few young people in the contemporary world. Once we recognize that it is language that carries the infection we may see more clearly both the positive contributions and possible distortions of language to cognitive states and their development. Unfortunately, for the most part developmental psychologists have been studying language as though it were a thing apart. It is time we studied it as a cultural tool of thought with all that implies, an entry point into the social mind, albeit occasionally a cultural weapon.

REFERENCES

Astington, J. W. (2001). The future of theory-of-mind research: Understanding motivational states, the role of language, and real-world consequences. *Child Development, 72,* 685–687.

Bloom, L. (2000). The Intentionality Model of Word Learning: How to learn a word, any word. In R. M. Golinkoff, K. Hirsh-Pasel, L. Bloom, L. B. Smith, A. L. Woodward, N. Akhtar, M. Tomasello, & G. Hollich (Eds.), *Becoming a word learner: A debate on lexical acquisition* (pp. 19–50). New York: Oxford University Press.

Bloom, L., & Lahey, M. (1978). *Language development and language disorders.* New York: Wiley.

Bloom, P. (2000). *How children learn the meanings of words.* Cambridge, MA: MIT Press.

Braine, M. D. S. (1976). Children's first word combinations. *Monographs of the Society for Research in Child Development, 41.*

Brown, R. (1973). *A First Language: The Early Stages.* Cambridge, MA: Harvard University Press.

Chomsky, N. (1988). *Language and problems of knowledge: The Managua lectures.* Cambridge, MA: MIT Press.

Clark, E. V. (1983). Meanings and concepts. In J. Flavell & E. Markman (Eds.), *Cognitive development. Handbook of child psychology* (4th ed., Vol. 3). New York: Wiley.

Damasio, A. (1999). *The feeling of what happens: Body and emotion in the making of consciousness.* New York: Harcourt.

Dennett, D. (1994). Language and intelligence. In J. Khalfa (Ed.), *What is intelligence?* (pp. 161–178). Cambridge, UK: Cambridge University Press.

Dickinson, D. K., & Tabors, P. O. (Eds.). (2001). *Beginning literacy with language.* Baltimore, MD: Paul H. Brookes.

D'Odorico, L., Carubbi, S., Salerni, N., & Calvo, V. (2001). Vocabulary development in Italian children: A longitudinal evaluation of quantitative and qualitative aspects. *Journal of Child Language, 28,* 351–372.

Donald, M. (1991). *Origins of the modern mind.* Cambridge, MA: Harvard University Press.

Fenson, L., Dale, P. S., Reznick, J. S., Bates, E., Thal, D. J., & Pethick, S. J. (1994). Variability in early communicative development. *SRCD Monographs, 59*(5).

Fodor, J. A. (1975). *The language of thought.* New York: Crowell.

Fontaine, R. G. (2002). *Children's understanding of stories in story-books: The role of genre, affect, and gender.* Unpublished PhD dissertation, City University of New York Graduate Center, New York.

Gentner, D. (1982). Why nouns are learned before verbs: Linguistic relativity versus natural partitioning. In S. A. I. Kuczaj (Ed.), *Language Development, Vol. 2: Language, thought, and culture* (pp. 301–334). Hillsdale, NJ: Lawrence Erlbaum Associates.

Golinkoff, R. M., Hirsh-Pasek, K., Bloom, L., Smith, L. B., Woodward, A. L., Akhtar, N., Tomasello, M., & Hollich, G. (2000). *Becoming a word learner: A debate on lexical acquisition.* New York: Oxford University Press.

Goody, E. N. (1997). Social intelligence and language: Another Rubicon. In A. Whiten & R. W. Byrne (Eds.), *Machiavellian Intelligence II: Extensions and evaluations* (pp. 365–377). Cambridge, UK: Cambridge University Press.

Halliday, M. A. K. (1975). *Learning how to mean*. London: Edwin Arnold.

Harris, P. L. (2000). *The work of the imagination*. Oxford: Blackwell.

Hart, B., & Risley, T. R. (1995). *Meaningful differences in the everyday experiences of young children*. Baltimore, MD: Paul B. Brookes.

Henseler, S. (2000). *Young children's developing theory of mind: Person reference, psychological understanding and narrative skill*. Unpublished PhD dissertation, City University of New York Graduate Center, New York.

Jusczyk, P. W. (1997). *The discovery of spoken language*. Cambridge, MA: MIT Press.

Lakoff, G. (1987). *Women, fire and dangerous things*. Chicago: University of Chicago Press.

Labov, W. (1972). *Language in the inner city*. Philadelphia: University of Pennsylvania Press.

Macnamara, J. (1982). *Names for things*. Cambridge, MA: MIT Press.

Mandler, J. M. (2000). Perceptual and conceptual processes in infancy. *Journal of Cognitive Development, 1*, 3–36.

Mandler, J. M., & McDonough, L. (1993). Concept formation in infancy. *Cognitive Development, 8*, 291–319.

Miller, P. J., Hoogstra, L., Mintz, J., Fung, H., & Williams, K. (1993). Troubles in the garden and how they get resolved: A young child's transformation of his favorite story. In C. A. Nelson (Ed.), *Memory and affect in development* (Vol. 26, pp. 87–114). Hillsdale, NJ: Lawrence Erlbaum Associates.

Nelson, K. (1973a). Some evidence for the cognitive primacy of categorization and its functional basis. *Merrill-Palmer Quarterly, 19*, 21–39.

Nelson, K. (1973b). Structure and strategy in learning to talk. *Monographs of the Society for Research in Child Development, 38* (1–2, Serial No. 149).

Nelson, K. (1974). Concept, word, and sentence: Interrelations in acquisition and development. *Psychological Review, 81*, 267–285.

Nelson, K. (Ed.). (1989). *Narratives from the crib*. Cambridge, MA: Harvard University Press.

Nelson, K. (1991). Remembering and Telling: A Developmental Story. *Journal of Narrative and Life History, 1*, 109–127.

Nelson, K. (1995). The Dual category problem in lexical acquisition. In W. Merriman & M. Tomasello (Eds.), *Beyond names for things*. Hillsdale, NJ: Lawrence Erlbaum Associates.

Nelson, K. (1996). *Language in cognitive development: The emergence of the mediated mind*. New York: Cambridge University Press.

Nelson, K. (2005). Language pathways into the community of minds. In J. W. Astington & J. A. Baird (Eds.), *Why language matters for theory of mind*. New York: Oxford University Press.

Nelson, K., & Fivush, R. (2004). Emergence of autobiographical memory: A social-cultural theory. *Psychological Review, 111*, 486–511.

Nelson, K., Hampson, J., & Kessler Shaw, L. (1993). Nouns in early lexicons: Evidence, explanations, and implications. *Journal of Child Language, 20*, 61–84.

Nelson, K., & Ware, A. (2002). The re-emergence of function. In N. Stein, P. Bauer, & M. Rabinowitz (Eds.), *Essays in honor of Jean Mandler*. Mahwah, NJ: Lawrence Erlbaum Associates.
Ogden, C. K., & Richards, I. A. (1923/1946). *The meaning of meaning*. London: Routledge & Kegan Paul.
Piaget, J. (1926). *The language and thought of the child*. New York: Harcourt, Brace.
Piaget, J. (1929). *The child's conception of the world* (J. A. Tomlinson, Trans.). New York: Harcourt Brace & World.
Piaget, J. (1962). *Play, dreams, and imitation in childhood*. New York: Norton.
Putnam, H. (1975). The meaning of meaning. In H. Putnam (Ed.), *Philosophical papers, Vol. 2: Mind, language and reality* (pp. 215–271). Cambridge, UK: Cambridge University Press.
Quine, W. V. O. (1960). *Word and object*. Cambridge, MA: MIT Press.
Saussure, F. D. (1959). *Course in general linguistics*. New York: The Philosophical Library. (Originally published in 1915)
Tomasello, M., & Kruger, A. C. (1992). Joint attention on actions: Acquiring words in ostensive and non-ostensive contexts. *Journal of child language, 19*, 313–333.
Vygotsky, L. (1962). *Thought and language* (E. Hanfmann & G. Vakar, Trans.). Cambridge, MA: MIT Press.
Walkenfeld, F. F. (2000). *Reminder and language effects on preschoolers' memory reports: Do words speak louder than actions?* Unpublished Ph.D. dissertation, City University of New York Graduate School, New York.
Wertsch, J. V. (1985). *Vygotsky and the social formation of mind*. Cambridge, MA: Harvard University Press.
Wertsch, J. (1991). *Voices in the mind*. Cambridge, MA: Harvard University Press.
Wittgenstein, L. (1953). *Philosophical investigations*. New York: Macmillan.

Chapter 2

Seeing Objects as Symbols and Symbols as Objects: Language and the Development of Dual Representation

Bruce D. Homer
New York University

Katherine Nelson
Graduate Center of the City University of New York

Beginning at birth, children are exposed to a diverse array of symbols, including pictures, writing, music, and, most importantly, language. These symbols and symbolic artifacts form the basis of human culture. For adults, the meanings of most symbols are transparent: Adults are able to "see through" symbols directly to meaning. For young children, however, this is not the case. Symbols are part of the "blooming, buzzing confusion" faced by children, and one of the central problems facing infants and young children is learning how to make sense of symbols and symbolic artifacts. Learning to understand and use symbols and symbolic artifacts is an essential component of children's becoming full-fledged members of their culture. Symbolic understanding allows children to negotiate their way in the "symbolic world" in which they live and gives them access to the vast array of knowledge that is represented in the symbols that surround them (Nelson, 2003).

Undoubtedly the most important development in the area of children's symbolic understanding is the acquisition of language. Many theorists have argued that language plays a central role in much of our advanced cognitive processes. Although few would disagree with the important function of language, learning to engage in other types of symbolic activities is also essential. All societies, to some extent, rely on modes of symbolic representation other than speech, whether it is lines drawn in sand to represent the flow of a river, notches on a stick to represent the passage of years, or marks on a sheet of paper to represent advanced mathematical formulas.

The exact nature of the relation between language and more general symbolic understanding has been the topic of much debate, with three possible relations proposed. The first is that language is just one expression of more general symbolic abilities. Piaget (1962), for example, suggested that children's acquisition of the semiotic function in the second year of life underlies all symbolic competencies, including symbolic play and language. Related to this perspective is research that has linked the emergence of symbolic play to subsequent linguistic developments (e.g., Casby & Corte, 1987). A second possibility is that language is more or less separate from other modes of symbolic activities. DeLoache (1991; 1995b; 2000), for example, has found that children's ability to use objects symbolically develops later than symbolic play and symbolic language and she has therefore tended to view this development as being independent of language. According to DeLoache, although children are able to engage in some modes of symbolic activity from an early age, true "symbol mindedness" develops only in the third year of life with the advent of *dual representation*, which is the ability to represent a symbol as both an actual object and as a representation of something else (DeLoache, 1995a, 1995b, 2000; DeLoache, Kolstad, & Anderson, 1991). A third possibility—the one supported in this chapter—is that although certain basic modes of symbolic activity are possible without language, once children acquire language it transforms their symbolic capabilities.

Drawing on the theoretical work of Nelson (e.g., current volume, 1996) and others who have emphasized the importance of language in cognitive development, it is argued that language plays a very important role in children's development of symbolic understanding. Specifically, it is argued that symbols are inherently social in nature and language provides a means for children to enter into the social, symbolic world. Furthermore, language functions to provide the "cognitive distance" that is required for children to engage in dual representation. Through language, symbolic artifacts, which are salient as physical objects, can be seen both as physical objects and as symbols.

This chapter explores children's development of symbolic understanding. First, an overview of the nature of symbolic representation is presented. It is then argued that there are regularities in the development of symbolic competencies in different domains, including language. Discussion then turns to the problems that children have with dual representation of both symbolic artifacts, which can be very salient as objects but are difficult for children to perceive as representations, and for language, which is extremely salient as symbol, but is difficult for children to contemplate as an object. We argue that for symbolic artifacts, language provides the "cognitive distance" that allows objects to be seen as symbols, whereas for language, writing provides the cognitive distance that allows linguistic forms to become "objects of thought" (Olson, 1994).

THE NATURE OF SYMBOLIC RELATIONS

Any attempt to explain how children develop symbolic understanding must first define what is meant by "symbol." At least part of the theoretical disagreement over how children develop symbolic understanding stems from inconsistencies in what is meant by this term. There are disagreements at the semantic level as well as deeper, theoretical differences in what constitutes a "symbol." In an effort to avoid these problems, DeLoache has adopted a broad definition of symbol as "something that someone intends to stand for or represent something other than itself" (DeLoache, 2002, p. 73). There are a number of strengths to this definition, such as the fact that it is inclusive and that it identifies several of the essential aspects of symbols (e.g., their representational and intentional nature). However, not addressed in DeLoache's definition is the fact that there are different ways in which symbols can be related to referents (i.e., the objects to which they refer). This is not to say that DeLoache is unaware of these differences (e.g., see DeLoache, 2002), but simply that this issue is not addressed in her definition, which is intentionally broad in order to encompasses different modes of symbolic representation.

Much of our current understanding of the nature of symbolic relations has been informed by the philosopher Peirce (1955). Peirce used the term *sign* as a more general term and used the term *symbol* to indicate a particular type of sign. In his theory of signs, known as *semiotics*, Pierce identified three types of signs that vary according to the nature of the relation between the sign and its referent: *icons*, *indexes*, and *symbols*. According to Peirce, *iconic signs* bear a physical resemblance to the objects that they represent: A similarity mediates the relation between an icon and its referent. Examples of iconic signs include pictures and drawings. *Indexical signs* have either a physical or temporal connection to the object that they represent. Often, there is a causal connection between an index and its referent. A thermometer is an example of indexical relation. As air temperature increases, it heats mercury in the glass tube causing it to expand and rise up the tube. The level of the mercury then serves as an index of air temperature. Finally, *symbolic signs* are arbitrary and have no direct connection to the object that they represent. Instead symbols are part of an interconnected system of signs and depend on social conventions for their meaning. Language is the quintessential example of a symbolic sign system.

Other theorists have made similar distinctions to those made by Peirce (1955), but have used different terms. Piaget (1962), for example, used *symbol* as the more general term and *sign* to denote arbitrary symbols that obtain their meaning through social convention. In their classic work on symbols, Werner and Kaplan (1963) use signs to refer to a more basic mode of representation and symbols to refer to more advanced mode of representation that entails a social component. For most theorists, regardless of the terminology used, the key distinction is between representations that obtain meaning through physical similarity or temporal/physical proximity and representations that are arbitrary in nature, obtaining their meaning through social convention. In the current chapter, Peirce's nomenclature will be adopted with a distinction being made between *icon*, *index*, and *symbol*, and with *sign* being used as the more general, superordinate term.

An essential aspect of Peirce's semiotic theory is that signs are always communicative: An object does not become a sign unless someone intends it to be so used and another interprets it as such. Deacon (1997) argues that we are engaging in "linguistic shorthand" when we call something an icon, index or symbol, and that what we really mean is that the object is likely to be interpreted by someone in that particular way (i.e., as an icon, index or symbol). In other words, being a sign is not a property of an object per se, it is a property of a person's interpretation of that object. Therefore an object is not an icon just because it bears a physical resemblance to something else, but only acquires this property when it is interpreted as an icon. For example, a red plastic disk only becomes an icon for "apple" when it is understood or interpreted by someone as standing for an apple.

An important implication of this interpretative feature of signs is that a single object can be an icon or index as well as a symbol, depending on how it is interpreted. As an example of this, Deacon (1997) refers to

American Sign Language (ASL). At one time, some linguists argued that ASL was only an iconic or indexical mode of communication because certain signs involve pantomime (icon) or pointing to objects or people (index). Now, however, it is clear that even though certain ASL signs can be interpreted in an iconic or indexical manner, to someone who is fluent in ASL, it is a fully symbolic mode of communication. Part of what makes ASL or other representational systems symbolic is that their signs are arbitrary, social conventions. Another key element is that the symbols are part of an interrelated system of signs. Symbols are part of an interconnected web of meanings, and therefore meaning derives not only from the world, but also from the symbol system itself. A sign then cannot be a symbol in isolation, but only as part of a system of signs, such as language. This in turn implies that as children acquire the first signs in a symbol system, such as language, the signs are not initially symbolic, but instead start out being iconic or indexical in nature and then develop into being fully symbolic.

ICON, INDEX AND SYMBOL: THE HIERARCHY OF SIGNS

Deacon (1997) claims that the hierarchy of signs laid out in Peirce's semiotics applies to both external, communicative signs and to internal, cognitive representations within the individual mind/brain. Deacon argues that more abstract signs are built up from lower-level forms, and conversely, that the interpretation of complex, abstract signs occurs by breaking them down into more basic signs. In other words, symbols—whether they are external in nature, such as written language, or internal, such as conceptual thought—are built up from sets of indices, and indices are built from sets of icons. Whereas the construction or acquisition of signs progresses from icon to index to symbol, the interpretation of signs involves breaking the system down from symbol to index to icon.

In stressing the hierarchy of signs, Deacon (1997) posits that iconic representation forms the basis of all higher-order representation. Deacon, similar to many other theorists, argues that the representation of direct experience is the most basic mode of representation. He speculates that each new experience is represented in the mind/brain, and that different aspects of each of our experiences are encoded within distinct sensory modalities. As the store of represented experiences grows, past experiences are called to mind when we are in a novel situation that shares some similarity with past, represented experiences. Because these representations of prior experience are related to one another based on similarity, Deacon argues that they are iconic in nature. Eventually, similar aspects of different experiences get linked to one another in an indexical way. The mental representation of specific types of objects (e.g., apples) involves the indexical linking of various experience-based, iconic features from different sensory modalities (e.g., "red and round" becomes associated with "tart and juicy"). Words can then become associated with the mental representation in an indexical manner, and, as language develops into a symbolic system, words also become associated with one another.

A more speculative component of Deacon's (1997) theory is that the hierarchy of signs (i.e., icon to index to symbol) is recapitulated in the neuronal structure of the brain. He points out that attempts to identify the brain structures that are associated with specific symbol tokens (e.g., words) seem to indicate that they are distributed across many areas of the brain, and are not isolated in a single neural substrate. Deacon argues that this is because symbols consist of a collection of indexical connections between various iconic representations. It is iconic representations of direct experiences, most likely within a single sensory modality, that are posited to map onto neuronal activity within a single region of the brain.

Although many of the details of Deacon's theory are speculative, there is a growing body of evidence indicating that children's symbolic understanding in different domains develops in ways that correspond to Peirce/Deacon's hierarchy of signs. This progression from less to more complex and abstract signs helps explain how children develop symbolic competencies: Signs that are symbols for adults are initially iconic or indexical for young children, and only gradually develop into being fully symbolic. We consider here two example of this development of symbolic understanding: children's acquisition of spoken language and children's acquisition of literacy.

Hierarchy of Signs in Language Acquisition

Children's acquisition of language is one of the most extensively researched areas in contemporary developmental psychology. Much of the work in this area has focused on accurately describing children's linguistic development, mapping out the sequence through which children move in learning to express and understand language at different ages. In addition to its inherent importance, language acquisition has also been studied because it provides fertile ground for investigating key theoretical issues regarding the nature of child development, such as the ways in which innate factors transact with children's sociocultural milieu in shaping development. Language acquisition also provides an interesting example of the hierarchy of children's symbolic understanding within a domain.

Language as a human universal, the communication system used in every human group, is the quintessential symbolic system. The words that form the lexicon of a language—its meaning units—are abstract, socially agreed upon, interrelated signs—symbols in the Peirce/Deacon sense. For young children who are just learning to communicate with language, however, words may not actually be symbolic in this sense. According to Deacon (1997), language signs have their basis in iconic representation of experiences. Unique representations are formed for the child for every acoustic experience of hearing a word spoken as well as for each experience with a reference. Similarities between the iconic representations of different specific experiences are recognized by the child and linked to representation of the word being spoken, creating an indexical link between the spoken word and the experience. Thus when the child first uses words, they are indexical in nature, serving as indexical signs or indices. It is only later, when relations between the indices (words) are linked, and when abstract hierarchical relations are established that language signs become truly symbolic. As Deacon emphasizes, it takes a great deal of experience with a sign system to move from the indexical to the symbolic level, where meaning depends upon the relations among signs as well as the relation of signs to the world. At what age this move may take place in language for children is not clear—it probably takes place gradually over the years from 2 to 3 as syntax is acquired and relations within the lexicon are established.

As an example of Deacon's (1997) proposal regarding changes in the representational nature of words, consider a mother teaching her young son the word, "juice." For the mother, "juice" is understood as a symbol because it is part of her symbolic system of language, but for the young infant, the word is initially meaningless. After repeated exposures, "juice" (both the word and object) becomes part of the child's experiential representations (which, according to Deacon, are iconic in nature). When the son hears his mother say "juice," it brings to mind other experiences when he has heard similar sounds (i.e., other times when mother or other people have said "juice"). Similarities in the contexts in which the sign, "juice," has been presented to the child are also brought to mind. Eventually, an indexical relation develops between the child's iconic representation of the sign, "juice" and his iconic representation of a specific feature of the contexts. For example, hearing the word "juice" becomes associated with a sweet liquid inside the child's cup. The final step occurs when the child develops a number of indexical relations for words, which then become related not only to experience, but also to one another. The sign, in this case, the word "juice," becomes enmeshed in a web of symbolic relations among the system of symbols, in this case, language. "Juice" is no longer associated with only specific objects or events in the world, but also to other signs (i.e., to other words), for example, "sweet" and "drink."

The idea that the meanings of words are different for children than for adults has been emphasized by Nelson (1996), who argues that language only gradually becomes fully symbolic for children. According to Nelson, infants' first representations of words are enmeshed in their representation of events. Children initially learn words as part of shared events that they experience with their parents (Levy & Nelson, 1994). At first, children will often use words to refer to an entire event (e.g., "bath" will refer to the entire experience of having a bath, not just a tub full of soapy water). At this very beginning stage of language learning, gestures and words are used interchangeably to refer to specific things in the child's environment. Children's gestures and first words are indexical in nature during the first years of learning language. The meaning of words and their representational nature becomes transformed for children as they interact with adults in the child's world who treat their utterances as having meaning and as being symbolic. However, because the early system of words and meanings is small and "gappy" it is likely that words retain an essential indexical character for several years.

Hierarchy of Signs in Literacy Acquisition

It may not be surprising that the representational nature of language—the first symbol system learned by children—only gradually develops into being fully symbolic. But what of symbol systems that children learn after they have acquired symbolic language? Is there a similar progression in the representational nature of signs in other domains? Research in the area of literacy acquisition seems to indicate that there is an analogous progression in this domain as well.

To understand transitions in the representational nature of writing, it is necessary to look at children's early understandings of writing. Although literacy acquisition is often thought of as something that occurs only when children begin school, the importance of earlier home factors for learning to read and write has been well documented. For example, the availability of reading material in the home, parental literacy activities, and attitudes toward literacy have all been found to predict children's later reading skills (e.g., Byrne, Fielding-Barnsley, Ashley, & Larsen, 1997; Daiute, 1993; Snow, Barnes, Chandler, Goodman, & Hemphill, 1991). These factors affect children before they begin school, a finding that has led to viewing literacy acquisition as an emergent process that begins well before formal instruction. The skills and knowledge that children acquire prior to formal instruction in school are necessary precursors for more formal modes of literacy (Clay, 1979; Teale & Sulzby, 1986; Whitehurst & Lonigan, 1998).

Within this emergent literacy framework, Emilia Ferreiro and her colleges have investigated what writing means for young children (e.g., Ferreiro, 1986, 1991, 1996; Ferreiro & Teberosky, 1982). Ferreiro, who has a Piagetian perspective on the nature of child development, characterizes children as actively attempting to understand their social and physical environments, including cultural objects such as literacy. According to Ferreiro, children are faced with a mass of "chaotic data" when they initially attempt to understand writing. Children form "theories" about the nature of writing in order to make sense of this data, and through their theory construction, children transform and eventually reconstruct literacy for themselves. For Ferreiro, young, preliterate children's attempts at reading and writing should not be characterized as being simply "mistakes," but instead provide insight into children's current "theories" of writing.

Ferreiro has developed a technique of asking children to write (or to "just pretend" if they say that they do not know how to write) and then asking them to "read" the different parts of what they have written. By analyzing commonalities in the progression of answers that children give in this paradigm, Ferreiro and others have been able to identify "levels of literacy" that children progress through in becoming literate. For Ferreiro (Ferreiro & Teberosky, 1982), the first step that children must make is to identify criteria for differentiating "writing" from other modes of graphical representation, such as drawing. Children do this by focusing on how the different elements of writing are arranged (i.e., in linear order), paying little attention to what is actually being written. Typically, this first step is achieved sometime around the age of four. Later stages involve children determining what constitutes "good writing" (e.g., a word must consist of different letters).

Ferreiro's work has been conducted primarily with Spanish-speaking children, but the methodology has also been used to study children learning to read and write in other languages, including English (Homer & Olson, 1999; Vernon, 1993), Hebrew (Levin & Landsmann, 1989), and Chinese (Homer, Xu, Lee, & Olson, 2005; Xue, Homer, & Fen, 2003). Although there are obviously important language-related differences in literacy acquisition, one common feature is that for children from a number of different cultures, writing is not initially understood as being symbolic, but instead children's first attempts at writing are iconic or indexical in nature. In early stages of literacy acquisition, the written signs of children do not convey meaning through abstract, conventional relations to spoken words, they convey meaning through iconic relations to objects. Children will alter properties of what is written to correspond to properties of the objects that are being written about. Because the representation is based on similarity, this early writing is iconic according to Peirce/Deancon's taxonomy of signs.

In their study with 5- and 6-year-old Israeli children, Levin and Landsmann (1989) found that the younger children manipulate properties of what they write to correspond with properties of the object being representing in the "writing." The authors asked children to write two nouns and then showed them two cards. One noun was printed on the first card and the other noun was printed on the second card. The two nouns where chosen to contrast in their "phonetic properties" (i.e., one was a "long" word and one was a "short" word) and the physical properties of their referents (e.g., the long word would refer to a "small" object while the short word would refer to a "big" object). An English example of this task would be to show children one card with "snake" written on it and a second card with "butterfly." Children who use an iconic strategy claimed that the card with "butterfly" written on it must say *snake* because it is a bigger object and therefore must be a bigger word. Similar findings have been reported in studies with children who speak other languages, including Italian (Pontecorvo & Zucchermaglio, 1988), Estonian (Tulviste, 1993), and English (Bialystok, 1986).

In a study on young children's understanding of writing, Homer and Olson (1999) adopted Ferreiro's technique of asking children to write and then "read" what they had written. Three- to 6-year-old English-speaking children were asked to write a series of phrases about dogs, which expressed either a negation (i.e., "no dog"), a quantity (i.e., "one dog," "two dogs"), or a quality (i.e., "red dog," "blue dog"). The children's attempts at writing were coded into three categories, based on the representational nature of the writing attempts. The youngest children would typically make a single, undifferentiated mark for each phrase that they were asked to write. When asked to "read" a segment of the mark, the children would repeat the entire phrase. These children differentiated writing from drawing, and knew that writing involves making marks on paper that can elicit speech, but writing did not appear to be representational for them; they related writing neither to the referent nor to speech. For a second group of children, writing was representational, but meaning was conveyed through iconic relations between what the children wrote and what they were attempting to represent. For these children, writing is an iconic system, in which a separate mark or token is used to represent each object mentioned in a written expression. For example, the children would represent "two dogs" with two marks, both of which would be identify as being "dog" (i.e., "two dogs" = "dog" "dog"). One interesting finding is that when children at this stage were asked to write, "no dogs," they would often say that "no dogs" could not be written or would make a mark and claim that it said something completely different (e.g., "cat"). For the third group, which consisted of older children, writing had become symbolic. Some of these children were able to write in conventional English, but others were still in the process of identifying how language is represented in text. These children would typically make a mark to represent each word of the expression they were writing. For example, they would make two marks for "no dogs," one for "no" and one for "dogs." There are two key transitions in this stage. First, the children are trying to represent spoken language, not meaning or objects. Second, the representational nature of their writing is symbolic, not iconic. Written marks are understood to be social conventions and the children have begun the task of learning the convention.

The studies just described provide support from the areas of language learning and literacy acquisition for the claim that there is a developmental transition from pre-symbolic to symbolic representation in different domains. When children first use words, their linguistic signs are indexical, not fully symbolic in nature. Similarly, when children first attempt to write, they are attempting to convey meaning through iconic or indexical representation, not through symbolic representation. But how do children learn to use symbols? How do children acquire symbolic understanding?

SYMBOLIC UNDERSTANDING AND THE DUALITY OF SIGNS

Using symbols requires a basic understanding of the nature of signs. In his theory of semiotics, Peirce (1955) identified several important aspects of signs, including their social and communicative nature, and the fact that there are different ways in which signs can obtain their referential meaning. An additional aspect of signs—one that children have particular difficultly with—is their inherent dual nature. Saussure (1959) characterized signs as being two-sided psychological entities made up of the signifier (*signifinant*) and the signified (*signifiè*). The signifier is the side of a sign that is an actual object, while the signified is the side that is the meaning represented by the sign. For example, in spoken language, the signifier is the sound that is heard when a linguistic sign is uttered and the signified is the concept that is being conveyed by the sign.

The signifier and the signified have been likened to two sides of a coin: they are inseparable, yet distinct. To fully understand signs requires being able to simultaneously perceive both the signifier and signified. DeLoache (1995a; 2002) has proposed that children's primary difficulty with signs is that they are unable to do this: They cannot perceive a sign as both a representation and as an object. DeLoache has called representing both sides of a sign *dual representation*, and claims that being able to use symbolic artifacts, such as models or maps, requires dual representation. She argues that the object side of a sign can be so salient for children that they are unable to think of the representation side of the sign. However, children's difficulty with dual representation can also come from the representation side of a sign being too salient—as is the case with linguistic signs once language becomes symbolic for children. The ability to think about the physical properties of language, or metalinguistic awareness, is a gradual and difficult achievement. There is evidence that representation in a second medium facilitates children's developing the ability to think about the representational side of symbolic artifacts and to think about the object side of linguistic signs. For symbolic artifacts, the second medium is language, and for linguistic signs, the second medium is writing. In the next sections, we examine how language and writing facilitate children's ability to engage in dual representation.

Seeing Objects as Symbols: The Role of Language

In numerous empirical studies, DeLoache and her colleagues (e.g., DeLoache, 1991, 2000; DeLoache & Burns, 1994; DeLoache & Marzolf, 1992) have investigated children's ability to use symbolic artifacts using the *model task*. In this task, children are shown a model of a room and told that it corresponds in every way to an adjacent, real room. For example, children are shown that every piece of furniture in the big room has a corresponding piece of toy furniture in the model room. The children are then shown a toy—usually a miniature doll—that is hidden in the model room. They are told that there is a similar, larger toy in the corresponding location in the real room. The children are then asked to find the larger toy in the real room. Success on the model task requires that children see the model not only as a physical object, but also as a representation of the room. Numerous studies with the model task have found that not until age 3 can a majority of children use the model to find the toy in the large room (DeLoache, 1995b; DeLoache & Burns, 1994). DeLoache has argued that the 2-year-olds' difficulty is due to an inability to engage in dual representation: Because the model is so salient as an object for children, (i.e., they perceive it as a toy), it difficult for them to also perceive the model as a representation.

DeLoache (2002) argues that being able to represent both the object and representational aspects of the model is a major development in children's acquisition of symbolic competencies and suggests that a number of factors are responsible for children's development of symbolic competencies (as indicated by success on the model task). These include: prior symbolic experiences, developmental increases in the basic amount of information that children can hold in mind, developmental increases in inhibitory control, and language development. DeLoache suggests that language developments may provide children with the "cognitive distance" that is required for engaging in dual representation. Although this is one important function, language also serves other vital functions in children's development of general symbolic competencies.

Language is the primary mode of human communication, and when children acquire language, it not only changes their communicative abilities but it also transforms many of their cognitive abilities (see Nelson, 1996). Although there are indications that children use some signs prior to language (e.g., indexical gestures), children's first truly symbolic activities can be seen in language. Although, as argued previously, initial language use is indexical, over time it develops to become a fully symbolic system. The emergence of syntax is an unequivocal indicator that language has become symbolic because it is based on an abstract structural system. Syntax develops during the third year of life from its beginnings in the conjunction of two words to the construction of complex sentences; basic grammar is generally evident by age 4 years. Independent symbolic play emerges about the same time. It is not until shortly after age two that children can use an object as a representation of something else in play (Tomasello, Striano, & Rochat, 1999).[1] The temporal coincidence of the emergence of symbolic language and symbolic play is not definitive evidence of a causal relation between them. However, converging evidence supports the claim that language plays a vital role in the development of symbolic understanding in terms of three key functions of language.

Language Provides Social Connection

One of the prime functions of language in the development of symbolic understanding is to provide a means for making the social connection that is required for the acquisition of symbols. By Peirce's definition, symbols are arbitrary social conventions and therefore, learning symbols requires social connection and communication to establish the con-

[1]There is some dispute about the age at which true symbolic play appears. Although naturalistic observations suggest that it emerges sometime around 18 to 24 months (e.g., Casby & Corte, 1987), Tomasello at al. (1999) argue that these observations are not true symbolic activity. Instead, Tomasello claims that young children use existing motor routines on objects with shared perceptual features (e.g., they move a block like a toy car because they are the same size and shape), or children's actions are guided by adults through example or verbal script.

ventional meanings of arbitrary forms. Once basic language is acquired it provides a medium through which other symbols systems, such as writing, mathematics and music, can be taught. Most of formal schooling can be considered as teaching children how to use different symbol systems, and this teaching occurs primarily through spoken language (with written language playing a more prominent role in later stages of education).

Although symbols are by definition social, other types of signs are also primarily social in function and language can facilitate the social interaction that occurs around these other signs. Even children's early symbolic play, which has often been characterized as an independent activity, is social in nature. Observational studies have found that children carry out a greater number of symbolic play acts and engage in more complex modes of symbolic play when their mothers are present (Fiese, 1990; Slade, 1987). Although there are a number of possible explanations for this observation, it is plausible that because of the social nature of signs and symbolic activities, children are more likely to engage in symbolic acts with another person present. Support for this claim comes from a study by Striano, Tomasello, and Rochat (2001) who found that children playing with objects were significantly more likely to turn and look at an adult immediately following a symbolic action (e.g., treating a block as a doll by putting the block/doll to bed) than following a non-symbolic action (e.g., hitting a peg with a hammer). The authors conclude that under the age of 3, symbolic play is primarily, if not exclusively, a social activity that takes place in a social context.

Language Provides a Means of "Scaffolding"

A second important function of language in the development of symbolic understanding is to support and direct children's action. With guidance, children's actions can be "scaffolded" so that they perform in ways that exceed their current independent level of development (Wood, Bruner, & Ross, 1976). This guided or scaffolded action provides an important mechanism for children's cognitive development. Tomasello et al. (1999) suggest that many of children's earliest symbolic actions are supported by adults who either model the symbolic actions or provide verbal scripts that guide children's actions. In the Tomasello et al. (1999) study of symbolic play, children participated in sessions divided into three 2-minute phases. An initial freeplay phase was followed by an experimenter demonstrating two symbolic actions and then observing the children for a second 2-minute play session. After the second observation period, an experimenter again modeled a symbolic act, but this time a verbal script was also provided. For example, the experimenter would take a block and push it along the table saying,

"Vroom! I'm going for a drive." After the linguistic modeling, there was a final 2-minute observation period. Tomasello et al. found that—using what they described as a "generous" coding scheme—2-year-olds produced very few symbolic acts during the initial 4-minute period (an average of less than 1), with 2.5-year-olds producing only slightly more (an average of about 2). In contrast, the 3-year-olds produced significantly more symbolic acts (an average of over 4). All age groups produced significantly more symbolic acts after they were provided with the experimenter's verbal script. In other words, the use of linguistic and physical modeling supported more symbolic acts, even for the youngest children. The authors conclude that children's attempts to imitate adult actions and understand adult language may be crucial for the development of symbolic understanding.

Language Provides Cognitive Distance

A third important function of language in the development of symbolic understanding is to provide a means of creating a "cognitive distance" to allow children to engage in dual representation. As described above, DeLoache has theorized that for 2.5-year-olds, difficulty with the model task is due in part to the fact that the "object" aspect of the model is so salient—the children can only see the model as a toy, not as a representation. Support for this claim comes from research showing that varying the degree of salience of the "object" side of the model has a direct effect on children's performance. For example, if children view the model from behind a glass window then performance of 2.5-year-olds is significantly improved, while having children play with the model for 10 minutes before testing makes the task significantly more difficult for 3-year-olds (DeLoache, 2000). In these examples, DeLoache affected children's ability to engage in dual representation in the model task by varying physical proximity to the model: By creating more physical distance, the object side of the model was less salient, which allowed children to engage in dual representation. In an analogous way, language can be used to create cognitive distance by mediating how children interact with signs.

Callaghan (1999, 2000) has argued that verbal labels facilitate young children's ability to engage in dual representation with pictures. Support for this claim come from a series of studies in which Callaghan (2000) showed 2.5- and 3-year-olds a picture and then asked them to identify which of two objects was identified in the picture. The experiment manipulated the availability of verbal labels either by using a target object for which the children would not know the name (e.g., a corkscrew), or by using a distracter object that came from the same basic-level category as the target object (e.g., if the target was a German

Shepard, the distracter would be a St. Bernard, both of which come from the basic-level category of "dog"). Callaghan found that the children performed significantly worse in the conditions in which they could not use verbal labels. She concludes that young children are not able to understand the symbolic nature of pictures without the use of language.

In our recent work (Homer & Nelson, 2003), we have investigated the influence of language on children's performance in the DeLoache model task in an experimental study with children ($N = 16$) who ranged in age from 2;4 to 3;5. All children were given a standardized language test (Dunn & Dunn, 1997) and one of two conditions of the model task: a standard condition (similar to DeLoache, 1991), and a language condition, which was the same except that it had an added linguistic scaffold. In both conditions, the children were shown a model of a room and then an actual room. The correspondence between the two rooms was pointed out to the children and they were then shown two dolls: "Little Mickey," who was in the model, and "Big Mickey," who was in the room. The children were told that whenever Little Mickey goes somewhere in the model, Big Mickey goes to the same location in the room. In the Standard condition, children then observed as Little Mickey was placed in a "hiding spot" in the model and then they were asked to find Big Mickey in the room. In the language version, the procedure was identical except that before being sent to find Big Mickey, children were asked, "Where is Little Mickey? Tell me where Little Mickey is hiding." This manipulation was intended to force the children to form a linguistic representation of Little Mickey's hiding spot, which could then be used to mediate their interactions with the model. As predicted, controlling for age, there was a strong positive correlation between language score and number of correct searches in the model task. Also as predicted, children in the language group were significantly more likely to succeed on the model task than were children in the standard group. The results support the claim that language mediates children's development of symbolic understanding.

These three functions of language—providing a social context, guiding and scaffolding behavior, and providing cognitive distance—are examples of the vital role played by language in children's development of symbolic understanding. The cognitive distance provided by language is particularly important for facilitating children's ability to engage in the dual representation of signs that are salient as objects (e.g., symbolic artifacts such as pictures or models). Language mediates representation of these signs and allows children to see beyond the object/signifier to the representation/signified. Although a majority of the research on dual representation has focused on children's difficulty with seeing the representation side of signs, for certain signs, children have difficulty with seeing the object/signifier side. This is particularly the case with linguistic signs when language has become a fully symbolic system for the child. When that occurs, linguistic signs are very salient as representations but are difficult for children to think about as objects in themselves. Whereas language facilitates the dual representation of symbolic artifacts, it is literacy that facilitates dual representation of linguistic signs, allowing language to become an "object of thought" (Olson, 1994).

Seeing Linguistic Signs as Objects: The Role of Literacy

For humans, language is the primary symbolic system. Normally, linguistic signs are "transparent" so that we see directly through linguistic signs to the meaning being conveyed without attending to the "object" properties of the signs. If necessary, adults can attend to the signifier side of linguistic signs, but for children this is very difficult. Even after children are fluent speakers, they find it difficult to "dual represent" linguistic signs: They can represent the signified but not the signifier. This is an ability that falls under the rubric of metalinguistic awareness.

Metalinguistic awareness is a term that has been used to convey a wide array of abilities, ranging from spontaneously correcting grammatical errors in speech to being able to express the nuances of different genres of writing. For the current discussion, we are interested in children's ability to reflect on the signifier side of linguistic signs. Children's awareness of the object/signifier properties of language can be considered to be present when they are able to spontaneously divide the continuous flow of speech into linguistic units such as phonemes or words. Doing so requires children to ignore the meaning being conveyed in speech, and instead focus on the properties of the actual linguistic signs that are being used.

Studies have typically found that children are able to divide speech into linguistic units such as words and phonemes sometime between the ages of 5 to 8 years, depending on the specific task used and the linguistic unit being assessed. Most theorists have focused on individual, cognitive factors to explain how children develop metalinguistic awareness. They have argued that metalinguistic awareness is either part of more general cognitive developments (e.g., Hakes, 1980; Piaget, 1929; Sinclair, 1978) or an aspect of language acquisition (e.g., Bialystok, 1993; Karmiloff-Smith, Grant, Sims, Jones, & Cuckle, 1996; Smith & Tager-Flusberg, 1982). There is considerable evidence, however, that literacy also plays a key role in facilitating the development of metalinguistic awareness.

This is an idea that was expressed by Vygotsky (1986), who argued that writing restructures the way that we think about language. His explanation focused on the differences between writing and speech. He argued that while speech is spontaneous and automatic, writing is an "abstract, voluntary, and conscious" activity and therefore it brings awareness to speech. For Vygotsky, it is the abstractness of writing that allows children to take cognizance of language: Writing "slows down" speech and provides a representation of language on which children can reflect. In other words, children can use the written representation to think about language signs. In this way, writing provides the cognitive distance that allows children to think about the object properties of linguistic signs.

A number of researchers have provided empirical support for the claim that children's metalinguistic awareness is strongly influenced by experience with writing (e.g., Bialystok, 1986; Downing & Leong, 1982; Ehri, 1985; Francis, 1975). Olson (1994), in his *model* theory of literacy, has argued that literacy plays a central role in the development of metalinguistic awareness. According to Olson, writing provides a model for understanding the structure of language; we become aware of the aspects of speech that are represented by our culture's script. Olson argues that writing is responsible for bringing aspects of language into consciousness by providing the set of categories that is used to reflect on and analyze speech.[2] Because the particular aspects of language that are brought into consciousness depend on the nature of the writing system, different writing systems will bring different aspects of language into consciousness. For example, the advent of writing systems that represented verbal form rather than meaning allowed for the differentiation between what is said and what is meant: What is said are the words written on the paper (i.e., the signifier), while what is meant is the intended meaning of the written words (i.e., the signified). Whereas the development of different scripts, different aspects of language are brought into awareness. For example, with syllabic scripts like Vai, the syllable becomes an object of thought, and with alphabetic scripts like Greek or English, phoneme-like sound units that correspond to letters become available for conscious reflection.

The model theory predicts that children's awareness of certain metalinguistic concepts should be related to literacy. Furthermore, both children and adults' metalinguistic awareness should be related to the particular script in which they are literate. Although few studies have been designed to explicitly test the model theory, there is considerable empirical evidence that supports predictions made by the model theory.

---

[2]Harris (1980, 1989, 1997) goes further and claims that writing is an idealized form of language that does not resemble actual speech and furthermore, linguistic categories such as phonemes and words are "second-order constructs" that are not brought into awareness, but are actually created by literacy.

For example, a number of studies have found that phonological awareness is related to learning to read an alphabetic script. Read, Zhang, Nie, and Ding (1986) investigated phonological awareness in an group of adult Chinese speakers, half of whom had previously learned an alphabetic script (i.e., Pinyin) in addition to learning traditional characters. The experimenters asked the participants to add and delete consonants in spoken Chinese words. (An English example of this task is to say "fish" without the "/f/.") Read et al. found that only those subjects with prior exposure to the alphabetic script Pinyin could segment words into phonemes. This effect was found even if exposure to the script had occurred many years previous and the subjects could no longer read or write in Pinyin.

Similar findings were reported by Huang and Hanley (1997) who carried out a longitudinal study with Chinese-speaking children. During their first year of school, the children were first taught a Chinese alphabetic script and then they were taught Chinese characters. The children were given phonemic awareness tasks several times throughout the school year: at the beginning of the year; 10 weeks later, after having been taught the alphabetic script; and a finally, after having been taught Chinese characters. Huang and Hanley found a significant increase in phonological awareness only after the children had been taught the alphabetic script, with no significant change after the children were taught Chinese characters (i.e., there was no increase in phonological awareness between Time 2 and Time 3). Based on their findings, the authors concluded that phonemic awareness is at least partially dependant on learning an alphabetic script.

This link between literacy and phonological awareness has also been found for children who are learning to read and write Spanish. In a study with Spanish-speaking children, Vernon and Ferreiro (1999) found that only when children had begun to relate letters to subsyllabic units (i.e., phonemes) could they pass a phoneme deletion task. The authors conclude that children's experience with writing affects their ability to analyze spoken language.

Perhaps the strongest evidence for a causal link between literacy and being able to dual represent linguistic signs comes from research on children's metalinguistic awareness of the concept of word. In one of the first empirical investigations of children's concept of word, Downing and Oliver (1974) presented 4- to 8-year-olds with a series of auditory stimuli and asked the children to identify which stimuli were words. In addition to words, the stimuli included distracters such as nonverbal sounds, phonemes, syllables, phrases and sentences. The researchers found that although all of the children overextended the use of word, there was a significant improvement at age 6, with the youngest age group (4- to 5-year-olds) making significantly more errors than the older groups.

Bialystok (1986) has also investigated children's concept of word using a number of Piagetian-style tasks. For example, in one task a sentence was read to children and they were asked to move a marker for each word in the sentence. In another task, children were asked to judge which of two spoken words was bigger: "train" or "caterpillar." This latter task is interesting because it explicitly pits the two sides of a linguistic sign against one another: It requires children to ignore the signified or representational side of the words (trains are bigger than caterpillars) and instead pay attention to the signifier or physical properties of the words ("caterpillar" is a bigger word than "train"). In both tasks, a significant improvement was found around age 6: The Grade 1 group performed significantly better than the Junior Kindergarten group. Both Bialystok and Downing and Oliver (1974) found that children demonstrate a marked improvement in their understanding of "word" at age 6, which is the same time that they begin school and start formal literacy instruction.

These types of tasks designed to test children's concept of word have been criticized by Karmiloff-Smith et al. (1996) as being too difficult for children; they designed a task that was intended to tap into children's "on-line" language processing capabilities. In their task, children were told a story, during which the experimenter would occasionally stop and ask the child to "repeat the last word." With the new task, preschool-aged children revealed some metalinguistic awareness of the concept of word, leading Karmiloff-Smith et al. to suggest that literacy is not causally involved in children's metalinguistic awareness. However, as noted previously, children begin the process of acquiring literacy prior to formal schooling and so emergent literacy may have played a role in the metalinguistic awareness of the children in Karmiloff-Smith et al.'s study.

Homer and Olson (1999) tested this idea by giving 4-, 5- and 6-year-olds a literacy task and a version of the Karmiloff-Smith et al. (1996) concept of word task. They found that about half of the 5-year-olds and a majority of the 6-year-olds passed the word-awareness task, and for all ages, the children who understood the concept of word in speech also understood "word" as a unit of text. The authors argued that this correlation between children's performance on the text-based and speech-based tasks supports the model theory of metalinguistic awareness. More recently, similar effects of literacy has been found for Chinese children's metalinguistic awareness of characters (Homer et al., 2005).

In the studies just reviewed, literacy was found to be linked to children's metalinguistic awareness, or their awareness of the object/signifier side of linguistic signs. Writing serves at least two related function. First, it provides children with cognitive distance that allows them not to be overwhelmed by the semantic or representational/signified side of linguistic signs, and instead to be able to contemplate the object/signifier side of language. A second function of writing is to provide a visually-fixed model of language that children use to divide up the continuous flow of speech, thus making children conscious of linguistic units that are found in their culture's language. In these ways, literacy facilitates the dual representation of language forms.

SUMMARY AND CONCLUSION

Children's acquisition of symbolic understanding is a complex process involving many different factors. It is not a uniform development, but instead children must learn to use and understand signs in different domains, with each domain providing unique challenges. Within the different domains, children's first use of signs is not symbolic, but instead involves iconic or indexical signs. This is true for signs that are learned earlier in development, such as words, as well as signs that are learned later on, such as literate graphic forms. One of the major difficulties faced by children in their acquisition of symbolic understanding is being able to engage in dual representation. Although symbolic development is domain specific, once symbol systems are learned then they can help facilitate the development of other domains. Both language and literacy facilitate the development of symbolic understanding in other domains. These two symbolic systems have been shown to be particularly important for providing the cognitive distance that allows children to engage in the dual representation and therefore see objects as symbols and symbols as objects. These effects of language and literacy are examples of the interplay between communication and cognition child development.

REFERENCES

Bialystok, E. (1986). Children's Concept of Word. *Journal of Psycholinguistic Research, 15*(1), 13–32.

Bialystok, E. (1993). Metalinguistic awareness: The development of children's representations of language. In C. Pratt & A. F. Garton (Eds.), *Systems of representation in children: Development and use* (pp. 211–233). John Wiley & Sons.

Byrne, B., Fielding-Barnsley, R., Ashley, L., & Larsen, K. (1997). Assessing the child's and the environment's contribution to reading acquisition: What we know and what we don't know. In B. Blachman (Ed.), *Foundations of reading acquisition and dyslexia: Implications for early intervention*. Mahwah, NJ: Lawrence Erlbaum Associates.

Callaghan, T. (1999). Early understanding and production of graphic symbols. *Child Development, 70*, 1314–1324.

Callaghan, T. (2000). Factors affecting children's graphic symbol use in the third year: Language, similarity, and iconicity. *Cognitive Development, 15*, 185–214.

Casby, M. W., & Corte, M. D. (1987). Symbolic play performance and early language development. *Journal of Psycholinguistic Research, 16*(1), 31–42.

Clay, M. (1979). *Reading: The patterning of complex behaviors*. Auckland: Heinemann.

Daiute, C. (Ed.). (1993). *The development of literacy through social interaction*. San Francisco, CA: Jossey-Bass Inc.

Deacon, T. W. (1997). *The symbolic species: The co-evolution of language and the brain*. New York: W. W. Norton.

DeLoache, J. S. (1991). Symbolic functioning in very young children: Understanding of pictures and models. *Child Development, 62*(4), 736–752.

DeLoache, J. S. (1995a). Early symbol understanding and use. *The Psychology of Learning and Motivation, 33*, 65–114.

DeLoache, J. S. (1995b). Early understanding and use of symbols: The model model. *Current Directions in Psychological Science, 4*(4), 109–113.

DeLoache, J. S. (2000). Dual representation and young children's use of scale models. *Child Development, 71*(2), 329–338.

DeLoache, J. S. (2002). The symbol-mindedness of young children. In W. Hartup & R. A. Weinberg (Eds.), *Child psychology in retrospect and prospect: In celebration of the 75th anniversary of the Institute of Child Development. The Minnesota symposia on child psychology, Vol. 32* (pp. 73–101).

DeLoache, J. S., & Burns, N. M. (1994). Symbolic functioning in preschool children. *Journal of Applied Developmental Psychology, 15*(4), 513–527.

DeLoache, J. S., Kolstad, V., & Anderson, K. N. (1991). Physical similarity and young children's understanding of scale models. *Child Development, 62*(1), 111–126.

DeLoache, J. S., & Marzolf, D. P. (1992). When a picture is not worth a thousand words: Young children's understanding of pictures and models. *Cognitive Development, 7*(3), 317–329.

Downing, J., & Leong, C. K. (1982). *Psychology of reading*. New York: Macmillan.

Downing, J., & Oliver, P. (1974). The child's conception of 'a word.' *Reading Research Quarterly, 4*, 568–582.

Dunn, L. M., & Dunn, L. M. (1997). *Peabody picture vocabulary test* (3rd ed.). Circle Pines, MN: American Guidance Service, Inc.

Ehri, L. C. (1985). Effects of printed language acquisition on speech. In D. R. Olson, N. Torrance, & A. Hildyard (Eds.), *Literacy, language and learning: The nature and consequences of reading and writing* (pp. 333–367). Cambridge: Cambridge University Press.

Ferreiro, E. (1986). *Proceso de alfabetizacion: La alfabetizacion en proceso [The process of alphabetization: Alphabetization in process]*. Buenos Aires: Bibliotecas Universitarias.

Ferreiro, E. (1991). Psychological and epistemological problems on written representation of language. In M. Carretero, M. Pope, R.-J. Simons, & J. I. Pozo (Eds.), *Learning and instruction* (Vol. 3, pp. 157–173). Oxford: Pergamon Press.

Ferreiro, E. (1996, August). *When is a word not a word?* Paper presented at the International Congress of Psychology, Montreal, PQ.

Ferreiro, E., & Teberosky, A. (1982). *Literacy before schooling* (S. Veintiuno, Trans.). Exeter, NH: Heinemann.

Fiese, B. (1990). Playful relations: A contextual analysis of mother-toddler interaction and symbolic play. *Child Development, 61*, 1648–1656.

Francis, H. (1975). *Language in childhood: Form and function in language learning*. London: Paul Elek.

Hakes, D. H. (1980). *The development of metalinguistic abilities in children*. New York: Springer-Verlag.

Harris, R. (1980). *The language-makers*. London: Duckworth.

Harris, R. (1989). How does writing restructure thought? *Language and Communication, 9*(2/3), 99–106.

Harris, R. (1997). From an integrational point of view. In G. Wolf & N. Love (Eds.), *Linguistics inside out: Roy Harris and his critics*. Philadelphia: John Benjamins Publishing Co.

Homer, B. D., & Nelson, K. (2003, April). *An experimental study of linguistic mediation in young children's symbolic understanding*. Paper presented at the Biennial Meeting of the Society for Research in Child Development, Tampa, FL.

Homer, B. D., & Olson, D. R. (1999). The role of literacy in children's concept of word. *Written Language and Literacy, 2*(1), 113–140.

Homer, B. D., Xu, F., Lee, K., & Olson, D. R. (2005). *The role of literacy in Canadian and Chinese children's metalinguistic awareness*. Manuscript submitted for publication.

Huang, H. S., & Hanley, J. R. (1997). A longitudinal study of phonological awareness, visual skills and Chinese reading acquisition among first-graders in Taiwan. *International Journal of Behavioral Development, 20*, 249–268.

Karmiloff-Smith, A., Grant, J., Sims, K., Jones, M.-C., & Cuckle, P. (1996). Rethinking metalinguistic awareness: Representing and accessing knowledge about what counts as a word. *Cognition, 58*, 197–219.

Levin, I., & Landsmann, L. T. (1989). Becoming literate: Referential and phonetic strategies in early reading and writing. *International Journal of Behavioral Development, 12*(3), 369–384.

Levy, E., & Nelson, K. (1994). Words in discourse: A dialectical approach to the acquisition of meaning and use. *Journal of Child Language, 21*, 367–389.

Nelson, K. (1996). *Language in cognitive development: The emergence of the mediated mind*. New York: Cambridge University Press.

Nelson, K. (2003). Making sense in a world of symbols. In A. Toomela (Ed.), *Cultural guidance in the development of the human mind* (pp. 139–162). Westport, CT: Greenwood.

Olson, D. R. (1994). *The world on paper: The conceptual and cognitive implications of writing and reading*. New York: Cambridge University Press.

Peirce, C. S. (1955). Logic as semiotic: The theory of signs. In J. Buchler (Ed.), *The philosophical writings of Peirce* (pp. 98–110). New York: Dover Books.

Piaget, J. (1929). *The child's conception of the world* (J. Tomlinson & A. Tomlinson, Trans.). London: Routledge & Kegan Paul.

Piaget, J. (1962). *Play, dreams and imitation in childhood*. New York: Norton.

Pontecorvo, C., & Zucchermaglio, C. (1988). Modes of differentiation in children's writing construction. *European Journal of Psychology of Education, 3*, 371–384.

Read, C. A., Zhang, Y., Nie, H., & Ding, B. (1986). The ability to manipulate speech sounds depends on knowing alphabetic reading. *Cognition, 24,* 31–44.
Saussure, F. d. (1959). *Course in general linguistics* (W. Baskin, Trans.). New York: Philosophical Library.
Sinclair, H. (1978). Conceptualization and awareness in Piaget's theory and its relevance to the child's conception of language. In A. Sinclair, R. J. Jarvella, & W. J. M. Levelt (Eds.), *The child's conception of language.* New York: Springer-Verlag.
Slade, A. (1987). A longitudinal study of maternal involvement and symbolic play during the toddler years. *Child Development, 58,* 367–375.
Smith, C. L., & Tager-Flusberg, H. (1982). Metalinguistic Awareness and Language Development. *Journal of Experimental Child Psychology, 34,* 449–468.
Snow, C., Barnes, W., Chandler, J., Goodman, I., & Hemphill, L. (1991). *Unfulfilled expectations: Home and school influences on literacy.* Cambridge, MA: Harvard University Press.
Striano, T., Tomasello, M., & Rochat, P. (2001). Social and object support for early symbolic play. *Developmental Science, 4*(4), 442–455.
Teale, W. H., & Sulzby, E. (Eds.). (1986). *Emergent literacy: Writing and reading.* Norwood, NJ: Ablex.
Tomasello, M., Striano, T., & Rochat, P. (1999). Do young children use objects as symbols? *British Journal of Developmental Psychology, 17*(4), 563–584.
Tulviste, T. (1993). The function of differentiating between a word and its referent. *Journal of Russian and East European Psychology, 31,* 27–39.
Vernon, S. (1993). Initial sound/letter correspondences in children's early written productions. *Journal of Research in Childhood Education, 8,* 12–22.
Vernon, S. A., & Ferreiro, E. (1999). Writing development: A neglected variable in the consideration of phonological awareness. *Harvard Educational Review, 69,* 395–415.
Vygotsky, L. S. (1986). *Thought and language* (A. Kazulin, Trans.). Cambridge, MA: MIT Press.
Werner, H., & Kaplan, H. (1963). *Symbol formation.* New York: Wiley.
Whitehurst, G., & Lonigan, C. (1998). Child development and emergent literacy. *Child Development* (69), 848–872.
Wood, D., Bruner, J., & Ross, G. (1976). The role of tutoring in problem solving. *Journal of child psychology and psychiatry, 17,* 89–100.
Xue, Q., Homer, B. D., & Fen, X. (2003, April). *Literacy and metalinguistic awareness in Chinese-English bilingual children.* Paper presented at the Biennial Meeting of the Society for Research in Child Development, Tampa, FL.

Chapter 3

*On the Possible Roots of Cognitive Flexibility**

Sophie Jacques
Dalhousie University

Philip David Zelazo
University of Toronto

ON THE POSSIBLE ROOTS OF COGNITIVE FLEXIBILITY

The ability to use human language is obviously dependent on both inherited cognitive systems and development in a social context. In turn, however, the emergence of language in childhood transforms these very same cognitive systems and social contexts. Although most researchers would agree that language has an impact on cognitive and social development, the nature of this impact is still being explored.

*The preparation of this chapter was funded by a research grant and postdoctoral fellowship from the Natural Science and Engineering Research Council (NSERC) of Canada. Correspondence concerning this chapter should be addressed to Sophie Jacques at Psychology Department, Life Sciences Centre, Dalhousie University, Halifax, NS, B3H 4J1 Canada or by email at sophie.jacques@dal.ca.

One of the earliest accounts of the role of language in development more generally comes from Lev Vygotsky (1934/1986). Vygotsky proposed that human cognitive development occurs as a result of two independent lines of development—the natural line of development in which maturation of the nervous system leads to developmental changes in basic cognitive processes such as memory or attention, and the cultural line of development in which children appropriate cultural tools and use them to control their thoughts and actions. By his account, language is the most important of these cultural tools and its appropriation makes possible the development of unique cognitive processes that are simply unavailable to other species.

Benjamin Whorf (1956) went further than Vygotsky in his claims about the role of language on cognitive development. He argued for the *linguistic relativity hypothesis:* that the language one speaks actually determines the kinds of thoughts that one can have. Both Vygotsky and Whorf clearly allowed for cultural learning to have a major impact on children's development (cf. Astington & Pelletier, this volume; Tomasello, 2003; Tomasello, Kruger, & Ratner, 1993). In contrast to nativist approaches to cognition, and to the idea that children's cognitive development depends mainly on interactions with the nonsocial environment (an idea often attributed to Piaget, 1964), the approaches promoted by Vygotsky and Whorf suggest that the course of cognitive development is influenced in important ways by children's interactions with other people. As children interact with other people, they rely on their own symbolic representations to appropriate (external) symbolic representations (especially language) from others, and doing so transforms the way in which they represent the world (see also Nelson, this volume).

A growing body of research on infancy has explored aspects of this dynamic, interactive process. For example, some researchers have investigated how early social understanding allows children to acquire language (e.g., Baldwin, 2000). Others, such as Xu (2002), have focused on how language, in turn, affects the way in which children represent the world. Xu (2002) found that the use of two distinct labels helped 9-month-olds succeed on an object individuation task that is usually difficult for children under 12 months of age. This provides an intriguing demonstration of the way in which language may shape cognition even in the very earliest stages of language acquisition.

In this chapter, we focus on the effects of language on cognitive function during the preschool period. In particular, we review the role that one aspect of language—labeling—might play in the development of one aspect of human cognitive function—the emergence of cognitive flexibility. Cognitive flexibility, or the ability to consider simultaneously multiple conflicting representations of a single object or event, is a hallmark of human cognitive function, and its consequences for behavior are clear. Among other things, cognitive flexibility is critical for such things as the development of a theory of mind and the development of set shifting (an aspect of executive function).

We begin by identifying various measures of cognitive flexibility, including measures that were not specifically designed to assess cognitive flexibility. We then discuss a basic difference between two kinds of measures of flexibility (viz. deductive vs. inductive measures), a difference that has important implications for assessing the role of language on the development of this ability. Next, we present findings from research on cognitive flexibility in which labels were manipulated. Thus, we review labeling effects in early work by Luria and his colleagues on rule use, work by the Kendlers and others on discrimination-shift learning, and work by Bruner and his colleagues on problem solving. We also review more recent labeling studies conducted by Gentner, Deák, and others, including our own research using a variety of labeling manipulations on the *Flexible Item Selection Task* (FIST; Jacques & Zelazo, 2001), a task that we devised specifically to assess flexible thinking. We show that not only does labeling affect performance on several measures of cognitive flexibility, but the impact of these labels appears to change with development, especially between 3 and 4 years of age.

MEASURES OF COGNITIVE FLEXIBILITY WITH CONFLICT

Before examining the effect of language on cognitive flexibility per se, we will first discuss measures of cognitive flexibility themselves. In the previous section, we defined cognitive flexibility as the ability to take multiple perspectives simultaneously on a single object or event. There are at least four dozen cognitive and sociocognitive tasks that we consider to be measures of flexibility according to this definition (see Table 3.1 for a listing of many of these). These tasks vary greatly in the content domain that they were specifically designed to assess. However, all tasks have a similar underlying structure such that if children approach the problem from one perspective, they will respond correctly, but if they approach it from another perspective, they will err. Moreover, adopting the incorrect perspective is easier or more natural. Only children with a "real" understanding of whichever concept is being tested by the investigators will adopt the more difficult perspective and therefore, respond correctly on the task. Thus, irrespective of the content domain, this particular task design allows investigators to identify exactly how children are solving the specific problem of interest.

For example, consider the false-belief task (Wimmer & Perner, 1983). In the change-of-location version of this task, children are told a story about a protagonist who mistakenly believes that an object is in a particular location, when in reality, it is in another location. Children are then asked to predict where the protagonist will search for the object. To succeed on the task, children must reason from the erroneous perspective of the protagonist while refraining from responding on the basis of their own current reality-informed perspective. In order for children to succeed on false-belief tasks, then, they necessarily need to be flexible in their thinking because they must consider a single object from two conflicting representations of its possible location. The Day-night Stroop-like task developed by Gerstadt, Hong, and Diamond (1994) is another example of a measure of flexibility. In this task, children are asked to say "Day" when presented with a picture of a moon and "Night" when presented with a picture of a sun. This is a measure of flexibility because it requires that children go against their pre-existing tendency to respond in a semantically congruent fashion when presented with each of the stimuli (e.g., to say "Day" in response to the picture of the sun).

For both false-belief tasks and the Day-night Stroop-like task (and many other measures of flexibility), investigators have capitalized on children's existing prepotent tendencies to favor a particular perspective over the other. In the false-belief task, if children do not understand the notion that people can hold false beliefs, they will respond on the basis of their own reality-informed perspective. In everyday life, children also have learned to associate the moon with nighttime and the sun with daytime.

In contrast, instead of capitalizing on children's existing prepotent response tendencies, others have taken a different approach by constructing tasks in which two equally salient perspectives are presented but one is made more salient during task administration. The *Dimensional Change Card Sort* (DCCS; Frye, Zelazo, & Palfai, 1995; Zelazo, Frye, & Rapus, 1996) is an example of such a task. In the DCCS, children are presented with two target cards (e.g., a red flower and a blue car), and they are asked to sort bivalent test cards (e.g., blue flowers and red cars), first by one dimension (i.e., preswitch phase; e.g., color) and then by the other (i.e., postswitch phase; e.g., shape). Sorting by the second dimension in the postswitch phase requires responses that conflict with those made in the preswitch phase. Children must be able to take two separate perspectives on the same test cards in order to sort correctly in both phases of the task.

Hence, on all measures of flexibility, children are required to respond either on the basis of a less preferred perspective or on the basis of *two* distinct perspectives. For the purpose of the current chapter, we denote trials on which children must adopt the more difficult of the two perspectives as *flexibility trials*. Therefore, on false-belief tasks, flexibility trials are those on which children must reason from another person's beliefs; on the DCCS, they are those on which children must sort by the second dimension, and so on.

Notice that in these examples, the distinct perspectives are in *conflict* and thus, lead to responses that are qualitatively different. This feature of the task makes it easy to identify which perspective children are adopting to perform the task. However, there are measures in which children can use multiple sources of information—or perspectives—to solve the task, but using all or only one of the sources leads to the same overt response (e.g., Uttal, Chiong, & Wilson, 2003). As a result, in order to assess flexibility on these kinds of tasks, researchers must rely on indirect means for determining which source(s) of information children actually used to solve the task (e.g., relying on children's verbal reports). Given the difficulty in establishing directly which perspective(s) children use to respond on these nonconflict measures of flexibility, however, we restrict our review to tasks in which different perspectives lead to different, conflicting overt responses patterns.

Deductive Measures of Flexibility

Two kinds of measures of flexibility with conflict can be distinguished: *deductive* and *inductive* measures. These measures differ in the amount and kind of information provided to children, and consequently, in the nature of the inferences that children must make (deductive vs. inductive inferences). In deductive measures of flexibility, all of the information necessary for solving the task is provided to children (see the first set of tasks in Table 3.1 for a listing of deductive measures of flexibility). To solve these tasks, children simply need to apply this information on specific trials. For example, as mentioned previously, in the DCCS, children are told to sort test cards according to one dimension in a preswitch phase and they are then told to sort by a different dimension in a postswitch phase. In the standard administration of the task, children are reminded of the rules on every trial in both phases so that all that they need to do to succeed is to apply the rules they are given. For example, on a given trial, children might be told, "Red ones go in this box and blues one go in that box. Here's a red one, where does it go?" As in all deductive measures, children simply need to deduce what to do on specific trials.

Nonetheless, despite being provided with relevant information, preschoolers exhibit substantial difficulties on deductive tasks. In general, across a wide range of deductive measures children's performance improves dramatically between the ages of 3 and 4 years (e.g., Day-night Stroop-like task, Gerstadt et al., 1994; DCCS, Frye et al., 1995; Go-No-Go, Luria, 1959; see Table 3.1). There are some notable exceptions, how-

TABLE 3.1 Measures of Cognitive Flexibility by Type

Task by Type	*Major Age-Related Change*	*Reference*
	(Standard Task Administration)	
Deductive		
Bear/Dragon Task	3.0 to 4.0	Reed, Pien, & Rothbart (1984)
Day-night Stroop-like Test	3.0 to 3.5 (for correct responding)	Gerstadt, Hong, & Diamond (1994)
Detour-Reaching Box	3.0 to 4.0	Hughes (1998)
Dimensional Change Card Sort	3.0 to 4.0	Frye, Zelazo, & Palfai (1995)
Go-No-Go Task	3.5 to 4.0	Luria (1959, 1961)
Spatial Conflict Task	2.5 to 3.0	Gerardi-Caulton (2000)
Luria Hand Game	3.0 to 4.0	Hughes (1996, 1998)
Luria Tapping Game Test	3.5 to 4.0 (for correct responding)	Diamond & Taylor (1996)
Match-Form-and-Content Task (Deductive)	3.0 to 5.0 (4-year-olds not tested)	Lourenco, Zelazo, & Liebermann (2005)
Moral Reasoning Task	3.0 to 4.0	Zelazo, Helwig, & Lau (1996)
Physical Causality (Ramp) Task	3.0 to 4.0	Frye, Zelazo, Brooks, & Samuels (1996)
Smarties Task	3.0 to 4.0	Müller, Zelazo, Leone, & Hood (2004)
Synonym Judgment Task	3.5 to 4.0	Doherty & Perner (1998)
Inductive		
Ambiguous Figures Task (Informed Cond.)	3.5 to 4.0	Gopnik & Rosati (2001)
Airplane-in-the-Sky Task	5.0 to 6.0	Martsinovskaya & Abramyan, in Luria (1961)
Appearance-Reality Task	3.0 to 4.0	Flavell, Flavell, & Green (1983)
Beaker Matrix Task	4.0 to 5.0	Bruner & Kenny (1966)
Number Conservation	3.0 to 4.0	Siegler (1981)
Quantity Conservation	6.0 to 7.0	Siegler (1981)
Cross-Mapping Task	4.0 to 5.0	Rattermann & Gentner (1998)
Deception/Sabotage Tasks	3.0 to 4.0	Hughes (1998)

Task by Type	Major Age-Related Change	Reference
	(Standard Task Administration)	
Deceptive Pointing Task	3.0 to 4.0	Carlson, Moses, & Hix (1998)
Discrimination Shift Learning Task	4.0 to 7.0 (5- & 6-year-olds not tested)	Kendler & Kendler (1961)
Double Categorization Task	4.0 to 5.0	Blaye, Jacques, Bonthoux, & Cannard (2003)
False Belief Task	3.0 to 4.0	Wellman, Cross, & Watson (2001)
Flexible Item Selection Task	4.0 to 5.0	Jacques & Zelazo (2001)
Future-Oriented Prudence Task	3.0 to 4.0	Thompson, Barresi, & Moore (1997)
Moving-Word Task	4.0 to 5.0	Bialystok (1991, 1997)
Visual Perspective Taking Task (Level 2)	3.0 to 4.0	Masangkay et al. (1974)
Match-Form-and-Content Task (Inductive)	3.0 to 5.0 (4-year-olds not tested)	Lourenco, Zelazo, & Liebermann (2005)
Matrix Classification Task	6.0 to 7.0	Inhelder & Piaget (1959/1964)
Novel Word Inference Task	3.0 to 4.0	Deák (2000)
Representational Change Task	3.0 to 4.0	Gopnik & Astington (1988)
Cross-Classification Tasks	6.0 to 7.0	Inhelder & Piaget (1959/1964)
Size-Judgement Task	3.0 to 4.0	Gelman & Ebeling (1989)
Spatial Analogy Task (Object Conflict)	4.0 to 5.0	Loewenstein & Gentner (in press)
Spatial Search Task (Indirect landmark)	3.0 to 5.0 (4-year-olds not tested)	Herman-Vazquez, Moffet, & Munkholm (2001)
Teddy-Bear Set Shifting Task	3.0 to 4.0	Hughes (1998)
Transposition Task	4.0 to 5.0	Kuenne (1946)
Windows Task	3.0 to 4.0	Russell, Mauthner, Sharpe, & Tidswell (1991)
Word-Size Problem	4.0 to 5.0	Bialystok (1991)

Notes. Tasks in bold are those for which labeling and nonlabeling versions have been compared directly (see text for a discussion of these findings).

(continued)

TABLE 3.1 *(continued)*

Notes: This list is not meant to be exhaustive. There are a number of other measures of flexibility that exist (e.g., Shift Attention, Courchesne et al., 1994; Forbidden Color Naming Task, Leontiev, 1932; Simon Task, Simon 1990; Simon Says Task, LaVoie, Anderson, Fraze, & Johnson, 1981; Strommen, 1973; Stop-Signal Paradigm, Logan, Cowen, & Davis, 1984; Stroop Task, Stroop, 1935; Visual Verbal Test, Feldman & Drasgow, 1951; Wisconsin Card Sorting Test, Berg, 1948; Grant & Berg, 1948), but that have not been used with preschoolers either because other task demands make them too difficult for use with children within this age range or the studies have not been done. In fact, some of the other tasks in this table have actually been designed as simplified versions of more complex tasks (e.g., Bear-Dragon Task for the Simon-Says Task; Day-Night Stroop and Smarties Task for the Stroop Task; Flexible Item Selection Task for the Visual Verbal Test; Spatial-Conflict Task for the Simon Task; Teddy-Bear Set Shifting Task for the Wisconsin Card Sorting Test). In addition, there are other tasks in the literature that meet our definition of measures of cognitive flexibility with conflict (e.g., see Carlson & Moses, 2001; Perner, Stummer, Sprung, & Doherty, 2002). However, many of these are variants of the tasks presented above and others like Delay (Reed, Pien, & Rothbart, 1984) and Delay-of-Gratification Tasks (e.g., Mischel, Shoda, & Rodriguez, 1989) use response times rather than correct responding as the primary dependent measure, making it difficult to compare them with the other tasks. Finally, other tasks exist (e.g., Deák, Ray, & Pick's, 2002, Object-Function Matching Task), which, in their original versions were not administered as measures of flexibility according to our definition, but could be easily adapted.

Finally, some of the names of the tasks provided in the table are not the actual names of the tasks that the authors devised, but rather, they are short acronyms that we are using for convenience. Moreover, where possible in the Reference column, we tried to cite the researchers who actually developed each task, however, it was not always possible to do so as we also wanted to cite the work of researchers who conducted research with children in the relevant age range. The age changes that we report in middle column are those reported by the researchers cited in the table.

ever. On the one hand, there are some tasks on which children's performance continues to improve beyond the age of 4 and are sometimes difficult even for adults (e.g., Stroop Task, Stroop, 1935; see MacLeod, 1991, for a review). However, these tasks appear to place high performance demands, such as requiring rapid, timed responses or requiring that children respond over a long series of trials. For example, children's performance on Luria's Tapping Test continues to show noticeable improvements in terms of response latencies well into children's sixth year, despite the fact that the largest improvement in *correct* responding on this task occurs between 3½ and 4 years of age (Diamond & Taylor, 1996).

On the other hand, younger children have been shown to perform well on other tasks that seemingly measure flexibility. For example, Gerardi-Caulton (2000) developed a spatial conflict task on the basis of the Simon Task (Simon, 1990) in which object and location information are pitted against each other. In Gerardi-Caulton's simplified spatial conflict task, 24- to 36-month-old children were presented with one of two items on a computer screen (e.g., lion vs. elephant) and children had to press one of two buttons, each with a picture of one of the two items (e.g., lion on the right button and the elephant on the left button), that matched the item presented on the screen. On spatial *compatible* trials, items were presented on the same side of the computer screen as the button with the picture of that item. On spatial *incompatible* trials, the items were presented on the other side of the screen. Gerardi-Caulton reported that by 36 months of age, children were accurate on over 90% of trials, despite being slightly slower on the spatial incompatible trials. However, despite the fact that this task appears to be a measure of flexibility, there are some slight, but important, differences between this task and other measures of flexibility.

Essentially, spatial information is not *inherently* present within the items (e.g., lion vs. elephant). Therefore, in the spatial conflict task, it may be possible to ignore spatial information and simply match the picture on the screen with the picture on the button. In other words, conflict may not truly be present in the spatial conflict task in the same way that it is in other measures of flexibility. However, it would be relatively easy to adapt Gerardi-Caulton's (2000) spatial conflict task to make it into a measure of flexibility with conflict. One way to do this would be to incorporate spatial information within the object information that could then be made to be incompatible with the spatial information provided by the location of the object on the screen. For example, children could be asked to select the left-hand button when they saw an elephant facing left and the right-hand button when they saw an elephant facing right, irrespective of which side of the monitor the elephant was actually located. An alternate way to construct a flexibility version of the spatial conflict task would be to keep the same task that Gerardi-Caulton created but have children use one kind of information (e.g., object information) first and then switch and use the other kind of information (e.g., location information).

Inductive Measures of Flexibility

Inductive measures differ from deductive measures in that children must make at least one inductive inference regarding how to go about solving the task: Children are not told explicitly *how* to solve the task. The false-belief task is one example of an inductive measure of flexibility. In the change-of-location false-belief task, children are told that the protagonist mistakenly believes that the object is in another location, but children are not told how to use this information to predict where the protagonist will look for the object.

Another example is the FIST (Jacques & Zelazo, 2001). On each trial of the FIST, children are shown three items (e.g., a small red boat, a small red shoe, and a small blue shoe), two of which match on one relevant dimension (e.g., the small red boat and the small red shoe match on color), and two of which match on another relevant dimension (e.g., the small red shoe and the small blue shoe match on shape). The other dimension is constant and irrelevant across the three items (e.g., size). Children are asked to select one pair of items that "go together in one way" (i.e., Selection 1). They are then asked to select a second pair of items that "go together but in another way" (i.e., Selection 2). Selection 1 responses measure primarily children's ability to abstract how two nonidentical items match on a particular dimension. In contrast, assuming good performance on Selection 1, Selection 2 responses serve primarily as flexibility trials. Because children are not told to select specific items by a specific dimension (e.g., "Show me the two red ones.") but instead must determine for themselves which pairs to select, the task is an inductive one.

As can be seen from Table 3.1, successful performance on many of these inductive measures of flexibility—including successful performance on the FIST—appears to occur at a later age than successful performance on the deductive measures. One reason for the décalage between successful performance on deductive and inductive measures may be due specifically to the deductive/inductive nature of the tasks: All else being equal, having to make inductive inferences may make inductive tasks necessarily more difficult than deductive tasks in which children are provided with all relevant information for completing the task at the outset. However, the inductive nature of the tasks alone appears to be insufficient to account for the décalage because 4-year-olds have been found do well on almost half of the inductive tasks, including false-belief tasks (Wellman, Cross, & Watson, 2001).

Alternatively, another difference between deductive and inductive tasks concerns the amount of relevant information that is explicitly *labeled* in each kind of task. In general, researchers label all relevant information in deductive tasks in the course of telling children what to do. In contrast, labeling relevant information is less likely to occur on inductive measures, although there are some tasks in which researchers do so anyway. On this analysis, it is possible that inductive measures of flexibility could be solved earlier if relevant information were labeled. For example, according to a recent meta-analysis by Wellman et al. (2001), the majority of 4-year-olds succeed on false-belief tasks, and when presenting false-belief stories to children, experimenters tend to label all relevant information (e.g., specific locations or specific contents), even if it is unnecessary to do so. If labeling relevant information is crucial for successful performance, this could explain why this particular kind of inductive measure is typically solved at a younger age than other inductive measures of flexibility. In fact, on this account, it might be possible to *worsen* the performance of 4-year-olds on these inductive measures of flexibility simply by limiting the use of relevant labels (see Jacques & Zelazo, in press, for a suggestion on how labels might be manipulated on false-belief tasks themselves).

As another example, in a different domain, Gelman and Ebeling (1989) attempted to delineate the development of preschoolers' understanding of different nonegocentric size standards including normative and functional standards. The task that they used to assess children's understanding of these different standards can also be considered to be a measure of flexibility. Specifically, they presented 3-, 4-, and 5-year-olds with a series of small and large objects. Half of the children were asked to make normative judgments for each object (e.g., "Is this a big or a little hat?"). The other children were asked to make functional judgments for each of these normatively small and large objects relative to a big or a little doll (e.g., "Is this hat big or little for the doll?). To answer the functional questions correctly they had to ignore the normative size of the objects (i.e., whether they were big or small) and instead focus on the size of the objects relative to the doll to which the objects were compared. The items were presented such that if children in the functional judgment condition judged normatively, then their responses would be different than if they judged functionally (e.g., a normatively small hat that was too big for a smaller doll). The authors found that 3-year-olds were at chance when judging the functional sizes of tools, whereas both 4- and 5-year-olds did well in both the normative and functional judgment conditions. Labels were not manipulated directly in these studies. In fact, all items were labeled for all children, which could explain 4-year-olds' good performance in both conditions.[1]

Summary of Findings with Flexibility Measures

Despite the fact that many of the tasks presented in Table 3.1 were not specifically intended to be measures of flexibility, and despite the fact

[1]In another experiment in the same paper, however, the authors assessed whether they could improve 3-year-olds' performance by modifying the instructions for the functional condition in such a way as to direct children's attention specifically to the functional aspects of the objects (e.g., "Is this hat *too* big or *too* little for the doll?"). Interestingly, this slight modification in the instructions significantly improved 3-year-olds' performance, perhaps by emphasizing the less salient perspective. This finding is reminiscent of a similar finding in the theory of mind literature that adding the word "first" in the false-belief test question helps 3-year-olds succeed on false-belief tasks (e.g., "Where will Jane look *first* for her kitten?"; Siegal & Beattie, 1991). As with the size-judgment task, the modifications in the instructions in the false-belief question appears to emphasize the less salient perspective.

that the tasks assess children's conceptual understanding in a wide range of content domains, preschoolers' performance on many of these tasks appears to be remarkably similar. In fact, recent studies have shown large correlations between performance on many of these tasks in both typically (e.g., Carlson & Moses, 2001; Carlson, Moses, & Hix,1998; Frye et al., 1995; see Perner & Lang, 1999; Zelazo & Jacques, 1997, for reviews) and atypically developing children (e.g., Hughes & Russell, 1993; Ozonoff, Pennington, & Rogers, 1991; Zelazo, Jacques, Burack, & Frye, 2002). In addition, there appears to be a difference in the age at which the majority of children succeed on deductive and inductive measures of flexibility. More specifically, significant changes seem to occur most often between 3 and 4 years of age on deductive measures of flexibility, whereas changes in performance on many inductive measures seem to occur between about 4 and 5 years (see Table 3.1). In the next section, we discuss existing evidence for the role of language in the development of cognitive flexibility.

LABELING EFFECTS ON MEASURE OF COGNITIVE FLEXIBILITY

There exists some correlational support for a link between language development and the development of flexible thinking in preschool children. In early work, Kuenne (1946) found age-related improvements in children's ability to solve complex transposition problems in which they had to select stimuli according to their relation with other items (e.g., the bigger of two items). Kuenne also found that children who could articulate exactly how they solved the transposition problem by using appropriate relational terms such as "smaller" versus "bigger" were able to succeed on all transposition problems, whereas those children who could not verbalize the rationale for their solutions could only solve simpler transposition problems, problems that even infra-human species can solve.

Likewise, Bruner and Kenny (1966) conducted an experiment in which they assessed children on their ability to reproduce nontransposed and transposed versions of a 3 × 3 matrix of nine clear-plastic beakers that varied on three possible heights and on three possible widths. To perform correctly on both versions, children needed to be flexible in how they represented the position of the beakers because they needed to consider two dimensions (height and width) simultaneously (as in Inhelder & Piaget's, 1959/1964, Matrix Classification Task). In addition, the transposed version was more difficult than the nontransposed version because the transposed version required that children determine the new correct positions of each beaker on both dimensions relative to the beaker(s) already in place while simultaneously suppressing their tendency to place each beaker back in its original position. Of particular interest were findings indicating differences in children's performance on both versions that correlated with their use of precise dimensional terms (e.g., "short" vs. "tall" for height or "skinny" vs. "fat" for width) or global, undifferentiated terms like "big" and "little" to refer to differences between beakers.

Similarly, in recent work, Hermer-Vazquez, Moffet, and Munkholm (2001) found that children who could reliably produce spatial terms like "left" and "right" in one task were able to solve another spatial reorientation task using only landmark information, even when this landmark information conflicted with geometric information. In contrast, children who failed to produce such labels performed at chance on the spatial reorientation task.

Finally, in the theory of mind literature, Astington and Jenkins (1999) found significant relations between language development and performance on standard theory of mind tasks including false-belief and appearance-reality tasks. Much research now exists that confirms this link between language and theory of mind development, although different researchers have emphasized different reasons for why language abilities might be related to developments within this content domain (see the volume by Astington & Baird, in press; and Astington & Pelletier, this volume). However, it is also possible to reinterpret this relation in terms of language-related effects on cognitive flexibility more generally, rather than on theory of mind development specifically (see Jacques & Zelazo, in press, for such an interpretation).

Although these results are interesting and are consistent with the hypothesis that language may affect the development of cognitive flexibility, there are many other reasons why measures of language development might predict performance on measures of cognitive flexibility. Thus, to circumvent problems of determining cause-and-effect using correlational findings, we limit the rest of our discussion to investigations in which language has been manipulated experimentally. In most of these studies, the language manipulations have been introduced as labeling manipulations in which labels are either introduced by the experimenter in certain conditions, or children themselves are asked to label specific information. As mentioned previously, for many of these studies, the tasks were not specifically designed to assess flexibility, and consequently, neither were the labeling manipulations. Nonetheless, the findings from both intended and unintended tests of labeling effects on measures of flexibility appear to be relatively similar across tasks, although there appears to be a real difference between labeling effects on deductive and inductive measures. As a result, we review these separately.

Labeling Effects on Deductive Measures

As noted, experimenters typically label all relevant information in deductive tasks. Nonetheless, researchers have introduced additional labeling manipulations on these tasks. In most instances they have done so by asking children *themselves* to label relevant information in addition to the experimenter's labels presented in the task instructions. For example, in an early study, Luria (1959, 1961) assessed the effects of labeling on a Go-No-Go Task. On this task, children were asked to press a bulb when a red light came on and they were asked to refrain from pressing when a blue light came on. Like measures discussed in previous sections, this is a measure of flexibility because within the same paradigm, children must do something under one condition, and they must do the reverse under another condition. Luria found that 3-year-olds had difficulty on the basic version of the task, whereas older preschoolers tended to do well. Moreover, when 3-year-olds were asked to accompany their manual responses (i.e., the response for which they were to press the ball) with self-directed commands like "press", they were better able to regulate their responses. In contrast, however, when 3-year-olds' were asked to accompany their *nonresponses* with self-directed commands like "don't press", their performance on no-go trials worsened. This was not true for older children, however. Their performance improved when they labeled both go and no-go trials. Luria argued that at age 3, children can direct their behavior using *impulsive* aspects of labels, but are still unable to govern their behavior using *semantic* aspects of labels; older preschoolers begin to use the meaning of labels to govern their behavior. We return to the issue of a possible qualitative change in how labels are used by 3- versus 4-year-olds in a later section.

Although Luria's work has been extremely influential, Western efforts to replicate Luria (1959, 1961) have only been partially successful. For example, Miller, Shelton, and Flavell (1970) were unable to replicate the age-related changes in the effects of labeling observed by Luria, even though they were able to replicate the basic age-related changes in manual responding on the task itself. In fact, they found that labeling seemed to disrupt children's performance across the entire age range of 3 to 5 years. They also found that children often labeled *after* they had pressed the bulb, and as a result, labels did not seem to help children control their manual responses. It is almost impossible to know exactly why Miller et al. (and other Western researchers) obtained results that differed from those of Luria given Luria's cursory descriptions of his methodologies. It may be that Miller et al. administered the task in some slightly different way and that may have had a crucial impact on their findings. Perhaps there are also cross-cultural or cross-linguistic differences in the effectiveness of labels. In any event, however, it remains unclear whether labels improve performance on this deductive measure of flexibility.

More recently, several researchers have conducted labeling experiments with the DCCS (Kirkham, Cruess, & Diamond, 2003; Lurye & Müller, 2003; Towse, Redbond, Houston-Price, & Cook, 2000; Yerys & Munakata, 2003), but the results of these experiments have also been mixed. For example, Kirkham et al. tested 3- and 4-year-olds in one of four versions of the DCCS, two of which are pertinent to the present discussion. In one of these conditions, children were tested in the standard version of the DCCS whereas in the other, children were also asked to label the stimuli in both the preswitch and the postswitch phases before sorting each of the test cards. That is, before each trial, when children were shown a test card that they had to sort, the experimenter asked, "What color (shape) is this one?" for the first trial in each phase, and then for the remaining trials in each phase, the experimenter asked children, "What's this one?" According to the authors, children labeled the correct dimension in both phases and on all trials within each phase in all but three instances. In addition, they found that 78% of 3-year-olds succeeded in sorting cards correctly in the postswitch phase compared to 42% in the standard version. Therefore, their results revealed that asking children to label the test cards in both the preswitch and postswitch phases helped 3-year-olds' performance on this task.

Towse et al. (2000, Experiment 4) also included a labeling manipulation on the DCCS. Unlike Kirkham et al. (2003), the experimenter asked only children who had failed the postswitch trials to identify test cards by asking the question, "What's this?" Unlike Kirkham et al., Towse and colleagues did not find that most 3-year-olds labeled appropriately when asked about the postswitch dimension. In fact, as the authors note,

> Despite being explicitly and repeatedly given the postswitch rules and despite completing six trials where the experimenter labeled cards with (just) the postswitch attribute, less than half the children ($n = 9$) identified the card solely in terms of its rule-relevant postswitch feature. (p. 359)

It is unclear why Towse et al. obtained different results from those obtained by Kirkham et al. Perhaps their results differed because of differences in when children were asked to label the stimuli and in how the experimenters worded the labeling questions.[2]

[2]Lurye and Müller (2003) also failed to find an effect of labeling on the DCCS, using the same procedure as Kirkham et al. In our own work, we found (like Towse et al., 2000) that the majority of 3-year-olds did not respond correctly when asked specific questions about the color, size, or shape of the stimuli on the FIST, whereas the majority of 4- and 5-year-olds could respond appropriately to such questions (Jacques et al., 2005; Experiment 1, irrelevant-label condition).

Using a different approach, Yerys and Munakata (2003) manipulated *experimenter* labels on the *preswitch* trials of the DCCS with 3-year-olds and assessed whether their performance differed on the *postswitch* phase. That is, the experimenter either labeled the relevant dimension in the preswitch phase or did not label it. For example, children in the labeling condition were told in the preswitch phase, "This is the color game. In the color game, the red ones go here and the blue ones go here. Here's a red one, where does it go?" Children in the no-label condition were told, "This is the sorting game. In the sorting game, this one goes here (the experiment waved a red truck) and this one goes here (the experimenter waved a blue flower). Here's one (the experimenter showed a red truck), where does it go?" In the postswitch phase, all children received the same labeled instructions. The authors found that a lack of labels in the preswitch phase *helped* 3-year-olds succeed on the postswitch phase. There are several possible explanations for this finding.[3] For example, it may be that not labeling the preswitch dimension made it easier for children to turn their attention to the relevant postswitch dimension (which *was* labeled). On this account, general attention-getting properties of labels might help explain why labeling in the preswitch phase hinders 3-year-olds' performance on the post-switch phase of the DCCS.

Using a different paradigm, Müller, Zelazo, Leone, and Hood (2004) also found that labeling helped 3-year-olds succeed on this deductive measure of flexibility by helping children redirect their attention to relevant information. In this task, children were shown five different colored Smarties that were placed on large mismatching colored cards (e.g., a green Smartie on a red card). They were also given a set of five small colored cards. In order to win the Smarties, the experimenter pointed to one of the Smarties and children were asked to give the experimenter one of the small colored cards that matched the color of the larger card on which that particular Smartie rested. In other words, children had to refrain from giving the experimenter a colored card that matched the color of the Smartie itself. Most 3-year-olds failed on the conflict version of the task but did well on a version in which the color of the cards did not conflict with the color of the Smarties. In contrast, 4-year-olds did well in both versions. However, even 3-year-olds did well when they were asked to label the color of the larger card before reaching for the small card. Having to label the larger card itself appears to have reoriented children's attention from focusing on the color of the Smarties to focusing on the color of the card, as they were required to do.

[3]For example, the authors used different kinds of stimuli from the ones used in previous studies with the standard version of the DCCS. In addition, removing labels may also have changed the preswitch phase from a deductive to an inductive task, which makes it difficult to determine whether or not it was the presence or absence of labels itself that led to performance differences.

Significant improvements in a pointing condition (Experiment 3) support this interpretation.

Labeling Effects on Inductive Measures

As with deductive tasks, perhaps the first experimental studies examining the effects of labeling on inductive measures of cognitive flexibility in preschoolers were done by Luria and his colleagues. In a simple yet telling study, Martsinovskaya (as cited in Luria, 1961) developed a task in which children were shown pictures of two simple colored circles on colored backgrounds (e.g., a red circle on a grey background and a green circle on a yellow background). Children were asked to squeeze a balloon on the right for the first picture and a balloon on the left for the second. Children easily learned to map the correct responses to the appropriate stimuli. Then, to determine whether the object in the foreground governed children's choices or whether the background color did, the experimenter presented children with stimuli for which the objects and backgrounds had been reversed (e.g., a red circle on a yellow background). Not surprisingly, children generally responded on the basis of the color of the object itself (foreground) and not the color of the background. In a separate experiment, Abramyan (also cited in Luria, 1961) attempted to determine whether language would reverse children's preexisting tendency to focus on the foreground object. To do so, Abramyan presented children with pictures of colored airplanes (instead of circles) on similar grey and yellow backgrounds. In addition, children were told to squeeze the right balloon when they saw the red plane on a yellow background because "the plane can fly when the sun is shining and the sky is yellow", and to squeeze the left balloon for the green plane on a gray background because "when it's rainy the plane can't fly and has to be stopped" (Luria, 1961, p. 6). When children were later asked to respond to the novel test stimuli (e.g., red plane on a gray background), the author found that this simple change in the instructions had caused children to focus their attention on the background color instead of the foreground color.

In another early demonstration of labeling effects, Inhelder and Piaget (1959/1964) realized that older preschool children's ability to change their classification criteria and to anticipate multiple ways of classifying objects in a cross-classification task appeared to depend on whether or not the experimenter named the objects when presenting the task. Unfortunately, however, Inhelder and Piaget were less interested in the effect of labeling than in children's inflexibility, and simply chose to present subsequent tasks without further labeling the items.

In contrast, experimental labeling manipulations became a popular research tool in the learning research literature in the 1960s, as researchers sought to investigate the contributions of verbal thought on learning in both adults and children. Several studies were conducted during this era using different variants of the discrimination-shift paradigm (see Esposito, 1975, for a review), a paradigm that can also be characterized as an inductive measure of flexibility. For example, Kendler and Kendler (1961) found clear effects of labeling when they asked 4- and 7-year-olds to label relevant or irrelevant aspects of the stimuli in a discrimination-shift learning paradigm. That is, 4-year-olds who labeled the relevant dimension on each trial learned the correct discrimination shift more rapidly than did children who were not asked to label. Relevant labels, however, did not help the performance of 7-year-olds relative to the no-label group, most likely because of a ceiling effect—both groups of 7-year-olds rapidly learned the correct discrimination. In contrast, irrelevant labels actually slowed learning down for both age groups, perhaps because these irrelevant labels focused children's attention away from the correct dimension.

More recently, Gentner and her colleagues have also used labeling manipulations on a variety of tasks, some of which also assess cognitive flexibility. For example, Rattermann and Gentner (1998) argued that with development, there is a shift in children's attention from object similarities to relational similarities. That is, early on, children focus on specific object properties when judging similarities between objects, whereas with development, they begin to pay attention to common relational structures between objects. To assess this shift in similarity judgments, Rattermann and Gentner devised a cross-mapping search task. In this task, 3-, 4-, and 5-year-olds were shown two sets of three toys, the experimenter's set (e.g., a smaller car, a medium cup, and a larger doll house) and the child's set (e.g., a medium cup, a larger doll house, and an even larger plant). On each trial, after seeing the experimenter place a sticker under one of the experimenter's toys, children were told to search for a sticker under one of their toys. The sticker could always be found under the toy that matched the experimenter's in terms of relational similarity, not object similarity. That is, if the experimenter hid the sticker under the largest item (i.e., the larger doll house), children could find the sticker under their largest item (the larger plant). Moreover, on each trial, object similarity and relational similarity were placed in conflict such that if children selected toys based on object similarity (e.g., searching under their larger doll house when the experimenter placed a sticker under the other larger doll house), they never retrieved the sticker correctly. However, if they chose the toy that corresponded to the experimenter's in terms of relative size (e.g., searching under their largest plant when the experimenter placed the sticker under the large doll house), they always found the sticker. Rattermann and Gentner found that both 3- and 4-year-olds searched incorrectly significantly more often than the 5-year-olds (Experiment 1). However, if the experimenter labeled each of the toys using relative-size labels (e.g., "Baby/Mommy/Daddy" or "tiny/little/big"), 3-year-olds' performance improved significantly (Experiments 2 and 3), and their performance continued to be high months later when they were presented with a similar cross-mapping task but with different objects and without labels. Similarly, Loewenstein and Gentner (in press) recently found that 4-year-olds (and for some kinds of labels, 3-year-olds) also benefitted from labels on a cross-mapped version of a *spatial* relational mapping task (see Jacques & Zelazo, in press, for a review of some of their findings).

In a separate line of investigation, Deák (2000) used an object selection task to assess whether or not 3-, 4-, and 6-year-olds could use predicate information to infer the meaning of novel words, and whether or not they could do so flexibly using different kinds of predicates. In this task, children were presented with a standard novel object and four test objects from which to choose. One of these test objects had the same body shape as the standard, the second object was made of the same material as the standard, the third had an identical affixed part as the standard, and the fourth was a foil object that shared no particular similarity with the standard. On each trial, children were asked to select an item. The experimenter labeled the standard using one of three predicates and a novel word (i.e., "This one *looks like* a _________.", "This one *is made of* ________.", or "This one *has a* ________."), and asked children to select an object using the same predicate and the same novel word (i.e., "Which one of these looks like/is made of/has a _________?"). The experimenter presented a block of six trials with one predicate, a second block with six trials with a different predicate, and a third block with the remaining predicate. Children's initial ability to select the appropriate match consistently for the predicate context used in Block 1 provided an indication of their ability to use predicate information in the face of alternate potential matches. Their ability to switch and correctly select items in the second and third blocks according to the second and third predicate contexts, respectively, provided an indication of their ability to use predicate information flexibly. Deák found that 4- and 6-year-olds, but not 3-year-olds, showed flexible use of predicate information to infer the meaning of novel words. That is, older children not only selected the correct object reliably above chance for the first predicate context to which they were exposed, but they did so correctly for the subsequent predicate contexts as well, suggesting that they could flexibly switch and use another kind of predicate context to infer the meaning of novel words. From our perspective, it is not surprising that 4-year-olds did well on this inductive measure of flexibility because the items that were presented were always labeled with novel words. Interestingly, in a third experiment with the use of the same predicate context but with the use of familiar words, even 3-year-olds had no difficulty switching between predicate contexts. However, it is debatable whether they needed to use predicate information at all to solve the task, given that the words were familiar to them. As a result, it was possible for children to ignore the predicate information and rely solely on their knowledge of the meaning of the words to select objects.

Finally, in our own recent work, we have attempted to investigate systematically the efficacy of different labels in improving the performance of preschoolers of different ages on the FIST (Jacques, 2001; Jacques, Zelazo, Lourenco, & Sutherland, 2005). As noted, on each trial in this task, children must select (from among three items) first one pair of items that match along one dimension and then a different pair that match along a different dimension. Children's ability to select both pairs correctly (Selection 1 and Selection 2) provides an index of their ability to switch flexibly between dimensions. In our first labeling experiment (Jacques et al., 2005, Experiment 1), we gave 3-, 4-, and 5-year-old children one of three versions of the task. In a relevant-label condition, after each of their selections, children were asked to label explicitly the dimension by which they selected items. Specifically, once children selected a pair for Selection 1, they were asked, "Why do these pictures go together?" To respond correctly, children had to identify the relevant dimension by which items matched. In an irrelevant-label condition, after each of their selections, we asked children to identify the irrelevant dimension. For example, if size was the irrelevant dimension on a particular trial, children were asked after they selected items for Selection 1, "What size are these pictures?" To answer correctly in this condition, children had to identify the irrelevant dimension. We also included a third condition in which children were given standard no-label instructions. Several findings emerged from this experiment. First, Selection 2 performance on the task was related to overall language abilities, irrespective of the condition in which children participated. Second, only 4-year-olds in the relevant-label condition benefitted on their Selection 2 performance from having labeled on Selection 1. The 3- and 5-year-olds in the relevant-label condition did not improve relative to children in the no-label condition, most likely as a result of floor and ceiling effects, respectively. Moreover, in the irrelevant-label condition, children did not benefit from the labeling manipulation at all in any age group, suggesting that it may be necessary to label relevant information for labels to be effective.[4] In a second experiment, we assessed 4-year-olds in one of five labeling conditions: a no-label condition, one of two

[4]Unlike the findings in the discrimination-shift literature, irrelevant labels did not *hinder* children's performance on the FIST at any age. This may be due to the fact that children were not asked to label the irrelevant dimension at the same time that they were asked to select items for Selection 2. In Kendler and Kendler's (1961) study, children were asked to label the irrelevant dimension for the same stimuli on which their performance was assessed, making it more likely that these labels interfered with their choices.

relevant-label conditions that differed in whether the experimenter labeled the dimension or specific attribute itself, and one of two irrelevant-label conditions that differed in an analogous manner. Unlike the previous study, it was the experimenter who selected items for Selection 1 and labeled them differently depending on the condition in which children participated. Children only selected items for Selection 2. As predicted, 4-year-olds in both relevant-label conditions outperformed those in the other three conditions.

A particularly important result of our studies is that because we introduced labeling manipulations on Selection 1 and assessed their impact on Selection 2 performance, we were able to eliminate general attention-directing effects of labels as a possible explanation for the effects of labels on this task. That is, by labeling after one selection, and assessing the impact of these labels on a separate selection, we ensured that children did not simply have their attention directed to the relevant information. So, unlike many of the results presented previously, especially those regarding labeling effects on deductive tasks (e.g., Müller et al., 2004; Yerys & Munakata, 2003), our results established that at least for this task, there is something about the influence of labels that goes beyond their possible role as simple attention-directing devices.

Summary of Labeling Effects With Flexibility Measures

Correlational findings from a wide range of domains and tasks suggest that language may be related to the development of cognitive flexibility. Experimental labeling manipulations have also been used with both deductive and inductive measures, although labeling effects have been more reliably detected with the inductive measures than with the deductive measures. For example, mixed results of child-produced labeling manipulations with 3-year-olds have been reported from studies using Luria's (1959, 1961) Go-No-Go task and the DCCS (Frye et al., 1995). It may be that labeling effects are less reliable with deductive tasks because in deductive tasks, the experimenter *already* labels relevant information when providing explicit instructions to children. Further research should be aimed at comparing children's performance on both deductive and (unlabeled) inductive versions of a particular task to another inductive version that includes labels. Such comparisons might help to establish whether or not it is the deductive nature of deductive tasks or the presence of labels that accounts for children's earlier success on deductive tasks. Lourenco, Zelazo, and Liebermann (2005) did devise deductive and inductive versions of their Match-Form-and-Content-to-Sample Task but they did not include an inductive version with labels. Thus, it is unclear from their studies whether children's better performance on the deductive version occurred because of its deductive nature or because of the presence of labels in this version but not in the inductive version.

In any case, however, it may be best to manipulate labels using inductive measures of cognitive flexibility. One can assess effects of labels on deductive measures by asking children to provide labels in addition to the experimenter's labels. However, it may never be clear whether children's successful performance in such cases occurs because they labeled the information themselves or because they were exposed to a *combination* of both the experimenter's and their own labels.

In contrast, labeling effects have been more consistently found with inductive measures and several general findings emerge from the review of the literature presented in previous sections. First, 4-year-olds appear to do better on inductive measures (e.g., false belief) in which it is standard practice for the experimenter to label relevant information when administering tasks. To determine whether this is truly the case, however, specific labeling manipulations need to be used.

Second, the results across several studies—in particular those that we conducted with the FIST—suggest that it may not matter who labels the relevant information (i.e., the experimenter or the child). However, experimenter versus child labels have never been tested within the same experiment, so it remains to be determined whether experimenter and child labels are truly equivalent.

Third, results from studies in which labeling has been manipulated experimentally have generally found that labeling effects are more consistent with children in the 4- to 5-year-old age range than with younger and older children (but see Loewenstein & Gentner, in press; Luria, 1961; Rattermann & Gentner, 1998, for evidence that 3-year-olds can also benefit from certain, but not all, labeling manipulations, and see Luria, 1961, for evidence that even older children can benefit from labeling). However, when a linguistic cue is used to highlight the more difficult perspective (e.g., "Is this hat *too* big or *too* little for the doll to wear?," in the size judgment task), even 3-year-olds appear to benefit from this kind of labeling manipulation. Moreover, certain labels also appear to influence (positively or negatively) 3-year-olds' performance, especially when they seem to focus children's attention toward or away from important information (e.g., Müller et al., 2004; Yerys & Munakata, 2003).

In contrast, results from our labeling experiments with the FIST (Jacques et al., 2005) indicate that attention-getting properties of labels are not sufficient to account for the labeling effects found with 4-year-olds on at least our inductive measure. It would seem, therefore, that the effects of labels may change qualitatively between 3 and 4 years of age. Luria also argued for such a change: He believed that children went from using impulsive to semantic aspects of labels across the two ages. Evidently, more theoretical and experimental work remains to be done to understand how and why the influence of labels might change between 3 and 4 years.

SOCIO-COMMUNICATIVE ROOTS OF COGNITIVE FLEXIBILITY

We have argued that language development makes possible the development of cognitive flexibility. The evidence for this seems clear. How best to interpret this evidence is currently less clear, however, and several possibilities exist. For example, Jacques (2001) argues that the use of arbitrary symbols creates natural psychological distance between the symbol user and the external stimuli that the symbols represent. This distance then allows these symbol users to be more flexible in their thinking because they are no longer bound to reason on the basis of the immediate environment. In contrast, Zelazo (1999) believes that labeling makes children's representations explicit, thereby allowing children to reflect on these representations, leading to greater flexibility. A third possibility is that other aspects of language development like syntax are crucial for the development of flexibility. For example, de Villiers and de Villiers (2003) posit that in order for children to pass false-belief tasks, they must be able to master syntactic complementation because on their account, this syntactic structure is the only means by which false propositions can be represented and still be true ("He believes *that* the toy is in his bedroom, but it is really in the yard.")

Unfortunately, empirical evidence that could be used to distinguish between these accounts is currently lacking. Clearly, the next step is to develop experimental procedures that will permit us to determine exactly how labeling comes to affect cognitive flexibility. Many questions still need to be answered. For example, what kinds of labels provide sufficient relevant information? What is meant by relevant information? What are the semantic, syntactic, symbolic, or pragmatic aspects of labels that are critical for effecting change?

In addition, despite the fact that we argue that language development is one of the proximal causes of developments in cognitive flexibility, there are likely other proximal causes, as well as distal ones. For example, Jenkins and Astington (1996) found that the presence of siblings in the family predicted false-belief understanding in children. Similarly, Dunn, Brown, Slomkowski, Tesla, and Youngblade (1991) found that child and mother discourse measures at 33 months predicted children's performance on theory of mind tasks at 40 months, as did measures related to interactions between children and their siblings. More recently, Landry, Miller-Loncar, Smith, and Swank (2002) also reported links between maternal scaffolding, language, and the development of executive function, including a spatial-reversal task that assesses flexibility.

These sociocommunicative influences on theory of mind and executive function could all contribute independently to developments in flexible thinking (cf. Jenkins & Astington, 1996). Alternatively, they could also affect developments in flexibility indirectly through their influence on children's language development or on the development of other cognitive abilities important for flexibility (cf. Landry et al., 2002). As we mentioned earlier, Vygotsky argued for this latter kind of influence. He argued that development moves from the inter- to the intra-personal domain. Children first appropriate cultural tools like language from their social interactions with others. They then internalize these tools and use them as cognitive tools (see also Astington & Pelletier, this volume; Nelson, 1996, this volume).

CONCLUSIONS

In this chapter, we have reviewed labeling effects on measures of cognitive flexibility. Given the wide range of tasks examined, the extent of the convergence in the results is quite remarkable. However, the nature of these effects remains a matter of debate, and there is still much to learn both about the role of labeling on the development of cognitive flexibility and about the multidirectional influences of language, cognitive, and social development on each other, more generally. For example, as mentioned in the previous section, social experiences could mediate effects of language on the development of cognitive flexibility or they could affect cognitive flexibility more directly. Longitudinal research may help to elucidate the role that social experience and or language plays in the development of this crucial cognitive ability. At present, however, the theoretical possibilities far outstrip the available data.

REFERENCES

Astington, J. W., & Baird, J. A. (Eds.). (in press). *Why language matters for theory of mind.* Oxford, England: Oxford University Press.

Astington, J. W., & Jenkins, J. M. (1999). A longitudinal study of the relation between language and theory-of-mind development. *Developmental Psychology, 35,* 1311–1320.

Baldwin, D. A. (2000). Interpersonal understanding fuels knowledge acquisition. *Current Directions in Psychological Science, 9,* 40–45.

Berg, E. (1948). A simple objective test for measuring flexibility in thinking. *Journal of General Psychology, 39,* 15–22.

Bialystok, E. (1991). Letters, sounds, and symbols: Children's understanding of written language. *Journal of Applied Psycholinguistics, 12,* 75–89.

Bialystok, E. (1997). Effects of bilingualism and biliteracy on children's emerging concepts of print. *Developmental Psychology, 33,* 429–440.

Blaye, A., Jacques, S., Bonthoux, F., & Cannard, C. (2003, August). *Switching between thematic and taxonomic relations in preschoolers: Is there more than cognitive flexibility?* Paper presented at the 11th European Conference on Developmental Psychology, Milan, Italy.

Bruner, J. S., & Kenny, H. J. (1966). On multiple ordering. In J. S. Bruner, R. R. Olver, & P. M. Greenfield (Eds.), *Studies in cognitive growth* (pp. 154–167). New York: John Wiley & Sons.

Carlson, S. M., & Moses, L. J. (2001). Individual differences in inhibitory control and children's theory of mind. *Child Development, 72,* 1032–1053.

Carlson, S. M., Moses, L. J., & Hix, H. R. (1998). The role of inhibitory processes in young children's difficulties with deception and false belief. *Child Development, 69,* 672–691.

Courchesne, E., Townsend, J., Akshoomoff, N. A., Saitoh, O., Yeung-Courchesne, R., Lincoln, A. J., James, H. E., Haas, R. H., Schreibman, L., & Lau, L. (1994). Impairment in shifting attention in autistic and cerebellar patients. *Behavioral Neuroscience, 108,* 848–865.

de Villiers, J., & de Villiers, P. (2003). Language for thought: Coming to understand false beliefs. In D. Gentner & S. Goldin-Meadow (Eds.), *Language in mind: Advances in the study of language and thought* (pp. 335–384). Cambridge, MA: MIT Press.

Deák, G. O. (2000). The growth of flexible problem solving: Preschool children use changing verbal cues to infer multiple word meanings. *Journal of Cognition and Development, 1,* 157–191.

Deák, G. O., Ray, S. D., & Pick, A. D. (2002). Matching and naming objects by shape or function: Age and context effects in preschool children. *Developmental Psychology, 38,* 503–518.

Diamond, A., & Taylor, C. (1996). Development of an aspect of executive control: Development of the abilities to remember what I said and to "Do as I say, not as I do." *Developmental Psychobiology, 29,* 315–334.

Doherty, M., & Perner, J. (1998). Metalinguistic awareness and theory of mind: Just two words for the same thing? *Cognitive Development, 13,* 279–305.

Dunn, J., Brown, J., Slomkowski, C., Tesla, C., Youngblade, L. (1991). Young children's understanding of other people's feelings and beliefs: Individuals differences and their antecedents. *Child Development, 62,* 1352–1366.

Esposito, N. J. (1975). Review of discrimination shift learning in young children. *Psychological Bulletin, 82,* 432–455.

Feldman, M. J., & Drasgow, J. (1951). A Visual-Verbal Test for schizophrenia. *Psychiatric Quarterly, 25(Suppl.),* 55–64.

Flavell, J. H., Flavell, E. R., & Green, F. L. (1983). Development of the appearance-reality distinction. *Cognitive Psychology, 15,* 95–120.

Frye, D., Zelazo, P. D., Brooks, P., & Samuels, M. (1996). Inference and action in early causal reasoning. *Developmental Psychology, 32,* 120–131.

Frye, D., Zelazo, P. D., & Palfai, T. (1995). Theory of mind and rule-based reasoning. *Cognitive Development, 10,* 483–527.

Gelman, S. A, & Ebeling, K. S. (1989). Children's use of nonegocentric standards in judgments of functional size. *Child Development, 60,* 920–932.

Gerardi-Caulton, G. (2000). Sensitivity to spatial conflict and the development of self-regulation in children 24–36 months of age. *Developmental Science. 3,* 397–404.

Gerstadt, C. L., Hong, Y. J., & Diamond, A. (1994). The relationship between cognition and action: Performance of children 3–7 years old on a Stroop-like day-night test. *Cognition, 53,* 129–153.

Gopnik, A., & Astington, J. W. (1988). Children's understanding of representational change and its relation to the understanding of false belief and the appearance-reality distinction. *Child Development, 59,* 26–37.

Gopnik, A., & Rosati, A. (2001). Duck or rabbit? Reversing ambiguous figures and understanding ambiguous representations. *Developmental Science, 4,* 175–183.

Grant, D. A., & Berg, E. A. (1948). A behavioral analysis of degree of reinforcement and ease of shifting to new responses in a Weigl-type card-sorting problem. *Journal of Experimental Psychology, 38,* 404–411.

Hermer-Vazquez, L., Moffet, A., & Munkholm, P. (2001). Language, space, and the development of cognitive flexibility in humans: The case of two spatial memory tasks. *Cognition, 79,* 263–299.

Hughes, C. (1996). Control of action and thought: Normal development and dysfunction in autism: A research note. *Journal of Child Psychology and Psychiatry and Allied Disciplines, 37,* 229–236.

Hughes, C. (1998). Executive function in preschoolers: Links with theory of mind and verbal ability. *British Journal of Developmental Psychology, 16,* 233–253.

Hughes, C., & Russell, J. (1993). Autistic children's difficulty with mental disengagement from an object: Its implication for theories of autism. *Developmental Psychology, 29,* 498–510.

Inhelder, B., & Piaget, J. (1964). *The early growth of logic in the child: Classification and seriation* (E. A. Lunzer & D. Pepert, Trans.). New York: Harper & Row. (Original work published in 1959)

Jacques, S. (2001). *The roles of labeling and abstraction in the development of cognitive flexibility.* Unpublished doctoral dissertation, University of Toronto.

Jacques, S., & Zelazo, P. D. (2001). The Flexible Item Selection Task (FIST): A measure of executive function in preschoolers. *Developmental Neuropsychology, 20,* 573–591.

Jacques, S., & Zelazo, P. D. (in press). Language and the development of cognitive flexibility: Implications for theory of mind. In J. W. Astington, & J. A. Baird (Eds.), *Why language matters for theory of mind.* Oxford, England: Oxford University Press.

Jacques, S., Zelazo, P. D., Lourenco, S. F., & Sutherland, A. (2005). *Age- and language-related changes in preschoolers' performance on the Flexible Item Selection Task: The roles of labeling and abstraction on the development of cognitive flexibility.* Manuscript in prep.

Jenkins, J. M., & Astington, J. W. (1996). Cognitive factors and family structure associated with theory of mind development in young children. *Developmental Psychology, 32,* 70–78.

Kendler, H. H., & Kendler, T. S. (1961). Effect of verbalization on reversal shifts in children. *Science, 134,* 1619–1620.

Kirkham, N. Z., Cruess, L., & Diamond, A. (2003). Helping children apply their knowledge to their behavior on a dimension-switching task. *Developmental Science, 6,* 449–467.

Kuenne, M. R. (1946). Experimental investigation of the relation of language to transposition behavior in young children. *Journal of Experimental Psychology, 36,* 471–490.

Landry, S. H., Miller-Loncar, C. L., Smith, K. E., & Swank, P. R. (2002). The role of early parenting in children's development of executive processes. *Developmental Neuropsychology, 21,* 15–41.

LaVoie, J. C., Anderson, K., Fraze, B., & Johnson, K. (1981). Modelling, tuition, and sanction effects on self-control at different ages. *Journal of Experimental Child Psychology, 31,* 446–455.

Leontiev, A. N. (1932). Studies on the cultural development of the child: III. The development of voluntary attention in the child. *Journal of Genetic Psychology, 40,* 52–83.

Loewenstein, J., & Gentner, D. (in press). Relational language and the development of relational mapping. *Cognitive Psychology.*

Lourenco, S. F., Zelazo, P. D., & Liebermann, D. (2005). *Preschoolers' sensitivity to the content and formal properties of pictures: Acquiring a dual representation.* Manuscript in prep.

Logan, G. D., Cowan, W. B., & Davis, K. A. (1984). On the ability to inhibit simple and choice reaction time responses: A model and a method. *Journal of Experimental Psychology: Human Perception & Performance, 10,* 276–291.

Luria, A. R. (1959). The directive function of speech in development and dissolution. Part I. Development of the directive function of speech in early childhood. *Word, 15,* 341–352.

Luria, A. R. (1961). *The role of speech in the regulation of normal and abnormal behavior* (J. Tizard, Ed.). New York: Pergamon Press.

Lurye, L., & Müller, U. (2003, April). *The effect of labeling on the performance in the Dimensional Change Card Sort Task.* Poster presented at the Biennial Meeting of the Society for Research in Child Development.

MacLeod, C. M. (1991). Half a century of research on the Stroop effect: An integrative review. *Psychological Bulletin, 109,* 163–203.

Masangkay, Z. S., McCluskey, K. A., McIntyre, C. W., Sims-Knight, J., Vaughn, B. E., & Flavell, J. H. (1974). The early development of inferences about the visual percepts of others. *Child Development, 45,* 237–246.

Miller, S. A., Shelton, J., & Flavell, J. H. (1970). A test of Luria's hypothesis concerning the development of verbal self-regulation. *Child Development, 41,* 651–665.

Mischel, W., Shoda, Y., & Rodriguez, M. L. (1989). Delay of gratification in children. *Science, 244,* 993–938.

Müller, U., Zelazo, P. D., Leone, T., & Hood, S. (2004). Interference control in a new rule use task: Age-related changes, labeling, and attention. *Child Development, 75,* 1594–1609.

Nelson, K. (1996). *Language in cognitive development: The emergence of the mediated mind.* Cambridge, UK: Cambridge University Press.

Ozonoff, S., Pennington, B. F., & Rogers, S. J. (1991). Executive function deficits in high-functioning autistic individuals: Relationship to theory of mind. *Journal of Child Psychology and Psychiatry and Allied Disciplines, 32,* 1081–1105.

Perner, J., & Lang, B. (1999). Development of theory of mind and executive control. *Trends in Cognitive Sciences, 3,* 337–444.

Perner, J., Stummer, S., Sprung, M., & Doherty, M. (2002). Theory of mind finds its Piagetian *perspective*: Why alternative naming comes with understanding belief. *Cognitive Development, 17,* 1451–1472.

Piaget, J. (1964). *Six psychological studies.* New York: Vintage.

Rattermann, M. J., & Gentner (1998). The effect of language on similarity: The use of relational labels improves young children's performance in a mapping task. In K. Holyoak, D. Gentner, & B. Kokinov (Eds.), *Advances in analogy research: Integration of theory and data from the cognitive, computational, and neural sciences* (pp. 274–282). Sophia: New Bulgarian University.

Reed, M. A., Pien, D. L., & Rothbart, M. K. (1984). Inhibitory self-control in preschool children. *Merrill-Palmer Quarterly, 30,* 131–147.

Russell, J., Mauthner, N., Sharpe, S., & Tidswell, T. (1991). The "windows task" as a measure of strategic deception in preschoolers and autistic subjects. *British Journal of Developmental Psychology, 9(Special Issue: Perspectives on the Child's Theory of Mind),* 331–349.

Siegal, M., & Beattie, K. (1991). Where to look first for children's knowledge of false belief. *Cognition, 38,* 1–12.

Siegler, R. S. (1981). Developmental sequences within and between concepts. *Monographs of the Society for Research in Child Development, 46*(2, Serial No. 189).

Simon, J. R. (1990). The effects of an irrelevant directional cue on human information processing. In R. W. Proctor & T. G. Reeve (Eds.), *Stimulus-response compatibility: An integrated perspective* (pp. 31–86). Amsterdam: North-Holland.

Strommen, E. A. (1973). Verbal self-regulation in a children's game: Impulsive errors on "Simon Says." *Child Development, 44,* 849–853.

Stroop, J. R. (1935). Studies of interference in serial verbal reactions. *Journal of Experimental Psychology, 18,* 643–661.

Thompson, C., Barresi, J., & Moore, C. (1997). The development of future-oriented prudence and altruism in preschoolers. *Cognitive Development, 12,* 199–212.

Tomasello, M. (2003). The key is social cognition. In D. Gentner & S. Goldin-Meadow (Eds.), *Language in mind: Advances in the study of language and thought* (pp. 47–57). Cambridge, MA: MIT Press.

Tomasello, M., Kruger, A. C., & Ratner, H. H. (1993). Cultural learning. *Behavioral and Brain Sciences, 16,* 495–552.

Towse, J. N., Redbond, J., Houston-Price, C. M. T., & Cook, S. (2000). Understanding the dimensional change card sort: Perspectives from task success and failure. *Cognitive Development, 15,* 347–365.

Uttal, D. H., Chiong, C., & Wilson, C. J. (2003). *Flexibility in spatial cognition: The development of the ability to communicate spatial information in different ways.* Manuscript in prep.

Vygotsky, L. S. (1986). *Thought and language* (A. Kozulin, Ed.). Cambridge, MA: MIT Press. (Original work published in 1934)

Wellman, H. M., Cross, D., & Watson, J. (2001). Meta-analysis of theory-of-mind development: The truth about false belief. *Child Development, 72,* 655–948.
Whorf, B. L. (1956). *Language, thought, and reality: Selected writings of Benjamin Lee Whorf* (J. B. Carroll, Ed.). Cambridge, MA: MIT Press.
Wimmer, H., & Perner, J. (1983). Beliefs about beliefs: Representation and constraining function of wrong beliefs in young children's understanding of deception. *Cognition, 13,* 103–128.
Xu, F. (2002). The role of language in acquiring object kind concepts in infancy. *Cognition, 85,* 223–250.
Yerys, B. E., & Munakata, Y. (2003, April). *Labels hurt but novelty helps: Factors influencing 3-year-olds' flexibility on a card sorting task.* Poster presented at the Biennial Meeting of the Society for Research in Child Development.
Zelazo, P. D. (1999). Language, levels of consciousness, and the development of intentional action. In P. D. Zelazo, J. W. Astington, & D. R. Olson (Eds.), *Developing theories of intention: Social understanding and self-control* (pp. 95–117). Mahwah, NJ: Lawrence Erlbaum Associates.
Zelazo, P. D., Frye, D., & Rapus, T. (1996). An age-related dissociation between knowing rules and using them. *Cognitive Development, 11,* 37–63.
Zelazo, P. D., Helwig, C. C., & Lau, A. (1996). Intention, act and outcome in behavioral prediction and moral judgement. *Child Development, 67,* 2478–2492.
Zelazo, P. D., & Jacques, S. (1997). Children's rule use: Representation, reflection and cognitive control. *Annals of Child Development, 12,* 119–176.
Zelazo, P. D., Jacques, S., Burack, J. A., & Frye, D. (2002). The relation between theory of mind and rule use: Evidence from persons with autism-spectrum disorders. *Infant and Child Development, 11,* 171–195.

Part II

Intentionality and Communication

Through participation in daily social exchanges, infants and young children come to appreciate that people can take on varying psychological and emotional perspectives towards objects and events; that motives, beliefs and desires underlie human actions and goal-directed behaviors; and that people are repositories of knowledge that is transmitted, negotiated and modified in the process of communication. The five chapters in this section offer complementary perspectives on the nature and meaning of these early emerging capacities. The order of the chapters roughly aligns with the ontogeny of children's abilities to process, understand, and intentionally regulate the emotions, actions, thoughts and goals of self and others. In the opening chapter, Walker-Andrews presents her programmatic research on young infants' impressive abilities to recognize and understand others' emotions. Next, Baldwin probes what is undoubtedly one of the most essential features to understanding others' intentions: babies' abilities to parse dynamic streams of action in ways that map onto adult meaning. Tamis-LeMonda and Adolph also address the intersection between action and intentions by examining when and how babies seek and use social information to make decisions about action under conditions of potential risk. Ahktar follows with a rigorous test of 2-year-olds' learning of new words from overheard conversations, thereby highlighting the indirect ways that children come to infer intentions and acquire language. Moore closes the section with his research on 3- and 4-year-olds' capacities to regulate behaviors in line with current and future goals. He emphasizes connections among children's developing theory of mind, social regulation, and attachment histories.

UNDERSTANDING OTHERS' EMOTIONS

Developmental theorists and philosophers have long espoused the functional adaptiveness of emotions. Infants' emotional displays regulate the actions of self and others and are a core feature of human communication and survival. Infants' cries signal hunger, pain, or discomfort, and their smiles communicate contentment or joy. For the most part, caregivers are highly attuned to the emotional content of infants' expressions. They rush to the assistance of distressed babies and respond to infants' delight with smiles, hugs, tickles, and enthusiastic words. Infants must also learn to respond to others' emotional messages. For the young, vulnerable infant who lacks the capacity to understand or produce words, the ability to recognize the emotional content of others' social messages is enormously adaptive. Adults' smiling faces and soothing voices convey comfort and safety, whereas fearful faces and anxious tones warn of potential danger.

Although infants are both communicators and recipients of emotions, early research on infants' emotional development predominantly emphasized the structural features of babies' emotional expressions. Much of this research focused on questions such as: Which emotions do infants display and at what ages, and how do caregivers respond to infants' expressions of hunger, pain, discomfort, and joy? However, methodological breakthroughs in infant perception paved the way for rigorous tests of infants' emotional understanding. By investigating how infants distribute their attention to competing visual and auditory stimuli, researchers are able to generate rich hypotheses about infants' knowledge and understanding of emotions.

In her chapter entitled *Perceiving Social Affordances: the Development of Emotion Understanding*, Walker-Andrews offers convincing evidence that young infants can discriminate, recognize, and respond appropriately to multimodal, emotional displays. Her review describes and contrasts studies of infants' discrimination (i.e., the ability to perceptually distinguish among two or more emotional expressions) and recognition (i.e., the ability to understand the meanings that underlie emotional expressions). She notes the conceptual limitations that continue to plague discrimination studies: an infant who can distinguish between two emotional displays does not necessarily appreciate the meanings conveyed by the different emotional expressions. In the absence of emotional understanding, adaptive use of emotional messages is tenuous. Walker-Andrews posits that matching studies, in contrast, tap infants' abilities to recognize and understand emotional expressions.

In a typical matching study, an infant views a visual display of two paired faces (e.g., happy and sad) and is simultaneously presented with a voice that expresses one of the two emotions. The infant's task is to match the auditory information to the correct display by looking at the face that is congruent with the vocal expression. Infants aged 4 months and younger are successful in these tasks. Walker-Andrews interprets this success as evidence that young babies detect invariant properties of emotions across modalities, and that they are able to use those properties to discover the meanings that are inherent in redundant emotional displays.

Walker-Andrews also demonstrates the importance of *context* in infants' emotional understanding. Infants are able to recognize emotional expressions in familiar settings and people before they are able to recognize the same emotions in unfamiliar settings or people. The developmental progression from understanding emotions in specific contexts to understanding emotions across contexts might also be adaptive. Very young infants rely on the emotional signals of familiar, trusted persons in situations of uncertainty. With development, babies increasingly decipher and benefit from information contained in the emotional displays of people who inhabit their wider social networks.

UNDERSTANDING OTHERS' ACTIONS

Infants' social cognitive abilities extend well beyond emotional discrimination and understanding. The capacity to infer others' intentions is fundamental to the development of social cognition and communication. In learning language, for example, infants must form conceptual connections between the words they hear and the actions they observe in self and others. Infants' capacity to process the available perceptual data in ways that "make sense" is a vital requisite to accurately deciphering others' intentions and linking those intentions to the words being used to describe them. In her chapter, *Discerning Intentions: Characterizing the Cognitive System at Play*, Baldwin tackles this uniquely human capacity of inferring intentions from peoples' actions. She convincingly argues that "action parsing" is fundamental to human communication. Her chapter appeals to the remarkable capacity of infants' cognitive system to analyze action sequences into discrete units.

Baldwin describes a series of studies in which she tests infants' capacities to parse visual streams into meaningful units. Because of infants' relatively meager knowledge base, virtually all actions are novel and implore interpretation. The simple act of an adult washing and peeling vegetables in preparation for dinner can be a visual enigma to the young infant. How do infants analyze this perceptually dynamic stream, and what cues do they use to process the available visual information? Baldwin takes a bottoms-up approach to this problem, noting that dynamic human action contains predictable and structured motion patterns. These predictable patterns map onto actors' underlying intentions and facilitate the processing of information by observers. Perceptual predictability is also evident in auditory streams of speech. Infants are keenly sensitive to the statistical properties of speech. If two sounds co-occur with a high degree of regularity, infants treat them as a unit, but if their co-occurrence is rare, infants treat the sounds as discrete units that demarcate the boundaries of words.

Baldwin's research reveals similar segmentation abilities in adults' and infants' processing of action streams. In her research with adults, participants viewed a series of novel action sequences in which the co-occurrence of certain actions was manipulated. When asked to identify "familiar" actions, adults relied on the statistical regularities of component actions. Action pairs that consistently co-occurred were rated as more familiar than those that infrequently co-occurred.

Baldwin extends this research to infants, asking about babies' natural proclivities to attend to statistical regularities when parsing action streams in visual displays. In a series of innovative studies, infants viewed a videotape that contained a sequence of logically ordered actions (e.g., a woman turning, looking to floor, picking up a towel, and placing towel on a rack). After viewing the videotape, infants saw two videotapes of the same event, with pauses inserted at different points. In certain instances, pauses occurred at "natural boundaries" (e.g., immediately after the woman picked up the towel) and in other instances pauses occurred at "illogical" boundaries (e.g., a pause in midair as the woman reached for the towel). Infants attended longer to the videotapes that contained illogical boundaries, suggesting that the positioning of pauses in the illogical condition differed from the way that infants would naturally segment the event. Moreover, Baldwin's ongoing research reveals that, like adults, infants rely on statistical information in their segmentation of event sequences.

However, as she points out, statistical cues are only one means for parsing actions and inferring others' intentions. Infants' own actions also form the basis for interpreting the actions of others. Through experiences with grasping at objects, for example, infants are able to process the action of grasping in others. Thus, self-produced action facilitates infants' recognition of actions in others, and ultimately equips infants with the necessary tools for drawing inferences about the intentions that underlie others' goal-directed actions.

SEEKING AND USING OTHERS' ADVICE

The chapters by Walker-Andrews and Baldwin highlight infants' capacities to understand and interpret others' emotions and actions, two cornerstones of infants' emerging social cognition and understanding of others' intentions. Both chapters point to the social necessity and adaptive value of these early emerging abilities. Infants must be able to recognize emotions such as "fear" in others' voices and tones and to process meaning from sequences of action if they are to incorporate social information into their own adaptive decisions. Tamis-LeMonda and Adolph, in their chapter entitled *Social Referencing in Infant Motor Action,* bridge the gap between social cognition and adaptive behavior by exploring the functional benefits of infants' social understanding in ambiguous, potentially dangerous situations—as infants decide whether or not to crawl or walk down slopes of varying degrees of risk.

They begin their chapter by noting that infants' emerging understanding of self and others as intentional, goal-directed actors enormously expands babies' opportunities for learning. Young infants, who are not yet aware of the potential benefits of others' communications, must learn through self discovery or else depend on the benevolence of others to offer unsolicited advice about how to respond in situations of uncertainty. Older toddlers, in contrast, are active participants in the construction of knowledge. By 18 months, if not sooner, infants intentionally solicit social information by gesturing, vocalizing, and looking to adults and other persons for advice, and are adept at using social information to clarify ambiguity. Tamis-LeMonda and Adolph suggest that infants' developing capacities to seek and use social information become especially important under conditions of potential risk, when the consequences of error can be serious.

An innovative aspect of their research is the merging of the social referencing and perception-action research. Perception-action research emphasizes how infants use perceptual information to make decisions about action, such as whether to reach, crawl, cruise or walk across an obstacle or ground surface. However, perception-action researchers treat infants as "solitary scientists" who perceive and act in a social vacuum. The social referencing literature, in contrast, stresses infants' use of social information in the decision-making process: that is, whether and how infants respond to mothers' advice about approaching or avoiding visual cliffs, scary toys or unfamiliar adults. However, social referencing studies take a "one-size-fits-all" approach to infants' use of social information, with all infants being exposed to the same visual cliff, stranger or toy.

The research presented by Tamis-LeMonda and Adolph builds on the strengths of perception action and social-referencing studies in ways that address the limitations of each. They adopt a psychophysical staircase procedure from perception-action research to determine individualized motor thresholds. Across dozens of trials, infants decide whether or not to crawl or walk down slopes of varying degrees, and a motor threshold is determined for each baby. This threshold represents the slope that is maximally uncertain for each infant, thereby demarcating the boundary between slopes that are "safe" and those that are "risky". This individualized approach moves beyond the "one-size-fits-all" definition of ambiguity that plagues social referencing studies. However, also recognizing the generally "a-social" nature of perception-action research, Tamis-LeMonda and Adolph manipulate mothers' social messages to their infants. Mothers are asked to either encourage or discourage their infants to crawl or walk down slopes that have been identified as safe, uncertain and risky during the psychophysical staircase procedure; in other conditions mothers are kept "occupied" as their infants are left to determine a course of action unassisted. By exploring when infants override versus defer to mothers' encouraging and discouraging advice, and when babies actively seek the advice of their "occupied" mothers, the authors formulate a theory on infants' developing ability to integrate knowledge about the self (i.e., recognizing whether a given slope is risky) with knowledge about the other (i.e., knowing that mothers' advice is useful to making a decision).

LEARNING FROM OTHERS' CONVERSATIONS

Beyond the social benefits that infants accrue through "direct" exposure to others' emotions, actions, and advice, infants' growing social-cognitive capacities in the second and third years of life enable them to profit from social exchanges in which they are not direct participants. In her chapter entitled *Is joint attention necessary for early language learning?*, Ahktar demonstrates that by two years, children are capable of learning words by observing the conversations of others. Moreover, children's expertise at culling meaning from overheard talk rivals the benefits of more direct forms of tutoring.

Ahktar begins her chapter with a brief review of classic studies in the area of joint attention. Strong associations exist between the time mothers and infants spend in joint attention and infants' early word learning. In Western cultures, mutuality in adult–child engagements is associated with the sizes of children's receptive and productive vocabularies, and a host of mechanisms have been proposed to explain these findings. Most notably, shared attention is thought to facilitate infants' referential understanding, the ability to map words to their real-life referents.

However, Ahktar notes that studies of joint attention, and the theories founded on their results, are based on research in societies characterized by child-focused interactions. In certain non-Western cultures, children are reared in environments where episodes of dyadic joint attention are rare. Rather, from an early age, children must learn how to effectively monitor others' interactions in order to actively participate in everyday social exchanges. In such cultures, overheard conversations are an essential source for children's language learning.

Ahktar and colleagues directly investigate the abilities of 2-year-olds to benefit from overhead conversations. Two-year-olds were exposed to novel words either through direct engagements or by observing conversations between an experimenter and adult confederate. Toddlers performed equally well in both conditions, demonstrating their ability to extract information about others' referential intentions by monitoring third-party conversations.

Ahktar's findings highlight cultural variation in the paths children take to learning language, and shift the responsibility for language learning from adults to children. Her constructivist approach to the communicative process offers a palatable explanation for the universal abilities of young children to learn language, despite enormous variation in the social environments of different cultures. Children display flexible adaptations to the conversational practices and communicative demands of their respective cultures.

REGULATING GOALS

In their chapter, *Attachment, Social Understanding and Delay of Gratification*, Moore and Symons move up the developmental ladder to focus on two aspects of preschoolers' social-cognitive development: theory of mind and future-oriented goals. By 4 years of age, children recognize that people can hold beliefs that differ from reality, enabling them to respond correctly to theory of mind tasks that tap the understanding of false beliefs. Thus, 4-year-olds can appreciate that "Person X will erroneously search for an object in location A if he or she is unaware that the location of the object has been switched from location A to location B."

Moore and Symons note that at roughly the same developmental period, children's understanding of goals and intentions in self and others takes a noteworthy leap. Children now appreciate temporal connections between behaviors and goals, namely, that behaviors can be directed towards immediate or long-term goals. As a part of this recognition, children are increasingly able to delay gratification; they will forego an immediate reward (e.g., one sticker now) in the expectation of receiving a larger reward in the future (e.g., two stickers later). Further still, children can direct immediate and long-term goals towards self or others. Thus, a child might choose to pursue an immediate goal that will benefit the self, an immediate goal that will benefit another person, a future goal that will benefit the self (future-oriented prudence), or a future goal that will benefit another person (future-oriented altruism).

Moore and Symons seek to understand similarities and differences in children's theory of mind and future-oriented thinking by investigating the roles of language, cognition and children's relationships with parents. Consequently, their chapter offers a unique integration of research on attachment with research on preschoolers' social cognition. They contend that despite developmental parallels in theory of mind and future-oriented thinking, each reflects distinct processes. Children's ability to conceptualize varying possibilities in theory of mind tasks strongly depends on cognitive achievements, whereas the ability to regulate behaviors in line with future-oriented goals is affected by social-emotional aspects of development and attachment relationships.

Their proposal is founded on two lines of evidence. First, they note that virtually all normally developing children are successful at classic theory of mind tasks by roughly 4 years of age, yet still vary substantially in their future-oriented prudence and altruism. This variation persists well beyond the preschool years, and is likely governed by processes beyond cognitive achievement. Second, and relatedly, the two sets of capacities are differentially linked to children's attachment histories. Although children's attachment status has been shown to predict theory of mind performance, these associations are short-lived. Once children are generally successful at false-belief tasks, attachment status no longer appears to matter. In contrast, the authors assemble a persuasive, empirically-supported argument for the role of attachment in future-oriented thinking. Children who display secure attachment behaviors were able to delay gratification by choosing to receive larger rewards at a later point in time, rather than a smaller reward immediately. Surprisingly, however, future-oriented altruism was not predicted by attachment security, although the authors attribute the lack of a finding to the task used rather than to the absence of a link per se.

SUMMARY

Together, the five chapters in this section offer a developmental window onto children's growing abilities to understand intentions in self and others—intentions that underlie others' emotions, actions and advice about ambiguous situations, and fuel goal-directed behaviors and future orientation. Additionally, this collection provides a valuable survey of paradigms that have been applied to the study of covert, social-cognitive processes in infants and young children. The methodological rigor of this research paves the way for future inquiry, and promises a fuller appreciation of the role that social context plays in the development of children's thinking.

Chapter 4

Perceiving Social Affordances: The Development of Emotion Understanding

Arlene S. Walker-Andrews
*Department of Psychology,
The University of Montana–Missoula*

During the first year of life, infants come to understand the emotional expressions of those around them, as information about future actions on the part of those individuals and as information about events in the world. This is a marvelous development that is important to social interactions and forming attachments, to comprehending critical aspects of the physical world and to acting on that world. For example, for the young infant interactions with others are mostly about communicating affect and the ability to discriminate and recognize emotional expressions is essential to such communication. With respect to information about the physical world, reading another's fearful expression as data about risks, such as that posed by a car speeding through an intersection, is beneficial as well.

How emotion perception develops and what influences that development are still puzzles. The development of infants' understanding of emotion appears to be a continual process that reflects changes in an infant's own perceptual, cognitive, and affective abilities. Indeed, it is difficult to determine when one can say that emotion recognition is present, given the complexity of that ability and the factors that will influence its development. Many researchers would concur that infants' ability to discriminate many emotional expressions seems well established by the second half of the first year (e.g., C. A. Nelson, 1987); however the literature is mixed when it comes to pinpointing when infants reliably discriminate particular emotional expressions and what factors influence infants' performance. That is, the ability to discriminate expressions is influenced by a number of variables such as fidelity of the expression, the mode (facial, vocal) of expression, the particular emotion that is being expressed, and perhaps who is portraying the emotion. There is little consistency across studies in the selection of emotional expression exemplars, the fidelity of those expressions, the age range of the infants, the mode of presentation, and other variables. A close reading of the literature suggests that the discrimination of dynamic facial expressions appears to begin at about 3 months of age, but discrimination of static representations of facial expressions (such as photographs) appears somewhat later (see Walker-Andrews, 1997, for a review). Particular facial expressions may be discriminated earlier than others, and particular pairs of facial expressions may be easier to discriminate from one another. That is, in most research reports, young infants seem to visually prefer happy facial expressions (e.g., LaBarbera, Izard, Vietze, & Parisi, 1976; Wilcox & Clayton, 1968). Furthermore, infants are more likely to give evidence of visual discrimination when happy facial expressions are paired with sad expressions, compared to when happy expressions are paired with angry facial expressions (Caron, Caron, & MacLean, 1988). To a large degree, this may reflect feature differences between facial expressions—for instance, the visible difference between a toothy smile and a compressed-lip frown may be conspicuous. Much less research has focused on infants' abilities to discriminate vocal expressions, but evidence suggests that the discrimination of vocal expressions of emotion may begin between 3 and 5 months of age as well (Fernald, 1992; Walker-Andrews & Grolnick, 1983; Walker-Andrews & Lennon, 1991).

Questions about more sophisticated abilities such as infants' recognition of others' emotions are still being posed. For recognition to occur, not only must the infant discriminate one expression from another expression, but also the infant must go beyond feature differences to some rudimentary identification of the emotion depicted by the expression (Nelson, 1987). Taking a moment to focus on definition, the perception of emotion may entail (a) detection of information that characterizes a particular emotion, (b) discrimination of two or more emotional expressions from one another, and (c) recognition of the underlying meaning of an emotional expression. Detection indicates simply the ability to pick out objects from the background. Discrimination refers to the ability to distinguish one object from another. Recognition requires more: "[At times] we must know exactly what a particular object is or who a particular person is. This third process we may call identification ... not only must one object be distinguished (discriminated) from among others, that object must also be recognized" (Sekuler & Blake, 1994, p. 141).

In part, as in the discrimination literature, questions about infants' abilities to recognize emotions remain because researchers have used different experimental methods and stimulus materials. Across studies the stimulus materials have ranged from very simple (line drawings, photographs, single syllables) to much more complex (videotaped expressions, live interactions). Methods have varied widely as well. For example, some researchers have used looking preferences (e.g., Barrera & Maurer, 1981; Kuchuk, Vibbert, & Bornstein, 1986; Wilcox & Clayton, 1968) or visual habituation methods (e.g., Caron, Caron, & Myers, 1985; Nelson, Morse, & Leavitt, 1979; Serrano, Iglesias, & Loeches, 1992; Young-Browne, Rosenfeld, & Horowitz, 1977) to determine whether infants can discriminate and/or recognize posed facial expressions. Others have examined infants' responses to emotional expressions presented during an ongoing interaction (e.g., Gusella, Muir, & Tronick, 1988; Haviland & Lelwica, 1987). A very few investigators have used operant procedures to determine whether infants prefer some emotional expressions to others (e.g., Everhart & Henry, 1992). Finally, researchers disagree about what it means to say that an infant recognizes an emotional expression (but see previous discussion). The stance that one takes regarding the definition of recognition is especially critical because it has repercussions for the selection of stimulus materials, the selection of methods, and the conclusions that are drawn from experimental results.

In this chapter, I propose that infants' recognition of emotional expressions entails detecting abstract information in expressions that potentially specifies the affordances of an emotional expression (Gibson, 1979; Walker-Andrews, 1997). To make such a claim, the researcher first must provide infants with tasks that require an infant to go beyond discrimination of expressions based on feature differences to detection of abstract, invariant information that can potentially guide behavior. For example, one method for asking whether infants recognize expressions is to determine whether their discrimination of two expressions persists over changes on some other dimension, such as in the identity of the person posing the expressions (e.g., Nelson, 1987). Therefore, the evidence I cite is drawn from experiments that use either an intermodal matching method in which infants must abstract intermodal correspondences or a generalization procedure in which infants must generalize across exemplars. Following presentation of these data, I offer evidence for recognition of expressions by infants as young as three months. In these more recent experiments the context for the expression was made more familiar, through the use of familiar persons as actors or by embedding the expressions in a familiar sequence, and the expressions were always presented bimodally. The data from these experiments suggest that infants can detect the affordances of emotional expressions at a very young age, provided such contextual information is provided.

To reiterate, for the recognition of emotional expressions to occur, it is not enough to simply detect feature differences, such as differences in the extent of eye opening or shape of the mouth (Caron, Caron, & Myers, 1985). Emotional expressions are socially communicative for infants to the degree that they foreshadow specific outcomes for the infants. For example, parental smiles are likely to be followed by positive caregiving interactions or experiences of being cuddled and played with. Frowns and other negative expressions are more likely to be followed by periods of isolation, muted interactions, or even harsh treatment. With experience with such patterns, infants may come to form expectations about the progression of events that begin with or are signaled by specific emotional expressions. Learning about the emotional expressions of others is a prime example of perceptual learning in which infants first learn expectations. These may underlie later discovery of more general causal relations such as intentions (Gibson & Pick, 2000; Walker-Andrews, Montague, & Kahana-Kalman, 2000)

There is controversy about how to measure infants' recognition of emotional expressions, or what evidence is necessary for the researcher to infer recognition of expressions. Although it is important to know whether infants can detect differences among emotional expressions, experimental procedures that test only infants' discrimination are not sufficient for determining whether infants understand emotional expressions. In my view, recognition of emotional expressions is demonstrated when infants (a) show that they detect a common affordance across facial and vocal expressions and (b) can generalize an emotional expression across persons, provided that the simple feature differences that often characterize those expressions but that are not emotion-specific are removed or controlled (Caron et al., 1985; Oster, 1981). The claim that infants recognize an emotional expression is strengthened when the experimenter finds that infants' own emotional responsivity is apposite as well. Research on mother-infant interactions has garnered some of the most convincing evidence that infants respond appropriately to others' emotional expressions, especially when those interactions are disrupted (e.g., Brazelton, Koslowski, & Main, 1974; Gusella, Muir, & Tronick, 1988; Haviland & Lelwica, 1987). Other methods for assessing infants' recognition of emotional expressions may be created, but based on the present literature, the most conservative reading is that infants begin to recognize some emotional expressions at about 7 months, although researchers have little idea how this ability develops (see Walker-Andrews, 1997, for a review).

RECOGNITION OF EMOTIONAL EXPRESSIONS—THE ROLE OF CONTEXT

After several decades of investigating infants' perception of emotional expressions I have come to believe that context—broadly defined to encompass both situations and persons—plays an especially important role in the development of emotion recognition during infancy. "Context" itself is a slippery term that encompasses a host of different possibilities. For example, K. Nelson and her colleagues (Nelson, 1986, 1993) emphasize that children participate in routine, culturally organized events that allow them to develop generalized event representations or scripts. In this view, the scripts are internalized mental structures that represent the context in which events normally occur. These scripts, in turn, allow children to explore the new features of an otherwise familiar event. As another example, research on infants' memories has found that placing an infant in a familiar context can cue the recall of an event formerly experienced in that same context (Howe & Courage, 1993; see also Bühler, 1930). In this case, the context refers to the actual physical setting. With respect to infants' perception of emotional expressions, infants seem to recognize the expressions of others most readily when those expressions are encountered as multimodal events and in familiar settings and displayed by familiar people. Each of these instances functions as a context: Each provides support for the detection of the information in an emotional expression that potentially specifies its meaning for the infant.

MULTIMODAL SPECIFICATION AS A CONTEXT

Much of my early research on the topic of infants' understanding of emotion focused on infants' perception of facial and vocal expressions presented together as a multimodal event, the first type of contextual support previously mentioned (Walker, 1982). The assumption was that when an infant observed a multimodal expression, in which facial, vocal, and perhaps haptic information is available, relational information would be highlighted and the common meaning of the emotional expression would be abstracted. That is, as a person displays an emotional expression, the voice is synchronized with the facial movements, the intensity of voice, face, and touch are likely to be correlated, and information specific to emotion is present in all modes. Such intermodal redundancy serves to guide infants' visual, acoustic, and tactual exploration of the event (Bahrick & Lickliter, 2000; Bahrick, Walker, & Neisser, 1981). Furthermore, faces and voices are typically experienced together, making the multimodal presentation a more ecologically valid stimulus display. In these initial experiments, infants did, indeed, detect relationships across modalities: When 5- and 7-month-old infants were presented happy and sad, happy and neutral, and happy and angry faces and voices in an intermodal preference procedure, infants increased their looking time to the faces that were accompanied by their affectively congruent vocal expressions (Walker, 1982; Walker-Andrews, 1986). This ability was demonstrated even when synchrony relations were disrupted (Walker, 1982), a portion of the face was occluded (Walker-Andrews, 1986), or featural information was removed (Soken & Pick, 1992). That is, even when some intermodal correspondences such as precise temporal synchrony were eliminated, infants appeared to detect the meaning that was common to the visual and acoustic displays, a more abstract but equally compelling relation. Lest one think that the infants were merely matching two events that had become associated in the past, one should note that the elimination of synchrony relations modified infants' looking preferences. Infants took far longer to show an intermodal looking preference when synchrony was disrupted, suggesting that infants attend to intermodal correspondences that include information such as synchrony and intensity as well as emotional meaning. They do not simply attend to the facial expression that is usually paired with a particular vocal expression as if exercising a reflex or exhibiting a learned association. Rather, infants seem to abstract information that is invariant across the optic and acoustic displays, including spatio-temporal correspondences such as synchrony along with other information that potentially carries the meaning of that expression. Faces and voices typically occur together. The infant does not form an association between the optic and acoustic information that happens to co-occur, but attends to a multimodal event (an emoting person) that offers a unique communicative affordance.

Others have shown that infants also demonstrate more sophisticated perceptual abilities when they are presented composite facial and vocal expressions. As one example, Caron, Caron, and McLean (1988) found that 4-month-olds discriminated happy and sad emotional expressions when these were presented as composite expressions, but not when happy and sad emotions were presented solely as facial expressions. Even at 7 months, infants did not discriminate happy and angry facial-only expressions, although they discriminated composite happy and angry expressions. The information for an emotion given across modalities permitted the infant to extract meaning from the multimodal display. Walker-Andrews and Lennon (1991) argued that the presence of a face acts as a setting that guides attention to the affective quality of the voice. They found that 5-month-olds failed to discriminate vocal expressions that were presented simultaneously with an unrelated visual stimulus, even though infants discriminated happy, angry, and sad vocal expressions when these vocal expressions were presented in the presence of a face. Multimodal stimuli provide a highly redundant presentation. They may also focus the perceiver's attention on the relevant aspects of a signal. Such effects may also characterize a mature perceiver's experience, both for multimodal and unimodal events. For example, Liberman, Cooper, Shankweiler, and Studdert-Kennedy (1967) reported that adult listeners hear an acoustic signal differently when the context indicates that the signal is an utterance, rather than noise. Listeners detect different information in the signal when it is perceived as speech. So, too, may infants attend to information that specifies an emotion if that information is made more salient by its presence in a socially relevant context.

Along these same lines, given that young infants' visual and auditory systems are still under development, the presence of multimodal information may aid in the detection of (degraded) unimodal stimulus information. That is, for an infant the visibility of facial features may be relatively poor and audibility may be compromised as well, but the presence of amodal information may function to enhance detection. For instance, if an event occurring at a distance is indistinct because it is barely within an observer's visible and audible range, a shared amodal property such as tempo or rhythm may enhance the detection of visual and auditory information. Similar effects can be found within as well as across modalities. For vision, recent research by Torralba and Sinha (2001) on the detection and recognition of faces by adults points to the enhancing effect of various types of optic information in visual recognition. Torralba and Sinha used a computer algorithm to "blur" images of faces and other objects. The perceiver viewed faces and objects that appeared to be out of focus to various degrees. As the defocusing became more pronounced, adults relied more and more heavily on contextual information such as location of the image in a scene, bounding contours, or photometric properties of the internal features of the image in order to identify a face as a face. This seemingly extraneous information could be used to determine whether a blurred image was of a face or some other object.

Analogously, as an example for how information across modalities aids perception, visual information improves the detection and recognition of speech by adult listeners. Adults who are allowed to look at a speaker's face while listening to a pure-tone auditory signal are markedly better at reporting what is being said than those who merely view the face without an acoustic signal or listen to the signal alone (Grant, Ardell, Kuhl, & Sparks, 1985). Bahrick and Lickliter (2000) reported recently that 5-month-olds who were habituated to a bimodally presented rhythm discriminated it from a novel rhythm, but failed to discriminate the same rhythms when these were presented unimodally (either visually or acoustically). To summarize, infants may realize improvements in the recognition of emotional expressions when information is provided across modalities because (a) intermodal redundancy guides attention and highlights important information, (b) multimodal presentations provide an ecologically appropriate setting for perception, and (c) multimodal specification enhances detection of information that may be near threshold for the infants' sensory systems.

FAMILIAR SITUATIONS AS CONTEXTUAL INFORMATION

Observing an emotional expression in the context of a familiar situation may also facilitate infants' detection of information specific to emotion. Montague and Walker-Andrews (2001) recently published a study in which infants as young as 4 months were presented with emotional expressions embedded in a familiar game. Specifically, these infants participated in a modified game of peek-a-boo. Peek-a-boo itself provides a rich, natural context that is characterized by substantial spatio-temporal structuring (Bruner & Sherwood, 1976). Moreover, it is explicitly multimodal: The initial effect of the game hinges on the presence not only of the reappearing face, but also the accompanying vocalizations of the mother or caregiver (Greenfield, 1972). In the study by Montague and Walker-Andrews, the experimenter, mimicking the typical hiding game in which parents and young infants engage, presented infants with happy/surprise facial/vocal expressions as she hid her face and then reappeared from behind a cloth. On designated reappearances she instead acted out an expression that would not typically occur in a peek-a-boo game (a sad, angry, or fearful facial/vocal expression).

As hypothesized, infants responded differentially to the disruptions in a typical peek-a-boo interaction. Infants in the angry and fearful conditions increased their looking time to these particular expressions, while those viewing either typical happy/surprise expressions or a sad expression on the designated trials decreased their looking time. Moreover, infants assigned to the angry condition increased their looking time on all trials, once the angry expression occurred, as if the occurrence of an angry expression increased their overall level of arousal. Finally, infants in the sad condition showed more lability in their own facial responses and more specific expressions identifiable as interest expressions (Izard, 1995). These results show that 4-month-olds are differentially responsive to composite facial/vocal expressions of emotion when the expressions are embedded in a familiar context, particularly one in which infants may already have expectations (Lewis & Goldberg, 1969; Muir & Hains, 1993; Rochat, Quierdo, & Striano, 1999). To summarize, increases in infants' looking time on the reappearance trials (for angry and fearful expressions) demonstrated that 4-month-olds could discriminate facial/vocal expressions that were presented multimodally and in a familiar context. The fact that infants also decreased their looking time to the sad emotional expressions and reacted with specific emotional responses to the expressions suggests that recognition may have occurred as well.

FAMILIARITY OF PERSON AS CONTEXTUAL INFORMATION

Familiarity of person may also provide contextual information that supports emotion recognition. Probably one of the more interesting and high frequency events in the life of a very young infant is the prolonged and reoccurring presence of the faces of his or her parents. Not only are these faces omnipresent, but they are especially salient because typically they are in motion and accompanied by speech and other sounds, nuzzles, and lots of tactile stimulation. What could be more exciting! These faces are contingent, reciprocal, expressive, evocative, and eventually signal all kinds of information to the infant. Whether one believes that faces are special at birth, it is clear that parental faces become (more) special very quickly. Infants are likely to observe a wide range of facial and vocal expressions in many, many situations displayed by persons who become very familiar to them.

The familiarity of a face is known to have effects in adults' face perception. Studies conducted with adults indicate that adults treat familiar faces differently than unfamiliar ones. For example, familiar faces are recognized more readily by internal rather than external facial features, but for newly encountered faces external and internal features are equally useful (Ellis, Shepherd, & Davies, 1979). This may be because of repeated attention to the expressive features of the face, given their importance to social interactions. Likewise, studies conducted with depressed and/or abusive mothers and their children suggest that characteristics of mother-infant interactions have effects on the ways in which infants and children perceive and react to emotions. For example,

Field and her colleagues have found that 3-month-olds display more sadness and anger and less interest than do infants of nondepressed mothers (Pickens & Field, 1993). These infants also show visual preferences for specific emotions (e.g., sadness) that may be different than those shown by children with nondepressed mothers (Field, 2000). In extreme cases of neglect or abuse, responses to happy, sad, fear, disgust, and angry facial expressions differ for abused, neglected, and nonmaltreated children (Pollak, Cicchetti, Hornung, & Reed, 2000). Given these findings, I and my colleagues have been looking at normative development to determine whether (a) young infants recognize the expressions of their parents, and (b) whether they can generalize from their parents' expressions to those of other, unfamiliar adults.

Emotional Expressions Portrayed by Mothers

In the first study, Kahana-Kalman and Walker-Andrews (2001) examined whether infants as young as 3 months could recognize the emotional expressions of their own mothers. The intermodal preference method was selected for this study because infants must detect abstract information that potentially specifies emotion in order to match facial and vocal expressions. As alluded to earlier, this method has been used successfully by several investigators to explore infants' recognition of emotional expressions at 5 to 7 months of age (Field, 2000; Soken & Pick, 1992, 1999; Walker, 1982; Walker-Andrews, 1986). By 7 months, infants appear to recognize happy, sad, angry, neutral, and fearful expressions when unfamiliar female adults portray these emotion expressions. At 5 months, infants may rely more on synchrony information than affective information in such tasks, however (Walker-Andrews, 1986). Soken and Pick have demonstrated that 7-month-old infants can use motion information alone to recognize happy and angry expressions (Soken & Pick, 1992) and to discriminate between facial expressions drawn from a positive or a negative set of expressions (Soken & Pick, 1999). In Kahana-Kalman and Walker-Andrews (2001), we presented infants with either their own mothers or an unfamiliar woman depicting happy and sad facial/vocal expressions. We also presented one group of infants with asynchronous pairings of the facial and vocal expressions to rule out the possibility that infants were using only temporal relations to determine which face and voice went together. We measured infants' looking time as well as their own facial affect.

Overall, Kahana-Kalman and Walker-Andrews found that when infants as young as 3 months observed emotional expressions portrayed by their own mothers, they detected intermodal correspondences between the facial and vocal displays, as demonstrated by their increased looking time to sound-specified films. Young infants perceived the components of the happy and sad expressions of their mothers as part of a unified, multimodal expression, even when the maternal facial and vocal expressions were presented out of temporal synchrony. Infants also looked preferentially to the happy facial expression when happy and sad films were presented simultaneously and in synchrony with the vocalization, indicating that infants found this filmed emotion the more compelling. Infants did not show by their looking patterns that they could detect any correspondence between vocal and facial displays of the same two emotions when these were portrayed by an unfamiliar woman, even though the vocal and facial displays were presented in temporal synchrony.

The affective responsiveness of the infants also differed across emotions and infants' familiarity with the person portraying the emotions (i.e., mother versus unfamiliar woman). When happy was the sound-specified emotion, infants were more expressive, they showed greater variability of affective expression, and increased the number of alternating expressions. Judges also rated infants as experiencing more positive affect and as more interested and engaged, particularly when the emotion displays were portrayed by the infants' mothers. Furthermore, more precise measures of infants' smiles and distress bouts revealed that infants who viewed their mothers spent more time smiling at the films than infants who viewed the unfamiliar woman; the groups did not differ in the duration of smiling when sad was the sound-specified emotion. Infants produced more full and bright smiles when happy was sound specified and particularly when they viewed the happy expressions of their mothers. Finally, the average duration of distress was longer for infants who observed the unfamiliar woman, than for those who observed their mothers.

Emotional Expressions Depicted by Mothers and Fathers

In a second study, the set of expressions was expanded, we included both mothers and fathers as actors, and we obtained information about levels of parents' involvement with their infants. In this study (Montague & Walker-Andrews, 2002), we also used the intermodal preference procedure, but each infant was presented with a series of intermodal trials. On some trials, the infant's mother and father were presented acting out happy and sad or happy and angry emotional expressions. On other trials, an unfamiliar male and an unfamiliar female acted out happy and sad expressions. In addition, the parents were interviewed to obtain information about their typical involvement with their infant. Specifically, a time diary was constructed from the descriptions parents provided about their activities on the most recent day during the week and during the weekend, and together the parents completed a questionnaire that asked about the percentage of time each parent performed each of 18 caregiver activities (e.g., feeding, bathing, playing with the baby). As in Kahana-Kalman and Walker-Andrews (2001), the infants were 3 months of age.

First, Montague and Walker-Andrews (2002) examined infants' overall visual preferences, because infants often show a preference for happy facial expressions regardless of which vocal expression is played concurrently. The infants looked proportionately longer at happy than sad facial expressions when these were presented together, but there were no such emotion preferences when happy and angry expressions were paired. The main question was whether a vocal expression influenced infants' preferential looking. Therefore, the next comparisons focused on whether a mother's vocal expression of emotion influenced her infant's looking preferences. Overall, infants looked differentially at the maternal facial expressions, depending on which vocal expression was played. For presentations in which the happy and sad facial expressions were viewed side-by-side along with a single vocal expression affectively matching one of the facial expressions, infants looked longer at the congruent facial expression. When they heard the happy vocal expression, they looked longer at the happy facial expression. When they heard the sad vocal expression, they looked proportionately longer at the sad facial expression. There was a different pattern of results when anger was one of the pair of facial expressions, however. Infants actually looked longer at the incongruent (non-sound-specified) facial expression in this case. When maternal happy and angry facial expressions were accompanied by a happy vocal expression, the infants looked longer at the angry expression. When the pair of expressions was accompanied by the angry vocal expression, the infants looked longer to the happy facial expression.

To reiterate, when infants saw their mothers' happy and sad or happy and angry facial expressions, their preferential looking was influenced by the vocal expression that was played. These effects were significant for all comparisons, but the preferences were in the opposite direction. When infants viewed happy and sad facial expressions, they looked proportionately longer at the affectively congruent (sound-specified) expression. When the paired facial expressions were happy and angry, infants looked proportionately longer at the affectively incongruent (non-sound-specified expression) facial expression. The typical pattern in intermodal matching experiments conducted with emotional expressions has been for infants to look longer at the congruent facial expression (see Walker-Andrews, 1997, for a review).

Montague and Walker-Andrews also looked at infants' patterns of looking to their fathers' expressions. Across all infants, none of the looking preferences were significantly increased for fathers' sound-specified emotional expressions. (As described later, for one group paternal vocal expressions did influence the infants' looking preferences.) Finally, infants did not show any sign of intermodal matching for the expressions portrayed by an unfamiliar male or female. As in the prior study (Kahana-Kalman & Walker-Andrews, 2001), infants did not make an intermodal match for expressions posed by an unfamiliar adult, although they did show a matching effect for their mothers' expressions.

Montague and Walker-Andrews then looked to the parent–infant interaction data to determine whether infants' looking preferences were related to these interaction patterns. As expected, mothers reported spending much more time with their infants than did fathers. In addition, there was a positive correlation between the amount of direct contact between mother and child and the infant's preference for the congruent, sound-specified sad expression. Conversely, there was a negative correlation between the amount of direct mother–infant interaction and looking time to the angry facial expression when it was accompanied by an angry vocal expression. For both mothers and fathers, greater parental involvement in a number of specific activities was related to the infants' intermodal matching. There were positive correlations with infants' preferences for the sound-specified expressions in the happy/sad combination; and negative correlations with preferences found for the happy/anger pairings. In addition, for the small subset of fathers who reported high involvement with their infants, infants' responses to paternal expressions paralleled those to maternal expressions.

Together, the results from Kahana-Kalman and Walker-Andrews (2001) and Montague and Walker-Andrews (2002) indicate that when infants observe emotional expressions portrayed by their own mothers and perhaps by their own fathers (at least for infants who have highly involved fathers), infants as young as 3 months detect the intermodal correspondences between the facial and vocal displays. Infants did not show by their looking patterns that they could detect the correspondence between vocal and facial displays of the same two emotions when these were portrayed by an unfamiliar woman or an unfamiliar man. The affective responsiveness of the infants also differed across emotions and familiarity with the person portraying the emotions (i.e., mother versus unfamiliar woman).

With respect to the interaction data from Montague and Walker-Andrews, examination of parent-child involvement patterns revealed many significant correlations with individual infants' sensitivity to parental expressions. Individual differences in family dynamics may be relevant to idiosyncratic patterns of responding by individual babies. Certainly this is an area that merits additional research.

In general, the results suggest an early sensitivity to expressions, especially when these are experienced as dynamic, multimodal, and familiar events. What is particularly interesting is that infants detected and responded to the affective correspondences in their own mothers' facial and vocal expressions even when synchrony relations between the face and voice were disrupted. They did not demonstrate a comparable capability with respect to the synchronously presented vocal and facial expressions of an unfamiliar woman (Kahana-Kalman & Walker-Andrews, 2001). This pattern implies that what accounts for infants' ability to detect correspondences between facial and vocal affective displays is their ability to extract a common meaning from the affective displays portrayed by their own mothers. Given infants' early ability to detect intermodal correspondences in multimodal events, I suggest that it is through the detection of intermodal invariants that infants also discover the meaning of emotional expressions. Infants may first detect the communicative affordance that is provided in a unified multimodal emotional expression, only later recognizing the same information for affect in vocal expressions and then facial expression alone. The results of this study provide further evidence that strengthens the proposal that multimodal information acts as a supportive context.

Generalization of Expressions Portrayed by Familiar Persons

If indeed infants first recognize the expressions of familiar persons, especially in familiar situations and when those expressions are depicted as multimodal, dynamic events, infants might be able to stretch their capabilities to the expressions of unfamiliar persons when all the circumstances are supportive. Just as young children seem to be able to exhibit more sophisticated cognitive abilities in some contexts such as pretend play (e.g., Dias & Harris, 1988) or when parental scaffolding is present (Vygotsky, 1978), perhaps infants can discriminate or even recognize the expressions of unfamiliar persons when these are viewed in supportive contexts.

Therefore, I recently embarked on a study in which infants were presented parental facial/vocal expressions followed by the expressions of an unfamiliar person in a visual habituation procedure. C. A. Nelson and his colleagues (Nelson, Morse, & Leavitt, 1979) first used the visual habituation procedure in this way, to examine infants' generalization of facial expressions across persons. In brief, in the Nelson et al. study 7-

month-olds were visually habituated to a series of slides showing different women posing a happy or fearful facial expression (a static pose). At test, the infants were shown either the same familiar expression posed by yet another female or the other (unfamiliar) expression. The infants increased their looking time to the unfamiliar expression, rather than responding with increased interest to changes in person. Others also have used this method, finding that infants can discriminate between photographs of different facial expressions, although infants seem to rely on feature information when it is available, rather than affective meaning before 7 months (Caron et al., 1985; but see Kestenbaum & Nelson, 1990). As mentioned earlier, Caron et al. (1988) demonstrated that if infants were shown dynamic facial-vocal expressions, infants as young as 4 months dishabituated to changes in happy and sad but in the happy to sad direction only; comparable performance for happy and angry was not found until 7 months (see also, Caron, 1988).

In the present experiment (Walker-Andrews & Pagan, 2002), we decided to test infants at 3 months of age to determine whether the use of familiar persons during the habituation sequence would enable infants to categorize expressions and generalize them to those of unfamiliar persons. We filmed the infants' own mothers and fathers acting out happy and sad facial/vocal expressions and then used these renditions as the presentations during the habituation phase. The parents were not trained to produce "perfect" expressions so that infants would view expressions as their parents typically present them. At test, infants participated in one of several groups. One group continued to see their own mother acting out the familiar expression (control group); another continued to see their own mother but she acted out the novel expression (emotion-only change). A third group of infants saw a female stranger acting out the familiar expressions (person-only change); and yet another group saw a female stranger acting out the novel expression (person and emotion change). The question was whether infants would generalize an expression across the familiar persons (mom and dad) and discriminate it from a new expression no matter who posed it. Looking time was the measure used to answer this question.

First, as expected, infants tended to look longer overall to the happy expressions during the habituation sequence and infants' looking time decreased over the habituation sequence for both sets of expressions. Group differences emerged on the test trials. In brief, infants in the control group who continued to view their own mother acting out the same familiar expression (happy or sad) showed a decrease in fixation time. Those infants who were presented changes at test showed increases in looking time. They increased their looking time to a change in emotion, whether their own mother or the unfamiliar woman presented the altered expression. They also increased their looking time when the unfamiliar person demonstrated the now-habituated emotional expression. Infants responded with increases in looking time to any change at test. In addition, infants who viewed the sad facial and vocal expressions first especially responded to the change in expression. The increases in looking time were approximately four times larger for the infants who first viewed parental sad expressions and then viewed a happy expression, compared to those for infants who viewed parental happy expressions during the habituation sequence. This confirms the assertion that order effects in studies using expressions are probably related to the meaning of those expressions (Walker-Andrews, 1997). One cannot expect that infants will show symmetry in their visual interest to all expression contrasts if meaning is detected.

To summarize, in this experiment infants were asked to abstract emotion information from a set of facial/vocal expressions presented by familiar individuals and generalize it to emotions portrayed by either a familiar or unfamiliar person. That is, the procedure itself highlighted the familiarity of person by presenting two very well-known individuals (Mom and Dad) and highlighted the emotion information by presenting two idiosyncratic portrayals of a dynamic, bimodal expression. Infants who saw these presentations for only a few minutes abstracted the emotion and person information, as indicated by their visual responsiveness on the posttests. They looked longer to a change in person, to a change in emotional expression, and to changes in both. As expected, they did not show visual dishabituation to the continued happy or sad expressions portrayed by their mothers.

What do these results say about infants' perception of emotional expressions? Overall, infants indicated by their looking time that changes in person and in expressions were detected. That is, infants seemed to discriminate happy and sad expressions when these were posed by familiar persons. They also discriminated familiar persons from a stranger, even when each person portrayed the same emotional expression. When infants viewed a unfamiliar person portraying a novel expression, they also increased their looking time, but is not clear from these data alone whether they were responding to the change in person or expression or both. The increases in looking time to changes in expression, person, or both indicate that infants can discriminate between happy and sad emotional expressions and between familiar and unfamiliar persons. Given specific patterns in infants' responsiveness, we speculate that the meaning of the emotional expressions may have been detected as well. This speculation rests primarily on the differences in responsiveness that infants showed to happy and sad expressions. Infants treated the change in expression from happy to sad differently from the change from sad to happy. The increase in looking time on the posttests when happy was the novel expression far exceeded the increase when sad was introduced. This was anticipated, because infants often look preferentially to happy expressions and because there are many order effects in the habituation literature when emotional expressions are used as the exemplars: (a) Caron et al. (1988) found that 4-month-olds would dishabituate to novel, bimodally presented expressions for happy and sad contrasts in the happy to sad direction; (b) Young-Browne et al. (1977) reported that infants increased visual fixation to surprise after being habituated to sadness, but did not dishabituate when these were presented in the opposite order; (c) similarly C. A. Nelson, Morse, and Leavitt (1979) reported that 7-month-olds would dishabituate to fearful expressions after being familiarized to happy, but not in the reverse order. These order effects undoubtedly relate to the "meaning of the expressions" rather than stemming from some irrelevant, chance occurrence.

In addition, the type of expression (happy or sad) also combined in an intriguing way with the identity of the persons portraying that emotional expression. Infants responded with extremely large increases in looking time to a person-only change after they viewed their parents' depictions of sadness during the habituation sequence. These infants showed a 10-fold increase in looking time. We speculate that there is something particularly aversive about parental expressions of sadness that lead to such a large increase in looking. These renditions may have been more meaningful to the infants because their own parents were the actors. To summarize, we infer that infants not only discriminated the happy and sad facial/vocal expressions, but that they also recognized these expressions. We speculate that 3-month-old infants were able to abstract emotional information from the expressions portrayed by their parents and generalize this information across both parents and to the expressions of an unfamiliar adult female. We are currently coding the infants' own emotional responsiveness to the posed expressions to determine whether this converging data will substantiate our view of the looking time results.

CONCLUSIONS REGARDING THE ROLE OF CONTEXT

A cultural-context perspective has recently resurfaced in the study of language (e.g., Tomasello, 1999) and other areas in development, such as autobiographical memory (e.g., Hudson, 1993). To make headway in the study of the development of emotion, taking a similar perspective is paramount. For the infant, affective communication is the primary mode of communication and even before words have meaning to an infant, adults in the environment place great stock in trying to communicate affectively with infants. In Western cultures at least, parents respond to infants as if they were intentional beings and attempt to engage their infants in affective interchanges. In an early study on mother–infant interactions Brazelton et al. (1974) described such interactions thusly:

The mother takes on facial expressions, motions and postures indicative of emotion, as though the infant were behaving intentionally or as though she and he were communicating. Frequently, in response to a motionless infant, she suddenly acquires an expression of great admiration, moving back and forth in front of him with great enthusiasm; or again in response to an unmoving infant, she takes on an expression of great surprise, moving backward in mock astonishment; or in the most exaggerated manner, she greets the infant and, furthermore, carries on an animated extended greeting interchange, bobbing and nodding enthusiastically exactly as though her greeting were currently being reciprocated. (pp. 67–68)

The experimental work reported here indicates that infants as young as 3 months are sensitive to the meaning of emotional expressions of others, at least when those expressions are encountered as multimodal events in familiar settings and/or portrayed by familiar individuals. The contributions of contextual information, such as intermodal correspondences and familiarity, to young infants' improved abilities are complex and reflect a number of processes. For example, the information provided by multimodal events may enhance the infants' perception in a number of ways: The presence of intermodal correspondences may highlight the abstract qualities of emotional expressions that carry the meaning of those expressions; the redundant information available across modalities may permit the detection of near-threshold information; and, finally, multimodal presentations are the norm. Observers rarely encounter mute faces with frozen expressions, nor do they routinely hear vocal expressions from an invisible person, at least when those vocalizations are directed to them (unless it is via telephone). Information presented redundantly across sensory modalities appears to selectively recruit attention and facilitate perceptual learning during infancy (Bahrick et al., 1981; Walker-Andrews, 1997). Certainly, the meaning of an emotional expression is not restricted to a single modality; information about that meaning is expressed across face, voice, and gestures.

Similarly, encountering an emotional expression in a familiar setting may provide contextual information that supports recognition of that expression. This should not be surprising: Encountering one's primary school teacher at the grocery store may hamper one's recognition of that individual. Conversely, observing a person in a familiar setting or engaging in a familiar activity is likely to facilitate recognition. Studies on adults' perception and memory substantiate these commonplace experiences. Similarly, research on infant perception indicates that newborn infants can recognize their mother's face under naturalistic conditions (Bushnell, Sai, & Mullin, 1989), that infants' memories are influenced by contextual information (Howe & Courage, 1993), and that infants can form expectancies during routine events (Lewis & Goldberg, 1969; Montague & Walker-Andrews, 2000).

Finally, in general, infants appear to recognize the emotional expressions of familiar others before they recognize those of unfamiliar individuals. For example, 3-month-old infants look longer to their mother's happy facial expression when they hear her happy vocal expression, though they do not show such intermodal matching for the facial and vocal expressions of a stranger (Kahana-Kalman & Walker-Andrews, 2001; Montague & Walker-Andrews, 2002). Why this occurs is not entirely clear. It may be that infants have had more opportunities to associate their mother's happy face with her happy voice, as the two are likely to co-occur and infants' mothers are apt to be the most frequent source of emotional information. This is a seductive argument: It places the infant's precocious intermodal matching behavior squarely in the literature on associative learning and it restricts the infants' behavior to a low-level ability. This explanation, however, does not address the finding that infants' intermodal matching is delayed when the face and voice are asynchronous (at least for strangers' faces and voices, Walker, 1982). Nor does it explain why preferential looking is attenuated when mother's face and voice are asynchronous (Kahana-Kalman & Walker-Andrews, 2001). In addition, Walker-Andrews and Pagan (2002) report that infants of the same age can generalize happy and sad expressions across their mothers and fathers and discriminate these expressions from one another. They may be able to generalize these expressions to those of a stranger, even at 3 months in a situation in which they observe the variability between mothers' and fathers' expressions beforehand. These abilities cannot be explained using the same appeal to association. Infants had to abstract emotional information that was presented across time and then (a) generalize it to another person and (b) discriminate it from a different emotional expression.

In closing, I submit that infants' developing perception of emotional expressions is an result of their more general perceptual learning and development. Sometimes it seems as if learning about persons is "special," but people are adept at entering into the infants' immediate environment. Perceptual learning itself is self-sustaining, and infants are prepared to learn about the affordances of others at birth. By the time they are born, infants have already been exposed to certain sounds, especially their mothers' voices, for many months (DeCasper & Fifer, 1980; DeCasper & Spence, 1986). This allows not only the recognition of her voice, but also some familiarity with intonation patterns and other suprasegmental information. Soon after birth, the familiar voice of the mother is heard in conjunction with the presence of her face and, most important to us here, the familiar tones of her voice are experienced along with the facial expressions she is producing. Initially, an infant will show a preference for his mother's voice (Cooper, 1997); and for her mother's face (Bushnell, Sai, & Mullin, 1989; Walton, Bower, & Bower, 1992). It seems that infants also are more adept at recognizing their mother's facial and vocal expressions.

Other adults in the environment also speak to infants while smiling or frowning at them. The amount of social information is vast, but infants appear to learn rapidly about the affordances that are made available in the multimodal communicative events in which they participate. By 5 months infants look longer at a video display of a facial expression that is synchronous with a soundtrack conveying the same affect vocally; and by 7 months infants show the same preferential looking even when the soundtrack is asynchronous with the ongoing facial expression. Thus these older infants detect correspondences specific to the meaning of the ongoing event in addition to the synchrony between the acoustic and optic information. They are differentiating the information specifying the affordance of the event rather than simply matching visible lip movements and voice sounds.

At the same time, infants are also detecting other types of social information. For example, infants show sensitivity to intermodal information specifying gender beginning at about 4 months (Walker-Andrews, Bahrick, Raglioni, & Diaz, 1991), as well as information about age (Bahrick, Netto, & Hernandez-Reif, 1998), and speech sounds (Kuhl & Meltzoff, 1982). Infants hone in on social information and learn rapidly about the affordances characterizing those events as they are also learning about the physical world. In many cases, this information is complementary. An incongruous event occurs and the infant's mother responds with surprise. A risky drop-off is encountered and the infant's mother displays fear.

Finally, infants themselves are active in their social worlds. They do not merely observe the expressions of others, but they evoke others' emotional responses by their own actions, including their own emotional expressions. Such interchanges are most common with the infant's mother and other significant persons. Infants learn to distinguish the emotions and moods of their caregivers, which have prospective meaning for what will happen next. In addition, these coordinated social interactions promote the learning of social routines, for example, the give-and-take of object exchanges or the give-and-take of a peek-a-boo game. The 3-month-old who recognizes the emotional expressions presented by caregivers is well on the way to achieving the capability for regulating and controlling interactions and learning about properties of objects and events, as well as people, by way of these early communicative interactions.

REFERENCES

Bahrick, L. E., & Lickliter, R. (2000). Intersensory redundancy guides attentional selectivity and perceptual learning in infancy. *Developmental Psychology, 36,* 190–201.

Bahrick, L. E., Netto, D., & Hernandez-Reif, M. (1998). Intermodal perception of adult and child faces and voices by infants. *Child Development, 69,* 1263–1265.

Bahrick, L. E., Walker, A. S., & Neisser, U. (1981). Selective looking by infants. *Cognitive Psychology, 13,* 377–390.

Barrera, M. E., & Maurer, D. (1981). The perception of facial expressions by the three-month-old. *Child Development, 52,* 203–206.

Brazelton, T. B., Koslowski, B., & Main, W. (1974). The origins of reciprocity: The early mother–infant interaction. In M. Lewis & L. A. Rosenblum (Eds.), *The effect of the infant on its caregiver* (pp. 49–76). New York: Wiley.

Bruner, J. S., & Sherwood, V. (1976). Peekaboo and the learning of rule structures. In J. S. Bruner & A. Jolly & K. Sylva (Eds.), *Play: Its role in development and evolution* (pp. 277–285). New York: Basic Books.

Bühler, K. (1930). The mental development of the child. New York: Harcourt, Brace & Company.

Bushnell, I. W. R., Sai, F., & Mullin, J. T. (1989). Neonatal recognition of the mother's face. *British Journal of Developmental Psychology, 2,* 11–17.

Caron, A. J. (1988). *The role of face and voice in infant discrimination of naturalistic emotional expressions.* Paper presented at the International Conference on Infant Studies, Washington DC.

Caron, A. J., Caron, R. F., & MacLean, D. J. (1988). Infant discrimination of naturalistic emotional expressions: The role of face and voice. *Child Development, 59,* 604–616.

Caron, R. F., Caron, A. J., & Myers, R. S. (1985). Do infants see emotional expressions in static faces? *Child Development, 56,* 1552–1560.

Cooper, R. P. (1997). An ecological approach to infants' perception of intonation contours as meaningful aspects of speech. In C. Dent-Read & P. Zukow-Goldring (Eds.), *Evolving explanations of development: Ecological approaches to organism-environment systems* (pp. 55–85). Washington, DC: American Psychological Association.

DeCasper, A. J., & Fifer, W. P. (1980) Of human bonding: Newborns prefer their mother's voices. *Science, 208,* 1174–1176.

DeCasper, A. J., & Spence, M. J. (1986). Prenatal maternal speech influences newborns' perception of speech sounds. *Infant Behavior and Development, 9,* 133–150.

Dias, M. G., & Harris, P. L. (1988). The effect of make-believe play on deductive reasoning. *British Journal of Developmental Psychology, 6,* 207–221.

Ellis, H. D., Shepherd, J. W., & Davies, G. M. (1979). Identification of familiar and unfamiliar faces from internal and external features: Some implications for theories of face recognition. *Perception, 8,* 431–439.

Everhart, V., & Henry, S. (1992). *Indicators of early empathy: Newborns learning the meaning of changes in facial expression of emotion within 5 minutes.* Paper presented at the International Conference on Infant Studies, Miami, FL.

Fernald, A. (1992). Human maternal vocalizations to infants as biologically relevant signals: An evolutionary perspective. In J. H. Barkow, L. Cosmides, & J. Tooby (Eds.), *The adapted mind: Evolutionary psychology and the generation of culture* (pp. 391–428). Oxford: Oxford University Press.

Field, T. M. (2000). Infants of depressed mothers. *Stress, coping and depression*, 3–22.

Gibson, E. J., & Pick, A. D. (2000). *An ecological approach to perceptual learning and development*. New York: Oxford University Press.

Gibson, J. J. (1979). *The ecological approach to visual perception*. Hillsdale, NJ: Lawrence Erlbaum Associates.

Grant, K. W., Ardell, L. A. H., Kuhl, P. K., & Sparks, P. W. (1985). The contribution of fundamental frequency, amplitude envelope, and voicing duration cues to speechreading in normal-hearing subjects. *Journal of the Acoustical Society of America, 77*, 671–677.

Greenfield, P. M. (1972). Playing peek-a-boo with a four-month-old: A study of the role of speech and nonspeech sounds in the formation of a visual schema. *The Journal of Psychology, 82*, 287–298.

Gusella, J. L., Muir, D., & Tronick, E. A. (1988). The effect of manipulating maternal behavior during an interaction on three- and six-month-olds' affect and attention. *Child Development, 59*, 1111–1124.

Haviland, J. M., & Lelwica, M. E. (1987). The induced affect response: 10-week-old infants' responses to three emotion expressions. *Developmental Psychology, 23*, 97–104.

Howe, M. L., & Courage, M. L. (1993). On resolving the enigma of infantile amnesia. *Psychological Bulletin, 113*, 305–326.

Hudson, J. A. (1993). Reminiscing with mothers and others: Autobiographical memory in young two-year-olds. *Journal of Narrative and Life History, 2*, 129–150.

Izard, C. E. (1995). *The maximally discriminative facial movement coding system (Max)* (rev. ed.). Newark, DE: University of Delaware, Information Technologies and University Media Services.

Kahana-Kalman, R., & Walker-Andrews, A. S. (2001). The role of person familiarity in young infants' perception of emotional expressions. *Child Development, 72*, 352–369.

Kestenbaum, R., & Nelson, C. A. (1990). The recognition and categorization of upright and inverted expressions by 7-month-old infants. *Infant Behavior and Development, 13*, 497–511.

Kuchuk, A., Vibbert, M., & Bornstein, M. H. (1986). The perception of smiling and its experiential correlations in three-month-old infants. *Child Development, 57*, 1054–1061.

Kuhl, P. K., & Meltzoff, A. N. (1982). The bimodal perception of speech in infancy. *Science, 218*, 1138–1141.

LaBarbera, J. D., Izard, C. E., Vietze, P., & Parisi, S. A. (1976). Four- and six-month-old infants' visual responses to joy, anger, and neutral expressions. *Child Development, 47*, 535–538.

Lewis, M., & Goldberg, S. (1969). The acquisition and violation of expectancy: An experimental paradigm. *Journal of Experimental Child Psychology, 7*, 70–80.

Liberman, A., Cooper, F., Shankweiler, D., & Studdert-Kennedy, M. (1967). The perception of the speech code. *Psychological Review, 74,* 431–461.

Montague, D. P. F., & Walker-Andrews, A. S. (2001). Peekaboo: A new look at infants' perception of emotion expression. *Developmental Psychology, 37,* 826–838.

Montague, D. P. F., & Walker-Andrews, A. S. (2002). Mothers, fathers, and infants: The role of person familiarity and parental involvement in infants' perception of emotion expressions. *Child Development, 73,* 1339–1352.

Muir, D. W., & Hains, S. M. J. (1993). Infant sensitivity to perturbations in adult facial, vocal, tactile, and contingent stimulation during face-to-face interactions. In B. de Boysson-Bardies, S. de Schonen, P. Jusczyk, P. MacNeilage, & J. Morton (Eds.), *Developmental neurocognition: Speech and face processing in the first year of life.* Dordrecht: Kluwer Academic Publishers.

Nelson, C. A. (1987). The recognition of facial expressions in the first two years of life: Mechanisms of development. *Child Development, 58,* 889–909.

Nelson, C. A., Morse, P. A., & Leavitt, L. A. (1979). Recognition of facial expressions by seven-month-old infants. *Child Development, 50,* 1239–1242.

Nelson, K. (1986). *Event knowledge: Structure and function in development.* Hillsdale: NJ: Lawrence Erlbaum Associates.

Nelson, K. (1993). The psychological and social origins of autobiographical memory. *Psychological Science, 4,* 7–14.

Oster, H. (1981). "Recognition" of emotional expression in infancy? In M. E. Lamb & L. R. Sherrod (Eds.), *Infant social cognition: Empirical and theoretical considerations* (pp. 85–125). Hillsdale, NJ: Lawrence Erlbaum Associates.

Pickens, J., & Field, T. (1993). Facial expressivity in infants of depressed mothers. *Developmental Psychology, 29,* 986–988.

Pollak, S. D., Cicchetti, D., Hornung, K., & Reed, A. (2000). Recognizing emotion in faces: Developmental effects of child abuse and neglect. *Developmental Psychology, 36,* 679–688.

Rochat, P., Quierdo, J. G., & Striano, T. (1999). Emerging sensitivity of the timing and structure of protoconversation in early infancy. *Developmental Psychology, 35,* 950–957.

Sekuler, R., & Blake, R. (1994). *Perception* (3rd ed.). New York: McGraw-Hill.

Serrano, J. M., Iglesias, J., & Loeches, A. (1992). Visual discrimination and recognition of facial expressions of anger, fear, and surprise in 4- to 6-month-old infants. *Developmental Psychology, 25,* 411–425.

Soken, N. H., & Pick, A. D. (1992). Intermodal perception of happy and angry expressive behaviors by seven-month-old infants. *Child Development, 63,* 787–793.

Soken, N. H., & Pick, A. D. (1999). Infants' perception of dynamic affective expressions: Do infants distinguish specific expressions? *Child Development, 70,* 1275–1282.

Tomasello, M. (1999). *The cultural origins of human cognition.* Cambridge, MA: Harvard University Press.

Torralba, A., & Sinha, P. (2001). Detecting faces in impoverished images. MIT AI Memo 2001–028, CBCL Memo 208.

Vygotsky, L. S. (1978). *Mind in society: The development of higher psychological processes.* Cambridge, MA: Harvard University Press.

Walker, A. S. (1982). Intermodal perception of expressive behaviors by human infants. *Journal of Experimental Child Psychology, 33,* 514–535.

Walker-Andrews, A. S. (1986). Intermodal perception of expressive behaviors: Relation of eye and voice? *Developmental Psychology, 22,* 373–377.
Walker-Andrews, A. S. (1997). Infants' perception of expressive behaviors: Differentiation of multimodal information. *Psychological Bulletin, 121,* 437–456.
Walker-Andrews, A. S., Bahrick, L. E., Raglioni, S. S., & Diaz, I. (1991). Infants' bimodal perception of gender. *Ecological Psychology, 3,* 55–75.
Walker-Andrews, A. S., & Grolnick, W. (1983). Discrimination of vocal expression by young infants. *Infant Behavior and Development, 6,* 491–498.
Walker-Andrews, A. S., & Lennon, E. (1991). Infants' discrimination of vocal expressions: Contributions of auditory and visual information. *Infant Behavior and Development, 14,* 131–142.
Walker-Andrews, A. S., Montague, D. P. F., & Kahana-Kalman, R. (2000, July). *Developing social expectations and understanding intentions.* Paper presented at the International Conference on Infant Studies, Brighton, UK.
Walker-Andrews, A. S., & Pagan, W. (2002, April). *Learning emotion at home: Young infants' generalization of parental emotional expressions.* Paper presented at the International Conference on Infant Studies, Toronto, Canada.
Walton, G. E., Bower, N. J. A., & Bower, T. G. R. (1992). Recognition of familiar faces by newborns. *Infant Behavior and Development, 15,* 265–269.
Wilcox, B., & Clayton, F. (1968). Infant visual fixation on motion pictures of the human face. *Journal of Experimental Child Psychology, 6,* 22–32.
Young-Browne, G., Rosenfeld, H. M., & Horowitz, F. D. (1977). Infant discrimination of facial expressions. *Child Development, 49,* 555–562.

Chapter 5

*Discerning Intentions: Characterizing the Cognitive System at Play**

Dare Baldwin
University of Oregon

Intentions are what define the meaning and value of human action. Our legal and ethical codes transparently reflect this—witness the pivotal role played by inferences regarding "malice aforethought" in judgments regarding legal culpability. In fact, our interpretation of virtually every social act we ever witness—from the tragic and the magnificent to the utterly mundane—hinges on the particular intentions we ascribe to the actors involved.

Gaining insight into others' intentions is as much a cognitive undertaking as a social one. Intentions are hidden, non-obvious things that we must somehow infer or recover from the dynamic flow of motion that we actually witness. It is clear that cognitive mechanisms of substantial complexity underlie this inferential or recovery process. And in turn, we reap

*Acknowledgments: This material is based in part upon work supported by the National Science Foundation under grant No. 0214484, and by the University of Oregon. Any opinions, findings, and conclusions or recommendations expressed in this material are those of the author(s) and do not necessarily reflect the views of the National Science Foundation. Many thanks to my research collaborators, to Catherine Tamis-LeMonda and Bruce Homer for editorial assistance, and to the many generous adults and infants who volunteered their assistance as participants in the research.

enormous cognitive benefits from intentional understanding: it supports our acquisition and use of language (e.g., Akhtar & Tomasello, 1998; Baldwin, 1991; Bruner, 1977, 1983; Snow, 1999; Tomasello, 1999), and expedites our acquisition of knowledge about the world (e.g., Baldwin, 2000; Baldwin & Moses, 1994; Tomasello, 1999; Tomasello, Kruger, & Ratner, 1993). Human cognition is thus fundamentally shaped by the central role that intentions play within our social intercourse.

To illustrate, imagine you observe someone carrying out an extended sequence of motions in which they move about a room, contact a series of objects, and bring some of these objects into contact with one another. On the description I've just given it would surely be difficult to encode, recall, and successfully reenact for oneself the sequence one observed. In fact, such a nondescript rendering of a lengthy and involved motion sequence might lead to encoding salient, but potentially irrelevant, occurrences within the stream—such as inadvertent loud sounds or large motions. But what if one recognized that this particular motion sequence was motivated by an overarching goal to set up a stage for an orchestral performance, with a set of subsidiary goals to arrange chairs in a particular array, set up music stands, and the like? Remembering and reenacting the motion sequence would be greatly facilitated; as well, memory wouldn't be needlessly guided by irrelevant factors such as noise level or range of motion. The basic idea is that inferences about goals and intentions help to organize processing of complex, dynamic motion, guiding structured interpretation, and hence encodability, of action sequences, thereby enhancing learning. As well, inferences about goals and intentions serve as a backdrop against which language that accompanies action can be interpreted. If you hear "Oh, geez" from an individual passing empty-handed in front of a gap in the line of music stands, you might infer chagrin that a music stand is lacking, but only if you'd appreciated what the goals and intentions of the overall motion stream were.

Although intentional understanding is clearly central to human social and cognitive functioning, as yet we know only a little about the nature of the actual cognitive abilities at play, and even less about their neurophysiological underpinnings. Children seem to acquire skills for interpreting others' intentions on a robust and predictable developmental schedule, but again, little is yet known about how such development takes place. It is rare, but the occasional individual seems to suffer deficits in interpreting others' intentions, sometimes as a result of a developmental disorder such as autism, and in other cases due to serious brain trauma occurring later in life. Sadly, such deficits profoundly disrupt these individuals' social and intellectual functioning. We do not yet understand the specific sources of these difficulties with intentional understanding, and thus we are uncertain how best to assist such individuals toward recovery.

This chapter focuses on what my own and others' current research is beginning to reveal about the cognitive underpinnings of intention detection. I outline a set of pressing questions about the nature of the system that makes intention detection possible, and offer some ideas about avenues along which investigation of these questions might usefully proceed.

COMPLEXITY OF ACTION AND THE POWER OF INTENTIONAL UNDERSTANDING

Humans in action present a potentially bewildering display of motion: limbs snake in and out, fingers wiggle about, heads bobble, torsos bend and twist. Meanwhile, in the midst of much travel hither and thither, objects of many sorts are contacted, handled in diverse ways, and then discarded, often in rapid succession. How do we make sense of this potentially bewildering muddle of motion? Given the complexities, it is striking that, more often than not, we all seem to achieve roughly the same analysis of the intentions underlying the actions we observe. Of course, there are exceptions to this, and our legal system directs a considerable amount of energy toward the resolution of disagreements concerning just what individuals did or did not intend on a given very specific occasion. Such disputed cases lie within the context, however, of a remarkable degree of agreement. On any given day each of us readily, and largely unconsciously, interprets a great variety of actions that others produce without encountering any contradiction to the intentions we impute. In fact, it is seldom that we experience any sense of ambiguity or uncertainty about our inferences regarding others' intentions. This is in itself surprising given that, in principle, an infinite number of possible intentions could underlie each and every motion sequence we observe (e.g., Searle, 1984).

In fact, we typically agree even when we observe people engaging in actions that are new to us. For example, you may never before have witnessed someone pitting cherries, but it is likely you would have little difficulty determining the relevant intentions on your first such opportunity. In cases of novelty we readily process the action, derive relevant intentions, and organize these into a larger appreciation of the overall goals. Together, these very basic observations all point to the existence of a cognitive system that supports inferences about intentions, and they clarify that this system is generative in kind. That is, the system generates systematic analyses of intentions even when the sequence of motions observed is novel. A first pressing issue for investigation is to flesh out this very skeletal outline about the nature of the cognitive system that makes intention detection possible.

CHARACTERIZING THE COGNITIVE SYSTEM FOR DISCERNING INTENTIONS

The overarching question I am concerned with is how we, as observers of others' motion, succeed in interpreting surface motion patterns in terms of latent, underlying motivators—goals and intentions—that give rise to those motions. This question is analogous to the fundamental question driving much of research in psycholinguistics; that is, the question of how we discover the latent structure and meaningful content underlying the complex auditory (or, for gestural languages such as ASL, visual/spatial) sequences characteristic of language. Psycholinguistics research cannot yet offer a comprehensive answer to this question, but at the very least this now extensive body of research clearly tells us that the answer is an involved one. In the following, I briefly sketch what generally are believed to be the broad outlines of our cognitive system for language processing; claims at this level are relatively uncontroversial among cognitive scientists. I then provide reasons—and a tiny amount of evidence—justifying the plausibility of these same phenomena in action processing. This is not to say that we should expect systems for processing language and action to be isomorphic in all respects. Clearly, these are distinct, and highly specialized cognitive systems processing different kinds of stimuli. At the same time, interesting parallels seem to hold. This makes it reasonable to conjecture that comparable processing solutions are achieved across these domains.

Language Processing Writ Large

Interpreting language seems to involve a plethora of mechanisms devoted to processing a variety of components of the linguistic signal. Processing seems to be massively parallel, with significant interaction occurring among multiple subsystems (Just & Carpenter, 1987). Processing also seems to involve parallel influence from both top-down and bottom-up sources of information (e.g., see Ashcraft, 1994). We are ubiquitously confronted with degraded speech, so language processing requires efficient extrapolation and "filling in" mechanisms that enable seamless processing in the less-than-utopian everyday speech environment. A significant degree of language processing is highly automatic, occurs outside conscious awareness, and is relatively impenetrable to introspection (e.g., see Tartter, 1986). Finally, language processing yields memory for "gist" or meaning; typically little is retained about the verbatim content of the surface form that speech actually took (Bransford & Franks, 1971; Butcher & Kintsch, 2003; Johnson, Bransford, & Solomon, 1973; Kintsch, 1998).

Action Parallels to Language Processing

As a stimulus, dynamic intentional action has important commonalities with linguistic behavior. Like talk, everyday action is rapid, largely continuous, multifaceted, and evanescent. And like talk, processing of action is oriented toward interpreting and encoding *meaning,* not toward detailed registration of the surface details of motion itself. Given these commonalities, it seems reasonable to expect important similarities between the cognitive systems that underlie processing in these two domains. Thus a reasonable starting hypothesis is that discerning intentions in dynamic human action involves parallel, highly interactive processing among multiple cognitive and perceptual subsystems. Curiously, there is relatively little empirical evidence to speak to this very basic hypothesis about the cognitive system underlying action processing. Action processing represents a singular gap in the investigative efforts of cognitive psychologists. Other fields, however—especially social psychology—have supplied at least a little relevant information that is generally consistent with the framework I am espousing. Here I flesh out hypotheses regarding action that are direct analogs to the linguistic phenomena just described, and note where some starting evidence bears out the plausibility of these hypotheses.

One specific hypothesis is that observers utilize both top-down and bottom-up information in parallel to jointly constrain analysis of the motion stimulus. Top-down information involves conceptual knowledge one possesses concerning the intentions actors are likely to enact in particular contexts. Such prior knowledge presumably influences what one selectively attends to within the motion stream, and may assist in the extraction and rapid identification of relevant actions. In fact, some years ago social psychologists Zadny and Gerard (1974) documented such a role for top-down information in action processing. They documented that observers' on-line inferences about what actors are doing can be systematically influenced by gifting them before-the-fact with top-down expectations about the actor's goals and intentions.

Top-down influences of this kind on action processing will likely predominate when observers watch well-known actors engage in highly predictable intentional acts in familiar contexts, such as when watching a family member brush teeth or unload the dryer.

Regarding bottom-up information, this is the idea that dynamic human action possesses inherent structural regularities—predictable motion patterns—correlated with intentions, and observers' sensitivity to these regularities facilitates processing of intentions. Along these lines, social psychologists Newtson and colleagues (Newtson, 1973; Newtson & Engquist, 1976) have shown that adults display a high degree of agreement in the way they segment ongoing intentional action into distinct acts, even when actions are relatively novel (e.g., assembling a saxophone). Given that adults would have little specific top-down knowledge on which to base their segmentation judgments for such novel intentional sequences, bottom-up processes presumably play a predominant role in locating segment boundaries within the motion flow. Recently we (Baldwin, Andersson, & Saffran, in prep; Guha, Baldwin, & Craven, in prep) and others (e.g., Martin & Tversky, 2003) have obtained additional evidence, to be described later, that sensitivity to "bottom-up" structure within the motion-flow assists adults' segmentation of dynamic human action. As well, Blythe and colleagues (Blythe, Todd, & Miller, 1999) recently documented in a simulation study that structural patterns within dynamic intentional action provide some direct information about the content of the intentions being enacted. Their PDP model showed a relatively high degree of accuracy in categorizing a small set of intentional actions (e.g., chase, tease) based solely on analysis of structural patterns within the motion flow. Finally, Zacks (2004) provided evidence for both top-down and bottom-up influences on event segmentation within one-and-the-same segmentation paradigm.

In the hurly-burly of the everyday world we often lack access to portions of a given action. For example, actors' motions frequently are partially or temporarily occluded by other objects or people. For this reason we should expect that mechanisms subserving action processing—like those known to support language processing—are capable of extrapolating and "filling in" to enable smooth and robust processing in the face of such stimulus degradation. An example that seems powerfully to capture our "filling in" skill is the explosive effect that the much-publicized video-tape depicting the beating of Rodney King had on Los Angeles residents when the police officers tried for his beating were initially acquitted of wrong-doing. In this short video clip, filmed at considerable distance with a consumer-grade camera, the scene was dark, the image was wildly jumpy, and the complex, rapidly unfolding event involved multiple people all moving simultaneously and frequently occluding one another from view. Despite these radical deficiencies as a visual stimulus, viewers readily processed the events and discerned hostile intentions at play. Such agreement in observers' interpretation of the intentional content of the highly degraded Rodney King video anecdotally supports the contention that powerful mechanisms of extrapolation facilitate action processing.

As with language, it also seems likely that much of action processing is automatic, implicit, and impenetrable to conscious introspection. It even has been argued that it is impossible to inhibit the act of interpreting the meaning of an utterance one happens to be privy to. Similarly, I suspect, it is impossible to consciously inhibit interpreting the intentions of an event one happens to witness.

Finally, we should expect a memory for gist phenomenon in action processing that is comparable to this phenomenon in language. That is, what people will remember in processing others' action will center around an interpretation of their goals and intentions—the "gist"—rather than the actual surface content of the motion itself. A tradition of research on eyewitness testimony within social psychology supplies an abundance of evidence that generally bears out this idea that intentions and goals are central among the things people encode about others' actions, not the motions themselves. It is reasonable to expect such a "memory for gist" phenomenon to be relatively reduced in children relative to adults—as has been documented in the language domain—given that children have less prior knowledge about intentions to guide top-down processing and in which to embed intentions they are able to discern and encode.

If the story I have been telling is correct, it is inferences about intentions that largely constitute our knowledge of others' actions—we remember what we thought people intended, not necessarily the details of what they actually did. This human propensity to take the "intentional stance" toward others' behavior (e.g., Dennett, 1987) seems to represent an arena of special expertise relative to other species (e.g., Povinelli, 2001; Tomasello, 1999), and Tomasello (1999) suggests that human intention-detection skill has been pivotal in the evolution of human cognition and culture more generally. Given the apparent centrality of skill at discerning intentions to cognitive and social functioning, a very important question is how human children come by their ultimate expertise at intention detection.

EMERGENCE OF SKILL AT DISCERNING INTENTIONS IN DYNAMIC ACTION?

At issue is whether skill at discerning intentions is something that develops, and if so, what the developmental course of such skill might be.

A sizable body of developmental research now indicates that skills for appropriate action-processing appear to be early developing (e.g., Wellman & Phillips, 2001; Woodward, 1998), with genuine inferences about intentions being within infants' grasp by the end of the first year of life (e.g., Baldwin, 2000; Tomasello, 1999). By 12–15 months, infants readily interpret basic intentions underlying novel sequences of action that unfold in complex ways over time (e.g., Akhtar & Tomasello, 1998; Meltzoff & Brooks, 2001; Woodward & Sommerville, 2000), and they weight information about intentions heavily in their response to others' behavior (e.g., Baldwin & Moses, 2001).

At the same time, developmentalists have long recognized that children's early understanding of intentions is limited in important ways, indicating that acquisition of the adult cognitive system for action processing undergoes extended development (e.g., Piaget, 1932). One kind of limitation on early action processing and intentional inference arises as a result of young children's apparent lack of conceptual understanding about certain kinds of mental states—specifically, "epistemic" mental states, such as beliefs or knowledge (e.g., Perner, 1991; Wellman, 1990). For example, as adults we think someone is unable to *intend* to do something if he or she lacks all knowledge of that thing, or believes that thing to be undoable. Lacking an understanding of epistemic states such as knowledge and belief leaves infants and young children unable to place such belief/knowledge constraints on their inferences about intentions (e.g., Moses, 2001). This conceptual deficit also leaves certain kinds of intentions opaque to young children, such as intentions that are motivated purely by the goal of gaining knowledge or altering others' beliefs.

Another kind of limitation on young children's early intentional understanding is also conceptual, but concerns their relative lack of knowledge about the world more generally (not just in the mentalistic domain). Understanding intentions depends heavily on knowledge of the objects and people involved in carrying out those intentions. Obvious examples of this are cases in which infants entirely lack any knowledge of the basic components involved in a given set of intentional acts, such as the intentions involved in financial transactions (depositing money, locking-in interest rates). It is highly unlikely that infants understand such intentions, given their profound lack of knowledge about monetary fundamentals. The implications of knowledge deficits are much the same for most other, everyday intentions. For example, it is unlikely that infants understand the intentions motivating such everyday actions as washing a dish in the way that you and I do, given that they likely know little of the role that soap and water play in sanitation processes, or the efficacy of bristly brushes for gunk removal. On the other hand, although infants may lack adult-level conceptual understanding of intentions, they may nevertheless be quite capable of engaging in a fair degree of appropriate *processing* of dish-washing actions. For example, infants might be able to segment the flow of dish-washing motions into relevant action segments—such as picking up a dish, turning on the water, scrubbing, rinsing, and the like—although they do not fully understand the *content* of the intentions motivating these acts. They probably also recognize that these actions are goal-oriented, even though specific rationales for these goals may escape them. In fact, skills that enable infants to achieve systematic, organized processing of the complex flow of motion seem likely to be crucial in making it possible for them ultimately to acquire a more sophisticated conceptual-level understanding of the intentions motivating action. In other words, action-processing mechanisms that are available early in development might bootstrap subsequent development of intentional understanding. This is a point to be elaborated in what follows. In any case, however, all evidence indicates that in human infancy, core components of intentional understanding are in place early—at least by the second year of life—but that such understanding nevertheless undergoes significant and protracted development. If this is correct, then the important question arises as to the nature of the mechanisms that support the emergence and development of skill at discerning intentions. This question of epigenesis is another pressing issue concerning the cognitive system for discerning intentions.

EPIGENETIC MECHANISMS FOR INTENTIONAL UNDERSTANDING?

I have likened action processing to language processing, at least along some dimensions. Pursuing the analogy, it is worth considering the extent to which theories of language acquisition might be relevant in constructing hypotheses about mechanisms enabling the acquisition of action-processing skills. Much is indeed relevant, I believe, but one prominent approach to language acquisition currently known under the guise of the learnability, UG, or principles and parameters approach (Chomsky, 1990; Crain & Pietroski, 2001; Pinker, 1994; Wexler & Culicover, 1980)—does not seem to be a good fit to the action domain. The core of this approach is a logical case (the poverty of the stimulus argument) pointing to a substantial, highly abstract, innate linguistic endowment in normally developing human infants. *Learning* of abstract grammatical structures is argued to be impossible given the absence of negative evidence in children's input regarding ungrammatical utterances, and thus learnability theorists have proposed that the human brain possesses innate, genetically-specified, language-specific representation of abstract, universal grammatical principles.

Is there a reason to make such a logical case for extensive innate endowment of action-processing abilities? Given that the logical case rests on the poverty of the stimulus argument, the first thing to consider is whether poverty of the stimulus concerns even arise in the case of intentional action. On Gold's theorem, the poverty of the stimulus argument is relevant only for the class of languages that is generative (in the sense of including recursive, embedded structures). There is reason to believe that intentional action meets this criterion. For example, we both engage in, and readily interpret when others engage in, intentional actions that involve recursive embedding. Consider a classic example of such recursive embedding: An Escher painting depicting a man holding a mirror such that he can view himself holding the mirror in another mirror. Watching himself watch himself watching himself continues ad infinitum within a series of increasingly tiny mirror images. From the standpoint of action processing, this is a man intentionally looking at himself intentionally looking at himself, in infinite recursion. Clearly, our action processing system possesses the recursive embedding structure that renders language subject to the poverty of the stimulus argument. Must we then posit genetically pre-specified and highly abstract innate intention representations as part of the evolutionary preparedness of the human brain?

I suspect this is unnecessary. Although intentional action is of the class of things to which the poverty of the stimulus argument might reasonably apply, the logical case for innate endowment is not a good fit to intentional action for other reasons. In possible contrast to language (but see, e.g., Tomasello, 2003, for discussion of this continuing controversy), there seems to be abundant negative evidence about the well-formedness of intentional acts in children's action input. This negative evidence seems to take a variety of forms. For example, children gain direct negative feedback from the world when their own intentional acts are ill-formed, because ill-formed actions usually fail to achieve the intended outcome. An interesting exception to this generality is slapstick comedy. Charlie Chaplin, for example, was a master at capturing the hilarity of bizarrely successful ill-formed intentional acts, as when he and a companion in *Modern Times* unwittingly brought cigars to one another's mouths and successfully smoked them, despite having each apparently intended to smoke his own cigar in the ordinary way.

In addition to direct feedback about the inefficacy of their own faulty intentional sequences, children likely also have abundant opportunity to observe potentially relevant clues from others (e.g., emotional responses such as laughter, epithets, and characteristic expressions, such as "Oops!") when their intentional acts are ill-formed. Adults also of course frequently make explicit remarks when children perform ill-formed intentional sequences (this is negative evidence) and provide indirect guidance by showing children how to recast the motion stream to gain the desired end. For these reasons, input regarding ill-formed intentional action sequences does not seem to be impoverished, undercutting any logical argument necessitating innate knowledge in this domain. This is one respect in which beliefs that some hold dear regarding acquisition processes in language seem not transferable to the domain of intentional action.

In contrast, in a number of other respects transfer from work on language acquisition to the acquisition of intentional understanding seems both sensible and beneficial. In particular, one popular contemporary approach to accounting for language development is to consider bootstrapping mechanisms that might help learners to break into appropriate processing of the complex linguistic input they encounter. This general notion that bootstrapping mechanisms likely play a crucial role in getting acquisition of the system off the ground seems worth pursuing in the domain of intentional action. As well, it is worth considering the possibility that *specific* bootstrapping mechanisms that have been identified in the language domain also play a role in bootstrapping children's processing of intentional action.

Bootstrapping Accounts

If we take seriously that much about adult-level action processing is *acquired,* then we need an account of (a) how infants break into organized processing of the motion stream, and (b) the mechanisms that transform infants' early, more primitive forms of analysis into the conceptually sophisticated form that we carry out as adults. In the language domain, a variety of bootstrapping mechanisms have been documented as playing just this kind of role. And some of the specific bootstrapping mechanisms known to operate in language acquisition seem potentially relevant to helping infants to achieve organized and appropriate processing of the motion stream, as well. To clarify this more general point, I offer two extended examples, only one of which is backed up by evidence as yet.

Just one among the issues to be dealt with in considering the origins of action processing is answering the important question of how tiny infants make any kind of start at dividing up, or "segmenting," the action stream to yield relevant units. Not just any units will do. For example, infants would have little chance of making sense of someone else's drinking-related motions if they were inclined to perceive half a grasp plus a third of a lift as a meaningful unit of motion. Put another way, infants need to pick out units that are generalizable across different action sequences and that thus can assist in processing novel actions encountered in the future. And, if intentional understanding is to develop, the segments infants detect within the motion stream must be useful, ultimately, to drawing inferences about intentions.

Segmentation in Language Acquisition

Research in the language domain has grappled with an analogous question about the origins of segmentation of the speech stream. Evidence now exists for at least two kinds of bootstrapping mechanisms operating to assist infants in extracting appropriate segments (e.g., words or clauses) within the complex, relatively continuous auditory flow. In particular, infants are sensitive to both configural and statistical regularities that are informative about segment boundaries. Regarding configural information, prosodic contours overlaid on speech—especially infant-directed speech—are highly correlated with clausal segments (e.g., Wanner & Gleitman, 1982), and infants are sensitive to these prosodically-driven segments even when they do not understand anything about the content or grammar of the speech at issue (e.g., Hirsh-Pasek, Kemler Nelson, Jusczyk, Cassidy, Druss, & Kennedy, 1987). Thus the prosodic patterns give infants probabilistic access to relevant units—clauses— within the speech stream, thereby supporting further appropriate analysis of linguistically-relevant segments.

Regarding statistical information, elements within speech that fall within a linguistically-relevant segment—such as a word—have relatively high rates of cooccurrence, whereas elements that are adjacent, but fall on either side of a linguistically-relevant segment, show relatively low rates of co-occurrence (Harris, 1955; Hayes & Clark, 1970). It turns out that infants are sensitive to these statistical properties of the speech stream: they can capitalize on co-occurrence rates to bind frequently co-occurring elements into coherent segments, and to detect segment boundaries where co-occurrence rates are low (e.g., Aslin, Saffran, & Newport, 1999; Saffran, Aslin, & Newport, 1996). Other research documents that infants can track statistical regularities for segmentation purpose with non-linguistic stimuli, as well, such as sequences of non-linguistic tones (e.g., Saffran, Johnson, Aslin, & Newport, 1999). Adults also are sensitive to statistical clues to segmentation, and presumably make use of such information to assist in their everyday segmentation of the speech stream (e.g., Aslin, et al., 1999).

Segmentation in Early Action Processing

My colleagues and I wondered whether infants initially segment dynamic intentional action by means of these same structure-detection mechanisms. We are in the midst of a research program testing infants' sensitivity to both configural and statistical regularities within the motion stream. At this point we have documented *adults'* sensitivity to both these forms of structure, making it at least plausible that infants may likewise possess such sensitivity.

Recent research of our own indicates that adults as well as 10- to 11-month-old infants are sensitive to relevant segments within dynamic intentional action—segments that are bounded by goal completion (Baird, Baldwin, & Malle, under revision; Baldwin, Baird, Saylor, & Clark, 2001; Baldwin, Pederson, Craven, Andersson, & Bjork, in prep). In the Baldwin et al. (2001) study with infants, for example, infants repeatedly watched a video display of continuous intentional action involving a woman turning, noticing a towel on the floor, moving to grasp the towel, then crossing the room to place the towel on a towel rack. Then infants watched two test videos in which an artificial 1.5 second pause was introduced into the same motion display. In the completing test video, the pause highlighted an action boundary, occurring just as the woman completed her grasp of the towel, before she picked it up to place it on the towel rack. In the interrupting test video, the pause interrupted an action segment midstream; for example, the pause occurred either just as the woman was in the midst of reaching to grasp the towel, or just as the woman was in the midst of picking the towel up. Infants displayed considerable interest (as measured by their looking times) in the interrupting test videos, in which action segments were interrupted, relative to the completing test videos, presumably because the interrupting test videos violated the way they themselves had segmented the videos during their prior viewing.

Research that is underway targets the mechanisms that may be operating to enable infants and adults to locate action segments within dynamic and continuous intentional action. Again, we suspect that both adults and infants may detect segments, at least in part, via their sensitivity to *structural* regularities within the flow of motion. Structural regularities can come in a variety of forms, and both the two forms already noted for language segmentation—configural and statistical—seem potentially relevant in the context of intentional action as well. One way that infants might identify relevant motion segments (distinct acts) would be to detect predictable configurations (clusters or sequences of features) within the motion stream that also happen to coincide with the movements linking the actor's initiation and completion of goals. Just as vocal intonation lays a configural "envelope" over speech that nicely coincides with linguistic segments such as the clause, so, too, do the dynamic properties of human motion in space seem to produce a predictable physical/temporal envelope within action as we move from initiating to completing object-directed intentions. For example, as a rule, an actor's change in gaze direction precedes both subsequent direction of movement, and contact with a new object targeted by gaze. This sequence of motions is not only predictable in ordering, it also possesses a characteristic temporal structure. As gaze fixates, the body is launched rather ballistically in the direction of the fixated object, with motion displaying a predictable form of acceleration and then deceleration. In many cases, this swath of action—for example, from the point at which gaze direction changes to target a new object to the point at which contact with the targeted object is achieved—encompasses what adults would pick out as a distinct act within the motion stream. Infants might note the configural predictability here, and thus extract the appropriate units, although they may not yet be conceptualizing the specific intention at play.

One way to test this possibility is to present viewers with dynamic intentional action in a format that preserves just the configural information, such as a point-light display. If sensitivity to configural structure can facilitate segmentation, then segmentation of dynamic intentional action should be possible even when viewing point-light displays of such action, in which configural information alone is available. A recent study with adults confirms this prediction, at least for one particular level of segmentation—what we have called the "small action" level (Guha, Baldwin, & Craven, in prep). That is, adults viewing a point-light version of the same dynamic action displays used in prior action segmentation research (e.g., an actor turns, notices a towel on the floor, moves toward it, grasps it, and then crosses the room to hang it on a towel rack) recall the location of tones that coincide with action boundaries (e.g., the point at which the towel is grasped) with significantly greater accuracy than tones that occur in the midst of ongoing action segments (e.g., a point midstream in the motion to hang the towel). These findings indicate that adults can readily segment small actions such as grasping, placing, pulling, pushing, and the like within a continuous motion stream via configural structure alone.

Research that is underway examines whether infants, likewise, can exploit configural structure to assist in extracting distinct acts within the motion stream. An ability to do so would enable them to begin appropriate segmentation of dynamic intentional action prior to actually understanding anything about the content of the goals and intentions motivating such action. These findings would thus help to explain how infants might get started at organized and appropriate processing of the dynamic action stream. Put another way, pattern recognition skills that enable infants to extract predictable configurations within the motion stream may bootstrap their ability to begin segmenting dynamic intentional action appropriately. Armed with the appropriate segments infants can go on to engage in further processing of these segments (e.g., discrimination, categorization, inferences about deeper commonalities—such as shared goals/intentions among actions of a given type, registration of relations to other actions) that will yield richer, more conceptual-level understanding about the actions that people undertake.

A second form of structural information that both adults and infants might utilize to assist in segmenting intentional action I call statistical, because it mirrors the statistical information shown to be exploited by both infants and adults for segmenting language. Of course the configural structure just described is also a form of statistical information (in that it represents recurring physical/temporal patterns within the motion stream). The configural patterns at issue there occur again and again across an enormous diversity of contexts—they are highly general indices of action segments. In contrast, what I am calling statistical structure concerns patterns of recurrence among highly specific motion elements. That is, certain motions within the stream of behavior co-occur more frequently than others, often because they are causally linked in achieving a goal (e.g., in preparing food for cooking, the motion of slicing a vegetable is frequently preceded by the motion of grasping a knife, whereas slicing a vegetable is only infrequently preceded by grasping a towel). From the observer's point of view, then, a history of low rates of co-occurrence for two particular adjacent motions is a potential clue to segmentation. In other words, low transitional probabilities among motion elements predict boundaries between intentional acts.

Research that my colleagues and I have just completed confirms that adults are able to utilize statistical regularities of this kind to discover segments within a novel and continuous sequence of intentional action (Baldwin, Andersson, & Saffran, in prep). We showed adults a 20-minute corpus of continuous motion consisting of twelve motion elements that displayed patterns of co-occurrence like those just described. Four three-motion combinations ("actions") recurred within the motion stream, and were randomly intermixed. Thus co-occurrence rates for motion elements within an "action" were 1.0, whereas co-occurrence rates for motion elements in differing "actions" were, on average, 0.33. To convey a sense of the stimuli we used, Figure 5.1 displays still images taken from the motion elements of two of the "actions" in the exposure corpus. If adults are sensitive to such statistical structure as a source of information for segmentation, they should come to recognize low co-occurrence rates as clues to segment boundaries over the course of observing the 20-minute exposure corpus.

A subsequent recognition test probed this possibility: Adults were shown pairs of video clips containing either (a) "actions" (combinations of motion elements with high co-occurrence rates) versus "non-actions" (new combinations of the same motion elements seen in the exposure corpus), or (b) "actions" versus "part-actions" (combinations of motion elements that linked the final element from one "action" with the first two elements of another "action," hence crossing a segment boundary). On seeing the pairs of video clips, adults were asked to indicate which in the pair seemed most familiar. They selected "actions" at significantly higher rates than chance would predict, regardless of whether the foils were "non-actions" (82%, $p < .0001$) or "part-actions" (73%, $p < .001$). These findings provide the first information to date that adults readily exploit statistical structure as a clue to segmenting continuous, intentional action.

A study that is currently underway investigates whether infants are also capable of capitalizing on statistical structure for segmentation purpose. If so, such findings will clarify that sensitivity to statistical structure facilitates segmentation of intentional action even in early childhood. This in turn will help to explain developments in skill at processing dynamic intentional action as children gain experience with the statistical structure inherent in the actions they witness over time. Again, then, sensitivity to structure—in this case statistical structure— may bootstrap initial segmentation of continuous motion into distinct acts, enabling infants to make a start at appropriate action processing even when they have little conceptual understanding of the actions they witness.

It is evident from the research we've described that dynamic intentional action contains at least some structural regularities, and that adults, at least, are sensitive to such structure, yet virtually nothing is known about details of the actual regularities to be found within everyday intentional action. There is pressing need for more information about the structural properties of dynamic action, and further investigation of which aspects of such structure observers are sensitive to, and to what purpose. Along these lines, it seems likely that different kinds of motion—for example, animate versus inanimate motion, and intentional versus unintentional action—display distinct patterns of structural regularity (e.g., Mandler, 1992; Premack & Premack, 1995). Observers' sensitivity to such structural differences could assist them in discriminating these contrasting motion categories, which would be of great significance in aiding rapid, automatic recognition of certain highly-relevant event distinctions.

Possible Assistance From Motionese

Within the category of dynamic intentional action, it seems possible that some intentional actions are more readily analyzable or "segmentable" for infants than others. In this respect, we all tend to interact rather differently with infants than with older children and adults. For example, we typically slow our motion, punctuate our movements, and exaggerate our facial displays of affect and line-of-regard. Perhaps our infant-directed motions maximize action segmentability for infants. Unconsciously, we may supply infants with simplified and highly recognizable action components. In effect, we may offer infants a form of action that is to the development of intentional understanding as "motherese" (child-directed speech) is to the development of language. The melodic intonational contours of child-directed speech appear to highlight certain aspects of the componential structure of language (e.g., Jusczyk, 1997; Wanner & Gleitman, 1982); likewise, infant-directed motion (we have coined the term *motionese*) may highlight the componential structure —the units of analysis—of intentional action. One of our recent studies confirms the basic phenomenon of motionese (Brand, Baldwin, & Ashburn, 2002), documenting that mothers indeed modify their infant-directed actions in ways that highlight the internal structure of the motion stream. In this study we asked mothers to demonstrate actions on novel toys either to their infant or to a highly familiar adult (spouse, close friend, or parent). With infant partners, mothers held objects close to the partner, and produced motion streams that were highly repetitive yet enthusiastic, simplified, broad in range (e.g., involving motion at the elbow and shoulders as well as wrist and fingers) and frequently punctuated by interactive exchanges with the partner. All of these modifications could assist infants in achieving an appropriate segmentation and intentional analysis of the motion stream. A study currently underway (Myhr, Baldwin, & Brand, in progress) examines whether infants who view novel intentional action sequences indeed benefit from motionese input. If so, infants who watch a motionese version of the novel sequence ought to be more successful at subsequently replicating that sequence themselves than infants who witnessed an unmodified, adult-directed version of the self-same novel sequence.

Back to Bootstrapping

The case of action segmentation helps to make clear, I hope, the value of importing the general idea of bootstrapping mechanisms to help account for the acquisition of action-processing skills. As well, our recent findings suggest that some of the specific bootstrapping mechanisms that have been shown to support language acquisition—sensitivity to configural and statistical structure—may likewise support acquisition in the domain of intentional action. These are important developments, but at the same time this bootstrapping account does not seem to speak directly to children's (or adults') ability to discern others' goals and intentions on witnessing their actions in the world. In other words, skill at picking out distinct acts from a motion stream seems an essential aspect of processing others' intentional actions, but appropriate segmentation does not translate inevitably into an understanding of the motivations and goals underlying such acts. Understanding the goals and intentions requires appreciating the *meaning* of the act, not just recognizing the act as a structural entity. This point may be easier to grasp through analogy to language. Segmenting a stream of speech into distinct words (e.g., "tupiro," "golabu" to borrow examples from the Saffran, et al. 1996 research) is a leg up toward making sense of that speech stream, but segmentation alone does not provide any information about what those words *mean*. Other inferential skills that promote acquisition of word meaning must be recruited to account for this discovery process. A substantial body of work now documents the role such inferential processes play in children's acquisition of word meaning (e.g., see volumes by Bloom, 2000; Golinkoff, et al., 2000; Hall & Waxman, in press; Markman, 1989; Tomasello, 1999).

Inferential Abilities Derive the Meaning of Action

Returning to the action domain, the question as I now frame it is how children move from working with a purely structural analysis of distinct acts and classes of acts to inferring the meaning of those acts—the goals and intentions that give rise to them. Baird and I have argued that accounting for inferences about goals and intentions requires granting children and adults inferential skills that operate in the action domain over and above structure-processing skills (Baird & Baldwin, 2001; Baldwin & Baird, 1999, 2001). In a related account, Povinelli and colleagues (e.g., Povinelli, 2001; Povinelli Bering, & Giambrone, 2000) likewise posit that humans read meaning—inferences about goals and intentions—into others' behavior, which requires going beyond a purely structural analysis of behavior. They argue that many, if not all, other species—even our closest phylogenetic relatives, the great apes—may lack the inferential skills that promote discernment of goals and intentions, and may thus be limited to a purely structural analysis of others' behavior (see Hare, Brown, Williamson, & Tomasello, 2002 for evidence that domesticated dogs may present an exception to this limitation). What Baird and I envision is that even infants possess inferential skills (such skills are also often termed "theory construction" abilities) that enable them to construct over time abstract notions about goals and intentions as hidden, non-obvious causes for action. Children's initial intuitions about goals and intentions may be fairly global—that is, they may not understand much about the diverse kinds of goals and intentions underlying different kinds of actions—but become increasingly refined and nuanced as they gain knowledge over time about objects, people, and how people relate to objects across differing contexts. Put another way, infants' theory-construction mechanism operates on segments and categories of action that initially may be largely structurally derived—via sensitivity to configural and statistical structure, for example. It takes these initially structural elements and generates explanations about the hidden, underlying causes of individual acts and of distinct classes of actions. Our assumption is that right from the start of infants' development, this inferential mechanism is working to "make sense" of the structural entities that arise from infants' processing of the complex, dynamic motion stream. That is, we suspect there is no point at which infants' action processing should be described as *solely* structural in kind, because as soon as structural regularities are registered by infants, their theory construction system will attempt to interpret those structural regularities in deeper, causal terms. At the same time, on this account early sensitivity to structural regularities is essential because it is what gives the theory construction mechanism useful data to "mine" for hypotheses about underlying causal factors such as ideas about intentions and goals.

This account is highly speculative, but clearly plausible. As described earlier, ongoing research provides dawning reason for believing that infants possess the structure detection abilities that would jump start appropriate perceptual-level processing of action segments. And recent research also provides at least starting support for the proposal that young children and even infants possess inferential skills that enable them to infer hidden, non-obvious causes, which is the basic skill that would be necessary to construct hypotheses about hidden causes such as intentions and goals. For example, Gopnik and colleagues (e.g., Gopnik, Sobel, Schulz, & Glymour, 2001), expanding on a substantial body of previous work on children's early causal understanding (e.g., Klahr, 2000; Kuhn & Pearsall, 2000) recently documented that 3-year-olds readily infer new, non-obvious causes based on a variety of systematic sources of evidence. Regarding the infancy period, my colleagues and I (Baldwin, Markman, & Melartin, 1993) found that infants as young as 9 months can draw inferences about hidden, non-obvious properties of objects. In that research, infants had 30 seconds of experience with a novel object that exhibited an unexpected novel property, such as a little can that "moo-ed" like a cow when turned over. On subsequently being given a similar, but non-identical can, infants across the 9–16 month age range immediately turned it over, and persisted in turning it over despite the can's failure to moo (the second can had been disabled to undercut its mooing capabilities, but this was not evident on the surface). Clearly, even 9-month-olds, and quite possibly younger infants, rapidly construct expectations about hidden, non-obvious properties based on relatively little, but telling, evidence. Two different research teams (Desjardins & Baldwin, 1992; Graham, Kilbreath, & Welder, 2002) modified the Baldwin et al. paradigm to examine whether providing a common label for objects that appear, on the surface, to be only moderately similar facilitates infants' inferences about hidden, non-obvious commonalities. They found that even infants at the earliest phases of language development—12-month-olds in the Graham et al. research and 16-month-olds in the Desjardins and Baldwin research—capitalized on language to guide inferences about deeper commonalities in just this way. Powerful inductive skills seem to be operative already in human infancy, lending plausibility to our speculation that such inferential abilities enable infants to construct ideas about intentions and goals as hidden, non-obvious causes for the regularities they detect in others' behavior.

Relations Between Producing and Comprehending Action

Any time inferential abilities are invoked, a thorny issue raises its head: the issue of under-determination. In the case of intentional action, the under-determination issue involves the question of how one resolves on a specific intention as the hidden, motivating force behind a particular motion stream, given that, in principle, an infinite number of possible intentions is actually consistent with that motion stream. To illustrate, consider Searle's (1984) amusing example: someone takes a walk through Hyde Park. Searle points out that this motion stream could arise from the actor's intention to walk through Hyde Park, or the intention to wear out the soles of his shoes, or the intention to walk in the general direction of Patagonia, or the intention to move a few air molecules, and on and on.

Each and every time infants (and adults, for that matter) are faced with a motion stream and activate inferential processes in an attempt to understand hidden motivations for that motion, they are faced with this potentially intractable inferential problem. How do they constrain their hypothesis space in drawing inferences about intentions? Self-produced action, coupled with (a) a general assumption that "others are like me" (Meltzoff & Brooks, 2001), and (b) some ability to map self action and other action (Barresi & Moore, 1996; Meltzoff & Brooks, 2001) might go a long way toward constraining inferences about the intentions underlying others' behavior streams. That is, in everyday action we typically know what it is that we intend to accomplish. For example, I might intend to grasp this glass, bring it to my lips, drink some water, and so on. When I observe others engage in motions involving glasses, water, hands, and lips, my knowledge of actions I have executed with these objects to obtain my own intentions could powerfully constrain the inferences I generate regarding others' actions involving these objects. Strikingly elegant studies by Woodward & Sommerville (2000) are consistent with this idea that self-produced intentional action may facilitate infants' understanding of others' intentional actions. These researchers developed a methodology that makes it possible to detect whether infants are construing a particular motion stream—I will concentrate on a "grasping" scenario, though they have studied several others—as "goal-directed." That is, infants will display a unique pattern of looking across several events if they are construing a grasping motion as directed toward contacting a specific object (see Woodward, 1998 for a detailed explanation of the methodology). With respect to grasping actions, they noted that infants typically first display a "goal-oriented" construal at roughly 5 months of age, which happens also to be the age at which infants themselves typically begin displaying success at voluntary grasping of objects. In subsequent research, Woodward and colleagues found a significant correlation between infants' own ability to achieve voluntary grasping of objects, and their tendency to construe another's grasping action as goal-oriented (Woodward, Sommerville, & Guajardo, 2001). However, such correlational findings don't support inferences about causation, so they also undertook an intervention study. They turned to investigating these abilities in 3-month-olds, none of whom were initially construing grasping actions of others as goal-oriented. Using a modification of Needham and colleague's methodology (e.g., Needham, Barrett, & Peterman, 2002), they supplied these 3-month-olds with "sticky mittens" (mittens coated with Velcro) and a set of objects coated with the complementary part of Velcro. The Velcro mittens enabled the otherwise inept graspers to successfully grasp, for the first time. Astonishingly, just five minutes' opportunity to play with Velcro mittens altered these 3-month-olds' processing of others' grasping actions. They now appreciated that another's grasping actions were specifically directed toward making contact with the object toward which the grasp was directed. These findings provide clear evidence that infants' own actions—and their success in executing these actions—influences their processing of others' actions. Clearly, self-produced action plays an important role—perhaps a key constraining role—in facilitating infants' understanding of action more generally.

Wrapping Up Regarding Epigenesis

In summary, although little is yet known about the mechanisms underlying children's acquisition of the cognitive system supporting analysis of intentions and goals, progress along these lines is underway. Bootstrapping mechanisms may operate to assist infants in detecting relevant structure within the motion stream, enabling them to get started on appropriate segmentation and categorization of distinct acts within the complex flow of dynamic motion. Inferential skills may enable infants to construct ideas about hidden causes—intentions and goals—for classes of actions that their structure detection skills pick out. Infants' own actions in the world may sharpen their attention to dimensions in others' motions that are relevant for interpreting goals and intentions, and/or help to constrain their inferences about the intentions and goals underlying specific acts others produce.

It is worth noting that the discussion thus far concerning the developmental emergence of intentional understanding rests on a hidden assumption: the assumption that a considerable degree of cross-cultural universality is to be expected in the arena of intentional understanding. Universally shared structure-detection skills would presumably give rise to similar perceptual analysis of the motion flow regardless of infants' culture, giving infants around the world similar segments and categories of action to draw intentional inferences over. In the next section, I consider directly the extent to which we should expect cross-cultural universality versus diversity in the arena of action processing and intentional understanding.

CROSS-CULTURAL UNIVERSALITY AND DIVERSITY?

The most basic skills for interpreting others' intentions are likely to be a universal aspect of human development, for all the reasons I have outlined. In brief, these skills are needed if infants and young children are to capitalize for learning purpose on the richness of information in their social milieu. Intentional understanding enables children to identify relevant relations amidst the richness and complexity of everyday language and action. And capitalize they do: rapid expansion of knowledge—about people, objects, and language—seems to be characteristic of infants across the world's cultures.

What is universal, I am suggesting, is a foundational cognitive system that makes possible the processing of others' actions in terms of underlying intentions. At its core, this system seems to support the development of at least two particular abilities: the ability to distinguish intentional from unintentional action, and the ability to derive basic inferences about the content of others' intentions based on their actions (e.g., inferences such as *she intends to talk about that object* versus *her talk is not about that object*). Western infants of 12–18 months have demonstrated both these abilities in existing research (e.g., Baldwin, Markman, Bill, Desjardins, Irwin, & Tidball, 1996), and it seems likely that infants of other cultural backgrounds would do so as well.

However, investigating this hypothesis of universality is fraught with some interesting complexities, for the very reason that cultural diversity is likewise present. Across cultures, one and the same action can carry very different value; for example, an utterance that counts as an entirely acceptable form of teasing in one culture may stand out as blatantly offensive in another. Clearly, our cultural context influences the way we interpret others' intentions and the value we assign to their actions. Recently, researchers have suggested that cultures may even differ in the extent to which individuals concern themselves with others' intentions at all (e.g., Lillard, 1997). In some cultures, for instance, focus seems to be centered primarily on the facts of action itself and there is little talk about the intentions motivating others' actions. As well, the action clues utilized in interpreting others' intentions differ to some degree cross-culturally. For example, gestures are more frequent and prominent in some cultures than others. We should therefore expect cross-cultural variability in how heavily children emphasize gestural cues to drive inferences about intentions. Just as a sighted child born to a blind parent in this culture needs to disregard gaze direction, which otherwise is a powerful clue to intentions, so children in different cultures need to become attuned to the particular clues that tend to provide good information about intentions within their culture.

Perhaps, then, we each possess a "native intentional system" (on analogy to a native language) that we have acquired by virtue of a range of culturally-driven experiences that helped to shape the way we interpret others' intentions. Core aspects of this native intentional system are likely shared across cultures—just as languages around the world share a variety of central, universal properties. For example, in any culture you can name, line-of-regard strongly supports inferences about the target of others' attention and intentions. At the same time, culturally specific principles for interpreting intentions would also operate for each of us, influencing the subtleties of intentional inference. Perhaps, as with language (e.g., Newport, 1990), early exposure to the relevant input for promoting acquisition of such skill enables greater fluency to be achieved. That is, those who belatedly enter a given cultural milieu may fail to achieve the native levels of fluency in intentional inference of those who have been immersed in that culture from an early age. To illustrate, detecting a liar in action is known to be a challenging inferential task under the best of circumstances (e.g., Malone & DePaulo, 2001), yet it may be considerably more difficult in a culture one entered first as an adult.

CONCLUSION

Intentions are the warp and weft of the fabric that is social functioning: They provide the basic structure for interpreting action. Complex cognitive abilities enable our recovery of the intentions motivating and binding others' actions, and such intentional understanding in return yields enormous cognitive benefits. Insight into intentions provides a framework for detecting relevant relations in others' language and action, fueling a uniquely human capacity for knowledge acquisition.

Much remains to be learned about intentional understanding and how it develops. I have outlined a number of pressing questions for investigation. Likely much new information soon will emerge on these fronts. I believe that this general research enterprise bids fair to illuminate the fundamentals of human sociocultural functioning. I hope too, that such knowledge will ultimately enable us to support enhanced social functioning for all, even those who face processing deficits that otherwise might limit opportunities for fully benefiting from their social and cultural milieu.

REFERENCES

Akhtar, N., & Tomasello, M. (1998). Intersubjectivity in early language learning and use. In S. Braten (Ed.), *Intersubjective communication and emotion in early ontogeny: Studies in emotion and social interaction* (2nd series, pp. xvi, 316–335, 454).

Ashcroft, M. H. (1994). *Human memory and cognition* (2nd ed.). New York: HarperCollins.

Aslin, R. N., Saffran, J. R., & Newport, E. L. (1999). Statistical learning in linguistic and nonlinguistic domains. In B. MacWhinney (Ed.), *The emergence of language* (pp. 359–380). Mahwah, NJ: Lawrence Erlbaum Associates.

Baird, J. A., Baldwin, D. A., & Malle, B. F. (under revision). Parsing the behavior stream: Evidence for the psychological primacy of intention boundaries.

Baird, J. A., & Baldwin, D. A. (2001). Making sense of human behavior: Action parsing and intentional inference. In B. F. Malle, L. J. Moses, & D. A. Baldwin. (Eds.), *Intentions and intentionality: Foundations of social cognition* (pp. 193–206). Cambridge, MA: MIT Press.

Baldwin, D. A. (1991). Infants' contribution to the achievement of joint reference. *Child Development, 62*(5), 875–890.

Baldwin, D. A. (2000). Interpersonal understanding fuels knowledge acquisition. *Current Directions in Psychological Science, 9*(2), 40–45.

Baldwin, D., Andersson, A., & Saffran, J. (in prep). *Adults extract statistics to segment dynamic human action.*

Baldwin, D. A., & Baird, J. A. (1999). Action analysis: A gateway to intentional inference. In P. Rochat (Ed.), *Early social cognition* (pp. 215–240). Hillsdale, NJ: Lawrence Erlbaum Associates.

Baldwin, D. A., & Baird, J. A. (2001). Discerning intentions in dynamic human action. *Trends in Cognitive Sciences, 5,* 171–178.

Baldwin, D. A., Baird, J. A., Saylor, M., & Clark, M. A. (2001). Infants parse dynamic human action. *Child Development, 72,* 708–717.

Baldwin, D. A., Markman, E. M., & Melartin, R. L. (1993). Infants' ability to draw inferences about nonobvious object properties: Evidence from exploratory play. *Child Development, 64,* 711–728.

Baldwin, D. A., Markman, E. M., Bill, B., Desjardins, R. N., Irwin, J., & Tidball, G. (1996). Infants' reliance on a social criterion for establishing word-object relations. *Child Development, 67,* 3135–3153.

Baldwin, D. A., & Moses, L. J. (1994). Early understanding of referential intent and attentional focus: Evidence from language and emotion. In C. Lewis & P. Mitchell (Eds.), *Children's early understanding of mind: Origins and development* (pp. xvi, 133–156, 493).

Baldwin, D. A., & Moses, L. J. (2001). Links between early social understanding and word learning: Challenges to current accounts. In A. Imbens-Bailey (Ed.), *Social Development, 10,* 309–329.

Baldwin, D., Pederson, E., Craven, A., Andersson, A., & Bjork, H. (in prep). *Change detection speeds up at intention boundaries.* Eugene: University of Oregon.

Barresi, J. Moore, C. (1996). Intentional relations and social understanding. *Behavioral & Brain Sciences, 19,* 107–154.

Bloom, P. (2000). *How children learn the meanings of words.* Cambridge, MA: MIT Press.

Blythe, P. W., Todd, P. M., & Miller, G. F. (1999). How motion reveals intention: Categorizing social interactions. In G. Gigerenzer & P. M. Todd (Eds.), *Simple heuristics that make us smart. Evolution and cognition* (pp. 257–285). Oxford, UK: Oxford University Press.

Brand, R., Baldwin, D. A., & Ashburn, L. (2002). Evidence for 'motionese': Modifications in mothers' infant-directed action. *Developmental Science, 5,* 72–83.

Bransford, J. D., & Franks, J. J. (1971). The abstraction of linguistic ideas. *Cognitive Psychology, 2*(4), 331–350.

Bruner, J. (1977). Early social interaction and language acquisition. In H. R. Schaffer (Ed.), *Studies in mother-infant interaction* (pp. 271–289). London: Academic Press.

Bruner, J. (1983). *Child's talk.* New York: Norton.

Butcher, K. R., & Kintsch, W. (2003). Text comprehension and discourse processing. In A. F. Healy & R. W. Proctor (Eds.), *Handbook of psychology: Experimental psychology, Vol. 4* (pp. 575–595). New York: John Wiley & Sons.

Chomsky, N. (1990). On the nature, use, and acquisition of language. In W. G. Lycan (Ed.), *Mind and cognition: A reader* (pp. 627–646). Cambridge, MA: Basil Blackwell.

Crain, S., & Pietroski, P. (2001). Nature, nurture and Universal Grammar. *Linguistics and philosophy, 24,* 139–185.

Dennett, D. C. (1987). *The intentional stance.* Cambridge, MA: MIT Press.

Desjardins, R., & Baldwin, D. A. (1992). *Infants' use of language to guide reasoning about the object world.* Paper presented at the biennial meeting Society for Infant Studies, Miami, Florida.

Golinkoff, R. M., Hirsh-Pasek, K., Bloom, L., Smith, L. B., Woodward, A. L., Akhtar, N., Tomasello, M., & Hollich, G. (2000). *Becoming a word learner: A debate on lexical acquisition.* New York: Oxford University Press.

Gopnik, A., Sobel, D. M., Schulz, L. E., & Glymour, C. (2001). Causal learning mechanisms in very young children: Two-, three-, and four-year-olds infer causal relations from patterns of variation and covariation. *Developmental Psychology, 37,* 620–629.

Graham, S. A., Kilbreath, C. S., & Welder, A. N. (2002). *The importance of being a FLUM: 12-month-olds rely on shared labels and shape similarity for inductive inferences.* Paper presented at the thirteenth Biennial International Conference on Infant Studies, Toronto, Canada.

Guha, G., Baldwin, D., & Craven, A. (in prep). *Finding structure in action.* University of Oregon.

Hall, G., & Waxman, S. (in press). *Weaving a lexicon.* Mahwah, NJ: Lawrence Erlbaum Associates.

Hare, B., Brown, M., Williamson, C., & Tomasello, M. (2002). The domestication of social cognition in dogs. *Science, 298,* 1634–1636.

Harris, Z. S. (1955). From phone to morpheme. *Language, 31,* 190–222.

Hayes, J. R., & Clark, H. H. (1970). Experiments in the segmentation of an artificial speech analog. In J. R. Hayes (Ed.), cognition and the development of language (pp. 221–234). New York: John Wiley & Sons.

Hirsh-Pasek, K., Kemler Nelson, D. G., Jusczyk, P. W., Cassidy, K. W., Druss, B., & Kennedy, L. (1987). Clauses are perceptual units for young infants. *Cognition. 26,* 269–286.

Johnson, M. K., Bransford, J. D., & Solomon, S. K. (1973). Memory for tacit implications of sentences. *Journal of Experimental Psychology, 98*(1), 203–205.

Jusczyk, P. W. (1997). *The discovery of spoken language.* Cambridge, MA: MIT Press.

Just, M. A., & Carpenter, P. A. (1987). *The psychology of reading and language comprehension.*

Kintsch, W. (1998). *Comprehension: A paradigm for cognition.*

Klahr, D. (2000). *Exploring science: The cognition and development of discovery processes.*

Kuhn, D., & Pearsall, S. (2000) Developmental origins of scientific thinking. *Journal of Cognition & Development. 1,* 113–129.

Lillard, A. S. (1997). Other folks' theories of mind and behavior. *Psychological Science. 8,* 268–274.

Malone, B. E., & DePaulo, B. M. (2001). Measuring sensitivity to deception. In J. A. Hall & F. J. Bernieri (Eds.), *Interpersonal sensitivity theory and measurement*. Mahwah, NJ: Lawrence Erlbaum Associates.

Mandler, J. M. (1992). How to build a baby: II. Conceptual primitives. *Psychological Review, 99*, 587–604.

Markman, E. M. (1989). *Categorization and naming in children*. Cambridge, MA: MIT Press.

Martin, B. A., & Tversky, B. T. (2003). *Segmenting ambiguous events*. Talk presented at the annual meeting of the Cognitive Science Society.

Meltzoff, A. N., & Brooks, R. (2001). "Like me" as a building block for understanding other minds: Bodily acts, attention, and intention. In B. F. Malle, L. J. Moses, & D. A. Baldwin (Eds.), *Intentions and intentionality: Foundations of social cognition* (pp. 171–191). Cambridge, MA: MIT Press.

Moses, L. J. (2001). Some thoughts on ascribing complex intentional concepts to young children. B. F. Malle, L. J. Moses, & D. A. Baldwin (Eds.), *Intentions and intentionality: Foundations of social cognition* (pp. 69–83). Cambridge, MA: MIT Press.

Myhr, K., Baldwin, D. A., & Brand, R. (in progress). *Infants benefit from motionese*. University of Oregon, Eugene, OR.

Needham, A., Barrett, R., & Peterman, K. (2002). A pick me up for infants' exploratory skills: Early simulated experiences reaching for objects using 'sticky' mittens enhances young infants' object exploration skills. *Infant Behavior & Development, 25*, 279–295.

Newport, E. L. (1990). Maturational constraints on language learning. *Cognitive Science, 14*, 11–28.

Newtson, D. (1973). Attribution and the unit of perception of ongoing behavior. *Journal of Personality & Social Psychology, 28*(1), 28–38.

Newtson, D., & Engquist, G. (1976). The perceptual organization of ongoing behavior. *Journal of Experimental Social Psychology, 12*(5), 436–450.

Perner, J. (1991). *Understanding the representational mind*. Cambridge, MA: Bradford Books/MIT Press.

Piaget, J. (1932). *The moral judgment of the child*. Kegan Paul.

Pinker, S. (1994). *The language instinct: How the mind creates language*. New York: William Morrow & Company.

Povinelli, D. J. (2001). On the possibilities of detecting intentions prior to understanding them. In B. F. Malle, L. J. Moses, & D. A. Baldwin (Eds.). *Intentions and intentionality: Foundations of social cognition* (pp. 225–248). Cambridge, MA: MIT Press.

Povinelli, D. J., Bering, J. M., & Giambrone, S. (2000). Toward a science of other minds: Escaping the argument by analogy. *Cognitive Science, 24*, 509–541.

Premack, D., & Premack, A. J. (1995). Intention as psychological cause. In D. Sperber & D. Premack (Eds), *Causal cognition: A multidisciplinary debate. Symposia of the Fyssen Foundation* (pp. 185–199). Clarendon Press.

Saffran, J. R., Aslin, R. N., & Newport, E. L. (1996). Statistical learning by 8-month-old infants, *Science, 274*, 1926–1928.

Saffran, J. R., Johnson, E. K., Aslin, R. N., & Newport, E. L. (1999). Statistical learning of tone sequences by human infants and adults. *Cognition, 70*, 27–52.

Searle, J. (1984). *Minds, brains, and science*. Cambridge, MA: Harvard University Press.

Snow, C. (1999). Social perspectives on the emergence of language. In B. MacWhinney (Ed.), *The emergence of language* (pp. 257–276). Mahwah, NJ: Lawrence Erlbaum Associates.

Tartter, V. (1986). *Language processes*. New York: Holt, Rinehart and Winston.

Tomasello, M. (1999). *The cultural origins of human cognition*. Cambridge, MA: Harvard University Press.

Tomasello, M. (2003). *Constructing a language: A usage-based theory of language acquisition*. Cambridge, MA: Harvard University Press.

Tomasello, M., Kruger, A. C., & Ratner, H. H. (1993). Cultural learning. *Behavioral & Brain Sciences, 16*(3), 495–552.

Wanner, E., & Gleitman, L. R. (1982). *Language acquisition: The state of the art*. Cambridge, MA: Cambridge University Press.

Wellman, H. M. (1990). *Children's theories of mind*. Cambridge, MA: MIT Press.

Wellman, H. M., & Phillips, A. T. (2001). Developing intentional understandings. In B. Malle, L. Moses, & D. Baldwin (Eds.), *Intentions and intentionality: Foundations of social cognition* (pp. 125–148). Cambridge, MA: MIT Press.

Wexler, K., & Culicover, P. (1980). *Formal principles of language acquisition*. Cambridge, MA: MIT Press.

Woodward, A. L. (1998). Infants selectively encode the goal object of an actor's reach. *Cognition, 69*, 1–34.

Woodward, A. L., & Sommerville, J. A. (2000). Twelve-month-olds interpret action in context. *Psychological Science, 11*, 73–77.

Woodward, A. L., Sommerville, J. A., & Guajardo, J. J. (2001). How infants make sense of intentional action. In B. Malle, L. Moses, & D. Baldwin (Eds.), *Intentions and intentionality: Foundations of social cognition* (pp. 149–169). Cambridge, MA: MIT Press.

Zacks, J. (2004). Using movement and intentions to understand simple events. *Cognitive Science, 28*, 979–1008.

Zadny, J., & Gerard, H. B. (1974). Attributed intentions and informational selectivity. *Journal of Experimental Social Psychology, 1*, 34–52.

Chapter 6

Social Referencing in Infant Motor Action

Catherine S. Tamis-LeMonda
Karen E. Adolph
New York University

INTRODUCTION

In this chapter, we adopt a novel approach to understanding the origins of social cognition. In contrast to typical studies that examine the development of social cognition and communication in the context of language and play, we examine how infants come to seek and use social information from their caregivers in the context of making decisions about challenging motor actions. Potentially risky motor situations heighten the relevance of caregivers' social information because infants' motor decisions have practical consequences for their safety. Moreover, the threat of physical harm provides a unique opportunity for investigating central issues in the literature on social referencing. In particular, how and when infants reference their caregivers as they plan a course of motor action has the potential to reveal new insights about babies' knowledge of self and others.

Our interest in the intersection of developmental changes in social cognition and motor action is dually motivated. First, on a developmental time scale, important strides in social cognition and motor abilities emerge in tandem (Campos et al., 2000). Most notably, between the ages of 8 and18 months, infants become independently mobile. Infants who could formerly interact with the world from a fixed position become mischievous crawlers, wobbly toddlers, and confident walkers over a relatively short time span. During this same developmental period, infants are increasingly able to capitalize on adults' knowledge. They follow adults' gaze, imitate adults' actions with novel objects, look toward adults in ambiguous circumstances, and vocalize and gesture to share experiences. These behaviors mark the start of a socio-cognitive revolution (Tomasello, Kruger, & Ratner, 1993).

A second motivation for studying social cognition in the context of motor action is that infants typically acquire new motor skills in a social context, supported by the encouragement and helping hands of their caregivers. Babies' first attempts to reach are likely toward a toy offered by a caregiver, their first experience standing is bouncing up and down on a caregiver's lap, their first crawling forays occur under their parents' watchful eyes, and their first walking steps are into a proud parent's open arms. Each motor action produces a rich, dynamic flow of perceptual and social information. The movements involved in reaching, sitting, bouncing, crawling, and walking generate visual, proprioceptive, vestibular, and auditory feedback about the position of the body relative to objects in the environment. At the same time, babies' movements are accompanied by the sights and sounds of caregivers' outstretched arms, smiling faces, and undulating voices expressing words of encouragement or warning.

In situations of potential motor risk, infants can gauge possibilities for action by looking at the obstacle, making physical contact through touching, testing the limits of their powers of strength and balance via swaying and rocking movements, and so on. Infants can also take an active role in ensuring their own safety by signaling their caregivers for information or help via puzzled or imploring looks, vocalizations, and gestures. Thus, infants' decisions about everyday motor challenges involve weighing and integrating perceptual information generated by their own exploratory movements with social information offered by their caregivers.

The transition from relying primarily on self-generated knowledge to becoming a savvy seeker and consumer of social information signals infants' entry into a world of social intentions (Baldwin, in this volume). Infants come to appreciate their caregivers as potential reservoirs of social information. Eventually, babies understand that people—themselves and others—can adopt varying psychological orientations toward objects and events (Moore & Corkum, 1994). This realization enormously expands infants' opportunities for learning. By capitalizing on the social information afforded by more expert caregivers, infants can acquire knowledge at a rate that was previously unfeasible (Baldwin et al., 1996; Tomasello et al., 1993).

Infants' social and motor achievements are not merely coincident in time; they are synergistic. Increasing postural control and the transition to mobility invite a new world of opportunities for learning and motivate fundamental changes in infants' interactions with caregivers (Campos et al., 2000). The ability to sit up and free the hands from supporting functions provides babies with enhanced opportunities to explore object properties and to engage in object-related social interactions. Independent locomotion summons new ways of communicating and sharing intentions from increasingly greater distances. The newfound independence and autonomy that accompany mobility instigate a venturous "love affair with the world" (Mahler, Pine, & Bergman, 1975). Crawling infants can initiate exploration away from their caregivers and begin to set new goals and directions of their own (Gustafson, 1984). Walking infants have a new perceptual and social vantage point on the world (Gibson, 1988). To parents' consternation, with the advent of upright locomotion and increased autonomy, infants are more likely to say "no" (Biringen, Emde, Campos, & Applebaum, 1995).

Independent mobility brings countless challenges waiting to be mastered and countless mishaps waiting to happen. Infants must figure out which actions are safe and which surfaces are risky. Parents must vigilantly encourage safe endeavors but discourage risky ones. The potential dangers inherent in locomotion mean that errors on either infants' or parents' part can be costly and potentially fatal (Rodriguez, 1990). Parents may inadvertently fail to take necessary precautions, remove children from hazards, provide the necessary hands-on support, or use effective social cues to ensure their infants' safety. Despite parents' use of barriers to safeguard their homes, their anticipation of falling accidents as they chase after their infants (Garling & Garling, 1995), and their perception that hands-on supervision decreases risk of injury (Garling & Garling, 1993) falling (along with burning, and poisoning) remains a primary household hazard for infants (Baker, O'Neill, & Ginsberg, 1992; Glik, Greaves, Kronenfeld, & Jackson, 1993). Although monitoring infants' whereabouts is a cornerstone of parents' interactions (Peterson & Stern, 1997), injuries to infants typically occur at home under parents' supervision (Rivera, Calonge, & Thompson, 1989; Shannon, Bashaw, Lewis, & Feldman, 1992). Young children may lack the physical size, locomotor experience, and cognitive ability to navigate potential environmental hazards on their own (Adolph, 2000; Glik et al., 1993).

Ironically, despite widespread agreement that motor and social developments are intertwined, research in these areas remains conceptually and empirically distinct. In particular, researchers know little about how infants weigh and integrate the perceptual information gleaned from their own exploratory activities with social information offered by their caregivers. What might the process of weighing competing sources of information under conditions of potential motor risk tell us about infants' emerging social understanding? In this chapter, we address this question by considering when and how infants seek and use social information as they make decisions about action.

SOCIAL REFERENCING

Seeking and using social information from caregivers is referred to as "social referencing". Infants *seek* social information by intentionally attempting to gather information via looking to a caregiver's face, vocalizing, and/or manually gesturing for help. *Using* social information entails that infants modify their emotions or behaviors in line with the social message. Thus, an infant who is wary of a stranger might seek social information by looking to mother in order to elicit her appraisal and use social information by reacting to mother's comforting smile with a decline in fearful expressions or by approaching the stranger.

Social referencing is a central milestone in the development of social cognition because it requires layers of knowledge about self, others, and the referential nature of social information. A common anecdotal example of social referencing is infants' stunned glance to their mothers after they fall down, as if to solicit mothers' advice about the seriousness of the injury. Mothers' assured smile signals to babies that "everything is okay" and a worried expression signals a more frightening interpretation of the event. The very core of social referencing is embedded in that slow-motion moment when babies decide whether to scream or to toddle off to their next adventure. Infants must recognize that they do not know how to behave or how to interpret an event and simultaneously recognize that their caregivers are valuable sources of advice about how to respond (Baldwin & Moses, 1996; Campos, 1983; Klinnert, Campos, Sorce, & Emde, 1983; Moore & Corkum, 1994).

Knowledge of Self

Because social referencing provides infants with useful information when their own knowledge is tenuous, *ambiguity* lies at the heart of social referencing. Infants should be more likely to seek social information or defer to unsolicited advice if they realize that they are unable to appraise the situation independently. Infants must possess a modicum of self-awareness to assess the situation as uncertain. Babies cannot judge a situation to be ambiguous without knowing on some level what they do and do not know or what they can and cannot do. They must realize that they are uncertain about the degree of risk, that they are unsure of the appropriate response, and that their own abilities are inadequate for generating the necessary information to deal with the situation.

Knowledge of Others

In addition to recognizing the limitations of their own knowledge, true social referencing requires infants to recognize that others are repositories of information. Infants cannot truly seek advice or understand the intentionality of parents' social messages until they appreciate the fact that more knowledgeable others can help resolve their own uncertainty about how to respond. Infants must understand the valence or content of others' messages, as well as connect those messages to the correct referent, in order to respond appropriately (Mumme & Fernald, 2003).

VISUAL CLIFF AND AMBIGUOUS TOY AND STRANGER PARADIGMS

Perhaps the most famous study in the social referencing literature examines 12-month-olds' reactions to mothers' emotional signaling on a modified visual cliff (Sorce, Emde, Campos, & Klinnert, 1985). In the classic visual cliff paradigm (Gibson & Walk, 1960; Walk, 1966), infants are placed on a centerboard dividing a glass table. To one side of the centerboard, the floor is visible 90 cm below the safety glass. To the other side, the apparent drop-off is only 3 cm. Mothers call to their infants from first one side, then the other. On the deep side of the standard visual cliff, most 12-month olds avoid crawling over the apparent precipice and on the shallow side most cross without hesitation (Richards & Rader, 1983; Walk, 1966).

In the Sorce et al. (1985), study, the apparent drop-off was set to 30 cm, a height that was designed to be ambiguous. Mothers were trained to pose static facial expressions (happy, fearful, interested, angry, or sad) for the duration of the trial. Infants were 12 months of age. Many infants (21%) formed their motor decisions without glancing toward their mothers' faces (an additional 19% could not be tested for other reasons). The 60% of infants who did look toward their mothers' faces were swayed by the emotional signals. Most babies crossed the 30 cm cliff when mothers posed positive expressions and avoided the drop-off when mothers posed negative expressions. On the 3 cm drop-off, 74% of infants immediately crossed without ever glancing at their mothers' face (an additional 9% were eliminated from testing for other reasons). Of the 17% who referenced their mothers' faces, mothers' fearful pose did not deter infants from crossing.

Given the centrality of this study for arguments about infants' social information seeking (Baldwin & Moses, 1996; Feinman, Roberts, Hsieh, Sawyer, & Swanson, 1992), it is surprising that more researchers have not used the visual cliff paradigm. The only additional study to test social referencing on the "ambiguous" 30 cm visual cliff failed to replicate Sorce's findings (Bradshaw, Goldsmith, & Campos, 1987). Only 27% of infants traversed the cliff when mothers posed positive expressions, suggesting that many infants relied on their own intuitions about safety, rather than mothers' advice, to make decisions.

The most common method for studying social referencing, however, entails exposing 9- to 14-month-old infants to a strange toy, animal, or person in the presence of their mothers (Feinman, 1982; Feinman et al., 1992), which avoids the requirement that researchers house a large unwieldy visual cliff apparatus in their labs. The key to the strange toy/person paradigm is that the novel objects or people are presumed to be ambiguous in nature, from babies' point of view, potentially alluring or frightening. Researchers have selected, for example, a motorized robot (Klinnert et al., 1983), large hairy spider (Zarbatany & Lamb, 1985), and a bunny in a cage (Hornik & Gunner, 1988).

As on the modified visual cliff, infants can solicit information from their mothers by looking toward them or engaging them in social interactions. Mothers, in turn, are coached to provide their infants with social information about how to interpret the stimulus by varying their facial expressions and vocalizations in line with prescribed scripts. Researchers gauge the effectiveness of mothers' social messages by observing infants' affective responses, proximity to their mothers, and proximity to the toy or stranger. However findings from these studies are based only on a subset of infants. Across studies approximately 20% never look towards their mothers and are eliminated from analyses (Feinman et al., 1992). Those infants who do look toward their mother tend to respond to the valence of their mothers' messages. Twelve-month-olds, for example, demonstrate modest changes in their proximity to the toy and/or their affective displays in response to their mothers' communications (e.g., Hirschberg & Svejda, 1990; Hornik & Gunner, 1988; Hornik, Risenhoover, & Gunnar, 1987; Mumme, Fernald, & Herrera, 1996; Stenberg & Hagekull, 1997).

THE PROBLEM WITH PREVIOUS PARADIGMS

Three interrelated problems plague extant studies of social referencing: (1) definitions of ambiguity are problematic; (2) the role of infants' experience and age are not adequately examined; and (3) the meaning of infants' responses on social referencing tasks is unclear.

Ambiguity

Despite the centrality of ambiguity in the social referencing literature, the construct has been ill defined. Weak results and conflicting findings across the strange toy/person and modified visual cliff paradigms may be the consequence of researchers' failure to achieve ambiguity in the displays. Previous researchers have relied on their own intuitions about ambiguity to select toys, animals, people, or the height of the drop-off on the visual cliff to use as stimuli. As Baldwin and Moses (1996) point out, the definition of ambiguity in traditional studies ends up being circular. We can only know that a stimulus is ambiguous if infants seek social support from their mothers and defer to mothers' social messages.

Thus, in some studies, infants may have considered the cliff/toy/animal/person to be perfectly safe. The visual cliff, for example, is indeed perfectly safe and infants can discover this fact after they touch the safety glass covering the drop-off. In such a case, infants may be oblivious to mothers' negative or prohibiting social messages. Or conversely, babies may have considered the hairy spider, bunny, or research assistant to be irrevocably scary. In this scenario, infants may ignore mothers' positive and encouraging social messages.

Experience and Development

Related to the issue of ambiguity, researchers rarely consider individual differences in infants' experience and development. Researchers typically take a "one size fits all" approach to ambiguity. Every infant in the sample is exposed to the same toy or the same 30 cm drop-off. This uniform approach is problematic in light of the vast individual differences in infants' experiences and reactions to novel toys and strangers, and babies' level of motor skill at the same chronological ages. A situation that is ambiguous to one infant might be perceived as unmistakably safe or dangerous to another. The role of infant experience is especially relevant to infants' referencing on motor tasks, because a few weeks of locomotor experience can change novice crawlers or walkers into experts who might shun their mothers' advice about how they should react to obstacles in their paths.

What Is the Meaning of Infants' Responses?

A true test of whether an infant is social referencing rests upon researchers' ability to gauge ambiguity for individual infants, independent of babies' response to the stimulus. However, without independent verification that a situation poses an ambiguous level of risk to individual infants, researchers cannot distinguish between true social referencing with all the cognitive underpinnings of self-other knowledge and communicative behaviors that lack the requisite layers of social knowledge. As Feinman (Feinman, 1982; Feinman et al., 1992) and others have pointed out, a host of nonreferential factors may cause infants to display social referencing-like behaviors. For example, babies may look to their mothers, vocalize, and gesture because they are aroused, seeking proximity or comfort, asking for hands-on assistance, or sharing affect. In such cases, these social behaviors can function as a bid for attention without infants possessing true referential knowledge. An infant who looks toward mother or vocalizes at the top of a stair may be checking on mother's whereabouts or may be merely aroused rather than seeking advice about whether to descend.

Just as nonreferential factors may explain apparent information seeking, nonreferential factors may also underlie apparent emotional and instrumental use of social information. Infants may be keenly receptive to parents' emotional displays in the absence of true social understanding. They may react to the emotional content of caregivers' messages through mood contagion or changes in mood states without understanding the referential nature of the social information. For example, a baby who freezes on the brink of a changing table as a parent expresses fear might be displaying emotional contagion, rather than using the information referentially to resolve uncertainty about the wisdom of leaping off the table. As yet, in the absence of objective criteria for quantifying ambiguity, we cannot distinguish among these various interpretations.

NEGOTIATING RISKY MOTOR TASKS

Recent work in our laboratory redresses problems in previous studies of social referencing. First, we tested infants in motor tasks where we objectively quantified ambiguity on an individual basis, rather than take a one-size fits all approach. Second, we considered the role of infants' locomotor experience. Finally, we considered various interpretations of infants' responses, including whether they were social referencing versus merely aroused or seeking proximity to their mothers.

Our general research strategy was to estimate psychophysical functions of actual risk levels for each infant, where risk varies from 0% (perfectly safe) to 100% (diabolically risky). Then, we determined the precision of infants' self-knowledge by examining whether their motor decisions were based on the degree of risk. Would babies limit themselves to situations that were completely safe? Would they be willing to incur small levels of risk? Or would they happily leap into the void?

More specifically, we challenged infants of different ages with varying levels of crawling and walking experience at the edge of shallow and steep slopes or small and large gaps in the floor (Adolph, 1995, 1997, 2000; Adolph & Avolio, 2000). As in the classic visual cliff paradigm, mothers beckoned their infants from the far side of the obstacle. Infants' task was to decide whether they could descend the slope or cross the gap so as to be reunited with their mothers. Unlike Sorce et al.'s (1985) famous visual cliff paradigm however, our slopes and gaps machines were adjustable rather than fixed at one setting. And, unlike the visual cliff paradigm, our test apparatuses had no safety glass covering the drop-off. Errors in judgment resulted in real life consequences: Babies could feel themselves lose balance and fall (an experimenter rescued them to prevent injury). Moreover, on the visual cliff, researchers were precluded from testing babies on multiple trials because babies learned after one exposure to the safety glass that the drop-off was actually safe. As a consequence of no safety glass, babies in our studies could be tested on dozens of trials without diminishing the strength of their avoidance response.

Figure 6.1 shows the adjustable sloping ramp and gaps apparatus. In the slope task, flat starting and landing platforms flanked a changeable slope. A motorized drive screw adjusted the height of the landing platform so that the slant could vary from 0–90° in 2° increments. In the gap task, babies decided whether to cross a gap with a vertical drop-off of 60 cm. Pulling the landing platform along a calibrated track varied the gap size from 0–90 cm in 2 cm increments.

We used a psychophysical staircase procedure to estimate each infant's ability to traverse the obstacle at each session (Adolph, 1995, 1997, 2000). As in perceptual psychophysics, the staircase procedure estimated a response function and a point estimate of a threshold along the curve. In this case, we estimated a motor function, the curve describing the changing probability of success for crawling or walking, from 100% success to 0% success. And, we derived a point estimate of a motor

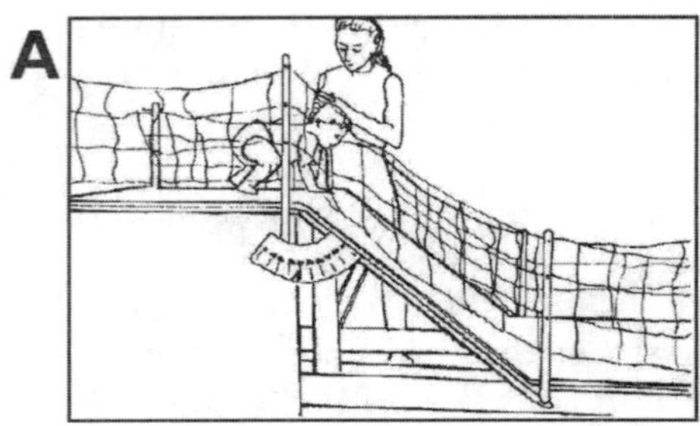

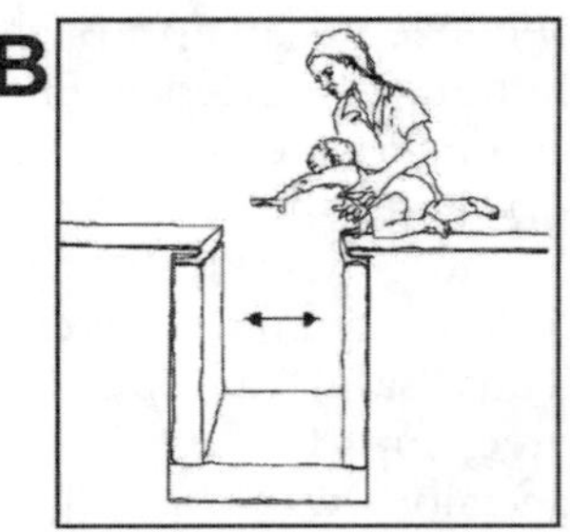

FIG. 6.1. (A) Slope apparatus. (B) Gap apparatus. In both tasks, infants began on a flat starting platform. Mothers (not shown) sat at the bottom of the landing platform and encouraged their infants to descend the slope or cross the gap. An experimenter (shown) followed alongside infants to ensure their safety.

threshold midway along the curve—the steepest slope each baby could crawl or walk down safely or the largest gap each baby could span successfully. The experimenter coded each trial on-line as either a successful outcome (baby crawled or walked safely) or an unsuccessful outcome (baby tried to crawl/walk but fell, or baby refused to crawl/walk). The slope angle for each trial was adjusted depending on the outcome of the previous trial. After successful trials, the experimenter presented steeper slopes or larger gaps. After unsuccessful trials, the baby was presented with shallower slopes or smaller gaps. The process continued until the experimenter converged on a crawling or walking threshold where the probability of successful crawling or walking was uncertain (< 100% and > 0%). Thus, the motor threshold could serve as an individualized, objective measure of risk and ambiguity. Slopes shallower than the threshold increment were increasingly safe by definition and slopes steeper than the threshold were increasingly risky.

A "go ratio" (number of attempts to crawl/walk divided by the total number of trials) indexed the level of infants' self-knowledge by the accuracy of their decisions at various increments of risk. If infants were aware of their abilities, they should attempt safe slopes where the probability of success was high (near 100%) and refuse to descend risky slopes where the probability of success was low (near 0%). Perfectly attuned self-knowledge would be evidenced by matching the go ratio (i.e., the probability of attempting) with the conditional probability of success.

Across studies, observations of hundreds of babies tested cross-sectionally or longitudinally revealed enormous variation across infants in their level of motor skill (e.g., Adolph, 1995, 1997; Adolph & Avolio, 2000; Adolph, Eppler, & Gibson, 1993) For example, at 9.5 months (± one week), infants' ability to crawl over gaps varied from 2 cm to 18 cm. At 14.0 months (± one week), infants' ability to walk down slopes varied from 0° to 28°. Gaps and slopes that were perfectly feasible for some infants were impossibly risky for others.

Individual variation in raw motor ability was matched by equally impressive variation in the precision of infants' self-knowledge. At every age group tested, some infants perfectly matched their go ratios to their crawling or walking thresholds. Other more hapless infants overestimated their abilities by attempting to traverse impossibly large slopes or gaps, seemingly oblivious to the potential danger and requiring quick rescue by the experimenter. And, still other infants underestimated their abilities by refusing to attempt slopes or gaps that were demonstrably safe.

What factors affected infants' motor thresholds and go ratios? At every age group, the strongest independent predictor of infants' motor skill level and precision of self-knowledge was the duration of their motor experience (Adolph, 1997, 2000; Adolph & Eppler, 2002). Across age groups and longitudinal observations, experience was a stronger predictor than age. Infants with more experience in crawling or walking navigated steeper slopes and larger gaps than novice crawlers or walkers. More importantly, the more experienced crawling and walking infants closely matched their decisions to go with the conditional probability of success. They attempted safe slopes and gaps but avoided risky ones by refusing to budge from the starting platform or by engaging in alternative locomotor strategies (e.g., backing down). In contrast, inexperienced infants displayed serious over-estimation errors. In the first weeks after they began crawling and walking, infants plunged headlong over the brink of impossibly steep slopes and large gaps on trial after trial. Error rates were typically between 75% and 100% on risky increments.

The central role of experience on the precision of infants' self-knowledge is illuminated in a longitudinal study of infants' locomotion over slopes (Adolph, 1997). Fifteen babies were observed from their first week of crawling until several weeks after they began walking. Fourteen babies in a control group were observed at three matched session times: in their first week of crawling, tenth week of crawling, and first week of walking.

At the emergence of crawling, babies went headfirst over safe and risky slopes alike. No infant displayed error rates under 50%. Over weeks of everyday locomotor experience, infants' motor decisions became increasingly accurate. After 22 weeks of experience, crawlers' motor decisions were virtually error-free (< 10%) (See Fig. 6.2). However,

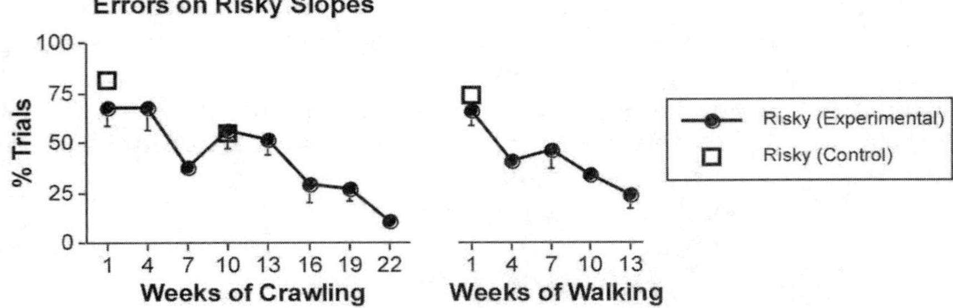

FIG. 6.2. Experience-related changes in infants' motor decisions on risky slopes. Curves represent the average proportion of trials on which infants erred by falling on impossibly steep slopes, requiring rescue by an experimenter. Error bars denote standard errors (Adolph, 1997).

once expert crawlers became novice walkers with a new upright posture, their error rates rebounded. Despite hundreds of trials over months of testing, there was no transfer between crawling and walking postures and learning was no faster the second time around. The infants in the control group showed nearly identical error rates at matched session times indicating that self-knowledge had generalized within postures from everyday experience with balance control to the laboratory slope task. However, self-knowledge did not transfer across developmental changes in posture.

IMPLICATIONS FOR SEEKING AND USING SOCIAL INFORMATION

Our findings of babies at the edge of slopes and gaps have important implications for conceptualizing and quantifying ambiguity, thereby providing an ideal context for studying the emergence of infants' social referencing. Whether and when infants seek and use social information will depend on their knowledge of self, as indexed in their evaluation of the situation as safe, ambiguous, or dangerous. To know that a situation is ambiguous, infants must be able to gauge the limits of their own abilities. *In the absence of self-knowledge, there can be no ambiguity.* At least for motor abilities, self-knowledge depends on the duration of infants' motor experience.

Following this logic, our data suggest that experienced crawlers and walkers know the limits of their abilities. Thus, for them the most ambiguous increments are those where the outcome is most uncertain, that is, where the probability of success is approximately 50%. Experienced infants should be most likely to seek and use social information from their caregivers at those ambiguous increments. In contrast, they should ignore social information at the increments on the tails of the response function (e.g., slopes that are relatively shallow or extremely steep). Caregivers' advice should be superfluous at those increments that babies deem to be clearly safe or dangerous, since the infant's perceptual exploration of the situation was, by definition, sufficient to make an adaptive decision.

What then of inexperienced infants? Why might they plunge over the brink when their mother beckons them from the far side of the obstacle? One possibility is that babies know on some level that they cannot accurately judge the limits of their own abilities. In that case, all slopes are ambiguous and babies should seek information from caregivers at every increment and blindly defer to their caregivers' advice. An alternative possibility is that babies do not realize that they lack self-knowledge. They may traipse over the brink of risky drop-offs because they mistakenly perceive the obstacle to be safe. Or, they may be oblivious about their ability to scale actions adaptively. On this account, infants should never socially reference their caregivers and any socially directed behaviors must be driven by some other factors. We are currently testing these hypotheses by examining the conditions under which infants of different ages and levels of locomotor experience seek and use social information in planning adaptive action.

SEEKING SOCIAL INFORMATION

How might experienced versus inexperienced infants differ in their *seeking* of social information across levels of risk? To explore this question, we are using the psychophysical staircase procedure to determine infants' crawling or walking thresholds on the slope apparatus. As in our previous research, mothers enthusiastically encourage their infants to crawl or walk down slopes until the experimenter converges on babies' motor thresholds. The point-estimate for the threshold is defined as the slope at which the probability for success is 50%.

Then, during test trials, we measure infants' appeals to their mothers at varying degrees of risk (100% success, 50% success, and 0% success). In contrast to the traditional toy, stranger, and visual cliff studies of social referencing, we aimed to test infants' social information seeking over multiple trials. We designed a set-up that would allow infants to tolerate mothers' inattention over repeated bids for assistance. Mothers sit caddy-corner at the bottom of the slope turned slightly to one side, occupied filling out forms. Our set-up is analogous to everyday situations in which mothers ignore bids from their infants such as when mother is occupied on the phone as her infant tugs at her skirt. The critical question is whether and how infants might seek information from their mothers by directing looks, vocalizations, or gestures in her direction.

Figure 6.3 depicts three possible outcomes depending on infants' locomotor experience and the level of risk. The solid line represents true social referencing behaviors, the long-dashed line represents social behaviors driven by arousal, and the dotted line represents social behaviors driven by proximity seeking. True social referencing with all the layers of self and other knowledge should differ in experienced and novice infants. If experienced infants appreciate the referential value of mothers' social information, they should seek social information only at ambiguous increments—where risk level is 50%—because they are able to accurately appraise the limits of their own abilities relative to risk level. If novices are aware that they do not know the limits of their own abilities, they should seek social information at all levels of risk. Alternatively, infants' communications to their mothers might merely signal arousal. In this case, experienced and novice infants alike should increasingly bid to their mothers as risk level increases. Finally, if infants are simply proximity seeking or "checking in," expe-

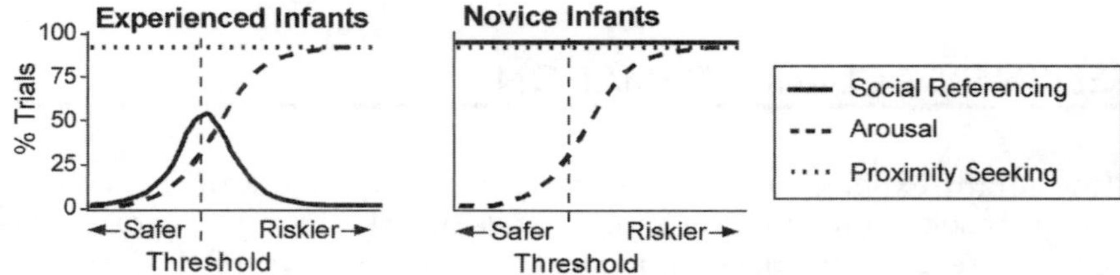

FIG. 6.3. Projected results for infants' bids toward mother (looks, vocalizations, gestures) on safe and risky increments for (A) experienced and (B) novice crawlers and walkers. Vertical dashed line = infants' motor threshold (normalized to each infant's demonstrated ability to descend slopes successfully). Solid lines = infants' pattern of responses if they were truly seeking social information from their mothers. Dashed lines = infants' pattern of responses if they were aroused. Dotted lines = infants' pattern of responses if they were seeking proximity to their mothers.

rienced infants and novices should look to their mothers at a constant rate across all levels of risk.

USING SOCIAL INFORMATION

What about infants' differential *use* of social information? In a second study, we are examining infants' responses to mothers' unsolicited encouragement (i.e., mothers coax their infants to walk or crawl down slopes) and discouragement (i.e., mothers prohibit their infants from walking or crawling down slopes) across levels of risk.

Our previous research shows a clear pattern of results under conditions of mothers' unsolicited encouragement: Infants' decisions about whether to attempt slopes or gaps depend on their motor experience and the relative degree of risk (solid lines in Fig. 6.4). When mothers urged their infants to cross novel obstacles in their path, at all ages between 8 and 18 months, infants with more everyday locomotor experience attempted safe increments and avoided risky ones, but novices attempted all increments indiscriminately (e.g., Adolph, 1997, 2000).

Possibly, all infants understood the referential quality of mothers' social messages. Experienced infants overrode mothers' advice on extremely safe or risky increments based on their own assessment of the situation. Inexperienced infants, aware that they lacked the ability to determine an appropriate course of action, deferred to their mothers' encouraging social messages at all increments.

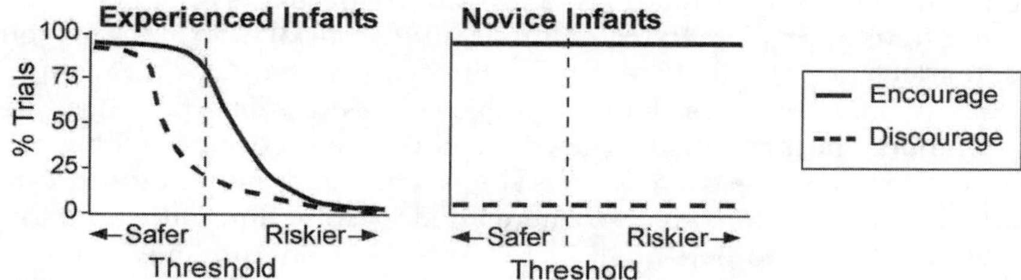

FIG. 6.4. Hypothetical results for infants' motor decisions on safe and risky increments for (A) experienced and (B) novice crawlers and walkers. Vertical dashed line = infants' motor threshold (normalized to each infant's demonstrated ability to descend slopes successfully). Curves represent infants' go ratios. Solid lines = results obtained in earlier work where mothers supplied unsolicited encouragement. Dashed lines = projected results if infants recognize their own inability to determine an appropriate course of action and defer to mothers' unsolicited prohibitions.

Equally plausible, however, is the possibility that infants *did not* understand the referential quality of mothers' messages. Expert crawlers and walkers could have based their decisions entirely on their own assessment of the obstacles rather than on mothers' advice. Their independent perceptual exploration might have afforded sufficient information about the slope's relative safety and mothers' stream of encouragement might have served no function at all. Inexperienced infants may have been blithely unaware of their own deficiencies in controlling actions adaptively. They might have resorted to a default behavior of going with little recognition of the value of mothers' encouraging advice. Alternatively, mothers' encouragement might have served a social function without providing real advice. Mothers may have provided a salient goal, drawn infants' attention to the far side of the obstacle, maintained infants' motivation to cross the obstacle over multiple trials, lifted infants' spirits via emotional contagion, comforted infants, regulated infants' arousal, or provided information about mothers' proximity. None of these alternative interpretations of mothers' seeming effectiveness require infants to appreciate the referential value of social messages.

In the absence of prohibitive social messages, however, we cannot distinguish among these alternatives. This limitation motivated an ongoing study of infants' responses to mothers' encouraging and discouraging messages. In the current study, we obtain individualized estimates of infants' crawling or walking thresholds using the staircase procedure. Then, in two blocks of counterbalanced test trials, mothers encourage and discourage their infants to descend slopes that are safe (100% probability of success), risky (0% probability of success), and set to infants' motor thresholds (50% probability of success).

If infants appreciate the referential value of social information, their motor decisions should be swayed in line with mothers' social message, but only on ambiguous slopes (see Fig. 6.4). Thus, for experienced infants should be most likely to go when mother says go and to stop when mother says no where ambiguous slopes surround their motor thresholds. In contrast, for novices where all slopes are ambiguous infants should defer to mothers at all increments. They should go when their mothers encourage them and remain on the platform when their mothers discourage them.

Alternatively, if infants' motor decisions are based *only* on experience and risk and not on mothers' social information there should be no effect for mothers' unsolicited advice in any of the contrasts. Experts and novices should attempt safe increments, but at risky increments, experienced infants should avoid and novices should go. In this scenario, responses for the encouraging and discouraging conditions would be identical and would follow the solid curves depicting encouragement in Fig. 6.4.

To date, predictions about the role of infant experience in babies' use of social information is supported by research in our laboratory. Eighteen-month-old walkers were most likely to defer to their mothers' advice at slopes at their thresholds, but to override mothers' advice to "not walk" at clearly safe increments and to "walk" at clearly risky increments. Novice walkers, in contrast, deferred to mothers advice at all levels of risk (Karasik et al., 2004; Lobo et al., 2003).

THE DEVELOPMENT OF SOCIAL REFERENCING

There has been a longstanding debate in the literature about when in development infants appreciate the referential value of others' advice and come to seek adults' input in making decisions. Most scholars agree that social referencing emerges sometime during infants' first 18 months, although the precise timing of its onset continues to be debated. Some researchers assert that 9-month-olds understand that others are useful sources of information and intentionally solicit social information to resolve uncertainty (Bretherton, 1992; Gopnik & Meltzoff, 1994). Infants' gaze following and pointing are offered as evidence for this 9-month sociocognitive revolution (Tomasello et al., 1993). On a more skeptical account, infants' intentional seeking of social information does not emerge until closer to 18 months, when infants are demonstrably cognizant of their own gaps in knowledge and the potential of others to address those gaps (e.g., Baldwin & Moses, 1996; Moore & Corkum, 1994).

We are contrasting the roles of infants' experience and age in all of our studies. Findings from our motor tasks promise to illuminate the developmental timing of infants' social understanding. If infants' social understanding of self and others changes dramatically between 8 and 18 months, infants' seeking and using of social information in motor tasks should vary across age. Younger infants should base their decisions on experience only, whereas older infants should be more adept at taking mothers' social information into account. By testing infants of different ages and levels of motor experience, we hope to pinpoint how and when infants integrate social information with their own perceptual exploration in planning adaptive action.

CONCLUSIONS

Social referencing is more than an instrumental response to an unsolicited social message. Infants' intentional seeking and use of social information in ambiguous situations lies at the heart of social referencing. To date however, investigators have adopted a one-size-fits-all approach to defining ambiguity. Consequently the developmental emergence of social referencing remains untested.

Potentially risky motor tasks render an ideal context for examining the phenomenon of social referencing. Our psychophysical staircase procedure, used with crawling and walking infants, enables us to quantify ambiguity on an individual basis and to examine how infants integrate perceptual and social information when making motor decisions. Whether infants attempt action under potential risk depends on their evaluation of the situation vis-à-vis their own motor abilities. Infants will seek and use social information differently under risky, safe, and ambiguous conditions. We are currently testing whether experienced and inexperienced infants of different ages display different patterns of social referencing at different levels of risk. This paradigm offers a new way to assess social referencing and bridges the long-standing divide between research on motor development and social cognition.

REFERENCES

Adolph, K. E. (1995). A psychophysical assessment of toddlers' ability to cope with slopes. *Journal of Experimental Psychology: Human Perception and Performance, 21*, 734–750.

Adolph, K. E. (1997). Learning in the development of infant locomotion. *Monographs of the Society for Research in Child Development, 62*(3, Serial No. 251).

Adolph, K. E. (2000). Specificity of learning: Why infants fall over a veritable cliff. *Psychological Science, 11*, 290–295.

Adolph, K. E., & Avolio, A. M. (2000). Walking infants adapt locomotion to changing body dimensions. *Journal of Experimental Psychology: Human Perception and Performance, 26*, 1148–1166.

Adolph, K. E., & Eppler, M. A. (2002). Flexibility and specificity in infant motor skill acquisition. In J. Fagen (Ed.), *Progress in infancy research* (Vol. 2, pp. 121–167). Norwood, NJ: Ablex.

Adolph, K. E., Eppler, M. A., & Gibson, E. J. (1993). Crawling versus walking infants' perception of affordances for locomotion over sloping surfaces. *Child Development, 64*, 1158–1174.

Baker, S., O'Neill, B., & Ginsberg, M. J. (1992). *The injury fact book*. New York: Oxford University Press.

Baldwin, D. A., Markman, E. M., Bill, B., Desjardins, N., Irwin, J. M., & Tidball, G. (1996). Infants' reliance on a social criterion for establishing word-object relations. *Child Development, 67*, 3135–3153.

Baldwin, D. A., & Moses, L. J. (1996). The ontogeny of social information gathering. *Child Development, 67*, 1915–1939.

Biringen, Z., Emde, R. N., Campos, J. J., & Applebaum, M. I. (1995). Affective reorganization in the infant, the mother, and the dyad: The role of upright locomotion and its timing. *Child Development, 66*, 499–514.

Bradshaw, K. D. L., Goldsmith, H. H., & Campos, J. J. (1987). Attachment, temperament, and social referencing: Interrelationships among three domains of infant affective behavior. *Infant Behavior and Development, 10,* 223–231.

Bretherton, I. (1992). Social referencing, intentional communication, and the interfacing of minds in infancy. In S. Feinman (Ed.), *Children's theories of mind: Mental states and social understanding* (pp. 57–77). New York: Plenum Press.

Campos, J. J. (1983). The importance of affective communication in social referencing: A commentary on Feinman. *Merrill-Palmer Quarterly, 29,* 83–87.

Campos, J. J., Anderson, D. I., Barbu-Roth, M. A., Hubbard, E. M., Hertenstein, M. J., & Witherington, D. C. (2000). Travel broadens the mind. *Infancy, 1*(2), 149–219.

Feinman, S. (1982). Social referencing in infancy. *Merrill-Palmer Quarterly, 28,* 445–470.

Feinman, S., Roberts, D., Hsieh, K. F., Sawyer, D., & Swanson, D. (1992). A critical review of social referencing in infancy. In S. Feinman (Ed.), *Social referencing and the construction of reality in infancy.* New York: Plenum Press.

Garling, A., & Garling, T. (1993). Mothers' supervision and perception of young children's risk of unintentional injury in the home. *Journal of Pediatric Psychology, 18,* 105–114.

Garling, A., & Garling, T. (1995). Mothers' anticipation and prevention of unintentional injury to young children in the home. *Journal of Pediatric Psychology, 20,* 23–36.

Gibson, E. J. (1988). Exploratory behavior in the development of perceiving, acting and the acquiring of knowledge. *Annual Review of Psychology, 39,* 1–41.

Gibson, E. J., & Walk, R. D. (1960). The "visual cliff". *Scientific American, 202,* 64–71.

Glik, D. C., Greaves, P. E., Kronenfeld, J. J., & Jackson, K. L. (1993). Safety hazards in households with young children. *Journal of Pediatric Psychology, 18,* 115–131.

Gopnik, A., & Meltzoff, A. N. (1994). Mind, bodies, and persons: Young children's understanding of the self and others as reflected in imitation and "theory of mind" research. In S. T. Parker, R. W. Mitchell, & M. L. Boccia (Eds.), *Self-awareness in animals and humans* (pp. 166–186). New York: Cambridge University Press.

Gustafson, G. E. (1984). Effects of the ability to locomote on infants' social and exploratory behaviors: An experimental study. *Developmental Psychology, 20,* 397–405.

Hirschberg, L. M., & Svejda, M. (1990). When infants look to their parents: I. Infants' social referencing of mothers compared to fathers. *Child Development, 61*(4), 1175–1186.

Hornik, R., & Gunner, M. R. (1988). A descriptive analysis of infants' social referencing. *Child Development, 59,* 626–634.

Hornik, R., Risenhoover, N., & Gunnar, M. (1987). The effects of maternal positive, neutral, and negative affective communications on infant responses to new toys. *Child Development, 58,* 937–944.

Karasik, L. B., Lobo, S. A., Zack, E. A., Dimitropoulou, K. A., Tamis-LeMonda, C. S., & Adolph, K. E. (2004). *Does mother know best? Infants' use of mothers' unsolicited advice in a potentially risky motor task.* Poster presented at the International Conference on Infant Studies, Chicago, IL.

Klinnert, M. D., Campos, J. J., Sorce, J. F., & Emde, R. N. (1983). Emotions as behavior regulators: Social referencing in infancy. In R. Plutchik & H. Kellerman (Eds.), *The emotion* (Vol. 2, pp. 57–86). New York: Academic Press.

Lobo, S. A., Karasik, L. B., Zack, E. A., Dimitropoulou, K. A., Tamis-LeMonda, C. S., & Adolph, K. E. (2003). *When do infants take mothers' advice?* Poster presented at the meeting of the Society for the Study of Human Development, Cambridge, MA.

Mahler, M., Pine, F., & Bergman, A. (1975). *The psychological birth of the human infant*. New York: Basic Books.

Moore, C., & Corkum, V. (1994). Social understanding at the end of the first year of life. *Developmental Review, 14*, 349–372.

Mumme, D. L., & Fernald, A. (2003). The infant as onlooker: Learning from emotional reactions observed in a television scenario. *Child Development, 74*, 221–237.

Mumme, D. L., Fernald, A., & Herrera, C. (1996). Infants' responses to facial and vocal emotional signals in a social referencing paradigm. *Child Development, 67*(6), 3219–3237.

Peterson, L., & Stern, B. L. (1997). Family processes and child risk for injury. *Behavioral Research & Therapy?, 35*, 179–190.

Richards, J. E., & Rader, N. (1983). Affective, behavioral, and avoidance responses on the visual cliff: Effects of crawling onset age, crawling experience, and testing age. *Psychophysiology, 20*, 633–642.

Rivera, F. P., Calonge, N., & Thompson, R. S. (1989). Population based study of unintentional injury incidence and impact during childhood. *American Journal of Public health, 79*, 990–994.

Rodriguez, J. (1990). Childhood injuries in the United States: A priority issue. *American Journal of Diseases of Children, 49*, 625–626.

Shannon, A., Bashaw, B., Lewis, J., & Feldman, W. (1992). Nonfatal childhood injuries: A survey at the Children's Hospital of Eastern Ontario. *Canadian Medical Association Journal, 146*, 361–365.

Sorce, J. F., Emde, R. N., Campos, J., & Klinnert, M. D. (1985). Maternal emotional signaling: Its effects on the visual cliff behavior of 1-year-olds. *Developmental Psychology, 21*, 195–200.

Stenberg, G., & Hagekull, B. (1997). Social referencing and mood modification in 1-year-olds. *Infant Behavior and Development, 20*, 209–217.

Tomasello, M., Kruger, A. C., & Ratner, H. H. (1993). Cultural learning. *Behavioral and Brain Sciences, 16*, 495–552.

Walk, R. D. (1966). The development of depth perception in animals and human infants. *Monographs of the Society for Research in Child Development, 31*(5, Serial No. 107), 82–108.

Zarbatany, L., & Lamb, M. E. (1985). Social referencing as a function of information source: Mothers versus strangers. *Infant Behavior and Development, 8*, 25–33.

Chapter 7

*Is Joint Attention Necessary for Early Language Learning?**

Nameera Akhtar
University of California, Santa Cruz

Beginning with Bruner's (1975, 1983) detailed descriptions of mother-infant interactions, many theorists have highlighted the importance of joint attention in early language learning.[1] The empirical work inspired by Bruner's ideas focuses on infants and children engaged in dyadic interactions with their caregivers. In these studies, joint attention has been defined as periods of time during which the caregiver and child are mutually focused on one another and on the same object or activity. The results show that dyads who engage in more episodes of joint attention generally have children with larger vocabularies (e.g., Tomasello & Farrar; 1986; Carpenter, Nagell, & Tomasello, 1998). Several ethnographic studies of families outside of the Western middle class context (e.g., Ochs, 1988; Schieffelin, 1990) indicate, however, that many of the world's children grow up in situa-

*Acknowledgments: Many thanks to Margarita Azmitia, Maureen Callanan, Maricela Correa-Chavez, Bruce Homer, Barbara Rogoff, Cathie Tamis-LeMonda, and Mike Tomasello for their comments on previous drafts.

[1]There is extensive research on the development of joint attention (see Butterworth, 2001, and Trevarthen & Aitken, 2001, for reviews) but I focus only on the work that makes an explicit link between joint attention and language development.

tions in which they experience relatively little joint attention—at least in the form in which it has been characterized and measured in dyadic interactions between parents and children. As these children all go on to speak and understand language, it is important to examine more closely the relation between joint attention and early word learning. That is the aim of this chapter.

Some researchers have posited that achieving joint focus is critical for word learning. For example, Akhtar and Tomasello (1998) claim that "to learn a new piece of language the child must in some sense enter into an intersubjective (joint attentional) state with a mature language user" (p. 317). The object or event being labeled does not have to be physically present (Akhtar & Tomasello, 1996), but most definitions of joint attention have emphasized the mutual engagement of adult and child as critical. That is, it is not considered enough for the two to simply be focused on the same thing at the same time; they must also be focused on one another.

In contrast, in a recent series of experimental studies (which is described in more detail later), my colleagues and I have shown that 24-month-olds are able to learn novel labels equally well when positioned as an onlooker to an interaction between two adults as when interacting directly with an adult (Akhtar, Jipson, & Callanan, 2001). These findings indicate that, at least in some circumstances, a young child and adult need not be intersubjectively engaged for the child to be able to learn a novel word that the adult uses. Of course the children who participated in these studies have a history of learning words in varied contexts, and these findings do not address whether joint attention (defined as mutual engagement) is perhaps required in the very earliest stages of word learning.

In this chapter, I review studies conducted in a variety of cultural contexts that demonstrate that, from a young age, children are quite good at tuning in to the attentional focus of others. That is, it is not necessary for them to be engaged in a reciprocal interaction with another person in order to focus on, comprehend, and learn from what that person is saying or doing. These findings, along with those demonstrating word learning through overhearing, suggest that early word learning may not require the intersubjective awareness that is often assumed to be an integral part of joint attention.

I begin with a look at how joint attention has been defined in studies of its relation to language development and review some of the data and arguments suggesting that it facilitates, and may even be necessary for, vocabulary learning. I then review briefly observational studies of infants' and toddlers' early interactions in several non-Western (often non-industrialized) contexts. These studies indicate that the kinds of dyadic interactions between infants and caregivers that have been the focus of joint attention research appear to be rare to non-existent in some societies, yet the children do not appear to be greatly delayed in language learning. Indeed, children growing up in these contexts seem to be quite good at monitoring others' interactions, which leads to the hypothesis that they may learn a great deal of language by attending to the conversations of others. I therefore examine the importance of overhearing or "listening in" (Rogoff, Paradise, Mejia Arauz, Correa-Chavez, & Angelillo, 2003) in language development more generally, and argue that our theories of "language input" and language learning are missing a great deal if they focus only on speech addressed directly to the language learning child. Finally, I return to the question posed in the title of this chapter—whether joint attention (defined as joint focus plus mutual engagement) is truly necessary for early language learning.

DEFINING JOINT ATTENTION AND ITS ROLE IN EARLY LANGUAGE

As Bruner (1995) has pointed out, what counts as joint attention varies at different stages of development. Thus, "at its most sophisticated level, joint attention ... depends not only on a shared or joint focus, but on shared context and shared presuppositions" (p. 6). In this chapter, however, as the focus is on children in the early stages of language learning I will concentrate on how joint attention has been defined during this early period, and only on how it has been defined in studies that also include measures of language development.

Building on the work of researchers studying the development of mother-infant interactions (e.g., Bakeman & Adamson, 1984; Trevarthen & Hubley, 1978), Tomasello and his colleagues (Tomasello & Todd, 1983; Tomasello & Farrar, 1986) were among the first to operationally define joint attention in studies of its relation to normal language development (but see Loveland & Landry, 1986, for an early study on the relations between joint attention and language in autistic children). In these studies, as in those that followed, joint attention was defined as episodes during which the parent (almost always the mother) and child were mutually engaged and focused on the same object or activity. Evidence of mutual engagement consisted of the child's alternating gaze between the parent's face and the object of common interest. Tomasello and Farrar (1986) explicitly excluded what they termed "mere onlooking"—episodes of joint focus on the same thing but without evidence of mutual engagement—from their definition of joint attention. The claim is that engaging in joint attention is different from onlooking in that "both participants are monitoring the other's attention to the outside entity" and both "know that they are attending to something in common" (Tomasello, 1995, p. 106). Similarly, whereas Baldwin (1995) has very clearly defined joint attention as the "simultaneous engagement of two or more individuals in mental focus on one and the same external thing", she also stresses the importance of the "intersubjective awareness that accompanies joint attention, the recognition that mental focus on some external thing is shared" (p. 132).

Using this definition—joint focus plus mutual engagement—many researchers have demonstrated a positive correlation between joint attention and early vocabulary size (Carpenter et al., 1998; Markus, Mundy, Morales, Delgado, & Yale, 2000; Tomasello & Todd, 1983). Another relevant finding is that toddlers tend to learn novel words best when an adult labels an object they are already looking at, rather than labeling an object which requires them to shift their attentional focus (e.g., Dunham, Dunham, & Curwin, 1993; Tomasello & Farrar, 1986). Although these studies support the idea that following the attentional focus of the child facilitates word learning, other studies have focused on the active role toddlers play in establishing joint attention with adults who utter novel words (e.g., Akhtar & Tomasello, 1996; Baldwin, 1991; 1993; Tomasello & Barton, 1994; for reviews, see Akhtar, 2004, and Tomasello, 2001). For example, upon hearing an adult utter a novel label for one of two possible novel objects (e.g., "It's a *toma*"), toddlers will check to see what the adult is looking at (Baldwin, 1991) rather than assume that the object they themselves are focused on is the one being labeled. In all of these studies, children are engaged in social interaction with the adult who is using the novel label. Indeed, they tend to resist word learning when the adult speaker is not interacting with them and shows no signs of attending to the object they are attending to; that is, when an adult who is not interacting with the child happens to utter a label while the child is focused on a novel object, the child will not attach the word to that object (Baldwin, et al., 1996).

If, however, the adult is not engaged with the child but is clearly labeling something she herself is attending to, it turns out that children as young as 24 months do learn the label for the object on which the adult is focused (Akhtar et al., 2001). To do this, they must be monitoring the adult's speech and attentional focus even when the adult is not interacting with them. This is an active form of "onlooking" that has been explicitly excluded from the definition of joint attention. That toddlers can learn words through overhearing suggests that mutual engagement with a speaker is not essential for word learning, at least not by 24 months. How can these findings be reconciled with the view that joint attention (joint focus plus mutual engagement) plays such an important role in early lexical acquisition?

One possibility is that mutual engagement plays a particularly important role earlier in the process, when children are learning their first words, and that by 24 months they have become so sophisticated at determining the referential intentions of adults that they do not need to be engaged with them to learn from them. This possibility is supported by a recent finding that individual differences in joint attention were related to individual differences in language development at 6 through 18 months, but not at 21 and 24 months (Morales, et al., 2000). In explaining a similar finding (i.e., a weakening of the relation between joint attention and language development over time), Carpenter et al. (1998) suggest that as children get older they become "better able to determine adults' focus of attention more reliably, even when it is discrepant with their own" (p. 118). The view then is that mutual engagement is most important in the very early stages of language learning, and may become less so as the infant matures and is better able to monitor others' interactions.

Alternatively, it is possible that mutual engagement is not critical and that from the earliest stages of language learning children are capable of tuning into what others are attending to. In other words, it may be the *child's* ability to determine a speaker's attentional focus that is critical in learning referential terms rather than joint attention per se; that is, the child has to be able to identify the speaker's focus, but the speaker may not have to be focused on the child. Indeed this is what is suggested by Akhtar and Tomasello (2000) when they claim that "when a child hears a speaker use an unfamiliar term, the child must use his or her understanding of the communicative situation to focus his or her attention on the same entity (object, attribute, action) on which the speaker is focused" (p. 116). This account of word learning is still profoundly social in that the child has to find a way to tune into the speaker's referential intentions (Tomasello, 2001) but it does not require the parental scaffolding that is generally associated with joint attention and other social approaches to word learning (see Bloom, 1993, for criticisms of the scaffolding model). However, because determining the speaker's focus is presumably easier for the child to do during periods of joint attention (the child has to expend relatively little effort because the speaker's focus coincides with his or her own), joint attention may be especially helpful in the earliest stages when the infant's sensitivity to various cues to another's focus of attention is not as well developed. This would explain the positive correlation between time spent in joint attention and early vocabulary; that is, whereas participating in joint attention may not be necessary, it may facilitate early language learning.

Before accepting this conclusion, however, it is important to examine cultures in which infants and toddlers generally do not participate in extended periods of joint attention—at least not as it has been defined in the research thus far; that is, in dyadic interactions with gaze alternation between partner and object. The goal is to determine whether the vocabulary learning of these children differs significantly from that of their counterparts who do experience lots of dyadic and didactic interactions. Unfortunately, the existing research does not allow a definitive answer to this question, mainly because studies of the relevant societies often do not contain quantitative descriptions of children's language development. Even in those studies in which language development is of interest, individual differences in the size and content of early vocabularies have not been systematically assessed (Lieven, 1994). Although this is clearly an important area for future research, it is worth noting that most researchers in these other cultural contexts have not remarked upon any great delay in language learning. One clear exception, however, is Brown (1998) who states that the Tzeltal Mayan children she studied are "often late starters in producing language, many hardly talking ... until age 2;0" (p. 201).

Before turning to a brief review of language learning in other cultural contexts, it is worth pursuing the implications of Brown's observation. First, even if it is true that children in these contexts are slower to produce words, it is also important: 1) to assess their comprehension abilities; and 2) to determine when these children "catch up" to their peers who experience more dyadic and didactic interactions with mature speakers. Brown's view is that, from about age 2 on, "the child's acquisition of her language, although slightly delayed in production vocabulary, is not out of line with that of Western children" (p. 201). Such a "delay" is likely of no consequence to the children who experience it; it is only in contexts in which faster is always viewed as better that beginning to speak a few months earlier might matter. The question of course is what implications would such findings (and it is important to keep in mind that they are not findings yet; only impressions) have for the relation between joint attention and early language learning. That is, even if children who experience less dyadic joint attention are slower to acquire vocabulary, does this necessarily mean that joint attention is critical for early language learning?

One reason why one cannot draw such a conclusion from findings of this kind is that there may be other factors that might explain the putative delay in vocabulary learning. For example, hearing (and presumably overhearing) less language is also associated with slower vocabulary acquisition (Hart & Risley, 1995). I know of no studies that have systematically explored the amount of language children in these other cultural contexts are exposed to compared to their Western counterparts. While they are directly addressed less often and may experience fewer dyadic language teaching interactions (see next section), they are still exposed to lots of language-rich interactions (Ochs & Schieffelin, 1995). In any case, amount of (dyadic) joint attention and amount of language exposure are orthogonal constructs, and the relative role each plays in individual differences in vocabulary acquisition has not yet been studied.

CULTURAL CONTEXTS OF LANGUAGE LEARNING

Many linguists and anthropologists who have studied language learning across a wide variety of cultural contexts have noted quantitative and qualitative differences in the speech directly addressed to infants and toddlers. Indeed, in some communities, infants and toddlers are rarely included as direct addressees in conversational interactions with adults, certainly not to the degree they tend to be in the Western middle-class context; see, for example, Brown (1998) on Tzeltal Mayans; Crago, Allen, and Hough-Eyamie (1997) on an Inuit community in northern Quebec; Schieffelin and Ochs (1983) on Papua New Guinea; Watson-Gegeo & Gegeo (1986) on the Kwara'ae of the Solomon Islands; and Lieven's (1994) review. In these contexts, young children are generally expected to take responsibility for monitoring the activities and conversations of others. Whereas siblings and other caregivers may play an important role in language socialization in these communities (Zukow-Goldring, 1995), most ethnographic reports suggest that young children experience far fewer one-on-one "language teaching" interactions than their counterparts in middle-class industrialized societies.

Indeed, multiparty or polyadic interactions seem to be the norm in many societies (Lieven, 1994; Tronick, Morelli, & Ivey, 1992).[2] Polyadic situations in general create different attentional demands than dyadic situations and how children from different cultural communities respond to those demands is instructive. Rogoff and her colleagues have shown that Guatemalan Mayan toddlers (and their mothers) maintained smooth simultaneous attention to multiple competing events, whereas European American toddlers (and their mothers) generally attended to one event at a time, often alternating attention between events (Chavajay & Rogoff, 1999; Rogoff, Mistry, Göncü, & Mosier, 1993). These patterns of attention are related to mothers' beliefs about how children learn; very young Guatemalan Mayan children are expected to be keen observers and to be able to coordinate attention to multiple par-

[2]Note that, especially if there is more than one child in the family, this is probably also true of the Western middle-class communities in which mother-infant dyads have been studied almost exclusively; see Barton and Tomasello (1991) on mother-infant-sibling triadic interactions, and Blum-Kulka and Snow's (2002) edited volume on multiparty conversations.

ticipants. It is important to note that, although there were cultural differences in children's attentional patterns in the polyadic context, all toddlers in both groups were actively engaged in monitoring multiple competing events.

These findings are significant because of their implications for studies of the relation between joint attention and language learning. Joint attention has always been assessed in dyadic contexts, but many (if not most) children spend a lot of their time in polyadic contexts. Although one might conclude that children experience less joint attention in polyadic contexts, it may be that the way joint attention has been measured in the Western middle class context is simply not the appropriate way to assess the same construct in different communities. As with any comparison across cultures, it is quite possible that other behaviors may fulfill the same function—in this case, the fact that a child does not systematically alternate gaze to his mother and to an object or event they are both interested in does not necessarily mean the child and mother are not mutually engaged. Other nonverbal gestures such as touch and posture, for example, may serve the engagement function that gaze does in traditional studies of joint attention (Chavajay & Rogoff, 1999; deLeon, 1998; Rogoff, 1990). Indeed Rogoff (personal communication) believes that there may even be *more* joint attention in the polyadic Mayan context she has studied than in the dyadic contexts that traditionally have been examined. In this context, both toddlers and their mothers almost continuously maintained attention to one another as well as to other people and objects (Chavajay & Rogoff, 1999). Thus, it is possible that joint attention does play a very important role in language learning, but the way it is achieved may be different in different cultural contexts.

It is also important to consider the possibility that children who are expected to keenly observe others (and have more practice doing so) may be much better at monitoring third-party interactions than children who are accustomed to having adults solicitously label things for them. These children may therefore not require the episodes of caregiver-initiated joint attention that seem to facilitate vocabulary learning in dyadic contexts, and may actually be better at learning words by attending to third-party conversations (Ochs & Schieffelin, 1995). Analogously, it is possible that children who are used to experiencing scaffolding may actually rely on it more both because they expect it and because they have not developed the monitoring skills of children who are expected to be keen observers. Clearly these are issues that future research will need to address.

It is commonly assumed that children in the communities that foster keen observation must initially learn some, if not most, of their language by overhearing it used by others. This process has been labeled "listening in" by Rogoff et al. (2003) to emphasize the active role children play in monitoring the interactions of others. Rogoff et al. argue that, although some communities may emphasize it more than others, in *all* cultures listening in plays an important role in learning language and other social-cognitive skills (see also deLeon, 1998; Forrester, 1988, 1993). Most studies of linguistic input, however, have examined only speech that is directly addressed to children. There are obvious practical reasons for this focus, yet there also appears to be an implicit assumption that children learn language mainly (if not solely) from speech directed to them by adults (but see Au, Knightly, Jun, & Oh, 2002). Given the findings that toddlers actively monitor others' interactions, it is important to examine whether they can learn new language from those interactions.

THE IMPORTANCE OF SPEECH NOT ADDRESSED TO THE CHILD

In order to learn a new word through overhearing, children must, at the very least, pay close attention to the conversations of others, and must be able to segment the target word from overheard speech. Although I know of no research on toddlers' ability to segment overheard speech (but see Saffran, Newport, Aslin, Tunick, & Barrueco, 1997, on this type of learning in 6-year-olds), there is plenty of evidence that they can and do monitor third-party conversations. For example, English-speaking 2- and 3-year-olds often interrupt conversations between their parents and siblings in relevant, topic-sensitive ways (Dunn & Shatz, 1989). Even younger children (19-month-olds) were more likely to join an ongoing conversation between their mother and older sibling than to initiate one themselves (Barton & Tomasello, 1991). These same children also responded appropriately to requests directed to another person, clearly indicating that they were attending to and comprehending language that was not addressed to them.

Research by Oshima-Takane (1988, 1999) suggests that overhearing plays a particularly important role in the acquisition of personal pronouns. Some children make reversal errors with personal pronouns; for example, referring to themselves as "you." One possible reason for these errors is that personal pronouns, along with other deictic terms, have shifting reference. Thus, when a mother speaks to her child, she refers to herself as *I* or *me* and the child as *you*, but when the child speaks, he or she has to reverse the usage of the pronouns. Consequently, the correct usage of personal pronouns depends on understanding the relations between the pronouns and speech roles. As Oshima-Takane points out, however, models for correct usage are not available in child-directed speech. For example, if a child only heard the word *you* in reference to herself, she might reasonably conclude that *you* is her name. But (over)hearing others addressing one another as *you* would lead to the more appropriate inference that *you* is a word used to refer to whoever is being addressed.

In this regard, it is particularly interesting that second-born children (who have more opportunities for overhearing speech) tend to have an advantage over first-borns in learning personal pronouns (Oshima-Takane, Goodz, & Derevensky, 1996). Although their overall rate of language development is equivalent to that of first-borns, second-borns are more likely to use personal pronouns correctly. Moreover, an examination of maternal speech in the triadic context (mother, first-born, and second-born) revealed that second-borns were exposed to more pronouns in overheard conversations than in speech directed to them. These findings support the hypothesis that second-born children's advantage in pronoun production is linked to increased opportunities to *overhear* pronouns being used in third-party conversations between their siblings and parents. What these studies do not address is whether children can learn new words (i.e., words they have never heard in speech directed to them) through overhearing.

In a series of experiments, Akhtar et al. (2001) directly examined whether young 2-year-olds could learn novel words when they only overheard them used in a third-party conversation. In each study, children were randomly assigned to one of two conditions: Addressed or Overhearing. In the Addressed condition, the experimenter played a game with the child and introduced a word for one of four unfamiliar objects. In the Overhearing condition, the child was positioned as an onlooker to an identical interaction between the experimenter and an adult confederate. In this condition, the experimenter introduced the novel word to the confederate instead of the child, and essentially ignored the child. In both conditions, the children were able to learn the word as shown in a subsequent comprehension test. Indeed, they performed equally well in these two conditions.

Although these findings are intriguing, one can question to what extent the experimental context approximates the everyday contexts in which children overhear novel words. In these studies, while children were seated as onlookers to the adults' interaction they had little to distract them from that interaction. To examine how well children this age might do in the presence of a potentially distracting activity, two more studies (Akhtar, 2005) were conducted, each with two within-subjects conditions. In the No-Distractor condition (which was essentially a replication of Akhtar et al.'s overhearing condition), children simply watched as two adults played with four novel objects and labeled one of them. In the Distractor condition, children were given an engaging toy to play with while the adults interacted. In both conditions, children monitored the adults' conversation and were able to respond appropriately on the comprehension test. In the second study, instead of the adult explicitly labeling the target object, she embedded the novel word in a directive to the confederate. In both studies, there was no difference in performance between the Distractor and No-Distractor conditions. Thus, even when another interesting activity was available, and even when the adults were not explicitly labeling the objects, 2-year-olds were able to learn words that were not addressed to them.

It is therefore clear that middle-class 2-year-old children learning English are able to monitor third-party conversations and can learn new labels from these conversations. They were not mutually engaged with the speaker, but were able to determine the speaker's referential intentions. It is important to be clear that they were not simply passively associating the words heard with some object they saw; in none of the studies were the objects perceptually available at the time the novel label was uttered. Thus, these children were intently monitoring the speaker's focus. It remains to be seen if younger children in this cultural context would do as well in this task, and whether children from communities in which keen observation is expected might outperform them at an earlier age.

In summary, although mutual engagement is probably a component of all children's interactions some of the time, it is important to bear in mind that there is a wide range of environments in which children are exposed to and learn language. Learning words through overhearing or "listening in" may play a particularly important role in communities in which children are expected to be keen observers of third-party interactions (Lieven, 1994).

IS JOINT ATTENTION NECESSARY FOR EARLY LANGUAGE LEARNING?

If we define joint attention as the state a child achieves when he or she discerns a speaker's focus when that speaker uses a new word, then yes, joint attention probably is necessary for early word learning. It is only by discerning the referential intentions of others in the contexts in which they use words that a child can determine the appropriate use of a conventional communicative symbol (Akhtar & Tomasello, 2000). However, if joint attention is defined—as it most often has been—as involving dyadic engagement of a child and speaker with one another as well as on some shared topic, then it is not clear that it is necessary. It certainly may be, but more research needs to be conducted on the earliest stages of language learning in a variety of cultural contexts. In particular, measures of joint attention that are appropriate for non-didactic polyadic contexts need to be developed to study the role that it might play in language learning in these contexts.

Although dyadic joint attention does seem to facilitate early vocabulary acquisition in the contexts in which it has been studied, it remains to be seen whether it has the same predictive relation to individual differences in vocabulary development in other cultural contexts. Studies conducted within the Western cultural context—where children's interactions are often (although certainly not exclusively) dyadic and didactic—indicate that very young children have impressive skills of observational learning that may obviate the need for benevolent "scaffolding" in the form of adults tuning in to and labeling what children are interested in. Toddlers can learn words when adults label things they (the toddlers) are not focused on (Baldwin, 1991) and even when the speaker is not interacting with them (Akhtar et al., 2001). Although it remains an empirical question, it seems reasonable to expect that children growing up in contexts in which they experience relatively few dyadic and didactic interactions would be even better at this type of learning through active monitoring and listening in. None of this diminishes the importance of the social contexts in which children encounter novel words nor the part played by adults who introduce those words. What I hope to have done, however, is to place more emphasis on the child's role in "making sense" of social interactions (Nelson, 1985), whether the child is directly participating in or intently observing those interactions.

REFERENCES

Akhtar, N. (2005). The robustness of learning through overhearing. *Developmental Science, 8*, 199–209.

Akhtar, N. (2004). Contexts of early word learning. In D. G. Hall & S. R. Waxman (Eds.), *Weaving a lexicon* (pp. 485–507). Cambridge, MA: MIT Press.

Akhtar, N., Jipson, J., & Callanan, M. (2001). Learning words through overhearing. *Child Development, 72*, 416–430.

Akhtar, N., & Tomasello, M. (1996). Two-year-olds learn words for absent objects and actions. *British Journal of Developmental Psychology, 14*, 79–93.

Akhtar, N., & Tomasello, M. (1998). Intersubjectivity in early language learning and use. In S. Braten (Ed.), *Intersubjective communication and emotion in early ontogeny: Between nature, nurture, and culture* (pp. 316–335). New York: Cambridge University Press.

Akhtar, N., & Tomasello, M. (2000). The social nature of words and word learning. In R. M. Golinkoff & K. Hirsh-Pasek (Eds.), *Becoming a word learner: A debate on lexical acquisition* (pp. 115–135). Oxford University Press.

Au, T. K., Knightly, L. M., Jun, S., & Oh, J. S. (2002). Overhearing a language during childhood. *Psychological Science, 13*, 238–243.

Bakeman, R., & Adamson, L. B. (1984). Coordinating attention to people and objects in mother-infant and peer-infant interaction. *Child Development, 55*, 1278–1289.

Baldwin, D. A. (1991). Infants' contribution to the achievement of joint reference. *Child Development, 62*, 875–890.

Baldwin, D. A. (1993). Infants' ability to consult the speaker for clues to word reference. *Journal of Child Language, 20*, 395–418.

Baldwin, D. A. (1995). Understanding the link between joint attention and language. In C. Moore & P. Dunham (Eds.), *Joint attention: Its origins and role in development* (pp. 131–158). Hillsdale, NJ: Lawrence Erlbaum Associates.

Baldwin, D. A., Markman, E. M., Bill, B., Desjardins, R. N., Irwin, J. M., & Tidball, G. (1996). Infants' reliance on a social criterion for establishing word-object relations. *Child Development, 67*, 3135–3153.

Barton, M. E., & Tomasello, M. (1991). Joint attention and conversation in mother-infant-sibling triads. *Child Development, 62*, 517–529.

Bloom, L. (1993). *The transition from infancy to language: Acquiring the power of expression*. Cambridge, UK: Cambridge University Press.

Blum-Kulka, S., & Snow, C. E. (2002). *Talking to adults: The contribution of multiparty discourse to language acquisition*. Mahwah, NJ: Lawrence Erlbaum Associates.

Brown, P. (1998). Conversational structure and language acquisition: The role of repetition in Tzeltal. *Journal of Linguistic Anthropology, 8*, 197–221.

Bruner, J. S. (1975). The ontogenesis of speech acts. *Journal of Child Language, 2*, 1–19.

Bruner, J. S. (1983). *Child's talk: Learning to use language*. New York: Norton.

Bruner, J. S. (1995). From joint attention to the meeting of minds: An introduction. In P. J. Dunham & C. Moore (Eds.), *Joint attention: Its origins and role in development* (pp. 1–14). Hillsdale, NJ: Lawrence Erlbaum Associates.

Butterworth, G. (2001). Joint visual attention in infancy. In G. Bremner & A. Fogel (Eds.), *Blackwell handbook of infant development* (pp. 213–240). Malden, MA: Blackwell Publishers.

Carpenter, M., Nagell, K., & Tomasello, M. (1998). Social cognition, joint attention, and communicative competence from 9 to 15 months of age. *Monographs of the Society for Research in Child Development, 63*(4), 176.

Chavajay, P., & Rogoff, B. (1999). Cultural variation in management of attention by children and their caregivers. *Developmental Psychology, 35*, 1079–1090.

Crago, M. B., Allen, S. E. M., & Hough-Eyamie, W. P. (1997). Exploring innateness through cultural and linguistic variation. In M. Gopnik (Ed.), *The inheritance and innateness of grammars* (pp. 70–90). New York: Oxford University Press.

deLeon, L. (1998). The emergent participant: Interactive patterns in the socialization of Tzotzil (Mayan) infants. *Journal of Linguistic Anthropology, 8*, 131–161.

Dunham, P. J., Dunham, F. S., & Curwin, A. (1993). Joint-attentional states and lexical acquisition at 18 months. *Developmental Psychology, 29*, 827–831.

Dunn, J., & Shatz, M. (1989). Becoming a conversationalist despite (or because of) having an older sibling. *Child Development, 60*, 399–410.

Forrester, M. A. (1988). Young children's polyadic conversation monitoring skills. *First Language, 8*, 201–226.

Forrester, M. A. (1993). Affording social-cognitive skills in young children: The overhearing context. In D. J. Messer & G. J. Turner (Eds.), *Critical influences on child language acquisition and development* (pp. 40–61). New York: St. Martin's Press.

Hart, B., & Risley, T. R. (1995). *Meaningful differences in the everyday experience of young American children*. Baltimore, MD: P. H. Brookes.

Lieven, E. V. M. (1994). Crosslinguistic and crosscultural aspects of language addressed to children. In C. Gallaway & B. J. Richards (Eds.), *Input and interaction in language acquisition* (pp. 56–73). Cambridge, UK: Cambridge University Press.

Loveland, K. A., & Landry, S. H. (1986). Joint attention and language in autism and developmental language delay. *Journal of Autism & Developmental Disorders, 16,* 335–349.

Markus, J., Mundy, P., Morales, M., Delgado, C. E . F., & Yale, M. (2000). Individual differences in infant skills as predictors of child-caregiver joint attention and language. *Social Development, 9,* 302–315.

Morales, M., Mundy, P., Delgado, C. E. F., Yale, M., Messinger, D., Neal, R., & Schwartz, H. K. (2000). Responding to joint attention across the 6- through 24-month age period and early language acquisition. *Journal of Applied Developmental Psychology, 21,* 283–298.

Nelson, K. (1985). *Making sense: The child's acquisition of shared meaning*. New York: Academic Press.

Ochs, E. (1988). *Culture and language development: Language acquisition and language socialization in a Samoan village*. Cambridge, UK: Cambridge University Press.

Ochs, E., & Schieffelin, B. (1995). The impact of language socialization on grammatical development. In P. Fletcher & B. MacWhinney (Eds.), *The handbook of child language* (pp. 73–94). Cambridge, MA: Blackwell.

Oshima-Takane, Y. (1988). Children learn from speech not addressed to them: The case of personal pronouns. *Journal of Child Language, 15,* 95–108.

Oshima-Takane, Y. (1999). The learning of first and second person pronouns in English. In R. Jackendoff, P. Bloom, & K. Wynn (Eds.), *Language, logic, and concept: Essays in memory of John Macnamara* (pp. 373–409). Cambridge, MA: MIT Press.

Oshima-Takane, Y., Goodz, E., & Derevensky, J. L. (1996). Birth order effects on early language development: Do secondborn children learn from overheard speech? *Child Development, 67,* 621–634.

Rogoff, B. (1990). *Apprenticeship in thinking: Cognitive development in social context*. New York: Oxford University Press.

Rogoff, B., Mistry, J., Göncü, A., & Mosier, C. (1993). Guided participation in cultural activity by toddlers and caregivers. *Monographs of the Society for Research in Child Development, 58*(8), 179.

Rogoff, B., Paradise, R., Mejia Arauz, R., Correa-Chavez, M., & Angelillo, C. (2003). Firsthand learning through intent participation. *Annual Review of Psychology, 54,* 175–203.

Saffran, J. R., Newport, E. L., Aslin, R. N., Tunick, R. A., & Barrueco, S. (1997). Incidental language learning: Listening (and learning) out of the corner of your ear. *Psychological Science, 8,* 101–105.

Schieffelin, B.B. (1990). *The give and take of everyday life: Language socialization of Kaluli children*. Cambridge, UK: Cambridge University Press.

Schieffelin, B.B., & Ochs, E. (1983). A cultural perspective on the transition from prelinguistic to linguistic communication. In R. M. Golinkoff (Ed.), *The transition from prelinguistic to linguistic communication* (pp. 115–131). Hillsdale, NJ: Lawrence Erlbaum Associates.

Tomasello, M. (1995). Joint attention as social cognition. In C. Moore, P. Dunham, & J. Philip (Eds.), *Joint attention: Its origins and role in development* (pp. 103–130). Hillsdale, NJ: Lawrence Erlbaum Associates.

Tomasello, M. (2001). Perceiving intentions and learning words in the second year of life. In M. Tomasello & E. Bates (Eds.), *Language development: The essential readings* (pp. 111–128). Malden, MA: Blackwell Publishers.

Tomasello, M., & Barton, M. E. (1994). Learning words in nonostensive contexts. *Developmental Psychology, 30,* 639–650.

Tomasello, M., & Farrar, M. J. (1986). Joint attention and early language. *Child Development, 57,* 1454–1463.

Tomasello, M., & Todd, J. (1983). Joint attention and lexical acquisition style. *First Language, 4,* 197–211.

Trevarthen, C., & Aitken, K. J. (2001). Infant intersubjectivity: Research, theory, and clinical applications. *Journal of Child Psychology & Psychiatry & Allied Disciplines, 42,* 3–48.

Trevarthen, C., & Hubley, P. (1978). Secondary intersubjectivity: Confidence, confiding and acts of meaning in the first year. In A. Lock (Ed.), *Action, gesture, and symbol: The emergence of language* (pp. 183–229). New York: Academic Press.

Tronick, E. Z., Morelli, G. A., & Ivey, P. K. (1992). The Efe forager infant and toddler's pattern of social relationships: Multiple and simultaneous. *Developmental Psychology, 28,* 568–577.

Watson-Gegeo, K. A., & Gegeo, D. W. (1986). Calling-out and repeating routines in Kwara'ae children's language socialization. In B. B. Schieffelin & E. Ochs (Eds.), *Language socialization across cultures* (pp. 17–50). New York: Cambridge University Press.

Zukow-Goldring, P. (1995). Sibling caregiving. In M. H. Bornstein (Ed.), *Handbook of parenting, Vol. 3: Status and social conditions of parenting* (pp. 177–208). Mahwah, NJ: Lawrence Erlbaum Associates.

Chapter 8

Attachment, Theory of Mind, and Delay of Gratification*

Chris Moore
University of Toronto

Doug Symons
Acadia University

INTRODUCTION

The theme of this volume and of the conference on which it is based is the relation between developing cognition, communication, and the culture in which development occurs. This is a broad theme and inevitably to make statements with any degree of precision, one has to focus in further on some particular aspect of the general theme. In our most recent work, we have been most interested in

*The work reported in this paper was supported by a grant from the Social Sciences and Humanities Research Council of Canada to the first author. The authors are grateful to Sandra Bosacki, Angela Ellsworth, Karen Lemmon, Shannon Macgillivray, Shana Nichols, Carol Thompson, Katie Walker for their assistance on the studies. This work would not have been possible without the dedication of our participant families to whom we are especially grateful. Address for correspondence: Chris Moore, Department of Psychology, Dalhousie University, Halifax, NS, B3H 4J1, Canada; e-mail: chris.moore@dal.ca. or Doug Symons, Department of Psychology, Acadia University, Wolfville, Nova Scotia, Canada; e-mail: doug.symons@acadiau.ca.

two parallel aspects of development during the preschool period—theory of mind and what we have termed future oriented prudence and altruism (Thompson, Barresi, & Moore, 1997). The notion of theory of mind is well known and appears in a number of other contributions to this volume. For the purposes of the current work, we take theory of mind to be the understanding of representational mental states that develops at about 4 years of age. A standard array of experimental tasks is used for theory of mind assessment, including various forms of false belief task.

Also during the preschool period, children start to develop the capacity to regulate their behavior consciously with respect to future goals. The classic case of this is delay of gratification, studied in detail by Mischel and his colleagues (e.g., Mischel, 1974; Mischel, Shoda, & Rodriguez, 1989). However, behavioral regulation does not only occur in relation to the future goals of self, what we have called "future oriented prudence" (Thompson, Barresi, & Moore, 1997), it also is important in relation to the goals of others. Thus an important condition for prosocial behavior is the ability to inhibit behavior directed at achieving one's own immediate goals in favor of behavior directed at facilitating the achievement of others' goals. We have referred to this ability as "future oriented altruism" (Thompson et al., 1997).

In order to study the development of future oriented prudence and altruism, we developed a modified delay of gratification procedure (Thompson et al., 1997). To date, the bulk of the research on delay of gratification has measured how long children can wait for a larger reward in the face of a smaller immediate reward and the kinds of cognitive and affective strategies employed by children who are able to delay longer (see e.g., Mischel et al., 1989). We modified the delay task to a trial based format so that different kinds of delay could be assessed in tandem. Thus, in addition to trials in which we asked children to choose between one sticker (the reward) now and two stickers later, we included trials in which there was no benefit to self in delaying but there was a benefit to another person. For example, in some cases children had to choose between one sticker for themselves now and two stickers shared between self and a play partner later. Over a series of trials children were asked to make choices between options that differ in terms of material reward (e.g., one versus two stickers), the time when the reward will be delivered (e.g., now or later), and to whom the rewards would be given (self only versus shared between self and other). Rather than being a task about coping with delay (as is Mischel's), our task was about the kinds of decisions children make when asked to weigh the relative value of immediate versus delayed reward and the relative value of the interests of self versus the interests of others. Over a series of studies, we have found that as children develop the ability to delay their own gratification, they also become able to inhibit their own immediate interests in favor of the interests of another person (see Moore et al., 1998; Moore & Macgillivray, 2004; Thompson et al., 1997). In short, future oriented decision-making develops during the period between 3;6 and 4;6 years.

The 4-year transition is, of course, also the period during which significant change in theory of mind tasks occurs (see, e.g., many chapters in Astington, Harris, & Olson, 1988). Although performance on theory of mind tasks and on future oriented prudence and altruism measures develop closely in terms of age and indeed measures of performance on these two types of task are correlated (Moore et al., 1998), our results have demonstrated that they probably reflect separable aspects of social-cognitive development during the preschool years. For one thing, correlations between theory of mind and delay of gratification do not survive control for more general aspects of development, such as verbal ability (Moore & Macgillivray, 2004). In addition, there is residual individual variability on our future oriented decision-making tasks after the point in time at which performance on the standard false belief task is close to complete. We have argued that the variability among participants in theory of mind tasks around age 4 years essentially reflects developmental differences, or differences in the rate of development among children. In contrast, the variability in our delay of gratification measures reflects both developmental and individual differences. Normally developing children acquire the ability to regulate their behavior in favor of future goals also around 4 years, but the degree to which they exercise this ability probably shows individual variability throughout life (Moore & Macgillivray, 2004).

In recent years, significant research attention has turned to how social context may influence theory of mind development (e.g., Slomkowski & Dunn, 1996; Jenkins & Astington, 2000). We have started to take an interest in how one component of the social context in which the child develops may play a role in the differences that may exist in theory of mind and future oriented decision-making during the preschool period. That component is the quality of the relationship between the developing child and the parents. In adopting this focus, we are following the lead of a small number of authors who have pointed to the attachment relationship as a potential influence on the young child's developing social understanding (e.g., Fonagy & Target, 1997; Meins, 1997) and delay of gratification (e.g., Jacobsen, Huss, Fendrich, Kruesi, & Zeigenhain, 1997; Sethi, Mischel, Aber, Shoda, & Rodriguez, 2000). In this chapter, we review the work that has been carried out to date on the link between attachment and theory of mind and between attachment and delay of gratification during the preschool period and then go on to report our recent research on the topic.

ATTACHMENT AND THEORY OF MIND

Since the classic work on parent–child attachment by Bowlby (1969/1997) and Ainsworth (e.g., Ainsworth, Blehar, Walters, & Wall, 1978), an enormous literature on the nature, antecedents, and sequelae of different attachment qualities has grown (see Cassidy & Shaver, 1999). Attachment quality in early development has long been assumed to be of profound significance for functioning in relationships throughout life. In theory of mind research, there also has been an assumption that understanding mental states must impact on meaningful aspects of social behavior (Moore & Frye, 1991), although this link is usually thought of in terms of interactions rather than relationships, and such data are currently sparse (see Astington, 2003, for a review). Only relatively recently have these two dominant lines of research on early social development been brought together. So how do attachment and theory of mind connect?

The first researchers to investigate the possible link between attachment and ToM were Fonagy and his colleagues. In an initial study, Fonagy, Redfern, and Charman (1997) found a significant association between belief-desire reasoning in 3- to 6-year-olds and attachment score derived from the Separation Anxiety Test, a projective test of security of attachment. In a later study, Fonagy, Steele, Steele, and Holder (1998) assessed attachment security in the strange situation at 12 months with mothers and 18 months with fathers. The children were then tested on their understanding of belief-based emotion at 5 years. The results showed a significant predictive association between security of attachment with mothers at 12 months and theory of mind at 5 years, although predictive relations of child-father were less clear.

Fonagy and his colleagues (especially Fonafy, Steele, Steele, & Holder, 1997; Fonagy & Target, 1997) have argued that the emotional characteristics of the attachment relationship are key for theory of mind development. Although a number of links between attachment and theory of mind are possible in theory, Fonagy and colleagues favor the idea that attachment reflects a quality of child–parent relationship that generates theory of mind. Parents who engage in the kind of sensitive caregiving that generates secure attachment tend to act towards their children in such a way as to lead the child to construct mental models of their own and others' mental states. Within a secure attachment, the infant feels safe in attributing mental states to others and to self to account for behavior. Children who are insecure are less able to do this. For example, avoidant children tend to reject the other and are therefore less likely to use mental state attributions of the other's behavior, although whether this reflects an inability or an unwillingness is unclear.

Meins and colleagues (Meins, Fernyhough, Russell, & Clark-Carter, 1998) also investigated the link between attachment and ToM. Their rationale was not as psychodynamic in orientation as Fonagy and colleagues but dwelt more on the potential role of parents in providing an explicit reflective social environment for their children. In the tradition of Vygotsky, Meins et al. (1998) propose that talking about mental states in conversation would foster children's participation in discourse about mental states and this interpersonal awareness of mental states would then yield an intrapersonal awareness through internalization. Further, they suggest that such "mind-mindedness" on the part of parents would be associated with secure attachment on the part of their children as well as the development of later social understanding of children (see Meins, 1999).

Meins et al. (1998) followed up a group of children who had been assessed in the strange situation at 12 months and classified as secure or insecure. The children were tested on a variety of ToM tasks at 4 and 5 years. The ToM tasks included a standard object displacement false belief task as well as Harris et al.'s (1989) belief-based emotion task which tests children's understanding that emotions such as happy and sad depend on people's beliefs about the world. Their results showed that children classified as secure at 12 months were much more likely to pass the standard false belief task at 4 and tended to do better on the belief-based emotion task at 5 years.

Home-based observations of parent–child relationships have also been related to theory of mind. In Symons and Clark (2000), attachment security at age five assessed with the Attachment Security Q-sort (AQS, Waters, 1987) was concurrently related to an aggregate of three different kinds of false belief tasks (see Symons, 2001). Overall observer AQS security scores at age two did not predict theory of mind at age 5. However, the AQS can be partitioned into a number of subscales relevant to security (see Waters, Vaughn, Posada, & Kondo-Ikemura, 1995). In a recent reanalysis of these data (Symons, 2001), a subscale was created of 9 items related to presence of secure base behavior and an absence of avoidance. This index of security at age 2 modestly predicted theory of mind at age 5, even controlling for concurrent secure base behavior.

Finally, a study by Laible and Thompson (1998) related attachment security using the AQS to affective perspective taking, particularly understanding negative emotions. This study used the AQS as a self report measure by having mothers describe their infant's own behavior, given that the maternal AQS is highly related to the observer AQS (see Pederson et al., 1990; Teti & McGourty, 1996). Recent research by DeRosnay and Harris (2002) has concurrently related emotional understanding to attachment security assessed with the Separation Anxiety Test. These authors use family discourse as a way to explain how these two constructs are related, an idea initially proposed by Dunn, Brown, and Beardsall (1991).

In summary, there is evidence from a variety of studies that security of attachment is related to theory of mind. In particular, children rated as more secure perform better on theory of mind tasks assessing both belief and belief-based emotion understanding. The origin of this relation may well have two sides. First, mothers of secure children are more likely to communicate about mental states more than mothers of insecure children and thereby create a communicative environment in which theory of mind can flourish (Meins, 1999). Second, secure children may be less defensive and thus more able to take the perspectives of others. Most likely both processes are at play. However, it is worth pointing out that what is being suggested here is influence over the rate of development of theory of mind. In the end all normally developing children, acquire theory of mind at least to the level of false belief.

ATTACHMENT AND DELAY OF GRATIFICATION

To date, there has been only a small amount of research directly assessing the link between attachment and delay of gratification. All have used waiting time in a situation in which the child has to resist the temptation of an immediately available smaller reward in order to receive a larger reward some time later.

The first study to directly assess the association between attachment and delay of gratification was by Jacobsen, Huss, Fendrich, Kruesi, & Zeigenhain (1997). They hypothesized that because attachment had been implicated theoretically in children's self-regulation, there should be an association between attachment and delay of gratification. They assessed attachment in late infancy using the strange situation and at 6 years using Main and Cassidy's (1988) method of microanalytical coding of the child's behavior in response to a reunion after a laboratory separation from the mother. Both the infancy and 6-year attachment assessments were used to assign children to the standard attachment categories—secure, insecure-avoidant, insecure-ambivalent and disorganized. Delay of gratification was assessed using a standard procedure from Mischel (Mischel et al., 1989) with length of delay time up to 15 minutes used as the measure. Comparison of the delay times across the attachment categories showed significant differences when the categories were derived at the 6-year session (i.e., concurrently) and also when the overall categorization from all attachment assessments was used. The main difference was between secure children who waited the longest and disorganized children who waited the least amount of time.

Sethi et al. (2000) were interested in how the cognitive-affective challenges presented by maternal separation may relate to the challenges presented by delay of gratification situations. They assessed 18-month-olds' responsiveness to maternal separation episodes in a laboratory situation similar to the classic strange situation. In addition to assessing the infants' strategies for dealing with separations and reunion bids, they also measured the degree of intrusive control that mothers exerted when interacting with their infants. At about 5 years, the children were given a standard Mischel (Mischel et al., 1989) delay of gratification procedure where they had the choice between taking a less preferred reward immediately or waiting for a more preferred reward 15 minutes later. The time of delay was measured as well as various strategies employed during the delay period, including "cooling" strategies such as distracting themselves from the immediately available reward and "hot" strategies such as focusing on the immediate reward.

Sethi et al.'s (2000) results showed that the extent to which the children had been able to engage in distracting strategies such as playing with toys during the separation episodes at 18 months predicted the amount of time they were able to delay at 5 years. However, there appeared to be more than one route to successful delay behavior. Children who as toddlers had tended either to avoid the bids of their more controlling mothers or approach the bids of their less controlling mothers were able to employ more cooling strategies during delay of gratification and to wait longer. Sethi et al. (2000) conclude that there are continuities between how toddlers deal with frustrations in interactions with significant others and how they later manage frustrations in goal attainment as 5-year-olds.

In sum, the small amount of evidence available does support the idea that attachment quality is related to delay of gratification. The association appears to exist across time so that attachment in infancy predicts delay of gratification in 5- to 6-year-old children. Although the research has yet to be done, it is possible that these effects continue throughout life, so that attachment style remains associated with individual differences in delay of gratification.

ATTACHMENT, THEORY OF MIND AND FUTURE ORIENTED DECISION-MAKING

In a recent study we sought to extend our knowledge of the links among attachment security, theory of mind, and delay of gratification by examining all the factors together and by examining not only delay time but also future oriented decision-making. A sample of preschool children were first tested at 3.5 years and followed up at 4 years. At each age they were given various tasks but in this report we focus on a measure of security of attachment taken when the children were 3.5 years and measures of theory of mind and future-oriented prudence and altruism taken at 4 years. The sample consisted of 49 children for whom all measures were completed. The children were all white and from middle class two-parent families.

During the 3.5-year visit, while the child was engaged in tasks with an experimenter, the mother completed the Attachment Q-sort (AQS; Waters, 1987). The AQS was used for reasons of convenience and efficiency because of its acceptable validity as a measure of attachment security and appropriateness for children of this age range (see Symons, Clark, Isaksen, & Marshall, 1998). As a control measure of verbal intelligence, one of the tasks given to the children at 3.5 years was the Peabody Picture Vocabulary Test (PPVT-III; Dunn & Dunn, 1997).

The AQS consists of 90 cards, each with a one sentence descriptive statement about the child. Although initially developed for use by trained observers of the child, the AQS has been used with parents completing the sort. The original sentences were modified so that all made reference to "your child" instead of "the child" and "mother" was replaced by "you." Although the mothers were not given the cards in advance of the sort, the task was explained to them by an experimenter who also sat with them as they sorted to provide the opportunity for assistance. Mothers were first asked to sort the 90 cards into three piles ordered from most to least like her child ensuring that they had 30 cards in each pile. They were then told to subdivide each pile into three further piles such that they ended up with 10 cards in each of nine piles. The nine piles were ordered and each card was given a score corresponding to the pile in which it had been placed. Thus cards in the pile corresponding to 'least like' were given a score of 1 and so on up to cards in the pile corresponding to 'most like' which were given a score of 9. The maternal sort was then scored according to standard procedure using security loadings in Waters et al. (1995). In this way, each child ended up with a score that could in principle range from –1.0 (completely opposite to the ideal sort) to +1.0 (exactly the same as the ideal sort). In this study scores from the AQS were all positive except for one (–.62). The latter child was excluded from analyses as an extreme outlier. Descriptive statistics for the AQS are shown in Table 8.1.

At the 4-year visit, children were presented with theory of mind, future oriented prudence and altruism tasks, and a simple measure of the ability to delay gratification. The theory of mind tasks were presented in commonly used format and included a displaced object task, and two misleading objects tasks. The misleading object tasks were presented in both self and other formats (see e.g., Gopnik & Astington, 1988). For the displaced object task, there were two containers and two toy characters (Barney and Elmo toys). A toy car was hidden in one container by one character, who then left the scene. The other character then moved the car from the original container to the other container and left the scene. Finally, the first character returned and the child was asked the test question, "where will he look first for his car." One of the misleading objects tasks involved misleading contents. Initially a band-aid box was shown to the child and he or she was asked what was inside. After answering the child was shown that in fact there was a small book inside. The book was replaced in the box, which was then closed. The child was then asked what another child who had not seen inside would think was in the box and what he or she had originally thought was in the box. The other misleading object task involved a deceptive object, namely a flashlight that looked like a pen. The task has a similar format to the misleading contents box and test questions about both the child's own previous belief and the beliefs of a naive other were asked. Children were given a score of 1 for each test question answered correctly yielding a possible score ranging between 0 and 5 (one possible point for the displaced object task and two possible points each for the misleading object tasks). The descriptive statistics for the theory of mind measure are shown in Table 8.1.

Along with the theory of mind measure, we also assessed future oriented decision-making using the task previously developed to assess future oriented prudence and altruism (Thompson et al., 1997). For this task, an additional female experimenter, who had previously played with the child, sat with the participant as a play partner. The task was explained to the child as a game in which they would make choices for stickers. The various options were explained to the child and they were shown that if they chose to take stickers immediately they could put them in a sticker book in front of them whereas if they chose to delay the stickers would be placed in an envelope to be saved for later. Children were presented with three trials of each of three trial types. Trials were presented in three blocks with one trial type in each block. The three trial types were:

- Two for self now or two shared with partner (now sharing)
- Two for self now or two shared with partner later (future oriented sharing)
- One for self now or two for self later (future oriented prudence)

The order of the two options within each choice was varied across blocks. The number of times the child chose to delay or to share for each of the three trial types was recorded, thereby yielding a score between 0 and 3 for each. Descriptive statistics are shown in Table 8.1.

Finally, we also presented children with a simple assessment of their ability to delay gratification. As we noted above, our future oriented decision making task differs from the traditional assessment of delay of gratification introduced by Mischel (e.g., 1974). Unlike Mischel we have not focused on the amount of time children can delay nor on the strategies they use to achieve delay. Yet, as we previously reviewed, Mischel and his colleagues have shown a relation between delay time in their task and how children cope with maternal separations and reunions. We therefore felt it was important to include a measure of delay. For this measure, we adopted the 'gift delay' task used by Kochanska, Murray, Jacques, Koenig, and Vandegeest (1996). In our version, once children had completed all of the other tasks they were told that were to receive a gift. They were then asked to turn around to face a blank wall and not peek while their gift was wrapped behind them. The wrapping was done with much noisy crunching of tissue paper and lasted for 60 seconds. During this time, we coded whether the child peeked around and the time in seconds until they first peeked. Children who did not peek at all were given a score of 60. Descriptive statistics for the delay to peek are shown in Table 8.1.

Our main interest was in how attachment as assessed by the AQS would relate to the 4-year measures. Zero order correlations and partial correlations controlling for PPVT-III between AQS and all of the relevant measures are shown in Table 8.2. Attachment correlated positively with all of the measures and significantly so with theory of mind, future oriented prudence and delay to peek at the gift. These correlations were

TABLE 8.1 Descriptive Statistics for the Measures of Vocabulary, Attachment, Theory of Mind, Future Oriented Prudence and Altruism and Delay of Gratification

Measure	*Mean*	*Actual range*
Vocabulary (PPVT-III)	105.7	75–139
Attachment (AQS)	.419	.074–.711
Theory of mind	2.69	0–5
Future oriented decision making		
Now sharing	1.69	0–3
Future sharing	1.15	0–3
Prudence	1.33	0–3
Delay to peek (secs)	42.19	0–60

Note. $N = 48$.

TABLE 8.2 Zero Order and Partial Correlations Between Attachment Q-Sort and Measures of Theory of Mind, Future Oriented Decision-Making and Delay

	Correlation with Attachment Q-sort	
	Zero order	*PPVT-III partialled*
Theory of Mind	.315*	.210
Now Sharing	.123	.039
Future Sharing	.276	.144
Future Prudence	.353*	.278
Delay to Peek	.421*	.375*

Note. $N = 48$; $*p < .05$.

reduced in magnitude after controlling for vocabulary, with only that between attachment and delay to peek remaining significant at a conventional level. This finding provides corroboration of the results of Sethi et al. (2000) and supports the idea that the manner of coping in a delay of gratification situation has some consistency with the coping evident in interactional situations. The partial correlation between attachment and future oriented prudence just failed to reach the $p < .05$ level of significance.

Examination of the correlations among the various 4-year measures showed that whereas there were some significant associations among these measures (for more discussion of the link between theory of mind and future oriented altruism see Moore & Macgillivray, 2004), the variables that were associated with attachment were not significantly associated with each other. This pattern implied that further investigation into the structure of the attachment measure and its association with the other measures was warranted. Although the AQS was developed as an overall measure of attachment security, recent work on the measure has started to explore possible subcomponents (see Baily, Waters, Pederson, & Moran, 1999; Symons, 2001; Waters et al., 1995). In line with this approach, we identified items in the Q-set that appeared to be more related to sensitivity to others' psychological states and items that appeared to be more related to secure base behavior. Our reasoning was as follows. As is well-known, theory of mind is about how sensitive children are to the diversity that exists in mental states across individuals and within an individual over time. Such sensitivity is intimately connected to the representational nature of mental states. Certain Q-set items appear to tap into the sensitivity of the child to others' psychological states and we grouped these items into a social understanding subscale (see Table 8.3; Symons, 2001).

TABLE 8.3 Attachment Q-Sort Items in the Social Understanding and Secure Base Scales

Social Understanding Scale	*Secure Base Scale*
1. Readily shares with you or lets you hold things if you ask to.	14. When your child finds something new to play with, he or she carries it to you or shows it to you from across the room.
18. Follows your suggestions readily, even when they are clearly suggestions rather than orders.	21. Keeps track of your location when he or she plays around the house. Calls to you now and then; notices you go from room to room. Notices if you change activities.
42. Recognizes when you are upset. Becomes quiet or upset him or herself. Tries to comfort you; asks what is wrong etc.	*25. Is easy for you to lose track of when he or she is playing out of sight.
47. Will accept and enjoy loud sounds or being bounced around in play if you smile and show that it is supposed to be fun.	*35. Is independent of you. Prefers to play on his or her own; leaves you easily when wants to play.
48. Readily lets new adults hold or share things he or she has, if they ask to.	36. Clearly shows a pattern of using you as a base from which to explore. Moves out to play; returns or plays near her; moves out to play again.
60. If you reassure your child by saying, "It's OK," or "It won't hurt you," your child will approach or play with things that initially made him cautious or afraid.	*43. Stays close to you or returns to you more often than the simple task of keeping track of you requires.
80. Uses your facial expressions as a good source of information when something looks risky or threatening.	*59. When finishes with an activity or toy, he or she generally finds something else to do without returning to you between activities.
	80. Uses your facial expressions as a good source of information when something looks risky or threatening.
	90. If you move very far, your child follows along and continues play in the area you have moved to.

Note. * denotes items that are inverse scored.

We also reasoned that future oriented prudence has a connection to secure base behavior in that both reflect the confidence to explore the more distant possibilities presented. In the case of classic secure base behavior in the strange situation, the secure infant is able to explore at a greater spatial distance from the mother. In the case of future oriented prudence the child's willingness to choose the delayed option can be seen as confidence to explore possibilities that are at a greater temporal distance. Waters et al. (1995) have previously identified items in the AQS that appeared to be more related to secure base behavior (see Table 8.3) and we followed their lead in generating a secure base subscale.

The actual score on the two subscales for each child was calculated simply by adding the item scores together, after reversing the score (i.e., subtracting the score from 10) for those items that should be negatively scored for the construct (indicated by an asterisk in Table 8.3). In this way we generated the two AQS subscale scores. Cronbach's alphas were calculated for the two subscales and were rather low (social understanding subscale, alpha = .44; secure base subscale, alpha = .45). However, because both scales had shown decent reliabilities and been used in previous research, we correlated them with the 4-year measures (see Table 8.4).

The results revealed some clear differences in the patterns of correlations with a strong dissociation in the manner in which the attachment subscales related to the 4-year measures. Even after controlling for PPVT-III score, the secure base scale score was significantly associated with future oriented prudence. Similarly, the social understanding scale score was significantly correlated with theory of mind. In contrast, secure base score was not associated with theory of mind and social understanding score was not associated with future oriented prudence. In short, there was a double dissociation between the two attachment subscales and the theory of mind and future-oriented decision-making scores. Interestingly, the two subscales scores were about equally

TABLE 8.4 Zero Order Correlations and Partial Correlations Between AQS Subscales and Theory of Mind, Prudence, and Delay Scores.

	Social Understanding Scale		*Secure Base Scale*	
	Zero order	*PPVT-III partialled*	*Zero order*	*PPVT-III partialled*
Theory of Mind	.416*	.375*	.044	–.046
Future Prudence	.207	.153	.459*	.428*
Delay to Peek	.309*	.276	.294*	.260

Note. N = 48; *$p < .05$.

strongly associated with the delay to peek measure and neither correlation was quite significant at conventional levels after controlling for PPVT-III score.

Our results show clear relations between attachment as assessed by the AQS and theory of mind, future-oriented prudence and delay of gratification. These findings both complement and extend earlier research on these variables. With respect to theory of mind, earlier studies have shown security of attachment, assessed in different ways, to be a predictor of theory of mind development at about 5 years. Whether behaviorally assessed as infants in the strange situation or assessed through observation and report as infants or preschoolers, those children classified as more secure appear to be facilitated in theory of mind acquisition (Fonagy et al., 1997; Meins et al., 1998; Symons & Clark, 2000). Our results extend this relation to attachment security as assessed by maternal Attachment Q-Sort at 3.5 years. One novel aspect of our findings here was that it was the social understanding components of the AQS that appeared related to theory of mind. This makes perfect sense in that the sensitivity to the attachment figure's psychological states revealed in the AQS is consistent with enhanced reasoning about mental states in theory of mind tasks. As a result, it provides more support for the idea that theory of mind is worked out within the context of close family relationships (e.g., Dunn, 1988, 2000).

Of course, the causal relation between attachment quality and theory of mind remains unresolved from this work. A variety of causal links between attachment and theory of mind have been proposed (e.g., Meins et al., 2002). First, secure relationships may develop in the context of sensitive mothering and it is the latter aspect of the familial environment that is important in promoting the development of the child. Second, there appears to be a link between security of attachment and mothers who are more aware of their children's mental states and who reflect these states back to their children in their communication (Meins, 1997). According to Meins (1997), it is this maternal mind-mindedness that leads their children to the understanding of mental states. Consistent with the latter account, Meins et al. (2002) recently found that after taking into account variability due to the child's own language, it was the extent to which mothers talked about mental states with their children earlier in life that best predicted the children's success on theory of mind tasks at 4 years.

It is worth reiterating that the relatively robust relations that appear to exist between attachment and theory of mind are between individual differences in attachment on the one hand and developmental differences in acquisition of theory of mind on the other. But all normally developing children acquire a theory of mind in the sense of understanding false belief and related psychological states, so it is certainly not the case that secure attachment is a necessary feature of theory of mind development.

The pattern of relations between attachment and future oriented prudence and delay of gratification is more interesting from our point of view. There has been very little research on this issue, despite the demonstrated importance of delay of gratification for adaptive function (Shoda, Mischel, & Peake, 1990). What has been shown is that the ability to cope with the frustration of having to wait for a superior reward is related to the patterns of dealing with challenges to easy interactions with the attachment figure (Sethi et al., 2000). Our results support this idea in that the ability to delay peeking at a temporally prohibited rewarding sight was related to overall security of attachment as measured by the AQS. What is novel in our results is that security of attachment was also related to the relative weighting of present and future rewards as measured by our future oriented decision-making task. The children who tended to opt for the superior delayed reward in favor of the lesser immediate reward were rated by their mothers as particularly high on the secure base subscale of the AQS. Thus children who have an appropriate level of secure base behavior (i.e., use a secure base but are not overly distant or clinging) are the ones most likely to maximize their rewards by choosing the larger but delayed reward when offered. Our interpretation of this finding is that future oriented prudence can be seen in terms of secure base exploration in time. Choosing future rewards is like exploring mentally beyond the secure base of the present so that those children who are high on security are more able to take advantage of opportunities that distant in time as well as space.

This explanation assumes that secure base behavior and future oriented choices reflect similar tendencies to explore opportunities away from the immediate environment. Again, the causal relation between attachment and future oriented decision-making is unclear. However, it seems less obvious that maternal mind-mindedness is playing a role as has been argued in the case of theory of mind (Meins, 1997). Instead, we suggest that the emotional regulation facilitated in secure attachment relationships plays a role in choosing future rewards over immediate ones. Children who are less concerned over the emotional conditions of the immediate will be more able to balance future and current rewards and respond appropriately in situations where prudence is warranted.

An intriguing prediction of this interpretation is that future orientation should vary with the same kinds of variables that affect secure base exploration in space. It is known for example that stressors, including novel people and environments, tend to increase proximity and reduce exploration in infants (Ainsworth et al., 1978). As the infant begins to feel more comfortable with the originally novel people and environments, exploration occurs along with regular checking of the attachment figure. Our prediction would be that a similar shifting pattern of present to future orientation would occur under similarly stressful circumstances at least in children who are classified as securely attached.

Finally, it is worth pointing out that we were surprised to find no evidence linking the attachment measures to our measure of altruism. Attachment security is supposed to have implications for how children treat others (see Weinfeld, Sroufe, Egeland, & Carlson, 1999) but the overall AQS score was not significantly related to sharing. However, it is possible that the quality of the relationship with the mother as assessed by the AQS is not such a good predictor of how children will behave toward others with whom there is no established relationship, as is the case in our future oriented decision-making task (cf. Thompson, 1999).

To conclude, a growing body of research reveals that security of attachment is related both to theory of mind and to delay of gratification. Our work both supports findings from earlier research and goes further in showing that different components of the quality of the attachment relationship may be related to different aspects of the social-cognitive changes that occur around four years of age. In general, then, we can have confidence that continued exploration of the quality of family relationships in association with social understanding and behavioral control will yield further insights into the nature of the development of these abilities during the preschool period.

REFERENCES

Ainsworth, M. D., Blehar, M. C., Waters, E., & Wall, S. (1978). *Patterns of attachment: A psychological study of the strange situation.* Hillsdale, NJ: Lawrence Erlbaum Associates.

Astington, J. (2003). Sometimes necessary, never sufficient: False belief understanding and social competence. In B. Repacholi & V. Slaughter (Eds.), *Individual differences in theory of mind: Implications for typical and atypical development* (pp. 13–38). New York: Psychology Press.

Astington, J., Harris, P., & Olson, D. (1988). (Eds.). *Developing theories of mind.* New York: Cambridge University Press.

Baily, H. N., Waters, C. A., Pederson, D. R., & Moran, G. (1999). Ainsworth revisited: An empirical analysis of interactive behavior in the home. *Attachment & Human Development, 1,* 191–216.

Bowlby, J. (1969/1997). *Attachment and loss: Attachment. Vol 1.* (2nd ed.) New York: Basic.

Cassidy, J., & Shaver, P. R. (1999). *Handbook of attachment: Theory, research, and clinical applications.* New York: The Guilford Press.

DeRosnay, M., & Harris, P. (2002). Individual differences in children's understanding of emotion: The roles of attachment and language. *Attachment and Human Development, 4,* 39–54.

Dunn, J. (1988). *The beginnings of social understanding*. Cambridge, MA: Harvard University Press.

Dunn, J. (2000). Mind-reading, emotion understanding, and relationships. *International Journal of Behavioral Development, 24,* 142–144.

Dunn, J., Brown, J., & Beardsall, L. (1991). Family talk about feeling states and children's later understanding of others' emotions. *Developmental Psychology, 27,* 448–455.

Dunn, L., & Dunn, L. (1997). *Manual for the Peabody Picture Vocabulary Test-III*. Circle Pines, MN: American Guidance Service.

Fonagy, P., Redfern, S., & Charman, T. (1997). The relationship between belief-desire reasoning and a projective measure of attachment security (SAT). *British Journal of Developmental Psychology, 15,* 51–61.

Fonagy, P., Steele, H., Steele, M., & Holder, J. (1997). Attachment and theory of mind: Overlapping constructs? *Bonding and Attachment, 14,* 31–41.

Fonagy, P., Steele, M., Steele, H., & Holder, J. (1998). Children securely attached in infancy perform better in belief-desire reasoning task at age five. Unpublished manuscript.

Fonagy, P., & Target, M. (1997). Attachment and reflective function: Their role in self-organization. *Development and Psychopathology, 9,* 679–700.

Gopnik, A., & Astington, J. W. (1988). Children's understanding of representational change and its relation to the understanding of false belief and the appearance-reality distinction. *Child Development, 59,* 26–37.

Harris, P. L., Johnson, C. N., Hutton, D., Andrews, G., & Cooke, T. (1989). Young children's theory of mind and emotion. *Cognition & Emotion, 3,* 379–400.

Jenkins, J. M., & Astington, J. W. (2000). Theory of mind and social behavior: Causal models tested in a longitudinal study. *Merrill-Palmer Quarterly, 46,* 203–220.

Jacobsen, T., Huss, M., Fendrich, M., Kruesi, M., & Zeigenhain, U. (1997). Children's ability to delay gratification: Longitudinal relations to mother-child attachment. *Journal of Genetic Psychology, 158,* 411–426.

Kochanska, G., Murray, K., Jacques, T., Koenig, A., & Vandegeest, K. (1996). Inhibitory control in young children and its role in emerging internalization. *Child Development, 67,* 490–507.

Laible, D. J., & Thompson, R. A. (1998). Attachment and emotional understanding in preschool children. *Developmental Psychology, 34,*1038–1045.

Main, M., & Cassidy, J. (1988). Categories of response with the parent at age six: Predicted from infant attachment classifications and stable over a one month period. *Developmental Psychology, 24,* 415–426.

Meins, E. (1997). *Security of attachment and the social development of cognition*. Hove, UK: Psychology Press.

Meins, E. (1999). Sensitivity, security, and internal working models: Bridging the transmission gap. *Attachment and Human Development, 1,* 325–342.

Meins, E., Fernyhough, C., Russell, J., & Clark-Carter, D. (1998). Security of attachment as a predictor of symbolic and mentalising abilities. *Social Development, 7,* 1–24.

Meins, E., Fernyhough, C., Wainwright, R., Das Gupta, M., Fradley, E., & Tuckey, M. (2002). Maternal mind-mindedness and attachment security as predictors of theory of mind understanding. *Child Development, 73,* 1715–1726.

Mischel, W. (1974). Processes in delay of gratification. In L. Berkowitz (Ed.), *Advances in experimental social psychology: Vol. 7* (pp. 249–292). New York: Academic Press.

Mischel, W., Shoda, Y., & Rodriguez, M. (1989). Delay of gratification in children. *Science, 244,* 933–938.

Moore, C., Barresi, J., & Thompson, C. (1998). The cognitive basis of prosocial behavior. *Social Development, 7,* 198–218.

Moore, C., & Frye, D. (1991). The acquisition and utility of theories of mind. In D. Frye & C. Moore (Eds.), *Children's theories of mind. Mental states and social understanding* (pp. 1–10). Hillsdale, NJ: Lawrence Erlbaum Associates.

Moore, C., & Macgillivray, S. (2004). Altruism, prudence, and theory of mind in preschoolers. In J. Baird & B. Sokol (Eds.), *Connections Between Theory of Mind and Sociomoral Development. New directions for child and adolescent development* Issue 103 (pp. 51–62). Jossey-Bass.

Pederson, D., Moran, G., Sitko, C., Campbell, K., Ghesquire, K., & Acton, H. (1990). Maternal sensitivity and security of mother-infant attachment. *Child Development, 61,* 1974–1983.

Sethi, A., Mischel, W., Aber, J., Shoda, Y., & Rodriguez, M. (2000). The role of strategic attention deployment in development of self-regulation: Predicting preschoolers' delay of gratification from mother-toddler interactions. *Developmental Psychology, 36,* 767–777.

Shoda, Y., Mischel, W., & Peake, P. (1990). Predicting adolescent cognitive and self-regulatory competencies from preschool delay of gratification. Identifying diagnostic conditions. *Developmental Psychology, 26,* 978–986.

Slomkowski, C., & Dunn, J. (1996). Young children's understanding of other people's beliefs and feelings and their connected communication with friends. *Developmental Psychology, 32,* 442–447.

Symons, D. (2001, August). Mother-infant relationship harmony and theory of mind development: The roles of sensitive parenting and attachment security. Paper presented at the Xth European Conference on Developmental Psychology, Stockholm Sweden.

Symons, D., & Clark, S. (2000). A longitudinal study of mother-child relationships and Theory of Mind in the preschool period. *Social Development, 9,* 3–23.

Symons, D., Clark, S., Isaksen, G., & Marshall, J. (1998). Stability of Q-sort attachment security from age two to five. *Infant Behavior and Development, 21,* 785–792.

Teti, D., & McGourty, S. (1996). Using mothers versus trained observers in assessing children's secure base behavior: Theoretical and methodological considerations. *Child Development, 67,* 597–605.

Thompson, C., Barresi, J., & Moore, C. (1997). The development of future-oriented prudence and altruism in preschoolers. *Cognitive Development, 12,* 199–212.

Thompson, R. (1999). Early attachment and later development. In J. Cassidy & P. Shaver (Eds.), *Handbook of attachment* (pp. 265–286). New York: Guilford Press.

Waters, E. (1987). *Attachment Behavior Q-set, Revision 3.0.* Unpublished, State University of New York at Stony Brook.

Waters, E., Vaughn, B., Posada, G., & Kondo-Ikemura, K. (Eds.) (1995). Caregiving, cultural, and cognitive perspectives on secure-base behavior and working models: New growing points of attachment theory and research. *Monographs of the Society for Research in Child Development, 60*(2–3, Serial No. 244).

Weinfeld, N., Sroufe, L., Egeland, B., & Carlson, E. (1999). The nature of individual differences in infant-caregiver attachment security. In J. Cassidy & P. Shaver (Eds.), *Handbook of attachment* (pp. 68–88). New York: Guilford Press.

Part III

Theory of Mind and Pedagogy

Teaching and learning epitomize the interconnectedness of communication and cognition. Teaching is communication that is explicitly intended to change the cognitions of a learner. The decision to teach someone something is based on a belief about that person's knowledge: We teach either because we believe that a person does not know something or because we believe that they have a false belief. Similarly, learners seek out instruction when they recognize their own ignorance or false belief. Furthermore, children learn quite early on to seek out information from the person that they think will be most likely to know the answers to their questions. The importance of social and cognitive factors in learning means that as children's cognitive and communicative skills improve, more complex modes of teaching and learning become possible. At the same time, complex modes of cognition and social interaction require learning on the part of children.

The three chapters in this section examine the interconnectedness of cognitive and communicative factors in teaching and learning. The first two chapters draw on concepts from research on children's theory of mind. Developing a theory of mind allows children to understand that people have beliefs about the world, which are sometimes false, and that people's actions are based on their beliefs. Theory of mind has been linked both theoretically and empirically to developments in children's communication, particularly linguistic developments. In their chapter,

Astington and Pelletier provide an overview of the mutual influences of theory of mind and language in early childhood. They argue that theory of mind and language development are integrally linked and together play a formative role in children's readiness for success in school. Frye and Ziv follow with a chapter on children's understanding of the intentional nature of teaching. They argue that the theory of mind construct provides a unique framework for analyzing children's understanding of the teaching process and they present a series of studies on 3- and 5-year-olds' understanding of the nature of teaching. Finally, in her chapter, Goldin-Meadow examines the potential use of gesture to facilitate teaching. She argues that gesture is a rich source of information and can play an important role in the learning process by providing indicators of when students are ready for cognitive change.

LANGUAGE, THEORY OF MIND AND SCHOOL READINESS

In their chapter entitled, *Theory of Mind, Language, and Learning in the Early Years: Developmental Origins of School Readiness*, Astington and Pelletier explore the interconnectedness of language and theory of mind in relation to children's learning. The authors point out that developments in both theory of mind and language are multifaceted and mutually influential throughout development. During early infancy, for example, awareness of other minds facilitates children's acquisition of language by allowing infants to connect spoken words to people's intentions. Later in development, language facilitates theory of mind development by providing a means for children to understand the actions and intentions of others. Astington and Pelletier review theoretical work that links the evolution of theory of mind and the development of more complex modes of teaching and learning (e.g., collaborative learning). The authors point out that developments in teaching and learning depend on the acquisition of a more sophisticated mentalistic language, and developing this metacognitive language is vital for advancing children's theory of mind.

Astington and Pelletier next examine the ways in which developments in language and theory of mind influence children's school readiness. Although children arrive at school with a great deal of understanding about thinking and learning, their knowledge is rather contextually dependent and embedded in everyday experiences. Success at school requires a more advanced understanding of the mind and of how knowledge is acquired. The authors conclude by presenting data from a recent longitudinal study that tracks children's theory of mind and metacognitive language as predictors of school readiness and success. They demonstrate how language and theory of mind influence children's abilities in a number of domains, including early reading, narrative understanding, scientific thinking and social competence.

THEORY OF MIND AND UNDERSTANDING THE INTENTIONALITY OF TEACHING

In their chapter entitled, *Teaching and Learning as Intentional Activities*, Frye and Ziv explore children's understanding of the intentional nature of teaching. They ask, when do children understand teachers' intentions and does this understanding alter how children participate in and benefit from the teaching process? The authors argue that children's theory of mind offers a new approach to explore these questions. In particular, with the acquisition of a theory of mind comes an appreciation of differences in self-other knowledge that is essential for understanding the reasons for teaching. Although it is not necessary to understanding teaching in order to benefit from it, not understanding teaching means that children cannot recognize "teaching moments", which may limit their contributions to the social exchange that constitutes teaching and learning.

To test their theories, Frye and Ziv conducted a series of studies on 3- and 5-year-olds' understanding of teaching. They found that both 3- and 5-year-olds understand that a person with knowledge is the one who should teach and that the person without knowledge is the one who should be taught. However, the younger children did not understand the behaviors of a teacher who tried to teach someone because the teacher had a false-belief about the learner's knowledge state, and both 3- and 5-year-olds had trouble understanding the intentional aspects of teaching. The authors conclude that educational practices should take advantage of our growing knowledge about children's understanding of the teaching process.

INTERPRETING GESTURE TO FACILITATE COGNITIVE CHANGE

In her chapter entitled, *Gesture in Social Interactions: A Mechanism for Cognitive Change*, Goldin-Meadow argues that gesture provides insight into speakers' thoughts, which can provide valuable information for bringing about cognitive change. Goldin-Meadow summarizes some of her previous work in which she has found that children who are on the cusp of a conceptual change will often display a mismatch between the information they provided in their verbal explanations and the information that they convey in their gestures. She then asks two important questions: Do children exhibit this "mismatch" in "real world" settings and can teachers "read" this mismatch in order to facilitate cognitive change.

To answer the first question, Goldin-Meadow provides evidence that children often convey information in their gestures that does not match the information contained in their verbal utterances. For example, Goldin-Meadow and her colleagues have found that prior to the emergence of two-word speech, children who combine gestures with words to provide non-redundant information are the first children to transition to two-word speech. Children's gesture, therefore, provides an indication of whether they are ready for cognitive change. Goldin-Meadow next asks if adults take advantage of this information when teaching children. She presents data from a study of teachers helping children learn to solve math problems. The teachers altered their teaching techniques as a function of the mismatch between the verbal response and gesture of the students. For example, teachers presented a greater variety of problem-solving solutions to those children who had a verbal/gesture mismatch. Goldin-Meadow concludes that gesture mediates the social interaction of teaching and learning in important ways and can be a critical tool for teaching children new concepts.

SUMMARY

The three chapters in this section provide examples of how developments in cognitive and communicative abilities alter children's participation in the teaching and learning process. As children come to know about the mind, they understand that the purpose of teaching is to change someone's beliefs. A greater understanding of teaching enables children to identify who needs to be taught, who can teach, and what constitutes good teaching. Also, as children's communicative skills develop, they are able to use both gesture and speech to influence their teachers, which transforms teaching and learning into an interactive process. As a whole, these chapters provide insight into the dynamic interactions between cognition, communication, and learning during children's development.

Chapter 9

Theory of Mind, Language, and Learning in the Early Years: Developmental Origins of School Readiness*

Janet Wilde Astington
Janette Pelletier
University of Toronto

For the past 2 decades, children's theory of mind has been a lively area of research in developmental cognitive science, investigating children's ability to interpret human behavior within a mentalistic explanatory framework. Initially, in the 1980s, research focused on demonstrating normative changes in preschool children's understanding of mental states, particularly as seen in their performance on experimental false-belief tasks. In the 1990s a new focus developed, investigating individual differences in theory-of-mind development, and the antecedents, correlates, and sequelae of this development. This

*We are grateful to the Social Sciences and Humanities Research Council of Canada, and the Natural Sciences and Engineering Research Council of Canada, for financial support for the research reported here. We are also grateful to Carla Baetz, Sandra Bosacki, Bruce Homer, Trudy James, Deepthi Kamawar, Barbara Schuster, and Jessica Sommerville for their assistance with the longitudinal project.

work broadened the scope of the research, extending the age range downwards into infancy and upwards into the school years, and expanding the field into areas such as children's emotion understanding, pretend abilities, narrative skills, and moral reasoning. Findings from these more recent investigations have shown that there is a strong relation between theory of mind and language in development. The nature and import of this relationship is currently a topic of vigorous debate (see Astington & Baird, 2005-b).

In the present chapter we explore one facet of this debate by examining the interconnection of language and theory of mind in relation to children's learning in the early years. We first discuss the interdependent nature of the relation between theory of mind and language in development. We then consider how developments in these two areas are linked to children's learning in the early years, first presenting a theoretical account of the relations among theory of mind, language, learning and teaching. This leads into a discussion of theory of mind as a developmental pathway towards school readiness, and a consideration of individual differences in theory-of-mind development at the time of transition to school. We focus on four specific areas: early reading, narrative development, scientific thinking, and social competence. We conclude by arguing that theory of mind is an important part of the developmental origins of readiness for school.

THEORY OF MIND AND LANGUAGE

The relation between language and theory of mind is complicated because both are multifaceted and because their development is intertwined. Language competence includes both lexical and syntactic knowledge and also the ability to express and interpret intended meanings in communicative exchanges. Theory-of-mind competence includes awareness of mental states (e.g., attention, perception, desire, intention, emotion, knowledge, belief) and the ability to use this awareness in interpreting, explaining, and predicting the behavior of self and others. Thus, because of the many facets of both language and theory of mind, there are many possibilities for their interconnection. There is now a burgeoning literature showing the interdependence of language and theory of mind in development.

The early reciprocal relation between theory of mind and language can be seen in infancy. For example, joint attention behaviors, developing at the end of the first year, underlie the acquisition of first words and the first awareness of others' mental states, although there is controversy over whether 12-month-olds actually are aware of other minds

(Moore, 1998; Tomasello, 1999). However, by 18 months of age, the child's recognition of speakers' referential intentions allows for accurate mapping of word-referent relations (Baldwin, 1993). At this early stage, theory-of-mind abilities facilitate language development. From this point on, language develops rapidly and is instrumental in the further development of theory of mind. In other words, initially language development requires a rudimentary theory-of-mind understanding in order to connect language to people's actions and intentions. Subsequent theory-of-mind development then requires language in order to understand actions and intentions at more advanced levels. For example, 2- and 3-year-old children acquire lexical terms to refer to mental states (Bartsch & Wellman, 1995), as adults use these terms to talk about the child's own and other people's mental states, allowing the child to map others' experience onto their own (Astington, 1996). Importantly, during this period, children's conversational skills develop. Conversation is of major importance in children's learning about others' beliefs, both *that* they have beliefs, as well as *what* those beliefs are about (Harris, 1996). Thus it is through language that children both learn about minds and begin to communicate about them.

The interrelation of language and theory of mind becomes more complex during the preschool years. There has been a focus of research on the period around 4 years of age, when children first understand that people may believe things that are not true, as evidenced by their successful performance on experimental false-belief tasks. In the classic task (Wimmer & Perner, 1983) the child has to predict where someone will look for an object that the child sees moved to a new location, but the person does not see it moved. In another frequently used task (Perner, Leekam, & Wimmer, 1987) the child has to predict what someone will say is inside a familiar container, such as a candy box, when the child has seen that the box contains pencils, not the expected candies, but the other person has not yet seen inside the box. In a variant of this procedure (Gopnik & Astington, 1988), children are asked to remember their own false belief, that is, what they thought was in the box before they looked inside it. Correct performance on these tasks depends on the child's understanding that people represent, and may sometimes misrepresent the world, and that it is people's representation of the world that determines what they say or do. For this reason, some researchers call the 4-year-olds' theory of mind a "representational theory of mind" (Perner, 1991). An important question concerns the precise aspects of language that children require in order to manage this level of representation (Astington & Baird, 2005a).

A number of studies using a range of false-belief and language measures has shown a relation between the two (Cutting & Dunn, 1999; de Villiers, 2000; Happé, 1995; Hughes, 1998; Jenkins & Astington, 1996).

One can simplify the false-belief task by simplifying its linguistic demands (Freeman, Lewis, & Doherty, 1991) but omitting language altogether in nonverbal tasks does not improve performance (Call & Tomasello, 1999; de Villiers, 2000). During this period it appears that language abilities facilitate theory-of-mind development. Astington and Jenkins (1999) have shown that changes in children's theory of mind in the preschool period are predicted by children's language competence, but there is no reciprocal relation, that is to say, language development is not predicted by theory-of-mind test scores. Further evidence for a causal link is provided by studies of deaf children and children with autism, whose language development and false-belief understanding are both delayed (de Villiers, 2000; Tager-Flusberg, 2000). Importantly, verbal ability appears to be the crucial factor determining if and when these children do pass false-belief tasks (de Villiers, 2000; Happé, 1995). Taken altogether, these findings support the idea that language development precedes and promotes theory-of-mind development during the preschool years.

The close association of language and theory of mind continues in the beginning school years, when children become able to deal with more complex representations that require double embeddings, for example, "He thinks that she thinks that ..."—such beliefs about beliefs are referred to as second-order beliefs. Research has shown that around 6 years of age children become able to represent and reason from second-order beliefs (Perner & Wimmer, 1985; Sullivan, Zaitchik, & Tager-Flusberg, 1994). Moreover, second-order belief understanding is as highly correlated with language ability as is first-order understanding (Astington, Pelletier, & Homer, 2002). Indeed, children with higher general language scores perform better on both first- and second-.order theory-of-mind tasks independent of non-verbal intelligence.

In the next section of the chapter we consider how these developments in theory of mind are linked to children's learning in the early years. We begin with an overview on learning and its relation to theory of mind. We then discuss how theory of mind is related to learning in the early school years.

THEORY OF MIND, LEARNING, AND TEACHING

Learning in a broad sense, that is, modifying behavior as a result of experience to acquire new skills and knowledge, begins even in utero (Hepper & Shahidullah, 1994). Subsequently, infants and children engage in social learning, in which the experience is provided by the social environment and much is learned observationally through modeling

(Bandura, 1986). Here, we are concerned with a particular type of social learning, referred to as cultural learning (Tomasello, Kruger, & Ratner, 1993). Learning often, although not necessarily, implies teaching, and researchers have linked the forms of learning described by Tomasello et al. to different forms of teaching, that is, to different pedagogical approaches (Olson & Astington, 1993a; Olson & Bruner, 1996).

The argument for the necessity of language in theory-of-mind development may be made clearer by considering teaching and learning among non-human species. Many animal species learn but only the human species teaches, or so a number of researchers would have us believe. Caro and Hauser (1992) provide a definition of teaching that does not require inferences about intentions to teach, but simply judges that teaching has occurred based on observable features of the interaction between two animals. That is, they say, teaching occurs if one animal modifies its behavior only in the presence of another, with no benefit to itself, encouraging, punishing, providing experiences for, or setting examples to the other, resulting in the other's acquisition of new knowledge or skill which it would not easily, if at all, acquire otherwise. In light of this definition, Visalberghi and Fragaszy (1996) examine supposed episodes of teaching in non-human primates and conclude that, although in many cases the social context supports individual learning, there is no good evidence of deliberate teaching. Likewise, Premack and Premack (1996) show that, despite the presence of a few examples of complex teacher-like behavior in laboratory-raised chimpanzees, only humans engage in real teaching episodes. They argue that chimpanzees have sufficient cognitive capacity to teach but lack the motivation to do so that exists in humans.

On the other hand, other researchers are more sanguine about the possibility of teaching in non-humans. Russon (1997), also citing Caro and Hauser's (1992) definition, concludes, in contrast to Visalberghi and Fragaszy, that "under this definition, some non-human primates teach" (Russon, 1997, p. 195). Caro and Hauser's own conclusion is that non-human primates do teach by providing others, usually their offspring, with opportunities to learn, even though more deliberate pedagogical techniques, such as shaping the other's behaviors using reinforcement or modelling the desired behavior, occur only rarely. Parker (1996) and Boesch (1996) also provide examples of what they describe as true teaching in chimpanzees and other great apes. It is evident that the area is controversial, to say the least. Call and Tomasello (1996), for example, are less inclined to give a pedagogic interpretation to the very same behaviors described by Parker and Boesch.

However this debate is resolved, it is clear that teaching is rare in non-humans, even if it is possible. Boesch (citing Olson & Astington, 1993a) counters the suggestion that primate teaching is unimportant because of its rarity with the argument that even in humans the amount of teaching differs among cultural groups and may be altogether absent in some groups. However, we did not say, as Boesch suggests that we did, that there is no teaching at all in some hunter-gatherer societies, such as the !Kung. The point we wanted to make was not that teaching does not occur in some cultures, but rather that different human societies go about teaching their young in different ways. It is the traditional Western didactic model that is not universal. Even in Western cultures, although didactic teaching is universal in schooling, there is more variability during the preschool years (Heath, 1983). Teaching does occur in all societies but it takes different forms in different social groups (Heath, 1986).

Thus, let us qualify the statement made at the beginning of this section: Many animal species learn, a very few might teach though rarely, but the human species regularly and universally teaches its young. Now to continue: Many animal species mentally represent objects and events, and many animal species communicate with conspecifics. However, only humans use the same system for both representing and communicating, that is, human language. Why might this be? That is, why do we find no language and no teaching in non-humans, and language and teaching together in humans? On our view, language, teaching, and theory of mind are intricately intertwined. In many instances teaching depends on language, but more fundamentally, both language and teaching depend on initial developments in theory of mind. However, equally important, later developments in theory of mind depend on language, and furthermore, new ways of teaching exploit these new levels of theory-of-mind development (Tomasello et al., 1993) and new levels of linguistic competence (Astington & Pelletier, 1996). Let us spell this out in more detail.

Cultural Learning

During the early years, language and theory of mind develop together and support one another to different degrees during different developmental stages, as previously described. Moreover, as these abilities develop, children become capable of different kinds of cultural learning, and are able to participate in different kinds of teaching/learning episodes. In an important paper, Tomasello et al. (1993) relate evolutionary developments in theory of mind to the evolution of culture. They conceive of the accumulation of culture as the product of cultural learning, a special kind of social learning which they say is dependent on understanding mental states in others. It depends on learning *through* another not just *from* another. By this Tomasello et al. mean that the learner is aware of the other's perspective and does not just copy the other's behavior or speech. This type of social learning thus depends on the learner's conception of the other's mind, which is what allows the learner to take the perspective of the other. Tomasello et al. describe three different levels of perspective-taking that enable children to participate in three different types of learning episodes.

The ability to take the other's visual perspective, as in joint attention and social referencing during infancy, allows children to understand people as intentional agents (he is trying to do *x*), which enables them to learn by imitation. The ability to contrast the other's conceptual perspective with one's own, as seen in false-belief tasks, allows the preschool child to understand people as mental agents (he thinks that *p*), which enables them to learn from instruction. The ability to integrate the other's perspective with one's own, as seen in second-order belief attribution, allows children to understand people as reflective agents (he thinks that I think that *p*), which enables them to learn collaboratively during the early school years. Tomasello et al. argue that as children develop these forms of understanding—at 9 months, 4 years, and 6 years, respectively—they become capable of the corresponding form of learning. In our commentary (Olson & Astington, 1993a) we distinguished between the learner's understanding of mind and that required by the teacher, specifically, the teacher's conception of the learner's mind. At the first level, in deliberately providing a model for imitation, the teacher recognizes the learner's inability (he does not know how to do *x*). Second, in order to instruct a learner, that is, to provide information, the teacher must recognize the learner's ignorance or false belief (he does not know that *p*). Third, collaborative learning requires both teacher and learner to reflect on the other's thoughts (he thinks that I think that *p*). It is important to note that higher forms of teaching do not necessarily replace earlier forms; rather they may be added on to earlier forms of teaching as children become developmentally ready to be taught at each level.

Olson and Bruner (1996; see also Bruner, 1996, chap. 2) extend this model by integrating folk psychology (that is, everyday conceptions of mind), with folk epistemology (that is, understanding what it is to know something and how one comes to know it), and with folk pedagogy (that is, ideas about how children learn and how they should be taught). They distinguish among four folk models of mind that they relate to four conceptions of what knowledge is and to four different modes of teaching and learning. They adopt Tomasello et al.'s (1993) developmental progression from the ability to learn by imitation, then via instruction, and then collaboratively, although they extend Tomasello et al.'s notion of collaborative learning as learning between peers, to include children's learning from adult teachers when this occurs via discourse and debate. Further, they add a fourth level: the ability to learn by participation in Popper's (1972) World Three culture of "justified knowledge", that which is based on evidence. This final level allows children to acquire objective knowledge from text, a step beyond knowledge based on personally held beliefs and opinions (Olson & Bruner, 1996).

We (Astington & Pelletier, 1996) added to Olson and Bruner's (1996) model the idea that the developmental progression is premised on the development of language, particularly the development of an increasingly explicit and sophisticated mentalistic or metalinguistic language. First, learning by imitation can be carried out without language. Second, learning by instruction requires the ability to comprehend language, to talk about the world, but requires no talk about the mind. Third, learning collaboratively requires a mentalistic language in order to talk about mutual understandings and misapprehensions. Terms are required to refer to one's own and one's partner's mental states. Fourth, learning from text also requires a mentalistic language. However, as well as mental state terms, it also requires metalinguistic terms (specifically, speech act terms) in order to distinguish what the author said from what he or she meant by it. This is important because authors, who may be far away or even no longer alive, cannot be questioned directly in the way that discourse partners can be during collaborative learning episodes.

This proposed sequence fits with data on linguistic development. Infants at first engage in intentional communication and imitation before they have any verbal language. Indeed, this is how both language and awareness of other minds are acquired. Second, the first words learned are concrete nouns, action verbs, and function words, with no mental terms initially. That is, children can talk about the world but not about the mind. Third, during the preschool years children begin to use a range of mental verbs (*want, like, think, know, guess, remember,* etc.). The age of acquisition does not quite fit Tomasello et al.'s model here, in that the child uses mental verbs before 4 years of age, but on their view he or she does not have a concept of the person as mental agent and engage in instructed learning before age 4. However, it is the case that the precise use of mental terms such as *think,* to explain actions based on mistaken beliefs, does not appear until about age 4 (Bartsch & Wellman, 1995) when children can perform correctly on false-belief tasks. Fourth, children use few speech act verbs until the school years: only *say, ask* and *tell* (and *ask/tell* are misunderstood until the school years; Chomsky, 1969). Speech act verbs are acquired throughout the school years (e.g., *promise, predict,* Astington, 1988; *assert, deny, concede, imply, confirm,* etc., Astington & Olson, 1990).

We (Astington & Pelletier, 1996) argue that this sequence also fits with data on children's understanding of teaching and learning. We have some preliminary evidence from a small study indicating that children first refer to teaching as showing, then telling, then helping, that is, collaborating. Moreover, children conceive of teaching as "showing" when they have no understanding of the other as a mental agent, that is, when they fail first-order false belief tasks. They understand teaching as "telling" when they acquire this understanding, that is, when they pass first-order false belief tasks. Then they understand teaching as "collaborating" when they understand the other as a reflective agent, that is, when they pass second-order false-belief tasks. Although we propose that children cannot conceptualize teaching as instruction or as collaboration before they have reached a certain level of understanding of mind, we do not suggest that this is a developmental sequence in which the new ways replace earlier ones, but rather new ways are added to earlier ones.

Thus, theory of mind and language develop together such that each supports the growth of the other, and further, their development allows the child to participate in more sophisticated teaching/learning episodes. One type of learning does not replace the earlier one but is added to it, so that by the beginning school years, children can learn by imitation, from instruction, and collaboratively. Turning now to the issue of school readiness, we argue that the development of theory of mind facilitates children's transition to school and their ability to act and interact in the school environment.

THEORY OF MIND AS A DEVELOPMENTAL PATHWAY TOWARDS SCHOOL READINESS

Formal schooling is an important sociocultural institution, at least in modern Western societies, although not only there. Much has been written about the relations among culture, cognitive development, and the factors whereby children are judged "ready for school" (Boyer, 1991; Saluja, Scott-Little, & Clifford, 2000). Our aim here is to contribute to the discussion by examining the relations among children's readiness for school and their theory-of-mind and language development. It may be that children's theory of mind—their ability to think about thinking—plays an important role in school readiness. As Jerome Bruner writes:

> Modern pedagogy is moving increasingly to the view that the child should be aware of her own thought processes, and that it is crucial for the pedagogical theorist and teacher alike to help her become more metacognitive—to be as aware of how she goes about her learning and thinking as she is about the subject matter she is studying. Achieving skill

> and accumulating knowledge are not enough. The learner can be helped to achieve full mastery by reflecting as well upon how she is going about her job and how her approach can be improved. Equipping her with a good theory of mind—or a theory of mental functioning—is one part of helping her to do so. (Bruner, 1996, p. 64)

Until the final sentence of this excerpt there is nothing that might not have been written more than twenty years ago, when the idea of metacognition was first introduced into educational circles—as knowledge about and monitoring of memory, comprehension, and other cognitive processes (Brown, 1978; Flavell, 1979). It is only Bruner's phrase "equipping her with a good theory of mind ..." that seems new, and perhaps puzzling in the context, because all the recent research on preschoolers' theory-of-mind development suggests that children arrive at school already "equipped" with a theory of mind.

Certainly, before formal schooling begins, children understand a great deal about thinking and learning in everyday social contexts (Astington, 1993). During the later preschool years they recognize that different people may have different beliefs about the same reality and that beliefs are subject to change, as seen in their successful performance on false-belief tasks, which we discussed in an earlier section. They also understand that people construct their knowledge through perception and communication, and that different information comes from different sensory modalities. They remember the source of their own beliefs. This is the understanding that children bring with them when they first make the transition to school.

Nonetheless, many young children, who learn so much, so quickly during their preschool years, find school learning difficult. Preschoolers can deal well with the world in situations that make human sense to them (Donaldson, 1978) but success in school depends on their ability to deal with representations of the world using unfamiliar symbol systems. Children from highly literate families seem to have less difficulty because such systems of symbolic representation are already somewhat familiar to them. Recently, early literacy programs have begun to provide all children, whatever their home background, with literate experiences that make sense to them, before they begin the process of becoming literate themselves (Dickinson, 1994).

A focus on literacy as the acquisition of reading and writing skills, however, may lessen the focus on language and thought, on how thoughts are expressed in language, and how different people may have different thoughts about the same thing. Furthermore, just as families provide different home literacy experiences, they differ too in the manner and extent to which they talk about people's thoughts. A contrast is often made between two styles of parenting: one that punishes bad behavior and demands obedience, and another that reasons with the child and explains people's different points of view in a situation (Baumrind, 1971). Talking about different viewpoints may well help children understand that people have beliefs about the world, that their beliefs may be different from those of others, and that beliefs may change when a person acquires new information. Indeed, Ruffman, Perner, and Parkin (1999) recently reported data supporting this suggestion. They asked mothers of 3- to 5-year-old children how they would respond to their child in five different disciplinary situations. The mothers sometimes said that they would ask children to think about how their hurtful actions made the other person feel. Ruffman et al. found that the number of such responses given by mothers correlated with their children's performance on standard tests of false-belief understanding, controlling for age and verbal ability. That is, children who are asked to think about situations from another person's perspective have a better understanding of false belief. It may be that such everyday metacognitive understanding helps children make sense of and succeed in school.

It is important to remember, however, that at this stage children's understanding is intuitive, embedded in their everyday social interaction. Does this intuitive theory of mind have any bearing on children's readiness for school and their first formal educational experiences? Strong claims have been made regarding the importance of theory-of-mind development for children's social behavior generally (Moore & Frye, 1991), and certainly, social maturity is an important aspect of school readiness. More specifically in relation to learning in school, as discussed earlier, Tomasello et al. (1993) propose that there is a relation between the level of children's theory-of-mind development and their ability to learn via imitation, instruction, and collaboration, all of which are important ways of learning in school. Theory-of-mind development also allows children to reflect on their own intentions and beliefs, which facilitates monitoring of their own cognitive activities. Such "self-monitoring" is an important aspect of success in school settings (Meichenbaum & Biemiller, 1998). Relatedly, self-reflection may allow children to think about what they know beyond what is currently perceived or activated in mind, thus fostering divergent thinking (Suddendorf & Fletcher-Flinn,1997).

Theory of mind may also play a role in children's narrative understanding (Astington, 1990), in particular, their ability to comprehend the "dual landscape" of narrative (Bruner, 1986) and to follow a story plot by linking the action script to the thoughts and motives of the characters. Both in comprehending and producing stories, and in understanding historical figures, attention must be given to people's motives and beliefs, in order to make sense of their actions (Gardner, 1991;

McKeough, 1992, 2000). Familiarity with stories and story telling is an important component of school readiness (Paley, 1994), providing a foundation for further development in the beginning school years. There may well be a two-way interaction involved, such that theory-of-mind understandings are crucial for story comprehension but also story reading enhances theory-of-mind development. Beginning in the preschool years children learn about mental states from stories that are read to them (Dyer, Shatz, & Wellman, 2000) and in the school years, story books continue to be an important source of mental state information (Cassidy et al., 1998). As Donaldson (1978) points out, young children rarely ask about the precise language used in a story, about word meanings, for example, but rather their attention is focused on the meaning of the story: "They ask many searching questions about the intentions and motives of the characters, the structure of the plot—if you like, the meaning of the story" (Donaldson, 1978, p. 91). Thus, theory of mind provides a foundation for narrative comprehension, which ultimately underlies a range of understanding in the humanities and social sciences.

Researchers also argue for a relation between theory of mind and the developmental origins of scientific thinking (Klein, 1998; Kuhn & Pearsall, 2000; Ruffman, Perner, Olson, & Doherty, 1993; Sodian, Zaitchik, & Carey, 1991). They postulate that children's theory of mind underlies an understanding of the nature and development of objective knowledge, including theories and the reasons for holding and believing them. For example, children who cannot represent and reason from second-order beliefs have difficulty reasoning about evidence, seen in their inability to distinguish between causes and reasons (Astington et al., 2002).

Thus, we have proposed relations between theory of mind and a number of factors, all of which are important in school readiness: social maturity, collaborative learning, cognitive monitoring, narrative comprehension, and the beginnings of scientific thinking. Taken together, these factors cover a lot of ground. What do they have in common? They all involve, indeed require, the ability to talk about one's own and other people's thoughts. That is to say, an appropriate metacognitive language is required for social maturity in order to explain and excuse oneself, and for collaborative learning in order to talk about mutual understandings and conflicts. It is also required in order to monitor one's own cognitive activity, to discuss story characters' motivations, and to generate and test scientific hypotheses. For all these purposes children need a language that is mentalistic and reflective, that gives reasons and asks for explanations. This is a metacognitive language, comprised of common terms such as *know, think, guess, remember,* and later, more formal ones such as *concede, assume, interpret, hypothesize,* and so on, all of which allow for reflection on thought and talk (Astington & Olson, 1990).

Metacognitive Language

It therefore seems likely that children's theory of mind is a developmental pathway to school readiness because it involves the acquisition of metacognitive language. We would argue that this is what Bruner meant when he said that teachers must equip children with a "good theory of mind"—it is their preschool social understanding, their theory of mind, made explicit in metacognitive language. It is an open question, in the examples given above, whether it is the theory of mind or the metacognitive language, that is important (if, indeed, they can be pulled apart). It is our suspicion that the language itself is important. That is, some children may be quite savvy in social situations but they may not talk much about people's thoughts, or only about the content of thought, not about thinking. They may well know that someone will look for an object in the place where he last saw it even though it is now moved, as tested in the classic false-belief task. However, they may be less inclined spontaneously to explain this in terms of the person thinking or assuming that is where the object is. It may be "talking the talk", that is, teacher talk or metacognitive language, that is important for school success. Bartsch and Wellman (1995) show that frequency of metacognitive term use by preschoolers is related to linguistic competence, measured by Mean Length of Utterance (MLU), independent of age. In other words, children who are generally more verbally able, tend to use more metacognitive language. However, the first appropriate use of a metacognitive term (indicating theory-of-mind understanding) is related to age, independent of MLU. That is, older children use more metacognitive language than younger children, independent of their general verbal ability. These findings suggests that theory of mind and frequency of metacognitive term use are different measures. So, although it is certainly likely that theory-of-mind task performance and metacognitive language use are closely related to one another, they may not be one and the same thing. It may be, as previously suggested here, that metacognitive language is an explicit way of expressing one's theory of mind, another example of the interweaving of levels of theory-of-mind development and language.

Thus, we would argue that preschool children's theory of mind provides a foundation for their initial learning in school and further development is enhanced through the learning of more complex metacognitive language. That is, schooling itself leads to further development in their theories of mind by making them more aware of thought and providing the opportunity and the vocabulary with which to talk about thought. Flavell, Green, and Flavell (1995, p. 91) suggest that participation in formal school activities may facilitate children's introspective abilities because children's thinking about school tasks may be overt and therefore easy for them to reflect on: "they can literally hear themselves thinking." Certainly, children do talk to themselves about tasks in the classroom. Moreover, competent children do this more than less competent ones, perhaps because not all their cognitive capacity is occupied by the immediate demands of the task, as Meichenbaum and Biemiller (1992) suggest. It may well be that such self-directive talk fosters children's awareness of their own thought processes and develops their ability to introspect. Indeed, Vygotsky argued that, "school instruction ... plays a decisive role in making the child conscious of his own mental activities" (Vygotsky, 1931/1962, p. 92).

Teachers' talk about mental activity might be important to further theory-of-mind development, although we do not know how much of this actually occurs in school classrooms (Olson & Astington, 1993b). In a study of kindergarten teachers' beliefs and practices, Pelletier (1994; see also Astington & Pelletier, 1996) examined teachers' use of metacognitive talk in two contexts: from observations of their regular teaching practices with children, and from a transcript of an interview conducted by an adult. Each session lasted approximately an hour. The teachers used metacognitive verbs more often during the interview with the adult than during teaching. Only 12 of 20 teachers used any metacognitive terms at all during teaching, and of those 12 teachers, there were only 31 terms total, that is an average of 2.6 terms each. In contrast, during the interviews, all teachers used metacognitive terms, for a total of 922—an average of 46.1 terms each. As in an earlier study (Feldman & Wertsch, 1976) teachers are more likely to use metacognitive terms with their colleagues than with students in the classroom. There was also some suggestion in Pelletier's study that the teachers' use of metacognitive terms was related to their teaching style, at least in English language classrooms, with greater use occurring in classrooms where the teacher took a constructive approach to children's learning.

Another likely important influence on further theory-of-mind development is the acquisition of literacy. Donaldson (1978) argues that when children first learn to read they gain a reflective awareness of language that leads them to reflective awareness of thought itself: "Those very features of the written word which encourage awareness of language may also encourage awareness of one's own thinking and be relevant to the development of intellectual self-control" (Donaldson, 1978, p. 95). Olson (1994) explores this idea in detail, investigating the ways in which literacy leads to the development of subjectivity, which he relates to self-consciousness, and which he defines as "recognition of one's own and others' mental states as mental states" (Olson, 1994, p. 234). He traces this development both in the individual child and in terms of cultural history. This leads to the question whether such self-reflection is universal or is peculiar to a literate theory of mind (Vinden & Astington, 2000). Perhaps it is the inclination to think about one's thinking that is essentially a product of Western socialization and schooling, rather then the ability to do so.

In this section we have argued that relations exist between theory-of-mind development and readiness for school, and that metacognitive language acquisition plays an important role, without providing much empirical evidence for these claims. In the next section, we summarize the results of a longitudinal study that we conducted, which was specifically designed to address this issue.

INDIVIDUAL DIFFERENCES IN THEORY-OF-MIND DEVELOPMENT AND READINESS FOR SCHOOL

In previous sections, we suggested that school readiness may be enhanced by having a theory of mind and that theory-of-mind development is further enhanced by schooling due to the focus on talk about thinking, knowing, and learning. In this section, we examine these suggestions more closely by delineating the independent factors that contribute to their association.

Children's school life begins at just about the time that they acquire a representational theory of mind, as marked by successful performance on false-belief tasks, that is, between 4 and 5 years of age. In kindergarten classrooms we find a range of performance on these measures but we do not know whether variation in false-belief understanding affects children's readiness for school, nor do we know whether earlier acquisition has consequences later, making a difference in terms of children's success in school. It is a well established fact that children's school success is predicted by their IQ and by the socioeconomic status (SES) of their family (Duyme, 1988; Neisser et al., 1996; Willms, 1999). Moreover, because there is clear evidence that false-belief task performance is related to general language ability (Jenkins & Astington, 1996), we can assume that children who do well on false-belief tasks are likely to do well in school, for the simple reason that language ability is an important component of IQ. In addition, language style is related to SES differences, with greater use of metacognitive terms by middle-class children, which is the group that fares better in school (Hall, Nagy, & Linn, 1984). Nonetheless, we need to know whether theory of mind and metacognitive language use themselves, independent of general language ability and SES, have any effect on school achievement. Even if they do not have any independent relation with school achievement, however, they may help explain the influence of IQ and SES. Although these variables are predictive, they are not explanatory in any precise way. It may be that theory of mind and metacognitive language use have a role to play in explicating the relation between IQ, SES, and school achievement. But is there any evidence in favor of this possibility? There is some evidence that theory-of-mind measures such as false-belief understanding and metacognitive language production and comprehension are related to the important school activity of reading (Anderson, 1998; Booth & Hall, 1994; Torrance & Olson, 1985, 1987). However, it is not clear to what extent, if any, this relation is independent of general language ability. In the next section we describe a longitudinal study that we conducted in order to address this issue.

Theory of Mind and Language at the Transition to School

Longitudinal work is crucial to understanding the developmental origins of school readiness and school success, helping to address issues of cause and consequence. Recently we followed two groups of children (N = 107) for 2 years during the transition to school. Participating children attended one of four schools; two public schools served a population of visible minority, recently immigrated families of lower SES, one public school served a primarily White, middle-class neighborhood, and the fourth school was a private university laboratory school serving middle- and upper-income families. At the start of the first year of the study the mean age of the younger group was 4 years, 4 months; these children attended "junior kindergarten" (for 4-year-olds). The mean age of the older group was 5 years, 4 months; these children attended "senior kindergarten" (for 5-year-olds). Both groups were in half-day kindergarten classes. In the second year, the younger group was still in a half-day kindergarten program, and the older group was in full-day first-grade classes. Children were tested once each term (i.e., fall, winter, and spring), over the 2 years, that is six times in all, on a variety of measures. Children were interviewed individually by a female researcher in a familiar room near the classroom. Our aim was to describe the pattern of relations among children's theory of mind, metacognitive language abilities, school readiness, and school performance, controlling for general language ability and family background, in order to determine whether children's understanding of mind makes a difference to their readiness for and success in school. Here we present a summary of some of our findings.

There are many aspects of school readiness, such as children's communicative skills, approaches to learning, cognition and general knowledge; as well as their social competence and emotional well-being, and the factors of age, health, and physical development (Kagan, Moore, & Bredekamp, 1995; Meisels, 1999). Here we consider the relation of theory of mind to communication and cognition in the domains of early reading, narrative, and scientific thinking. We also consider the relation between theory of mind and children's social competence and emotional well-being. The children's theory-of-mind development was assessed at the beginning of the project using first-order false-belief tests and later in the project using second-order tests.

Early Reading

We found that first-order false-belief understanding predicts early reading ability, measured by standard reading test scores (Reid, Hresko, & Hammill, 1981). However, this relation is explained by the false-belief test's acting as a measure of the child's language ability. When general language competence is controlled, the correlation between reading test scores and false-belief test scores is non-significant. Metacognitive language comprehension and production are also related to reading ability, but again the correlation is non-significant when general language competence is controlled. However, we have some evidence that metacognitive language may play a role. That is, children's performance on the metacognitive language tests makes a small but significant contribution to prediction of the *change* in reading test scores from the first year to the second year of the project, even when general language ability is controlled. This provides some support for the idea that children's ability to use metacognitive language helps them to make progress at the start of schooling.

Story Narrative

At this early stage, reading tests primarily measure children's understanding of the conventions of print, knowledge of the alphabet, and ability to read individual words (Reid et al., 1981). Theory-of-mind abilities are likely to play a more important role later on, in reading comprehension, especially story narrative comprehension where understanding the plot depends on integrating the action of the story with the characters' motives and thoughts (Bruner, 1986). We assessed this aspect of children's narrative abilities by asking them to retell two wordless picture book stories (Pelletier & Astington, 2004): one story that was first told to the child by the experimenter, and another that was first told by the teacher to the whole class group. Illustrations for both stories included "thought-bubbles" that depicted the characters' thoughts and plans.

We used Bruner's (1986) notion of the dual landscape of narrative to develop a coding scheme for the story retelling transcripts, in order to measure the child's ability to understand the two landscapes of narrative by linking story events and actions to characters' thoughts and motives. We counted the number of references to action, to thought, and to thought/action, as follows:

- *Action:* refers to setting, events or actions (e.g., "and they're running away").
- *Thought:* refers to the content of the thought-bubble without mentioning the character who holds the thought (e.g., "the squirrel looks underneath and gets it"—the illustration shows a boy whose thought-bubble depicts the squirrel's action).
- *Thought/Action:* refers in the same utterance to the character and the content of his or her thought-bubble (e.g., "he had an idea how he could get that bunny in the pot"—the illustration shows the character with a thought-bubble depicting the bunny in the pot).

All children retold simple descriptions of setting, events and actions, that is, Bruner's (1986) landscape of action. They also reported the action taking place in the thought-bubbles. From our perspective, this is Bruner's landscape of consciousness. However, for some children it appeared to be simply part of the story action, that is, they retold events and actions depicted in thought-bubbles, with no mention of the character who held the thought. At a more advanced stage children did refer to the character who held the thought when they referred to actions depicted in thought-bubbles, that is, they had the ability to integrate the landscapes of action and consciousness, although they did not do this all of the time. The most advanced group of children always referred to the character who held the thought whenever they referred to actions depicted in thought-bubbles.

In order to examine the characteristics of this development, we computed a proportional score that indicated reference to Thought/Action as a proportion of total reference to Thought plus Thought/Action, independent of the actual number of such references. Children who referred only to the content of thought-bubbles, with no mention of the character holding the thought, received a score of zero, whereas children who always mentioned the character when referring to thought-bubble content, received a score of 1. The remainder of the children received a proportional score that indicates their success at achieving integration of the landscapes of action and consciousness.

We found that children's performance on this measure was significantly related ($p = .052$) to false-belief understanding, controlling for age and general language ability. This finding provides evidence of a relation between theory of mind and the ability to comprehend the dual landscape of narrative that is independent of purely linguistic ability. This finding is in keeping with McKeough's (1992) work that views story narrative understanding as the integration of events (plot) and perceptions (consciousness).

Scientific Thinking

Bruner (1986) draws a distinction between narrative and paradigmatic thought, both of which are crucial to success in school. As we have seen, narrative thought is concerned with psychological causes, with motives and beliefs. Paradigmatic thought, on the other hand, is concerned with physical causes, with scientific reasoning in matters of evidence and truth. At the end of the second year of the project we assessed children's understanding of evidence, that is, their ability to distinguish between the physical cause of an event and a person's reason for believing it (Astington et al., 2002). A reason is essentially a belief that provides the evidence for another belief (i.e., a second-order belief) and so we argued that children's understanding of evidence would depend on their ability to represent and reason from second-order beliefs. We showed that children's performance on the evidence test was related to their performance on the second-order false-belief test, although performance on both tests was related to general language and non-verbal abilities. However, a significant proportion of variance in the evidence scores was accounted for by second-order false-belief understanding, over and above that accounted for by general language and non-verbal abilities. This finding provides clear evidence of a relation between theory of mind and the scientific concept of evidence. Although the correlational result implies no causal direction, we would argue for a direction of effect from theory of mind because it is more generally fundamental to scientific reasoning, underlying not just children's understanding of evidence, but also their ability to make truth value judgments (Homer, 1995).

Social Competence and Emotional Well-Being

So far we have focused on cognitive aspects of children's readiness for school but their social competence is an equally important factor (Astington, 2003). In the middle of the first year of the project, we used Lalonde and Chandler's (1995) teacher rating scale to assess the children's social competence. We found that false-belief task performance was significantly related to social competence, controlling for age, but the relation was no longer significant after controlling for general language ability. However, the scale can be divided into two subsets: the first consists of social convention items, such as saying please and thank you, and the second consists of items that require thinking about other people's point of view, such as explaining one's reasons in a conflict situation. We found that false-belief understanding was significantly related to both subset scores. However, after controlling for age and language ability, only the relation with the second set remained significant. This shows that children's theory of mind is particularly important in social situations that require attention to others' thoughts and wishes.

At the end of the second year of the project the children's teachers completed a different rating scale (Cassidy & Asher, 1992), from which we computed a composite measure of social competence. We also computed a composite false-belief measure using children's scores on the first-order false-belief tasks given at the start of the first year, and the second-order false belief tasks given at the end of the second year. In addition, we had a measure of children's spontaneous use of metacognitive terms (e.g., *think, know, remember*) from the story retelling task given in the middle of the second year. In a hierarchical regression analysis, we found that false-belief understanding accounted for unique variance in the teacher rating of social competence, after accounting for age and language ability. Beyond this, however, children's spontaneous production of metacognitive terms in the story retelling task explained additional variance in the social competence scores. Perhaps this is because metacognitive language plays a useful role in resolving conflicts in a manner that socially competent children use (e.g., "He didn't know you thought it was my turn").

As well as being rated by their teachers at the end of the second year of the project, the children themselves were interviewed (based on Donelan-McCall & Dunn, 1997) to assess their perceptions of peer relations, teacher-child interaction, and school work. Children's responses were coded for affective content, in order to measure the emotional tone of their school experience. We found that children's reports of positive and negative experiences were related to their false-belief understanding, independent of language ability. Their reports were also consistent with the teacher ratings of social behavior. That is, children who were happy in school had higher false-belief scores and were more likely to be rated socially competent by their teachers. Children who were unhappy in school scored lower on the false-belief tasks and were less likely to be judged by teachers as socially competent. Thus children's theory of mind is related to their emotional well-being, as well as to their social competence, and both of these factors are important in children's readiness for school and success in school.

CONCLUSION: DEVELOPMENTAL ORIGINS OF READINESS FOR SCHOOL

In this chapter, we have outlined a developmental framework for the relation among theory of mind, language, and school readiness. We discussed learning in the broad context that is defined by human culture and by the culture of teaching and learning. We put forward the proposal that theory of mind and language development represent a tightly-woven set of constructs, each powerfully affected by age and general cognitive ability, yet mutually tied to each other. Initially language development requires a theory-of-mind like capability in order to engage in interactions with members of one's culture. However, further theory-of-mind development depends on language, as evidenced repeatedly in research. We claim that although general language development is critical to theory-of-mind development, it is a special "language of mind" (Astington & Pelletier, 1996) that is important for further theory-of-mind development and for schooling. This metacognitive language is the language of thinking, knowing, and learning, the language used by teachers to teach and by learners to express their learning across a range of domains in school. We then provide evidence for how the relation between theory of mind and language plays out during the early school years—in early reading, in story narrative understanding, in scientific thinking, in social competence and emotional well-being. In each area, we witness the contribution of theory of mind to early learning. Furthermore, we witness the bond between theory of mind and general language in the preschool years, and theory of mind and metacognitive language in early schooling. Taken together, the evidence strongly suggests that the relation between theory of mind and language is at the origin of children's developmental readiness for school and continues to set the framework for ongoing success in school.

REFERENCES

Anderson, W. B. (1998). *An investigation of the relationship between literacy, verbal ability and metarepresentational ability in normal young readers.* Unpublished doctoral dissertation, Fordham University, New York.

Astington, J. W. (1988). Children's understanding of the speech act of promising. *Journal of Child Language, 15,* 157–153.

Astington, J. W. (1990). Narrative and the child's theory of mind. In B. Britton & A. Pellegrini (Eds.), *Narrative thought and narrative language* (pp. 151–171). Hillsdale, NJ: Lawrence Erlbaum Associates.

Astington, J. W. (1993). *The child's discovery of the mind*. Cambridge, MA: Harvard University Press.

Astington, J. W. (1996). What is theoretical about the child's theory of mind A Vygotskian view of its development. In P. Carruthers & P. K. Smith (Eds.), *Theories of theories of mind* (pp. 184–199). Cambridge, UK: Cambridge University Press.

Astington, J. W. (2003). Sometimes necessary, never sufficient: False belief understanding and social competence. In B. Repacholi & V. Slaughter (Eds.), *Individual differences in theory of mind: Implications for typical and atypical development* (pp. 13–38). New York: Psychology Press.

Astington, J. W., & Baird, J. A. (2005-a). Introduction: Why language matters. In J. W. Astington & J. A. Baird (Eds.), *Why language matters for theory of mind* (pp. 3–25). New York: Oxford University Press.

Astington, J. W., & Baird, J. A. (Eds.). (2005-b). *Why language matters for theory of mind*. New York: Oxford University Press.

Astington, J. W., & Jenkins, J. M. (1999). A longitudinal study of the relation between language and theory of mind development. *Developmental Psychology, 35*, 1311–1320.

Astington, J. W., & Olson, D. R. (1990). Metacognitive and metalinguistic language: Learning to talk about thought. *Applied Psychology: An International Review, 39*, 77–87.

Astington, J. W., & Pelletier, J. (1996). The language of mind: Its role in learning and teaching. In D. R. Olson & N. Torrance (Eds.), *The handbook of education and human development: New models of learning, teaching and schooling* (pp. 593–619). Oxford, UK: Blackwell.

Astington, J. W., Pelletier, J., & Homer, B. (2002). Theory of mind and epistemological development: The relation between children's second-order false-belief understanding and their ability to reason about evidence. *New Ideas in Psychology, 20*, 131–144.

Baldwin, D. A. (1993). Early referential understanding: Infants' ability to recognize referential acts for what they are. *Developmental Psychology, 29*, 832–843.

Bandura, A. (1986). *Social foundations of thought and action*. Engelwood Cliffs, NJ: Prentice-Hall.

Bartsch, K., & Wellman, H. M. (1995). *Children talk about the mind*. New York: Oxford University Press.

Baumrind, D. (1971). Current patterns of parental authority. *Developmental Psychology Monographs, 4*(1, Part 2).

Boesch, C. (1996). Three approaches for assessing chimpanzee culture. In A. E. Russon, K. A. Bard, & S. T. Parker (Eds.), *Reaching into thought: The minds of the great apes* (pp. 404–429). Cambridge, UK: Cambridge University Press.

Booth, J. R., & Hall, W. S. (1994). Role of the cognitive internal state lexicon in reading comprehension. *Journal of Educational Psychology, 86*, 413–422.

Boyer, E. L. (1991). *Ready to learn: A mandate for the nation*. Princeton, NJ: The Carnegie Foundation for the Advancement of Teaching.

Brown, A. L. (1978). Knowing when, where, and how to remember: A problem of metacognition. In R. Glaser (Ed.), *Advances in instructional psychology* (Vol. 1). Hillsdale, NJ: Lawrence Erlbaum Associates.

Bruner, J. (1986). *Actual minds, possible worlds*. Cambridge, MA: Harvard University Press.

Bruner, J. (1996). *The culture of education*. Cambridge, MA: Harvard University Press.

Call, J., & Tomasello, M. (1996). The effect of humans on the cognitive development of apes. In A. E. Russon, K. A. Bard, & S. T. Parker (Eds.), *Reaching into thought: The minds of the great apes* (pp. 371–403). Cambridge, UK: Cambridge University Press.

Call, J., & Tomasello, M. (1999). A nonverbal false belief task: The performance of children and great apes. *Child Development, 70*, 381–395.

Caro, T. M., & Hauser, M. D. (1992). Teaching in nonhuman animals. *The Quarterly Review of Biology, 67*, 151–174.

Cassidy, J., & Asher, S. (1992). Loneliness and peer relations in young children. *Child Development, 63*, 350–365.

Cassidy, K. W., Ball, L. V., Rourke, M. T., Werner, R. S., Feeny, N., Chu, J. Y., Lutz, D. J., & Perkins, A. (1998). Theory of mind concepts in children's literature. *Applied Psycholingustics, 19*, 466–470.

Chomsky, C. (1969). *The acquisition of syntax in children from 5 to 10*. Cambridge, MA: MIT Press.

Cutting, A. L., & Dunn, J. (1999). Theory of mind, emotion understanding, language and family background: Individual differences and interrelations. *Child Development, 70*, 853–865.

de Villiers, J. G. (2000). Language and theory of mind: What are the developmental relationships? In S. Baron-Cohen, H. Tager-Flusberg, & D. J. Cohen (Eds.), *Understanding other minds: Perspectives from developmental cognitive neuroscience* (pp. 83–123). Oxford, UK: Oxford University Press.

Dickinson, D. K. (Ed.). (1994). *Bridges to literacy: Children, families, and schools*. Cambridge, MA: Blackwell.

Donaldson, M. (1978). *Children's minds*. Glasgow: Fontana.

Donelan-McCall, N., & Dunn, J. (1997). School work, teachers, and peers: The world of first grade. *International Journal of Behavioral Development, 21*, 155–178.

Duyme, M. (1988). School success and social class: An adoption study. *Developmental Psychology, 24*, 203–209.

Dyer, J. R., Shatz, M., & Wellman, H. M. (2000). Young children's storybooks as a source of mental state information. *Cognitive Development, 15*, 17–37.

Feldman, C. F., & Wertsch, J. V. (1976). Context dependent properties of children's speech. *Youth and Society, 7*, 227–256.

Flavell, J. H. (1979). Metacognition and cognitive monitoring: A new area of cognitive-developmental inquiry. *American Psychologist, 34*, 906–911.

Flavell, J. H., Green, F. L., & Flavell, E. R. (1995). Young children's knowledge about thinking. *Monographs of the Society for Research in Child Development, 60* (1, Serial No. 243).

Freeman, N. H., Lewis, C., & Doherty, M. J. (1991). Preschoolers' grasp of a desire for knowledge in false-belief prediction: Practical intelligence and verbal report. *British Journal of Developmental Psychology, 9*, 139–157.

Gardner, H. (1991). *The unschooled mind*. New York: Basic Books.

Gopnik, A., & Astington, J. W. (1988). Children's understanding of representational change and its relation to the understanding of false belief and the appearance-reality distinction. *Child Development, 59*, 26–37.

Hall, W. S., Nagy, W. E., & Linn, R. (1984). *Spoken words: Effects of situation and social group on oral word usage and frequency*. Hillsdale, NJ: Lawrence Erlbaum Associates.

Happé, F. G. E. (1995). The role of age and verbal ability in the theory of mind task performance of subjects with autism. *Child Development, 66,* 843–855.

Harris, P. (1996). Desires, belief, and language. In P. Carruthers & P. K. Smith (Eds.), *Theories of theories of mind* (pp. 200–220). Cambridge, UK: Cambridge University Press.

Heath, S. B. (1983). *Ways with words.* Cambridge, UK: Cambridge University Press.

Heath, S. B. (1986). What no bedtime story means: Narrative skills at home and school. In B. B. Schieffelin & E. Ochs (Eds.), *Language socialization across cultures* (pp. 97–124). Cambridge, UK: Cambridge University Press.

Hepper, P. G., & Shahidullah, S. (1994). The beginnings of mind: Evidence from the behaviour of the fetus. *Journal of Reproductive and Infant Psychology, 12,* 143–154.

Homer, B. (1995). *Children's attribution of second-order mental states and truth value judgement.* Unpublished master's thesis, Ontario Institute for Studies in Education.

Hughes, C. (1998). Executive function in preschoolers: Links with theory of mind and verbal ability. *British Journal of Developmental Psychology, 16,* 233–253.

Jenkins, J. M., & Astington, J. W. (1996). Cognitive factors and family structure associated with theory of mind development in young children. *Developmental Psychology, 32,* 70–78.

Kagan, S. L., Moore, E., & Bredekamp, S. (Eds.). (1995). *Reconsidering children's early development and learning: Toward common views and vocabulary* (Report of the National Education Goals Panel, Goal 1, Technical Planning Group). Washington, DC: Government Printing Office.

Klein, P. D. (1998). The role of children's theory of mind in science experimentation. *Journal of Experimental Education, 66,* 101–124.

Kuhn, D., & Pearsall, S. (2000). Developmental origins of scientific thinking. *Journal of Cognition and Development, 1,* 113–129.

Lalonde, C. E., & Chandler, M. (1995). False belief understanding goes to school: On the social-emotional consequences of coming early or late to a first theory of mind. *Cognition and Emotion, 9,* 167–185.

McKeough, A. (1992). The structural foundations of children's narrative and its development. In R. Case (Ed.), *The mind's staircase: Exploring the conceptual underpinnings of children's thought and knowledge* (pp. 171–188). Hillsdale, NJ: Lawrence Erlbaum Associates.

McKeough, A. (2000). Building on the oral tradition: How story composition and comprehension develop. In J. W. Astington (Ed.), *Minds in the making: Essays in honor of David R. Olson* (pp. 98–114). Oxford, UK: Blackwell.

Meichenbaum, D., & Biemiller, A. (1992). In search of student expertise in the classroom: A metacognitive analysis. In M. Pressley, K. Harris, & J. Guthrie (Eds.), *Promoting academic competence and literacy: Cognitive research and instructional innovation* (pp. 3–53). New York: Academic Press.

Meichenbaum, D., & Biemiller, A. (1998). *Nurturing independent learners: helping students take charge of their learning.* Cambridge, MA: Brookline Books.

Meisels, S. J. (1999). Assessing readiness. In R. C. Pianta & M. J. Cox (Eds.), *The transition to kindergarten* (pp. 39–66). Baltimore, MD: Paul H. Brookes.

Moore, C. (1998). Social cognition in infancy (commentary on "Social cognition, joint attention, and communicative competence from 9 to 15 months of age," M. Carpenter, K. Nagell, & M. Tomasello). *Monographs of the Society for Research in Child Development, 63*(4, Serial No. 255), 167–174.

Moore, C., & Frye, D. (1991). The acquisition and utility of theories of mind. In D. Frye & C. Moore (Eds.), *Children's theories of mind* (pp. 1–14). Hillsdale, NJ: Lawrence Erlbaum Associates.

Neisser, U., Boodoo, G., Bouchard, T. J. J., Boykin, A. W., Brody, N., Ceci, S. J., Halpern, D. F., Loehlin, J. C., Perloff, R., Sternberg, R. J., & Urbina, S. (1996). Intelligence: Knowns and unknowns. *American Psychologist, 51,* 77–101.

Olson, D. R. (1994). *The world on paper.* Cambridge, UK: Cambridge University Press.

Olson, D. R., & Astington, J. W. (1993a). Cultural learning and educational process (commentary on "Cultural learning," M. Tomasello, A. C. Kruger, & H. H. Ratner). *Behavioral and Brain Sciences, 16,* 531–532.

Olson, D. R., & Astington, J. W. (1993b). Thinking about thinking: Learning how to take statements and hold beliefs. *Educational Psychologist, 28,* 7–23.

Olson, D. R., & Bruner, J. S. (1996). Folk psychology and folk pedagogy. In D. R. Olson & N. Torrance (Eds.), *The handbook of education and human development: New models of learning, teaching and schooling* (pp. 9–27). Oxford, UK: Blackwell.

Paley, V. G. (1994). Every child a storyteller. In J. F. Duchan, Hewitt, L. E., & R. M. Sonnenmeier (Ed.), *Pragmatics: From theory to practice* (pp. 11–19). Englewood Cliffs, NJ: Prentice-Hall.

Parker, S. T. (1996). Apprenticeship in tool-mediated extractive foraging: The origins of imitation, teaching, and self-awareness in great apes. In A. E. Russon, K. A. Bard, & S. T. Parker (Eds.), *Reaching into thought: The minds of the great apes* (pp. 348–370). Cambridge, UK: Cambridge University Press.

Pelletier, J. (1994). *Children's understanding of school and teachers' beliefs and practices in French immersion and regular English language kindergarten.* Unpublished doctoral dissertation, University of Toronto (OISE).

Pelletier, J. & Astington, J. W. (2004). Action, consciousness and theory of mind: Children's ability to coordinate story characters' actions and thoughts. *Early Education and Development, 15,* 5–22.

Perner, J. (1991). *Understanding the representational mind.* Cambridge, MA: Bradford Books/MIT Press.

Perner, J., Leekam, S., & Wimmer, H. (1987). Three-year-olds' difficulty with false belief: The case for a conceptual deficit. *British Journal of Developmental Psychology, 5,* 125–137.

Perner, J., & Wimmer, H. (1985). "John *thinks* that Mary *thinks* that ..." Attribution of second-order beliefs by 5- to 10-year-old children. *Journal of Experimental Child Psychology, 39,* 437–471.

Popper, K. (1972). *Objective knowledge: An evolutionary approach.* Oxford, UK: Clarendon.

Premack, D., & Premack, A. J. (1996). Why animals lack pedagogy and some cultures have more of it than others. In D. R. Olson & N. Torrance (Eds.), *The handbook of education and human development: New models of learning, teaching and schooling* (pp. 302–323). Oxford, UK: Blackwell.

Reid, D. K., Hresko, W. P., & Hammill, D. D. (1981). *The Test of Early Reading Ability (TERA).* Austin, TX: Pro-Ed.

Ruffman, T., Perner, J., Olson, D. R., & Doherty, M. (1993). Reflecting on scientific thinking: Children's understanding of the hypothesis-evidence relation. *Child Development, 64,* 1617–1636.

Ruffman, T., Perner, J., & Parkin, L. (1999). How parenting style affects false belief understanding. *Social Development, 8,* 395–411.

Russon, E. A. (1997). Exploiting the expertise of others. In A. Whiten & R. W. Byrne (Eds.), *Machiavellian intelligence II: Extensions and evaluations* (pp. 174–206). Cambridge, UK: Cambridge University Press.

Saluja, G., Scott-Little, C., & Clifford, R. (2000). Readiness for school: A survey of state policies and definitions. Washington, DC: Office of Educational Research & Improvement. In Early Childhood Research and Practice: An Internet Journal on the Development, Care and Education of Young Children (Fall), 59 pages.

Sodian, B., Zaitchik, D., & Carey, S. (1991). Young children's differentiation of hypothetical beliefs from evidence. *Child Development, 62,* 753–766.

Suddendorf, T., & Fletcher-Flinn, C. M. (1997). Theory of mind and the origin of divergent thinking. *Journal of Creative Behavior, 31,* 169–179.

Sullivan, K., Zaitchik, D., & Tager-Flusberg, H. (1994). Preschoolers can attribute second-order beliefs. *Developmental Psychology, 30,* 395–402.

Tager-Flusberg, H. (2000). Language and understanding minds: Connections in autism. In S. Baron-Cohen, H. Tager-Flusberg, & D. J. Cohen (Eds.), *Understanding other minds: Perspectives from developmental cognitive neuroscience* (pp. 124–149). Oxford, UK: Oxford University Press.

Tomasello, M. (1999). *The cultural origins of human cognition.* Cambridge, MA: Harvard University Press.

Tomasello, M., Kruger, A., & Ratner, H. H. (1993). Cultural Learning. *Behavioral and Brain Sciences, 16,* 495–552.

Torrance, N., & Olson, D. R. (1985). Oral and literate competencies in the early school years. In D. R. Olson, N. Torrance, & A. Hildyard (Eds.), *Literacy, language and learning: The nature and consequences of reading and writing* (pp. 256–284). Cambridge, UK: Cambridge University Press.

Torrance, N., & Olson, D. R. (1987). Development of the metalanguage and the acquisition of literacy. *Interchange, 18,* 136–146.

Vinden, P. G., & Astington, J. W. (2000). Culture and understanding other minds. In S. Baron-Cohen, H. Tager-Flusberg, & D. J. Cohen (Eds.), *Understanding other minds: Perspectives from developmental cognitive neuroscience* (pp. 503–519). Oxford, UK: Oxford University Press.

Visalberghi, E., & Fragaszy, D. M. (1996). Pedagogy and imitation in monkeys: Yes, no, or maybe? In D. R. Olson & N. Torrance (Eds.), *The handbook of education and human development: New models of learning, teaching and schooling* (pp. 277–301). Oxford, UK: Blackwell.

Vygotsky, L. S. (1962). *Thought and language* (E. Hanfmann & G. Vakar, Trans.). Cambridge, MA: MIT Press. (Original work published 1931)

Willms, J. D. (1999). Quality and inequality in children's literacy: The effects of families, schools, and communities. In D. P. Keating & C. Hertzman (Eds.), *Developmental health and the wealth of nations* (pp. 72–93). New York: The Guilford Press.

Wimmer, H., & Perner, J. (1983). Beliefs about beliefs: Representation and constraining function of wrong beliefs in young children's understanding of deception. *Cognition, 13,* 103–128.

Chapter 10

Teaching and Learning as Intentional Activities

Douglas Frye
University of Pennsylvania

Margalit Ziv
Tel Aviv University

One of the most obvious forms of communication that affects children's cognition is teaching. Children experience teaching as a common sociocultural activity. It defines school and, to some degree, preschool, but is not restricted to those settings. Teaching frequently occurs at home and on the playground. Parents, siblings and peers teach children numerous things from academic skills to household chores to sports. Although we can justifiably claim to know much about the knowledge and skills that can be learned through teaching, it is less clear what makes this sociocultural practice possible. When do children recognize teaching as an identifiable activity, especially when a "teaching moment" may be inserted without ceremony into the ongoing flow of behavior? When do they have the cognitive prerequisites to understand teaching, given that the objective of the activity is to convey knowledge, and hence may require theory of mind? And, once they do understand what teaching is, does that change how they can participate in and benefit from it?

Teaching is possible as a sociocultural practice because we can detect differences in knowledge and engage others in activities to diminish those differences. The reason for teaching cannot be grasped if it is not possible to recognize differences in other people's knowledge compared to our own (Olson & Bruner, 1996). Nothing could be done about those differences unless there were activities—demonstrating, describing, guiding—that allowed one member of our species to alter the knowledge of another. Absent those activities, we would simply have to wait until others' experience caused their knowledge to change. Taking these points together, teaching can be seen to be an intentional activity that is pursued in order to increase the knowledge of another (see also Kruger & Tomasello, 1996).

Children's theory of mind offers a new approach to interpreting children's understanding of teaching (Tomasello, Kruger, & Ratner, 1993). The primary interest of the recent, intensive research on theory of mind has been to determine when children can appreciate differences in knowledge. The entire line of inquiry in theory of mind began with the discovery of preschool changes in children's understanding of inaccurate knowledge or false belief (Wimmer & Perner, 1983) and their slightly earlier recognition of the absence of knowledge or ignorance (Hogrefe, Wimmer, & Perner, 1986). Although the continued concentration on this one aspect of theory of mind may be limiting (Schwitzbegel, 1999; Ziv & Frye, 2003), it is precisely relevant to the understanding of teaching. Understanding differences in knowledge should be a prerequisite to understanding what teaching is.

There are strong arguments for regarding teaching as being intentional (Macmillan & McClellan, 1968; Scheffler, 1960). Research on theory of mind may help to illuminate how children understand the intentional aspect of teaching. There are changes in the understanding of intention that occur as a part of the preschool development of theory of mind (Astington, 1991). Those changes could allow children to see the point of teaching, that it is directed toward sharing knowledge, as well as help them pick out exactly what it is that the teacher is attempting to convey. In addition, the child's theory of mind becomes important in another way. Because the teacher is acting intentionally, the teacher's conception of the child can be heeded to guide how the teaching should occur. Strauss and Shilony (1994) have identified the implications of this possibility. Because education is a social exchange, both the child's and the teacher's theory of mind become relevant.

DIFFERENCES IN KNOWLEDGE

It is important to establish that teaching depends on a difference in knowledge and the exercise of intention. The basic necessity of a difference in knowledge between two parties is clear. When a difference exists, the knowledgeable or skillful person can assume the role of teacher in order to provide knowledge or skills to the other. The other may be ignorant or lack knowledge—as when children do not know why leaves turn yellow—or hold a false belief—as when children think subtraction should be commutative because addition is. In order for teaching to occur, both the conditions of knowledge on the teacher's part and ignorance or false belief on the learner's part have to occur. When someone does not now how to read, only a person who has this knowledge can teach the person and only the person who lacks the knowledge can be taught.

The difference in knowledge states is not restricted to instances in which teachers or other adults are knowledgeable and therefore can teach, while children are ignorant and therefore can only be learners. Teaching is a role rather than the characteristic of an individual. The skillful or knowledgeable person can be any adult, not necessarily a teacher, or it could be a child. Consequently, a professional teacher may be the right person to teach math, a parent may be more suitable for teaching how to ride a bike, an older sibling might be appropriate for teaching basketball skills, and a peer might be best for teaching cartwheels.

It is not enough, however, that a difference in knowledge states exists for teaching to occur, the critical component is that there must also be an *awareness* of the difference. The teacher needs to be aware of the knowledge difference in order to recognize the need for teaching. Without a sense of the other's ignorance or false belief, there is no need to provide information. For example, when preschoolers learn something new, they often assume that they have known the information for a long time and that other children know it as well, even when the information is novel like why cats have whiskers (Taylor, Esbensen, & Bennett, 1994). The assumption that new information is already known by other people will make it seem unnecessary to communicate about it. A similar lack of sensitivity to the knowledge difference will prevent a knowledgeable person from teaching because he or she does not recognize the need.

Awareness of the knowledge difference operates somewhat differently for the learner. The learner may or may not be aware of the knowledge difference. Even without that awareness, it should be possible to learn. All that is necessary is that the learner sees something he or she would like to do. However, an inability to conceive of differences in knowledge would make it impossible for the learner to recognize or make sense of what teaching is. Without an understanding of the knowledge difference, the learner should not be able to appreciate what makes teaching different from some other conversation or social exchange. Consequently, a learner in this position should not identify a teaching episode as teaching. Learning should still be possible; however, failure to recognize the episode will limit the extent to which the learner can actively cooperate in the didactic exchange with the teacher and may restrict the contribution of the teaching. A similar occurrence, perhaps, is that it is possible to find a new location without a map but having one is likely to help.

The question of children's first awareness of knowledge state differences is the focal point of the most common theory of mind tasks. For example, in the classic change-of-location false belief task (Wimmer & Perner, 1983), children must recognize that their knowledge of the location of an object is different from that of a character in a story. In the familiar scenario, a boy named Maxi places an object in one location, after which it is moved to another place without his knowledge. The child can then be asked a question about Maxi's ignorance, "Does Maxi know where the chocolate is?" or a one about his false belief, "Where does Maxi think the chocolate is?" Some 3-year-olds and many 4-year-olds can correctly answer the ignorance question (Hogrefe et al., 1986). In contrast, correct answers to the false belief question typically occur 6 months to a year later (see Flavell & Miller, 1998 for a review). At about the same time, children can correctly report their own, prior false beliefs (Gopnik & Astington, 1988) and begin to say accurately when they learned something new (Taylor et al., 1994). Success may be delayed until 6 years when the false belief concerns something other than the physical state of the world (Nguyen & Frye, 1999; Symons, McLaughlin, Moore, & Morine, 1997).

Not surprisingly, these results verify that adults should have little trouble determining the need for teaching. They should readily be able to detect the knowledge difference when someone lacks, or has a mistaken belief about a topic. Children may be different. Certainly children younger than 3 years should not see the point of teaching or understand the concept of it, if their understanding of mind does not include an awareness of differences in knowledge. Young children should be unable to teach for this reason. They may also fail to recognize what teaching is, and potentially be less likely to benefit from it. On the other hand, the change in theory of mind during the period from 3 to 6 years could allow children to recognize teaching, see the point of it, and perhaps even attempt it themselves. If so, there would be evidence that children have an understanding of teaching well before they enter formal schooling.

It may be somewhat ironic, but this analysis suggests that false belief will be important for teaching in another way. If the *awareness* of a knowledge difference, and not just the existence of the knowledge difference, is what is important for teaching, then the possibility arises that the person about to teach may be mistaken about the knowledge difference. The teacher's *belief* about the knowledge difference will determine whether teaching is provided. However, successful teaching will only occur on the basis of an accurate belief. For example, if a teacher thinks a child does not know how to read when, in fact, the child can read, the teacher may attempt to teach the child, but in reality no teaching or no successful teaching will take place. Similarly, if a teacher thinks a child knows how to read when, in fact, the child cannot read, the teacher will decide there is not a need and again no teaching will occur. Should these more complicated patterns arise, and be understood by children, they too will serve as evidence that children understand that teaching depends on the awareness of the knowledge difference.

To summarize, four aspects of the knowledge difference required for teaching have been put forward: that there is a knowledge state difference, that teaching is a role and not a characteristic of the individual, that there must be an awareness of the knowledge difference, and that the teacher's awareness must be accurate for teaching to succeed. As was proposed earlier, these conditions should be considered prerequisites for teaching. Yet, even when these conditions are met—when there is an awareness of the knowledge difference and the knowledgeable person has an accurate belief about it—these prerequisites must be followed by an intentional action in order for teaching to come about.

THE INTENTIONALITY OF TEACHING

For an activity to qualify as teaching it must be intentional. Suppose a novice watches an expert do something new and learns how to do the same thing as a consequence. The meaning of this advance will change entirely depending on whether the expert does or does not know that the other person is watching. If the expert has no idea that the novice is watching, then it does not make sense to call the episode an instance of teaching. Teaching only occurs when what someone does is being directed toward increasing the knowledge or understanding of the other person. Although exactly the same events happen in the two versions of this example, teaching cannot come to pass when the expert does not know about the presence of the novice because the expert's actions cannot be directed toward enhancing the novice's understanding.

It should not be surprising that the general characteristics of intentional action (Anscombe, 1957; Searle, 1983) apply readily to teaching. Teaching is done with the goal in mind of changing another's understanding, and what is being done is directed towards accomplishing that goal. Because there is a goal, the person can say, if asked, why they are carrying out the activity. In addition, it is not necessary for the goal to be satisfied. The activity is still teaching even if—as may too often be the case—it does not succeed. This characteristic begins to indicate the difference between an intentional interpretation of teaching and a functional or mechanical one. In a functional definition of teaching (Caro & Hauser, 1992), the learner's behavior must change as a consequence of something the teacher does (with several other restrictive conditions). However, because the functional definition does not incorporate intention, it cannot identify instances in which teaching was attempted but was unsuccessful on that occasion.

The most important aspect of the intentional view of teaching is that it can help to explain the process involved. Under the intentional characterization, the teacher is aware of both the goal and the activity directed toward it, thus it is possible to recognize when the activity does not succeed. That recognition can guide the activity, given that it is intentional. Should the teaching activity initially fail, then it can be continued until it has an effect. For the same reason, it is also possible to select another, potentially more effective instructional approach and try it. In each case, it is the awareness that the activity is directed toward a goal that can explain why the activity will be stopped, continued, or altered according to its observed effects.

Although there is not as much research in theory of mind on children's understanding of intention as there is on their understanding of differences in knowledge, intention is seen as being an equally important topic (Astington, 1991; Zelazo, Astington, & Olson, 1999). There are several empirical results indicating when children recognize intention, and hence when they might begin to recognize the intentionality of teaching. Children as young as 3 years can determine when a simple action has a goal and whether the goal has been fulfilled or not (Shultz & Wells, 1985; Wellman & Woolley, 1990). However, Astington (1991) has argued that young children's early judgments of intentionality may be based on a matching strategy according to which an outcome is identified as being intentional if it matches a goal and unintentional if it does not. This strategy would not allow children to appreciate that a desirable outcome which occurs accidentally is unintentional. Astington's findings suggest that it is not until about 4 years, approximately the same time as the understanding of false belief, that children begin to understand that the origin of the action (and not its outcome) determines its intentionality.

Oddly enough, the research topic in theory of mind that is perhaps most relevant to the understanding of teaching is its opposite—the understanding of deception. The two are closely related concepts. Deception is an intentional action to maintain someone's ignorance or give them a false belief. Teaching is an intentional action to remove someone's ignorance or correct a false belief. The two are alike in that they both are directed toward knowledge, rather than some other mental state, and both involve a deliberate attempt to manipulate that state. They differ only in the intended direction of the outcome. In one, it is to produce beliefs that are further from reality. In the other, it is to produce ones that are closer to it.

An example of where teaching has gone wrong can help to underscore the similarity between teaching and deception. Imagine an instance in which someone uses a long out-of-date map to trick someone into believing that Philadelphia is the capitol of Pennsylvania. Compare that to an instance in which someone mistakenly uses the same map to *teach* someone that Philadelphia is the capitol. (This is still a case of teaching.[1] A certain percentage of what we teach at any given time is likely to be wrong.) The outcome in both instances is exactly the same. Each recipient has a false belief about Philadelphia. To distinguish the two cases, it is necessary to consider the intent in each. The intent of the deception was to distort the other's knowledge. The intent of the teaching, although clearly unfulfilled, was to enhance it. The two actions are the same except for this one feature.

Research findings on children's understanding of deception may help to predict their understanding of teaching. Wimmer and Perner's (1983) initial paper on false belief initiated the study of deception with theory of mind. Hiding games have typically been used in the deception studies. Several experiments (Hala, Chandler, & Fritz, 1991; Sullivan & Winner, 1993) have found evidence for an understanding of deception in children as young as 2.5 to 3 years of age. However, the majority of studies examining preschoolers' deceptive abilities reveal the usual theory of mind change, with 3-year-olds having very limited capacities for comprehending deception and 5-year-olds being well aware of it (Leekam, 1991; Ruffman, Olson, Ash, & Keenan, 1993; Sodian & Frith, 1992; Sodian, Taylor, Harris, & Perner, 1991). In addition, it has been found that young children's ability to engage in deception does not seem to be delayed relative to their ability to understand it (Peskin, 1992; Russell, Mauthner, Sharpe, & Tidswell, 1991).

The conceptual similarity between teaching and deception would suggest that, everything else being equal, there should be a change in children's understanding of teaching between 3 and 5 years, just as there is in the understanding of deception. It also hints that children's own participation in teaching may not be long delayed after their first understanding of it. Hence, 5-year-olds ought to be able to determine what is being intended in simple teaching situations and respond accordingly. Three-year-olds may also be able to recognize the intention of teaching in some situations. However, they may be misled, as the research on the understanding of intention illustrates (Astington, 1991),

---

[1]We thank Ed Modestino for suggesting this possibility.

when there is an accidental match between an outcome and the goal of teaching. In other words, when there has been an observable change in someone's understanding, 3-year-olds may over-attribute the change to the effects of teaching, even if teaching was not involved.

Although teaching and deception share a close conceptual relation, the one difference between them, the intent either to increase or limit knowledge, may have unexpected implications. Apart from teaching being a generally good thing and deception being a generally bad one, the intent of each puts a different pressure on the child's understanding and the knowledge exchange. Teaching has the effect of drawing the parties involved into similar mental states, whereas deception has the effect of separating them in different ones.

When deception is successful in maintaining someone's ignorance or giving them a false belief, a necessary outcome is that the deceiver and the person deceived are placed in different knowledge states. One person knows the truth of the situation, the other does not. The difference has several likely effects. It will restrict future exchanges. The most probable form that any further interaction will take will be to maintain the difference. A deviation from that pattern runs the risk of exposing the original deception. The cause of the difference will also work to limit the deceived person's awareness. Deception is best, of course, when the other person does not even suspect they have been deceived. Becoming aware of the knowledge state difference opens the possibility that the deception will unravel.

The tendency is the opposite in the case of teaching. When teaching is successful, the knowledge state difference between the teacher and the student is reduced, and may even be removed. The outcome can result in the sharing of mental states or having a "meeting of the minds" (Olson & Bruner, 1996). Here, awareness of both the difference and subsequent change in knowledge states can only contribute to diminishing the difference further. As a teacher and student approach a shared understanding, it becomes easier to see and address any incongruities that may remain. Joint awareness should also make possible forms of reciprocal or cooperative teaching (Brown & Palincsar, 1989) in which both parties in the exchange can work to increase their shared understanding. These outcomes are a possibility in teaching, but not deception, because both parties can be aware of the goal of decreasing the knowledge difference, and so both can coordinate their actions toward that end.

It can be seen that awareness of a knowledge difference and intention are both necessary for teaching. Intent is what differentiates doing something and doing that same thing to show someone else how to do it. From the standpoint of theory of mind, teaching and deception are very similar because both are intentional actions to manipulate a knowledge state. They differ in whether the intent is to increase someone's knowledge or restrict it. Increasing the student's knowledge as a consequence of teaching has the effect of reducing the knowledge difference between the teacher and learner, thus making it more likely that they will share the same knowledge state. The potential for teaching to lead to shared knowledge states is what makes special forms of teaching and learning possible.

TYPES OF TEACHING AND LEARNING

The characteristics of awareness of a difference in knowledge and intention can help to distinguish the different forms of teaching and learning. The present analysis of teaching generates a classification system that partially overlaps with the others that have been proposed. Tomasello et al. (1993) divided cultural learning into imitative, instructed, and collaborative learning according to the development of perspective-taking abilities of the learner. In the first to appear, imitative learning, learners adopt the behavioral strategies of others in doing something. The next, instructed learning, depends on learners following the directions of others and then internalizing those directions to regulate their own learning later. Finally, collaborative learning requires participants to take each other's perspectives in order to construct new knowledge. In each of these, it is assumed that the learner must take the point of view of the other, and how extensively that can be done determines the type of learning that can occur.

Olson and Bruner (1996) have proposed a related scheme in which the type of teaching that can be pursued is governed by the type of theory of mind that the learner can hold. Or, in other words, folk pedagogy rests on folk psychology. In this approach, the learner follows a progression of doer, knower, thinker, and expert. The learner changes from knowing how to do something or procedural knowledge, to knowing facts or declarative knowledge, to understanding beliefs or interpretative knowledge, and, finally, to knowing what is known or cultural knowledge. The teacher's role changes similarly from demonstrating actions for the learner to imitate, to presenting facts for the learner to comprehend, to collaborating in interpreting ideas to form beliefs, and, finally, to serving as a consultant when the learner attempts to add to the corpus of what is known. Astington and Pelletier (1996, this volume) have identified changes in language necessary for each of the categories in this scheme.

When awareness of knowledge differences and intention are used to analyze teaching and learning, slightly different categories are formed than have been considered thus far. The main difference is that intention helps to draw a distinction between teaching and learning because it applies to each differently. According to the current approach, teaching must be intentional. Teaching depends on the goal of enhancing someone's knowledge. The same is not true for learning. Although much of our learning is intentional—we deliberately attempt to acquire new knowledge or a new skill—there are also times when we learn incidentally or, in other words, without trying. For learning to occur, there merely has to be a change in the person's understanding, regardless of how the experience is brought about.

On the basis of this difference in intention, four possibilities emerge for how teaching and learning can correspond to each other. Premack and Premack (1996) noted three of the possibilities. The full set is no teaching and non-intentional learning, no teaching and intentional learning, teaching and non-intentional learning, and teaching and intentional learning. These four possibilities compare in interesting ways with the cultural learning account (Tomasello et al., 1993) and with Olson and Bruner's (1996) further analysis of folk pedagogy.

No Teaching and Non-Intentional Learning

Infants learn about the world and about the culture that they are growing into from birth. This learning occurs through interactions between a knowledgeable person, at first mainly an adult, and the child, who is less knowledgeable. Language acquisition serves as an example of such learning. Despite the adults' awareness of ignorance on the baby's part, most of the learning does not involve engagement of the adult in intentional teaching. As Tomasello et al. (1993) point out, children usually do not learn new pieces of language in intentional linguistic sessions, but rather do so while engaged in everyday routine situations, such as feeding, diaper changing, book reading, taking a walk or playing hide and seek. Although no intentional teaching is involved, the adult does provide cues that the child's learning relies on, such as the tone of voice, direction of gaze, behavior towards objects, and so on.

On the baby's part, there is not likely to be explicit learning. Infants probably do not realize that there is a gap or difference in their knowledge that they must fix. Yet, implicit learning can occur and it relies on new skills. Tomasello et al. (1993) refer to a number of perspective taking behaviors that emerge at around 9 months of age—for example, joint visual attention and social reference—that enable this learning. These behaviors reflect, according to the authors, an understanding of persons as intentional agents that are clearly different from inanimate objects. Baldwin (this volume) describes evidence showing babies at about this age segment the stream of other people's intentional behavior and may begin to infer the goals of the behavior. Whereas Tomasello et al. suggest that this learning at this point relies on imitation, we would propose to distinguish between the kind of implicit learning that is manifested in language acquisition versus the imitation proper of specific behaviors. The latter, we propose, often involves an established understanding of intentionality and is discussed in the next section.

To summarize, in situations of no teaching and non-intentional learning there is a knowledge state difference; however, the learner may not be aware of it, and learning relies on naturally occurring situations and interactions in which neither party is explicitly trying to teach or to learn. Intention may be involved in these situations, as when there is intentional communication between the two, nonetheless there is no explicit intention to instruct the other or learn something new.

No Teaching and Intentional Learning

Young children often want to learn something that another person, whether an adult or another child, knows how to do and they do not. One of the common ways children do so is by watching the other person and attempting to imitate the person's behavior. The person who serves as the source of knowledge, or object of imitation, may or may not be aware that there is a knowledge difference. Even if the person is aware of the knowledge difference, and hence recognizes the prerequisite necessary for teaching, the person may not choose to do so. Thus, the intention to learn a new skill may drive the learner to engage in imitation without a corresponding intention to teach on the part of the knowledgeable person. Examples for this kind of relation between no teaching and intentional learning are not unusual. They include a child who tries to learn to tie his or her shoelaces by watching older siblings routinely tie their own laces, or children who watch a parent assemble a toy in order to learn how to do so themselves.

There are two aspects of intention that have to be involved in order for a learner to engage in imitation, or learn without intentional teaching. First, obviously, the learner has to have the intention to acquire some new knowledge. It is the driving force for the learning and the reason for engaging in imitation. Second, the learner must successfully be able to make the distinction between means and goals in the other's behavior. Searle (1983) emphasized that a goal is accomplished intentionally only if the person who has that goal is responsible for the means to achieve it. This relation has also been described as the self causal nature of intention (Astington, 1991). When watching another person perform an action, understanding the causal nature of intentional acts allows the distinction between the action's outcome on the one hand, and the intention, or goal on the other. Being able to make this distinction reduces the possibility of copying unrelated behavior that may be occurring at the same time, and enables imitation of the behaviors that are relevant to the intended act.

There is mixed evidence regarding the age at which children come to understand the means-goal distinction. There is evidence for early understanding of the means-goal distinction in a study in which 16- and 24-month-old infants could adjust the means they used in order to accomplish a required outcome, namely retrieving a toy from a distant location (Frye, 1991). Meltzoff (1995) provided a strong demonstration that 18-month-old infants could infer and re-enact a person's intended act, even when they watched failed attempts to perform this act, indicating their ability to differentiate between the intended outcome and the means employed to achieve it.

Astington (1991) reports several studies that suggest that children develop a full understanding of intention, including both the distinctions between intentional and non-intentional acts and between goals and means, only at around the age of 4 years or about the same time as they come to understand false belief. Before this age, children cannot distinguish, for example, between an intentional and non-intentional act when both result in a similar outcome. Young children may also not be able to distinguish between prior intention and a subsequent action. When asked about prior intentions using pictures of actions, 3-year-olds picked a picture depicting the actual action rather than a picture of the person preparing to perform the act. In contrast, 5-year-olds distinguished between the picture depicting the preparation for action and the picture of the action itself.

Despite the different indications in the research on when children show a full understanding of intention, there is a general acceptance that during the second year of life children develop sufficient understanding of people as intentional agents to engage in successful (intentional) imitation.

Intentional Teaching and Non-Intentional Learning

Teaching and learning situations are often determined primarily by a knowledgeable person, a teacher, who defines the goal of his or her activity as teaching another person, or causing another person to learn. This kind of teaching does not rely on the learner's intentional learning in order to accomplish the goal of teaching. The teaching is expected to have an effect whether the learner is interested, or engaged in intentional learning or not. Although the learner does not necessarily engage in explicit learning, the intention, or goal of teaching is always to cause a learner to learn. Thus, it is possible to imagine instances in which the teacher scaffolds experiences and the other learns as consequence even without trying. Examples are plentiful. Having children play a board game to learn counting, assemble puzzles to improve spatial reasoning, or follow baking recipes to gain experience with fractions are all instances in which the learning comes as a consequence of the scaffolded activity rather than the learner seeking the target skill.

In accord with Olson and Bruner's analysis, defining the goal of teaching, or the expected change in the learner, may differ depending on teacher's view of learners, as doers or knowers (or, alternatively can integrate both views). Perceiving children as doers leads adults to demonstrate skills for children to imitate. Conceiving of children as knowers leads adults to provide learners with knowledge of facts, principles, and rules. Both views consider children as passive in determining the goal and process of learning. In theory of mind terms, it just sees them as lacking knowledge (ignorance) or holding false beliefs that have to be corrected.

In summary, intentional teaching that does not rely on intentional learning consists of a knowledge difference between the teacher and learner, the teacher's awareness of this difference and the teacher's directing of the situation by applying their beliefs about learners' minds and defining the teaching's goals and means.

Intentional Teaching and Intentional Learning

In this category, the teaching-learning process relies on both the teacher's and the learners' intentional engagement. As in the previous level, the teacher's goal is to create a change in the learner; this feature is definitional for intentional teaching. Here, however, in contrast to the previous level, the learner shares this goal with the teacher and assumes an active role in attempting to accomplish it.

The nature of the change that the teacher defines as the goal of teaching can be similar to the change discussed in the previous level, namely, acquiring a skill or knowledge. The learner's intentional learning may influence the process by making the teaching more effective or by deepening the learner's understanding of what is taught. For instance, the goal of learning to count may be the same as in the example of the board game at the previous category. However, the course of the learning is likely to be different when children know they cannot count, or recognize the knowledge difference, and want to remove it. The learners' active seeking of the goal does not change the goal, but it can change how involved they are in the process, what they try to do to accelerate the process, and whether they are satisfied with the outcome.

It is also possible when the teaching and learning are both intentional that the goal or nature of the desired change can take a different configuration from the previous level. The teacher's goal in scaffolding was to transfer knowledge, or skill from a knowledgeable, authoritative person to an ignorant, or less knowledgeable individual. In contrast, the teacher's goal, when relying on active participation and a corresponding intention on the part of the learner may be to create a shared discourse in which the relation between beliefs and evidence are actively explored (Olson & Bruner, 1996).

Accomplishing this goal relies on a reciprocal, rather than teacher-directed process. It depends on an interaction between teacher and learner (as well as among learners), or between teachers' and learners' ideas and opinions. In theory of mind terms, teachers' and learners' beliefs and desires play a mutual role in the process of creating the shared discourse. Consequently, as Olson and Bruner have proposed, teaching and learning take place in the forms of discussion, collaboration, and negotiation in which different ways of construing the subject are encouraged.

Interestingly, although the roles of teacher and learner are usually defined on the superficial level and the intention of one is to teach and the other to learn, at a deeper level the distinction may not be as clear, or as important. When the situation is reciprocal, both parties affect and are changed by each other, and in a real sense the two can serve both as teachers and learners at the same time. In other words, in addition to the teacher's intentional engagement in teaching and the learner's intentional and active engagement in learning, both also participate in the opposite role, the teacher implicitly learning and the learner implicitly teaching.

This sharing of roles does not remove the requirement of a knowledge difference. The difference remains a prerequisite for any kind of teaching, although not necessarily for learning. However, the knowledge difference is not dominant in determining the goal, namely providing knowledge or changing the knowledge state of the learner. The knowledge state of the two parties becomes part of a broader perspective in which the knowledge, beliefs, opinions of both parties serve as the base for a collaborative process. In theory of mind terms, both parties' beliefs about the world, about the process of teaching and learning (and about each other) are recognized and come into play in the teaching-learning situation.

CHILDREN'S UNDERSTANDING OF TEACHING

The proposed analysis suggests that teaching has two main components. First, existence of a difference in the state of knowledge of two parties has been considered a prerequisite for all of the four teaching–learning conditions described. In addition, out of the four possible relations between teaching and learning, the pattern between the intention of the teacher and the intention of the learner determined the type of educational interaction that will occur. In order to understand children's possible participation in these different types of educational exchanges it is necessary to know what comprehension they have of the two components of teaching—the difference in knowledge and the intention to eliminate that difference.

Only a few previous empirical studies have tested the relation of children's understanding of teaching to their theory of mind. Astington and Pelletier (1996) explored Olson and Bruner's (1996) proposal that children's conceptions of learning and teaching may be related to their level of understanding of mind. They observed children in three situations—spontaneous pretend play of school, pretend play of school scenarios prompted by the experimenter's questions about learning and teaching, and modeled teaching followed by children teaching their peers. They found that children who did not yet understand false belief tended to talk about teaching as showing, those who understood false belief tended to describe teaching as telling, and those who had an even more advanced theory of mind tended to characterize teaching as helping or collaboration. This pattern agreed with Olson and Bruner's analysis that understanding people as intentional agents allows learning by imitation, understanding of people as mental agents enables learning from instruction, and understanding people as reflective agents enables collaborative learning.

Wood, Wood, Ainsworth and O'Malley (1995) investigated children's peer tutoring ability at 3, 5, and 7 years of age. Children were first taught how to carry out a construction task and were then asked to teach a peer how to do the same. The results revealed significant age-related differences in tutoring strategies, verbal instruction, and contingency of teaching. The authors suggest that, in accord with the cultural learning account of Tomasello et al. (1993), children's effective tutoring depends on their second-order perspective-taking skills. Effective tutoring requires the tutor to reason about the tutee's performance with respect to his or her previous attempt at instruction as well as about modifying the next instruction in light of it.

Ashley and Tomasello (1998) examined children's teaching during the period of the initial changes in theory of mind. Same-age pairs of 24-, 30-, 36- and 42-month-olds played with a mechanical device that required coordinating two different actions (pulling a lever and turning a handle). Each of the pairs worked at one of the actions, they then switched roles, and finally each was put with another child who had no previous experience with the device. Only the oldest three groups succeeded on the task. They displayed a steady increase in coordination with age. The 30- and 36-month-olds exhibited some differences in behavior when paired with an uninitiated child; however, only the 42-months gave any evidence of teaching. This age corresponds to when children begin to improve on theory of mind.

We have carried out a preliminary investigation of children's understanding of the basic components of teaching—awareness of a knowledge difference and the intention to diminish it. The study was conducted by presenting preschool children with stories about instances of teaching. Each story asked a single question about teaching. The first three asked children about separate aspects of the knowledge difference prerequisite, and the last two explored children's understanding of the role of intention in teaching. Together these tasks provide some indication of children's conceptions of the teacher's mind and may show the significance of theory of mind to real life teaching-learning experiences. Information about children's conceptions of teachers and teaching must be integrated with evidence of teachers' conceptions of learners (Strauss & Shilony, 1994) to better understand and improve the interaction between teachers and children.

EVIDENCE OF CHILDREN'S AWARENESS OF THE KNOWLEDGE DIFFERENCE REQUIRED FOR TEACHING

Who Should Be Taught?

A basic understanding of the knowledge difference required for teaching includes understanding of both the ignorance of the learner and of the knowledge held by the teacher. The initial task in the study was designed to explore whether 3- and 5-year-old children understand the first of these points, namely that something can be taught only to a person who lacks a certain knowledge of skills or facts. Do young children understand that in deciding whether and whom to teach, the teacher has to identify the person who lacks the knowledge or, in other words, distinguish between children who have the specific knowledge and those who do not?

This question was investigated by presenting children with a story about two children, one who knows how to read and the other who does not. The children were asked to judge whom the teacher would teach to read. If young children's understanding of teaching relies on the knowledge, role, or authority of a teacher, then they might suggest that the teacher who "teaches how to read" will teach both children, whether they know how to read or not. However, if they appreciate the importance of the state of knowledge, or lack of knowledge on behalf of the learner, as critical for determining who to teach, they will correctly say that the teacher will teach only the child who does not know how to read.

Thirty-two children from two preschools in Pennsylvania participated in the study. There were sixteen 3-year-olds and sixteen 5-year-olds. The children were presented with a story acted out with miniature dolls and miniature books. The task was arranged so that the gender of the dolls matched the child's. The story was:

> Tom and Michael go to the same school. Tom knows how to read. Michael does not know how to read, he just looks at the pictures. Here is the teacher. He teaches how to read. Who will the teacher teach how to read? Will he teach Michael, Tom, or will he teach them both?

The majority of 3-year-olds and all 5-year-olds correctly said that the teacher would teach only the child who did not know how to read (*Ms* = 75% and 100% for the 3- and 5-year-olds, respectively). This result indicates that already at the age of 3 years children understand that teaching is not determined by the teacher's state of knowledge only (the fact that the teacher knows how to read and teaches children how to read), but in addition requires consideration of the knowledge state of the learner. Only an ignorant learner when paired with a knowledgeable person (e.g., teacher) can create a teaching situation.

Who Can Teach?

The results of the first task showed that children as young as 3-years-old appreciate that teaching requires consideration of the knowledge state of the learner and is directed towards an uninformed, rather than a knowledgeable person. It may be, though, that children assume that this difference in knowledge states can occur only between a teacher or adult on the knowledgeable side and a child on the ignorant side. Whereas children realize that they (or their peers) can be knowledgeable or ignorant about a certain topic (and require teaching or not accordingly), they may still conflate the role of teacher with an adult's authority or age. Consequently, young children may not realize that in certain circumstances they, rather than an adult, can have the needed knowledge and assume the teaching role. In these circumstances, a knowledgeable child could teach an ignorant peer. Moreover, a knowledgeable child could teach an ignorant adult. Do children discriminate between the teacher's authority and knowledge states, and understand the dominance of the knowledge state over age and authority in determining who can teach?

Although understanding of the relation between knowledge states and teaching has not been directly investigated, previous comments and research about children's understanding of sources of knowledge may be of interest. Olson and Bruner (1996) have suggested that young children (no age was specified) assume that teachers have the knowledge and pass it on to the class. Only later do they learn that others in the class might have knowledge too. Wimmer, Hogrefe, and Perner (1988) suggest that young children may over-attribute knowledge to teachers, reflecting a tendency to regard adults as omniscient.

Pillow and Weed (1997) directly investigated children's understanding of the relative importance of perceptual knowledge and age for assessing another's knowledge. Children were asked whether a child or adult knew the identity of a hidden object after either the child or the adult had looked inside the container in which the object was hidden. In contrast to Wimmer et al. (1988), children's responses indicated that 3- and 4-year-olds did not automatically attribute knowledge on the basis of adult status alone, and that they treated perceptual access as more important than age in determining a person's knowledge.

In order to investigate children's understanding of the importance of knowledge over age for teaching, children in the current study were presented with a story about a child (e.g., Rachel) who wants to learn to make a paper airplane. The teacher does not know to make these airplanes, whereas another child in the story does. Children were asked who would teach Rachel how to make the airplane. In addition, they were asked whether the child who was said to know how to do it could teach the teacher.

The same 32 children were presented with the following story:

> One day Rachel comes to school and sees a paper airplane. Rachel says, "I want to make an airplane like this". The teacher does not know how to make paper airplanes. Andy, Rachel's friend, knows how to make them. Who can teach Rachel how to make the airplane? Can Andy teach Rachel or can the teacher teach her? Can Andy show the teacher how to make a paper airplane?

The majority of 3-year-olds and all of the 5-year-olds answered both questions correctly. They said that Andy, Rachel's friend, and not the teacher would teach Rachel how to make a paper airplane (*M*s = 73% and 100% for the 3- and 5-year-olds, respectively). Both the 3- and 5-year-olds also said that Andy could teach the teacher how to make the airplane (*M*s = 69% and 94% for 3- and 5-year-olds, respectively).

Already at the age of 3 years, children did not assign the teaching role solely to the teacher. Rather, they assigned teaching to the person holding the knowledge, a child in this case, indicating that they understood the relation between knowledge and teaching. In other words, 3- and 5-year-olds seem to understand the greater importance of knowledge over age or status for teaching. Therefore, depending on their knowledge, adults and children can teach, and knowledge can be passed through teaching from a child to an adult.

In their response to the present task, children also did not show a tendency to view adults as omniscient. As Pillow and Weed (1997) found, they may view teachers as knowledgeable in certain domains, but not in all. By the age of 4 years, children may begin to differentiate specific from overall knowledge, and may use age as a basis for attributing overall knowledge but not necessarily for attributing specific knowledge. Children's perception of the relation between teaching and specific versus overall knowledge merits further investigated.

Teacher's Belief About the Learner's Knowledge

The first two tasks have shown that when the difference in states of knowledge is clear, children as young as 3-years-old can correctly infer both who requires teaching—the ignorant and not the knowledgeable person—and who will assume the teaching role—the knowledgeable and not the ignorant person. However, the knowledge status of learners may not always be transparent or known to the potential teacher. Teachers must make decisions about teaching based on their *belief* about learners' knowledge. This belief can correspond to the actual knowledge status of the learner, meaning that the teacher actually knows whether the learner understands the material that is about to be taught or not. However, there is also a possibility that the teacher is misinformed about the actual knowledge status of the learner, or, in other words, has a false belief about learners' knowledge.

As in the traditional false belief tasks, this situation creates a conflict between reality and a person's belief. The question is whether children realize that the teacher's decision of what to teach is based on the teacher's belief about the learner's knowledge or lack of it, and not necessarily on the actual knowledge state of the learner. On the basis of the extensive literature on false belief understanding (Flavell & Miller, 1998), it is expected that there will be a difference between 3- and 5-year-olds in their judgments of teachers' false beliefs about learners' knowledge. However, detecting such a difference in regards to a teaching scenario rather than the traditional hiding-of-object task, should help to extend the findings about the false belief development to a new area.

Children were presented with a story about a teacher who thinks a student (e.g., Eric) does not know how to read when in fact the student does know how to read. As in Wellman and Bartsch's (1988) explicit false belief task, the children were not required to infer the teacher's belief, but were explicitly told what the teacher thinks. They were then asked to infer, or predict the teacher's action—whether the teacher will try to teach the child (who knows how to read) to read or not. The story was as follows:

> Eric knows how to read. But the teacher never saw Eric reading. The teacher thinks Eric does not know how to read. Will the teacher try to teach Eric how to read or not? Does Eric really know how to read?

Children who understand the teacher's false belief should say that the teacher will teach Eric how to read. In contrast, children who do not understand the teacher's false belief will predict the teacher's action using the real state of affairs, namely that Eric can read. Thus, they should say that the teacher will not teach Eric how to read.

As expected, there was a significant difference between 3- and 5-year-olds' responses on the task ($t = -3.42$, $p < .005$, *M*s = 31%, 75% for 3- and 5-year-olds, respectively). Three-year-olds, who typically perform poorly on traditional false belief tasks, said that the teacher will not try to teach Eric to read. In contrast, 5-year-olds, similar to their better performance on traditional false belief tasks, said that the teacher (who thinks that Eric does not know how to read) will teach him to read (even though in reality Eric knows how to read). Thus, 5-year-olds showed an understanding of teachers' possible false beliefs about learners' knowledge, as well as the implication of that belief for the decision of whether to teach or not.

These results, although preliminary, suggest that between the ages of 3 and 5 years children come to understand that merely identifying a knowledge state difference is not sufficient to determine engagement in teaching. Five-year-olds appear to realize that in addition to the actual state of affairs, an important component for determining an intentional engagement in teaching is the teacher's belief about the learners' knowledge. Thus, expanding false belief testing to scenarios that go beyond a search for physical objects has revealed new information about the significance of false belief understanding for an important type of social exchange.

Of course, this finding requires further study. One possibility would be to present children with additional scenarios regarding teachers' beliefs about children's knowledge. For example, a scenario could describe the opposite situation to the one currently described; namely, it would depict a teacher who thinks a child cannot read when in fact the child can. In this case, the teacher's false belief will lead to a decision not to teach, and consequently the child will not be provided with an opportunity to learn how to read.

If the current findings are supported, they indicate that during the preschool years, when children come to understand physical false belief, they also begin to understand potential for discrepancies between teachers' beliefs and reality or, in other words, between teachers' and learners' perspectives.

EVIDENCE FOR CHILDREN'S UNDERSTANDING OF TEACHING AS AN INTENTIONAL ACTIVITY

Understanding the Critical Role of Intentionality in Teaching

As discussed previously, the teaching-learning continuum produces four possible relations between teaching and learning. Whereas learning occurs in all four possibilities and will not take place without a knowledge difference, intentional teaching is involved only in two—one that does not necessarily rely on intentional learning and the other in which intentional teaching takes advantage of and is affected by intentional learning. Thus, all four possibilities share the prerequisite of the knowledge difference and may result in a similar outcome, namely acquiring a new skill, fact, or understanding. However, they may differ in the intentionality component, whether an intention to teach exists as the mediating link between the prerequisite (knowledge difference) and the outcome (reducing the knowledge difference).

The next task in the study provided a preliminary exploration of the question whether young children can make the distinction between (intentional) teaching and no teaching when the learning outcome is accomplished. An example of a learning situation that does not involve intentional teaching is learning through imitation of a person who does not assume the role of teacher (i.e., no teaching and intentional learning). For instance, a child in a story watches another person perform a certain skill that the child does not know how to do. By imitation and practice (intentional learning) the child acquires the new skill. How do preschool children judge this situation? Do they consider it to be an instance of teaching or not? In other words, when asked, will children say that teaching has occurred because of the intentional learning and successful outcome or will they notice that no intentional teaching actually took place?

Children were presented with the following story:

> Michael does not know how to tie his shoelaces. Michael's sister knows how to tie her shoelaces. Every day Michael watches his sister tie her

> shoelaces and Michael tries to tie his own. Now Michael can also tie his shoelaces. Did Michael's sister teach Michael how to tie his shoelaces?

If children consider the intention to teach as critical for determining whether the situation depicts teaching, they will say that Michael's sister did not teach him how to tie his shoelaces. However, if intentional learning accompanied by a successful outcome leads children to judge a situation as teaching, the fact that Michael practiced and learned how to tie his shoe laces will lead them to say that Michael's sister taught him to do so.

Both 3-and 5-year-olds found this task difficult and said that Michael's sister taught him how to tie his shoelaces, indicating a possible difficulty in reconciling the outcome of acquiring the skill of tying shoelaces with the absence of an intention to teach that outcome. Previous research has suggested that 3- but not 5-year-olds have difficulty distinguishing between intentional and non-intentional action when the outcome in the world is the same (Astington, 1991). Applying the same distinction to teaching may be more difficult because teaching and learning are related in a causal, goal-outcome relation in a way that other intentional actions with physical outcomes may not be. Children may also be more aware of instances in which others engage in explicitly teaching them than of instances in which they engage in learning on their own. Thus, preschoolers may tend to associate learning with teaching and, as a result over-generalize the concept of teaching to include situations in which only learning occurs.

Additional tasks would be helpful in supporting this preliminary finding. It would be useful to present children with two scenarios that share a similar outcome, one involving intentional teaching and the other of imitation without intentional teaching. Such a comparison may highlight the critical role of intentionality in teaching and make clearer the distinction between intentional teaching and learning without such teaching. In order to make sure that such tasks can indeed reveal a developmental change in understanding teaching, it might also be helpful to present the stories to older children, ones who are at least 6 or 7 years old, or even to adults.

In addition, it is not clear whether children judged the current situation as teaching because they placed weight on the process of watching and practicing or on the outcome of acquiring the new skill. Tasks that separate these the two elements—practice and outcome—could be informative for better understanding of children's conceptions of teaching. For example, children could be presented with a story similar to the current one but the outcome would be omitted. Children would be asked to judge whether this instance was teaching, based only on information about attempts to imitate and practice. In another task, children could be presented with a story about a child who watches a knowledgeable person, engages in imitation and practice but does not acquire the desired skill. Would children consider this scenario to be teaching? Finally, the significance of the learning outcome alone for children's teaching judgments could be investigated by presenting a story, opposite to the previous one, In it, there would be a person who performs a certain skill. Another character would not be able to perform the skill and does not watch the knowledgeable person or practice. Nevertheless, after some time the character is said to possess the new skill, Again, children would be asked if the knowledgeable person taught the character or not.

Understanding the Goals and Means of Teaching

In addition to distinguishing between intentional teaching and learning, the distinction between means and end is important for understanding intentional action in general, and teaching specifically. This distinction is important for understanding teaching because it often involves engagement in a large variety of activities and techniques that serve as a means to achieve the goal of transference of knowledge or skills. For example, teachers may choose to play (didactic) games with children in order to practice a certain skill, such as reading letters or counting, as a means to achieving the goal of teaching that skill. Teachers do not usually inform young children of the rationale or the academic goal of the activities or games they play with them. When a teacher plays such games with young children, what do children think? Do they assume that the teacher, like them, merely enjoys playing the game? Or do they understand that the teacher actually has a goal beyond the particular activity she engages in?

As mentioned earlier, previous research suggests that children come to a full understanding of the distinction between means and ends at the same time as they develop the understanding of false belief, namely at around the age of 4 years (Astington, 1991). The current task was designed to serve as a preliminary investigation of children's understanding of this distinction as related to teaching. In other words, can children distinguish between a teacher's goal on the one hand, and the means that are used to achieve the goal on the other?

Children were presented with a story about a teacher who teaches children to read numbers and plays a number game with them. They were then asked whether the teacher really wants to play the game or to teach numbers? Note that whereas children were directly presented with the teacher's action, they were not explicitly told about the goal or the outcome of the action (i.e., learning to read numbers). Consequently, they could not use the strategy of matching a goal with outcome, as 3-year-olds are reported to do (Astington, 1991). Rather, they had to infer the teacher's intention by integrating the information provided about the teacher's everyday act of teaching numbers with the specific act of the teacher's playing a game with the children.

The female-teacher version of the story was as follows:

> Here is Ms. Katy. Ms. Katy is a teacher. Every day Ms. Katy, the teacher, teaches the children in her class how to read numbers. One day, Ms. Katy, the teacher, brings a game to class. Ms. Katy says to the children, "Today we're going to play the number game. In this game every child gets a card and has to read the number on the card. The child who gets the biggest number wins the game." Now the teacher and the kids are playing. When the teacher plays the game, what does the teacher really want? Does the teacher really want to play cards with the kids or does the teacher really want to teach the class numbers?

A significant difference was found between 3- and 5-year-olds ($t = -2.10$, $p < .05$, *Ms* = 38%, and 75%, for 3- and 5-year-olds, respectively). Three-year-olds said that the teacher really wanted to play the game, whereas 5-year-olds correctly said that the teacher really wanted to teach the class numbers.

The younger children in this instance seemed to base their judgments on the action the teacher was involved in, and did not make an inference about the goal of this action or about the teacher's intention. It could be that they were truly unaware that the teacher had a goal beyond playing the game, and thus could not infer the intentional cause of the action when it was not directly provided to them. In contrast, 5-year-olds seemed to be aware of and could infer the teacher's intention, as well as distinguish between the teacher's goal and means. This finding, if confirmed, suggests that when entering elementary school children understand an important aspect of teaching and teachers' minds. They realize that much of what teachers do is directed towards supporting learning, even when it may not appear to be.

CONCLUSION

The initial results of this set of studies indicate that even 3-year-olds have a beginning understanding of the components of teaching—a knowledge difference and the intention to reduce it—but that there are also changes in this understanding over the preschool period. Three-year-olds appear to be able to recognize the differences in knowledge that make teaching possible. They understand that the teacher must know the material to be taught and that the learner cannot know it if teaching is to occur. On the other hand, 3-year-olds' appreciation of this relation appears to be entirely at the level of reality. They do not appear to realize that it is the teacher's and learner's awareness of the knowledge difference that will actually determine what they try to do. As would be expected from the extensive research on false belief understanding, 3-year-olds did not recognize that a teacher could be mistaken about the learner's knowledge state—that the teacher could mistakenly assume that a child does not know something—and that the teacher's false belief will affect the decision to teach. This understanding changes over the preschool period because 5-year-olds were able to predict accurately what the misinformed teacher would do.

The results indicated less of a firm grasp of the intentional component of teaching. The children's incomplete understanding of intention caused them to both over-generalize and under-generalize the concept of teaching. Both the 3- and 5-year-olds over-generalized teaching to include a situation in which a child intentionally learned the skill of tying shoelaces but was not taught it. At the other extreme, 3-year-olds under-generalized the notion of teaching in a situation in which a teacher introduced a game to practice number magnitude comparisons. Five-year-olds were able to recognize the instructional intent of this activity. This improvement again suggests that changes in children's theory of mind allow them to enter primary school with a working understanding of teaching.

There is a good chance as a consequence that educational practices can be advanced if they begin to take into account children's particular understanding of teaching and the more we can learn about it. Astington and Pelletier (this volume) have identified several non-exclusive ways in which theory of mind may be important for school readiness, including its relation to language, reading and narrative comprehension, its account of evidence in scientific reasoning, and its contribution to social and emotional competence. It may be that another important component of school readiness is children's understanding of teaching itself, specifically their awareness of differences in knowledge and their growing understanding of teaching's intentionality. These changes may help school-age children grasp teaching, but they may also allow teachers to approach children as partners in the process of accomplishing shared goals—enhancing children's knowledge and at the same time learning with each other.

REFERENCES

Anscombe, G. E. M. (1957). *Intention*. London: Blackwell.

Ashley, J., & Tomasello, M. (1998). Cooperative problem-solving and teaching in preschoolers. *Social Development, 7*, 143–163.

Astington, J. W. (1991). Intention in the child's theory of mind. In D. Frye & C. Moore (Eds.), *Children's theories of mind*. Mahwah, NJ: Lawrence Erlbaum Associates.

Astington, J. W., & Pelletier, J. (1996). The language of mind: Its role in teaching and learning. In D. R. Olson & N. Torrance (Eds.), *The handbook of education and human development: New models of learning, teaching, and schooling* (pp. 593–619). Cambridge, MA: Blackwell Publishers.

Brown, A. L., & Palincsar, A. S. (1989). Guided, cooperative learning and individual knowledge acquisition. In L. B. Resnick (Ed.), *Knowing, learning and instruction: Essays in honor of Robert Glaser* (pp. 393–451). Hillsdale, NJ: Lawrence Erlbaum Associates.

Caro, T. M., & Hauser, M. D. (1992). Is there teaching in nonhuman animals? *Quarterly Review of Biology, 67*, 151–174.

Flavell, J. H., & Miller, P. H. (1998). Social cognition. In D. Kuhn & R. S. Siegler (Eds.), *Handbook of child psychology, Volume 2: Cognition, Perception, and Language* (pp. 851–898). New York: John Wiley & Sons.

Frye, D. (1991). The origins of intention in infancy. In D. Frye & C. Moore (Eds.), *Children's theories of mind: The development of social understanding of others* (pp. 15–38). Hillsdale, NJ: Lawrence Erlbaum Associates.

Gopnik, A., & Astington, J. W. (1988). children's understanding of representational-change and its relation to the understanding of false belief and the appearance-reality distinction. *Child Development, 57*, 36–37.

Hala, S., Chandler, M., & Fritz, A. S. (1991). Fledging theories-of-mind: Deception as a marker three-years-olds' understanding of false belief. *Child Development, 62*, 83–97.

Hogrefe, G.-J., Wimmer, H., & Perner, J. (1986). Ignorance versus false belief: A developmental lag in attribution of epistemic states. *Child Development, 57*, 567–582.

Kruger, A. C., & Tomasello, M. (1996). Cultural learning and learning culture. In D. R. Olson & N. Torrance (Eds.), *The handbook of education and human development: New models of learning, teaching, and schooling* (pp. 369–387). Cambridge, MA: Blackwell Publishers.

Leekam, S. R. (1991). Jokes and lies: Children's understanding of intentional falsehood. In A. Whiten (Ed.), *Natural theories of mind*. Oxford: Basil Blackwell.

Macmillan, C. J. B., & McClellan, J. E. (1968). *Can and should means-ends reasoning be used in teaching?* In C. J. B. Macmillan & Thomas W. Nelson (Eds.), *Concepts of teaching: Philosophical essays*. Chicago: Rand McNally.

Meltzoff, A. N. (1995). Understanding the intentions of others: Re-enactment of intended acts by 18-month-old children. *Developmental Psychology, 31*, 838–850.

Nguyen, L., & Frye, D. (1999). Children's theory of mind: Understanding of desire, belief, and emotions with social referents. *Social Development, 8*, 70–92.

Olson, D. R., & Bruner, J. S. (1996). Folk psychology and folk pedagogy. In D. R. Olson & N. Torrance (Eds.), *The handbook of education and human development: New models of learning, teaching, and schooling* (pp. 10–27). Cambridge, MA: Blackwell Publishers.

Peskin, J. (1992). Ruse and representations: On children's ability to conceal information. *Developmental Psychology, 28,* 84–89.

Pillow, B. H., & Weed, S. T. (1997). Preschool children's use of information about age and perceptual access to infer another person's knowledge. *Journal of Genetic Psychology, 158,* 365–376.

Premack, D., & Premack, A. J. (1996). Why animals lack pedagogy and some cultures have more of it than others. In D. R. Olson & N. Torrance (Eds.), *The handbook of education and human development: New models of learning, teaching, and schooling* (pp. 302–323). Cambridge, MA: Blackwell Publishers.

Ruffman, T. K., Olson, D. R., Ash, T., & Keenan, T. (1993). The ABCs of deception: Do young children understand deception in the same way as adults? *Developmental Psychology, 29,* 74–87.

Russell, J., Mauthner, M., Sharpe, S., & Tidswell, T. (1991). The "windows task" as a measure of strategic deception in preschoolers and autistic subjects. *British Journal of Developmental Psychology, 9,* 331–350.

Scheffler, I. (1960). *The language of education.* Springfield, IL: Charles C. Thomas.

Schwitzgebel, E. (1999). Representation and desire: A philosophical error with consequences for theory-of-mind research. *Philosophical Psychology, 12,* 157–179.

Searle, J. R. (1983). *Intentionality: An essay in the philosophy of mind.* New York: Cambridge University Press.

Shultz, T. R., & Wells, D. (1985). Judging the intentionality of action-outcomes. *Developmental Psychology, 21,* 83–89.

Sodian, B., & Frith, U. (1992). Deception and sabotage in autistic, retarded, and normal children. *Journal of Child Psychology and Psychiatry, 33,* 591–605.

Sodian, B., Taylor, C., Harris, P. L., & Perner, J. (1991). Early deception and the child's theory of mind: False trails and genuine markers. *Child Development, 62,* 468–483.

Strauss, S., & Shilony, T. (1994). Teachers' models of children's minds and learning. In L. A. Hirschfield & S. A. Gelman (Eds.), *Mapping the mind: Domain specificity in cognition and culture* (pp. 455–473). New York: Cambridge University Press.

Sullivan, K., & Winner, E. (1993). Three-year-olds' understanding of mental states: The influence of trickery. *Journal of Experimental Child Psychology, 56,* 135–148.

Symons, D., McLaughlin, E., Moore, C., & Morine, S. (1997). Integrating relationship constructs and emotional experience into false belief tasks in preschool children. *Journal of Experimental Child Psychology, 67,* 423–447.

Taylor, M., Esbensen, B. M., & Bennett, R. T. (1994). Children's understanding of knowledge acquisition: The tendency for children to report that they have always known what they have just learned. *Child Development, 65,* 1581–1604.

Tomasello, M., Kruger, A. C., & Ratner, H. H. (1993). Cultural learning. *Behavioral and Brain Sciences, 16,* 495–552.

Wellman, H., & Bartsch, K. (1988). Young children's reasoning about beliefs. *Cognition, 30,* 239–277.

Wellman, H., & Woolley, J. (1990). From simple desires to ordinary beliefs: The early development of everyday psychology. *Cognition, 35,* 245–275.

Wimmer, H. M., Hogrefe, G.-J., & Perner, J. (1988). Children's understanding of informational access as a source of knowledge. *Child Development, 59,* 386–396.

Wimmer, H. M., & Perner, J. (1983). Beliefs about beliefs: Representation and constraining function of wrong beliefs in young children's understanding of deception. *Cognition, 13,* 103–128.

Wood, D., Wood, H., Ainsworth, S., & O'Malley, C. (1995). On becoming a tutor: Toward an ontogenetic model. *Cognition and Instruction, 13,* 565–581.

Zelazo, P. D., Astington, J. W., & Olson, D. R. (1999). *Developing theories of intention: Social understanding and self-control*. Mahwah, NJ: Lawrence Erlbaum Associates.

Ziv, M., & Frye, D. (2003). The relation between desire and false belief in children's theory of mind: No satisfaction? *Developmental Psychology, 39,* 859–876.

Chapter 11

*Gesture in Social Interactions: A Mechanism for Cognitive Change**

Susan Goldin-Meadow
University of Chicago

When people talk they gesture, and the gestures they produce often reflect thoughts that they do not express in their words. Gesture thus has the potential to provide for the listener unique insight into a speaker's thoughts. The question I address in this chapter is whether listeners take advantage of this potential and, in so doing, contribute to cognitive change in the speaker.

As an example, consider problem-solving by school-aged children. When children are asked to explain their solutions to a problem, some produce gestures that convey different information from the information they convey in their speech. Interestingly, it is these children who are particularly ready to make progress when given instruction in the task (Church & Goldin-Meadow, 1986; Perry, Church, & Goldin-Meadow, 1988).

*The research described in this chapter was supported by grants from the National Institute of Child Health and Human Development (RO1 HD18617, RO1 HD31185, ROI HD47450), the Spencer Foundation and from the March of Dimes.

Might the "mismatch"[1] between the information conveyed in gesture and in speech somehow signal for the adult that a child is open to instruction? Specifically, if adults were able to "read" the information conveyed in the child's gestures and appreciate the mismatch, they might alter their interaction with the child, providing input particularly well suited to that child's cognitive state. In this way, children could help shape their own learning environments just by moving their hands.

In order to convince ourselves that gesture really does play this kind of role in the adult-child learning interaction, we need to verify three points. First, children must produce gestures that reflect their cognitive state in their naturalistic interactions with adults. Second, adults must be able to interpret children's gestures and alter their responses to the children accordingly. Finally, the adults' responses must be effective in promoting learning. Note that this process demands quite a lot from adults. Not only must they be able to understand the gestures children produce in conversation, but they must also know how to use that information to respond appropriately and effectively to promote learning. If adults are capable of this type of sensitivity and adjustment, they could be the force behind a powerful learning mechanism, one that is potentially at work all of the time and is social by design.

My goal in this chapter is to provide evidence for each of these three steps, and thus provide evidence that gesture, when produced in social interaction, can bring about cognitive change. I begin by reviewing literature on the role that the social environment can play in fostering cognitive change. I then provide evidence in three domains (language, reasoning about quantities, and math) that the spontaneous gestures children produce (when interpreted in relation to the speech they accompany) do predict which children are particularly likely to learn. I next show that adults appreciate the mismatches between gesture and speech that children produce and, in response, adults offer input that is effective in facilitating cognitive growth in the children. I complete this section by demonstrating how both children and adults use their hands to work together to promote learning.

It is worth noting that gesture has the potential to play a role in bringing about cognitive change not only indirectly, as I hope to demonstrate in this chapter, but also more directly by having an impact on learners themselves. I end the chapter with a brief discussion of the more direct effects gesture can have on cognitive change.

---

[1]The term *mismatch* adequately conveys the notion that gesture and speech convey different information. However, for many, *mismatch* also brings with it the notion of conflict, a notion that I do not intend. The pieces of information conveyed in gesture and in speech in a mismatch need not conflict and, in fact, they rarely do. There is almost always some framework within which the information conveyed in gesture can be fitted with the information conveyed in speech, as I make clear later in the chapter.

THE ROLE OF THE SOCIAL WORLD IN FOSTERING COGNITIVE CHANGE

The social world may be particularly well suited to induce cognitive change for two reasons. First, the social world may be more difficult to ignore than the physical world. That is, there is a social obligation to consider information presented by a person that does not arise when information is offered by the physical world (Doise, 1985). Second, people can adjust their responses to a learner in a way that the physical world cannot. In other words, the social world can (although it need not) react in a fashion that is tailored to the learner's level of understanding.

Social interaction can provide input that brings about cognitive change even if the partner's intent is not to instruct. In fact, the information to which a learner is exposed by a social partner need not even be correct in order for cognitive progress to occur (Perret-Clermont & Brossard, 1985). For example, when children who fail on Piagetian reasoning tasks are exposed to the different but also incorrect reasoning of a peer, they are often able to profit from the two wrongs and right their performance on the reasoning task (Ames and Murray, 1982).

However, children do not benefit from just any input—input must be appropriate to the child's needs in order for learning to occur (e.g., Perry, Church & Goldin-Meadow, 1992). Indeed, the most effective input is likely to be input aimed just above the child's current level of understanding. In a study designed to test this hypothesis, Kuhn (1972) provided children with instruction in classification that was one level below their level, at their level, one level above their level, or two levels above their level. She found that the greatest tendency for change was among the children who had received input one level above their own level. Turiel (1969) found the same result when he gave children instruction in moral reasoning one level below their current level, one level above, and two levels above. Thus, children appear to be particularly likely to experience cognitive change if exposed to a view that is discrepant from, and slightly in advance of, their own.

The problem, of course, is how to maximize the fit between social input to the child and the child's level of understanding—in Vygotsky's (1978) terms, how to maximize the chances that the adult and child will be interacting within the child's "zone of proximal development." A child's zone of proximal development contains abilities that the child has not yet mastered but is actively working on—abilities that are ripe for change. But how is an adult to know which skills a given child is working on? In order for the zone of proximal development to be more than just a descriptive tool and to actually play a role in developmental change, children must be able to give off reliable cues to their cognitive state and do so in everyday social interactions. Moreover, adults must be able to interpret and respond to those cues.

Children indicate that they are having difficulty with a problem when they solve the problem incorrectly or when they offer incorrect verbal explanations for their solutions. In addition to these rather obvious cues, children can use nonverbal means to provide more subtle cues to their lack of understanding. For example, children ages 4 to 8 take longer to respond, shift their bodies more frequently, and move their hands more often when responding to messages they don't understand than to messages they do (Patterson, Cosgrove, & O'Brien, 1980). First grade children exhibit less direct eye contact with the speaker, more head tilting, excessive hand movements, and agitated body movements when listening to a difficult lesson than when listening to an easy one (Machida, 1986). Kindergarten and second grade children produce distinctive facial, manual and bodily expressions of puzzlement, manual vacillation, hesitations, and pauses in activity when asked to follow inadequate instructions (Flavell, Speer, Green & August, 1981).

Nonverbal cues of this sort can tell us that a child is at a loss and needs help with a particular task. However, these cues don't tell us whether the child is particularly ready to make use of instruction in the task, nor do they tell us which parts of the task (if any) the child is actively working on. To learn this type of information, we can turn to a different type of nonverbal behavior—gesture. In the next section, I provide evidence that gesture not only tells us whether a child is ready to learn the task at hand, but also what the child is just beginning to understand about the task. In the remainder of the chapter, I show that adults seem to be perfectly capable of interpreting this information and using it to good effect.

GESTURE CAN TELL THE WORLD THAT A CHILD IS READY TO LEARN

The gestures that speakers produce along with their talk are symbolic acts that convey meaning. It is easy to overlook the symbolic nature of gesture simply because its encoding is iconic rather than arbitrary. A gesture often looks like what it represents—for example, a twisting motion in the air resembles the action used to open a jar—but the gesture is no more the actual act of twisting than is the word *open*.

Because gesture can convey substantive information, it can provide insight into a speaker's mental representation (Kendon, 1980; McNeill, 1992). For example, a speaker in one of McNeill's (1992, p. 12) studies says "and he bends it way back" while his hand appears to grip something and pull it from a space high in front of him back and down to his shoulder. The speaker is describing a scene from a comic book in which a character bends a tree back to the ground. The gesture reveals the particular point of view that the speaker takes to the event—he is gripping the tree as though he were the tree-bender, making it clear by his actions that the tree was anchored on the ground. He could, alternatively, have represented the action from the point of view of the tree, producing the same motion without the grip and perhaps in a different space (one that was not tied to his shoulder), a movement that would have conveyed the tree's trajectory but not the actions performed on it.

Children, too, often use hand gestures as they speak (Jancovic, Devoe, & Wiener, 1975), gesturing when asked to narrate a story (e.g., McNeill, 1992) or when asked to explain their responses to a problem (e.g., Church & Goldin-Meadow, 1986). The gestures children produce in a problem-solving situation provide insight into the way they represent those problems. For example, Crowder and Newman (1993) found that gestures were a frequent mode of communication in a sixth grade science lesson on the seasons, and that the gestures the students produced revealed their knowledge of the factors that create seasonal change. In one case, a child used both hands to produce a symmetrical gesture, laying down temperature bands on either side of the equator, and thus revealing through her hands knowledge of the symmetry of the hemispheres.

These examples from both adults and children make it clear that gesture can convey meaning and can offer a view of the speaker's mental representation. But gesture has the potential to do much more. When considered in relation to the speech it accompanies, gesture can provide a view of the speaker's cognitive stability—how open that individual is to new input. We have found gesture to be a reliable index of readiness-to-learn in three distinct domains.

Language: The Transition to Two-Word Speech

At the early stages of language development, children are able to produce words one at a time, but are not yet able to combine those words into even very short two-word sentences. We observed six children longitudinally as they made the transition from one- to two-word speech and found that gesture featured prominently during this transitional period (Goldin-Meadow & Butcher, 2002). The first interesting point is that, at the beginning of this period, children seem to find it difficult to combine *gestures* with words. During our initial observations, the children were producing words and they were producing gestures. However, they did not combine those words and gestures together into a single utterance. Moreover, this hole in their repertoires was not because the children were unable to make sounds while gesturing—the children did combine their gestures with non-meaningful sounds, just not with meaningful words. Thus, producing a gesture-plus-word combination itself seems to be a developmental milestone.

When children do begin to produce gesture-plus-word combinations, those combinations are of two types: (1) combinations in which the gesture conveys information *redundant* with the information conveyed in speech; for example, pointing at an object while naming it (de Laguna, 1927; Greenfield & Smith, 1976; Guillaume, 1927; Leopold, 1949); and (2) combinations in which the gesture conveys information that is *different* from the information conveyed in speech; for example, gesturing at an object while describing the action to be done on the object in speech (pointing to an apple and saying "give"), or gesturing at an object and describing the owner of that object in speech (pointing at a toy and saying "mine"; Goldin-Meadow & Morford, 1985; Greenfield & Smith, 1976; Masur, 1982, 1983; Morford & Goldin-Meadow, 1992; Zinober & Martlew, 1985).

Note that in this second type of combination, the child is expressing two semantic elements, one in gesture and one in speech. If gesture and speech are considered a single system, these combinations are, in effect, short one-proposition sentences. We found that the children in our study used gesture-speech combinations of this type to convey a wide range of propositions (Goldin-Meadow & Butcher, 2003). For example, one child pointed at a drawer and said "open" (thus conveying the proposition *open drawer*); another pointed at a turtle and said "go" (conveying the proposition *turtle goes*); yet another produced a clawing gesture and said "bear" (conveying the proposition *bear claws*); finally, one child produced a gesture for big and said "monster" (conveying the proposition *monster is big*).

Combinations in which gesture and speech convey different (and, in this sense, mismatching) information could be a stepping-stone on the way to two-word combinations expressing these same propositions. And, indeed, we found that all of the children produced gesture-speech combinations of this type *before* they produced their first two-word utterance—a child might say "dada" and point not at dad but at his hat an average of 2.3 months (SD = .88, range 1 to 3) before producing "dada hat." More impressive is the fact that the age at which the children first produced these mismatching gesture-speech combinations *correlated* with the age at which they first produced two-word utterances ($r_s = .90$, $p < .05$; Goldin-Meadow & Butcher, 2003). Thus, the children who were first to produce mismatching gesture-speech combinations were also first to produce two-word utterances.

Importantly, the correlation between gesture-speech combinations and two-word speech was specific to utterances in which gesture and speech conveyed *different* information—we didn't find the pattern for utterances in which gesture and speech conveyed the *same* information (i.e., matches, e.g., "hat" + point at dad's hat). The correlation between the onset of matches and the onset of two-word utterances was much lower and unreliable (r_s = .46, ns).[2] Thus, it appears to be the ability to use gesture and speech to convey different components of a proposition—and not just the ability to use gesture and speech in a single utterance—that predicts the onset of two-word utterances (see also Capirci, Montanari, & Volterra, 1998; Goodwyn & Acredolo, 1998; Iverson & Goldin-Meadow, in press).

We have found that the relation between gesture and speech can tell us who is ready to take advantage of input when that input comes naturally through the child's interactions with the world. As seen in the next sections, we find the same effect even when input is administered by an experimenter.

Reasoning About Quantities

When children are asked to justify responses to a series of Piagetian tasks, they gesture (Church & Goldin-Meadow, 1986). Moreover, they use those gestures to convey substantive information about the task. Take, for example, a liquid conservation task. A child is shown two identical glasses containing the same amount of liquid. The liquid from one glass is poured into a short wide dish, and the child is asked whether the glass and the dish contain the same amount of water. Nonconservers say "no" and justify this judgment by explaining that "it's a different amount because you poured it." At the same time, many children augment this verbal response by producing a pouring motion in gesture.

Interestingly, however, some children do not use their hands to express the same information that they express in speech. They use them to convey additional information. For example, a child again says, "it's a different amount because you poured it," but this child gestures the shape of the container rather than the pouring action (i.e., two C-shaped hands positioned with fingertips touching to form a round circle). The

[2]One of the children was substantially older than the others and at the top of the scale on all measures. However, even without this outlier, the correlation between onset of gestures conveying *different* information from speech and onset of two-word speech was .82. Importantly, when this outlier was removed from the correlation between onset of gestures conveying the *same* information as speech and onset of two-word speech, the correlation dropped to .03.

child has focused on the experimenter's pouring motions in speech, but on the shape of the container in gesture—the child has produced a gesture-speech mismatch.

Note that, in this example, the information conveyed in gesture is different from the information conveyed in speech but does not contradict it. In most cases of mismatch, we can imagine a framework within which the pieces of information conveyed in gesture complement and can be integrated with the pieces of information conveyed in speech (in this case, understanding that pouring water into a different shaped container has no effect on the amount of water). However, it is very likely that the speaker who has produced the mismatch is not yet able to appreciate that framework. Indeed, grasping the framework within which gesture and speech can be integrated may be the first step in resolving a mismatch and making progress on the task (see Goldin-Meadow, 2003, for discussion).

We guessed that children who produce many gesture-speech mismatches might differ from children who produce few in their potential for learning, and we conducted a training study to test this hypothesis (Church & Goldin-Meadow, 1986). We first gave fifty-two 5- to 8-year-old children a pretest of six quantity problems to assess their understanding of conservation. We also used the pretest to determine whether the children produced primarily gesture-speech matches (and called those children "matchers") or produced primarily gesture-speech mismatches (and called them "mismatchers"). We then gave all of the children instruction in the task—half were given explicit instruction in conservation, and half were given experience in manipulating the task objects but no training or feedback. After the instruction session, the children were again given the six conservation problems, and we assessed their improvement, if any, from pretest to posttest. We assessed progress in two ways: producing six (out of six) correct judgments on the posttest; and producing a new correct explanation on the posttest, one that the child had not produced at any point before instruction.

We found that, not surprisingly, children given explicit instruction made more progress than children given only the opportunity to manipulate the objects (e.g., none of the manipulators ended up producing six correct judgments on the posttest). However, the important point is that, no matter what type of instruction the children received, mismatchers made significantly more progress than matchers (Church & Goldin-Meadow, 1986). In both instruction groups, significantly more mismatchers than matchers added a new correct explanation to their repertoires (.86 vs. .37, $p = .03$, in the explicit instruction group; .40 vs. .00, $p < .05$, in the manipulation group) and, in the explicit instruction group, significantly more mismatchers than matchers produced six correct judgments (.36 vs. .06, $p = .05$).

Thus, gesture-speech mismatch in a child's explanations of conservation is an excellent sign that the child is ready to learn conservation. Gesture not only reveals a child's unspoken thoughts about quantities, but it also can give us notice that the child may be ready to make progress on the task. To push the boundaries of the phenomenon even further, we set about exploring a second problem-solving task—mathematical equivalence—which is typically mastered by older children (9- to 10-year-olds).

Mathematical Equivalence

Mathematical equivalence is the notion that the two sides of an equation must be equivalent. We used addition problems of the following sort to tap this notion: $4 + 5 + 3 = \_\_ + 3$. Fourth grade children in the United States typically have trouble figuring out that 9 is the number that ought to go in the blank. Children can easily solve simple problems such as $4 + 5 + 3 = \_\_$ and thus, on the surface, *appear* to understand that the two sides of an equation must add to the same amount. However, in these simple problems, children may be getting the right answer for the wrong reason. For example, a child may interpret the equal sign as an instruction to add all of the numbers in the problem, and not as an instruction to make both sides of the equation equal (cf. Behr, Erlwanger, & Nichols, 1980; Ginsburg, 1977; Kiernan, 1980). The fact that children cannot solve the more complex addition problems suggests that this is so. Indeed, fourth grade children typically make two types of errors on the complex problems: they add all of the numbers in the problem (an add-all-numbers strategy), or they add the numbers on the left side of the equation (an add-to-equal-sign strategy).

We videotaped children explaining how they solved the complex addition problems, and found that most children produced gestures along with their explanations (Perry, Church, & Goldin-Meadow, 1988). The children who knew how to solve the problems gave correct explanations in both speech and gesture—"4 plus 5 plus 3 equals 12, so to make the other side equal 12, you need 9 more," said while gesturing: sweep across the 4, 5, and 3 on the left side of the equation, point at the equal sign, sweep across the blank and 3 on the right side of the equation. In this example, the child focuses on the fact that there are two parts to the problem that need to be treated alike (an equalizer strategy) in both modalities. Other children gave incorrect explanations in both speech and gesture—"I added 4 plus 5 plus 3 plus 3 equals 15," while pointing at the 4, the 5, the 3 on the left side of the equation, the 3 on the right side of the equation, and the blank. Here, the child is saying that he added all of the numbers in the problem (an add-all-numbers strategy) in both speech and gesture.

We also found that some children produced gesture-speech mismatches. For example, one child said, "I added 4 plus 5 plus 3 plus 3 equals 15," while pointing with a V-shaped hand at the 4 and the 5 and then pointing at the blank. The child produced an add-all-numbers strategy in speech, but in gesture focused on the two numbers that can be grouped and summed to get the correct answer (a grouping strategy). The child produced an incorrect strategy in speech, but a correct one in gesture. Children also produced mismatches containing two incorrect strategies—"I added 4 plus 5 plus 3 equals 12," while pointing at the 4, the 5, the 3 on the left side of the equation, the 3 on the right side of the equation, and the blank. The child produced an incorrect add-to-equal-sign strategy in speech, but an incorrect add-all-numbers strategy in gesture.

We then conducted a training study comparable to our conservation study (Perry et al., 1988). We gave 37 children in the fourth and fifth grades a pretest of six addition problems to assess their understanding of mathematical equivalence and divide the children into matchers and mismatchers. We then gave the children instruction in the principle underlying the addition problems—the children were told that the goal of the problem was to make both sides of the equation equal. After the instruction session, the children were again given six addition problems and a series of novel addition and multiplication problems that tested their ability to generalize what they had learned.

As in our conservation study, significantly more mismatchers were successful on the posttest and generalization test than matchers (.62 vs. .25, $p < .03$, Perry et al., 1988). The mismatchers had not only learned how to solve the equivalence problems, but also to extend that knowledge to different problem types. Again, mismatch predicted who would learn and who would not.

Interestingly, most of the children who were mismatchers on the pretest produced explanations in which they expressed an incorrect strategy in speech (e.g., an add-to-equal-sign strategy) and a different yet also incorrect strategy in gesture (e.g., an add-all-numbers strategy), as in the example previously described ($4 + 5 + 3 = \_ + 3$). On the surface, these two strategies seem to conflict (they even lead to different solutions, 12 for the add-to-equal-sign strategy and 15 for add-all-numbers strategy). However, note that in order to fully understand mathematical equivalence, a child must understand the premises that underlie both strategies—that the equal sign breaks the equation into two parts (the premise underlying the add-to-equal-sign strategy) and that there are numbers on both side of the equation (the premise underlying the add-all-numbers strategy). As noted earlier, there is in this example (as in most examples of mismatch) a larger framework within which gesture and speech can be integrated. The child who produces the mismatch is not yet aware of that framework, but with instruction comes to appreciate it and make progress on the task.

ADULTS TEACH CHILDREN DIFFERENTLY AS A FUNCTION OF THEIR GESTURES

We now know that information about a child's readiness-to-learn is available in the gestures that children spontaneously produce. Experimenters trained in the art of gesture-coding can make use of this information to predict who will profit from instruction and who will not. The question is whether individuals who are not trained gesture coders can interpret the gestures that children spontaneously produce. The answer is clearly "yes"—at least in experimental situations.

A number of recent studies have shown that adults, and even children (Kelly & Church, 1997, 1998), can interpret the spontaneous gestures that children produce when those gestures are selected by an experimenter and shown twice on videotape (Alibali, Flevares, & Goldin-Meadow; 1997; Goldin-Meadow, Wein, & Chang, 1992; see also Beattie & Shovelton, 1999a; McNeill, Cassell, & McCullough, 1994; Thompson & Massaro, 1986). Indeed, adults can even read children's gestures when the gestures are unedited and observed "live" (Goldin-Meadow & Sandhofer, 1999). But reading gesture as an observer of an interaction is not the same as reading it as a participant in the interaction. Nor do we know from these studies whether adults profit from the information they glean from a child's gestures and use it to alter the way they teach that child.

We decided that the best way to explore this issue was to observe adults instructing a child in a concept. We therefore set up one-on-one math tutorials to determine whether adults give children who produce gesture-speech mismatches different instruction than they give to children who do not. We asked eight math teachers to individually instruct 9- and 10-year-old children whom they did not know in mathematical equivalence (Goldin-Meadow & Singer, 2003). Each teacher instructed from 4 to 6 children. A total of 38 teacher-child pairs were observed. The teacher watched while an experimenter gave the child a pretest consisting of six mathematical equivalence problems. Children who solved even one problem correctly were eliminated from the study. The teacher then instructed the child using any techniques that he or she thought appropriate. After the tutorial, we gave the child a posttest comparable to the pretest. We found that, on the basis of the explanations they produced during the pretest and training, the children could be divided into three groups: those who never produced mismatches at any point during the testing or instruction (*N* = 12); those who produced mismatches only during instruction (*N* = 12); and those who produced mismatches during the pretest (and typically during instruction as well, *N* = 14).

The interesting result is that the children's posttest scores reflected these gesture-speech groupings: Children who produced gesture-speech mismatches on the pretest and during instruction solved 3.2 problems correctly on the posttest (out of 6), children who produced mismatches only during instruction solved 2.1 correctly, and children who never produced mismatches solved 0.5 correctly (Goldin-Meadow & Singer, 2003). Thus, the children who produced mismatches were far more likely to profit from the teacher's instruction than the children who did not. We have once again replicated the basic phenomenon—children who produce gesture-speech mismatches are particularly likely to profit from instruction. Of course, at this point in our analyses, we cannot yet tell whether the mismatchers learned because they were ready to, or because the teachers provided them with just the right instruction. In fact, we will find that *both* the child's state and the teacher's instruction may be important in creating learning.

Let's first look at the teacher's instruction. To determine how sensitive the teachers were to the presence or absence of gesture-speech mismatch in a child's explanations, we calculated how many different types of correct and incorrect strategies each teacher produced when instructing children in the three groups. The number of different types of strategies gives us some idea of how diversified the teacher's lesson was. We found that teachers used significantly more different types of both correct and incorrect strategies when teaching children who produced mismatches during pretest and instruction (1.9 correct, *SD* = .53; 1.0 incorrect, *SD* = .78) and only during instruction (2.0 correct, *SD* = .43; 1.5 incorrect, *SD* = .80) than when teaching children who produced no mismatches at all (1.2 correct, *SD* = .62; 0.6 incorrect, *SD* = .51). In all cases, the teachers used their incorrect strategies to instruct children in what not to do (e.g., "you don't add up all of the numbers in the problem," or to comment on what a child had just done (e.g., "you just added up all of the numbers in the problem"). The incorrect strategies thus seemed to be part of the teacher's instructional plan.

Another index of variability, this time within an utterance rather than across them, is gesture-speech mismatch. At times, the teachers produced mismatches of their own, conveying one strategy in speech and a different strategy in gesture (often both strategies were correct, yet different). Indeed, all 8 teachers produced mismatches and, in fact, they produced mismatches in 34 of the 38 teaching sessions they conducted with the children. However, the teachers produced significantly more mismatches when teaching children who themselves produced mismatches during pretest and instruction (.08, *SD* = .06, of their strategies contained mismatches) and during instruction alone (.12, *SD* = .07) than when teaching children who produced no mismatches at all (.04, *SD* = .03).

Two points are important to make at this juncture. First, this difference rests on the *variety* of correct and incorrect strategies in a teacher's lesson, not the tokens of correct and incorrect strategies. We looked at the proportion of correct and incorrect strategies that the teachers produced, counting each token of a correct and incorrect strategy rather than each type. Not surprisingly, the teachers produced many more correct than incorrect strategies when teaching the children. The important point, however, is that they used the same distribution of strategies when teaching children in all three groups—the proportion of correct strategies the teachers produced did not differ across the three child groups, nor did the proportion of incorrect strategies.

Second, the teachers really did seem to be responding to the children's gesture-speech mismatches. We calculated the number of different types of correct and incorrect strategies the children themselves produced during instruction, and also the proportion of correct and incorrect tokens they produced. There were no reliable differences across the three child groups in either types or tokens of correct and incorrect strategies. The *only* difference that we could find across these three groups of children was their production of gesture-speech mismatches.[3]

Thus far, we have learned that teachers spontaneously provide a more diversified and variable input when teaching children who produce gesture-speech mismatches than when teaching children who don't produce mismatches. Is there any reason to believe that variability is good for learning? We know that when children who cannot solve the mathematical equivalence problem are given repeated trials with the problem but no instruction at all, they make no progress on the task (Alibali, 1999; Goldin-Meadow & Alibali, 2002). Thus, the teachers' in-

[3]Further evidence that the teachers were reacting to child mismatch comes from the fact that the variables the teachers altered during instruction (the number of different types of strategies they produced, and their own mismatches) correlated with child mismatch during instruction. The more mismatches a child produced during instruction, the more different types of strategies ($r_s = .39$, $p = .01$) and the more mismatches ($r_s = .58$, $p < .001$) a teacher was likely to produce during instruction. However, the number of different types of strategies the children produced was *not* significantly correlated with either teacher types ($r_s = .18$, ns) or teacher mismatch ($r_s = .13$, ns). Adjustments in teacher instruction thus correlated only with child mismatch.

struction did make a difference. But was the highly variable instruction that the teachers gave the mismatching children particularly effective in promoting learning?

Note that the phenomenon that we have discovered—that teachers tailor their input to child initial state—makes it difficult to use naturalistic teaching interactions to assess whether teacher instruction has an impact on learning above and beyond the effect of the child's initial knowledge state. Because teachers tailor their input to the children they teach, teacher instruction and child initial state are confounded. To explore whether the variable instruction that the teachers in our study spontaneously gave children is generally good for learning, we need to manipulate instruction experimentally.

We therefore gave 160 children in the 3rd and 4th grades instruction in mathematical equivalence and varied the number of problem-solving strategies taught in speech and the types of gestures that accompanied those strategies (Singer & Goldin-Meadow, 2005). Children were taught either 1 or 2 strategies in speech accompanied by no gesture, gesture conveying the same strategy (matching gesture), or gesture conveying a different strategy (mismatching gesture). The first interesting result is that children solved significantly fewer problems correctly on the posttest when they had been taught two strategies in speech (1.25) than when they had been taught one (2.10). Variability in terms of speech was *not* good for learning. However, variability in terms of gesture was. Children taught one strategy in speech accompanied by mismatching gesture solved significantly more problems correctly on the posttest (3.00) than children taught one strategy in speech accompanied by matching gesture (1.75) or no gesture (1.33; none of the children had solved any problems correctly on the pretest). We found the same pattern in terms of gesture when children were taught two strategies in speech (1.81 mismatching gesture, 1.15 matching gesture, .75 no gesture). Thus, two strategies were not effective in promoting learning when they were both taught in speech, but they were effective when one of the strategies was taught in speech and the other was taught in gesture (i.e., in the one strategy in speech plus mismatching gesture condition). Children profited from instruction in gesture but primarily when it conveyed a different strategy from speech.

Gesture-speech mismatch in instruction appears to promote learning. But does it promote learning for all children? Does the child's state matter? To find out, we used the pretest data to assess whether a child was in a mismatching or a matching state prior to instruction, and then calculated posttest scores for the two groups of children. We found that children in a matching state prior to instruction profited differentially from the different types of gestures in the instruction—they solved more problems correctly on the posttest when instructed with mismatching gesture (2.68) than with matching gesture (1.53) or no gesture (0.57). In contrast, children who were in a mismatching state prior to instruction profited from instruction no matter which gestures they were taught (1.70 mismatching gesture, 1.37 matching gesture, 1.90 no gesture; Singer, 2004). Recall that the teachers in the original Goldin-Meadow and Singer study (2003) instinctively produced mismatches with children who themselves produced mismatches. But it turns out that they did not need to—the mismatching children learned whether or not they were given mismatches in instruction. It was the matching children who required mismatching input to succeed on the task. Our mismatching instruction had turned children who were not quite ready to learn the task into learners.

CHILDREN AND TEACHERS WORK TOGETHER TO PROMOTE LEARNING—AND USE THEIR HANDS TO DO SO

The findings I have presented thus far suggest that gesture mediates the give-and-take between teacher and child—that teachers are sensitive to their students' gestures, and vice versa. However, there could conceivably be other cues that go hand-in-hand with gesture-speech mismatch (e.g., hesitancy in the speaker's voice) and mediate the interchange between teacher and child. We would have a stronger case that gesture-speech mismatch is, in fact, mediating the exchange between teacher and child if we had direct evidence that the teachers noticed and picked up information from the children's gestures, and vice versa.

To get this evidence, we first asked whether the gestures that accompany a child's speech affect the message that the teacher takes from that speech (Goldin-Meadow & Singer, 2003). If, for example, gesture conveys a different message from speech, the teacher might be *less* likely to receive the spoken message than if speech were accompanied by no gesture at all. Conversely, if gesture conveys the same message as speech, the teacher might be *more* likely to receive that message than if speech were accompanied by no gesture at all. To test this hypothesis, we needed a measure of the teacher's reception of the message conveyed in speech, and we chose a conservative one—we counted a spoken strategy as "received" if the teacher repeated that strategy in his or her own words or in gesture.

We calculated the proportion of teacher responses that were repetitions following three types of child utterances: those in which the strategy children expressed in speech (1) matched the strategy expressed in gesture, (2) was accompanied by no gesture, and (3) did not match the strategy expressed in gesture. Teachers did indeed vary their repetitions as a function of type of child utterance. Teachers were significantly *less* likely to repeat a spoken strategy when it was accompanied by mismatching gesture than by no gesture at all (.08 vs. .29 strategies repeated). However, they were no more likely to repeat a spoken strategy when it was accompanied by matching gesture than by no gesture at all (.28 vs. .29). Teachers seem to react to child mismatches but not to child matches.

Gesture thus affects how teacher listeners interpret their student's words. But do those listeners also glean substantive meaning from the gestures themselves? In a gesture-speech mismatch, the child is providing a strategy in gesture that is not conveyed anywhere in speech. If the teacher were to repeat that strategy (in gesture or in speech), we would have evidence that the teacher is indeed gleaning meaning from the child's gestures. We found that teachers did repeat the strategy that the children produced in the gestural component of a mismatch in .10 of their responses—as often as they repeated the strategy that the children produced in the spoken component of a mismatch (.08). Teachers can glean substantive information from their students' gestures.

Are children sensitive to their teacher's gestures? We did precisely the same analysis on the children's responses to teacher utterances. Children varied their repetitions as a function of type of teacher utterance. They were significantly *less* likely to repeat a teacher's spoken strategy if it was accompanied by a mismatching gesture than by no gesture at all (.13 vs. .28 strategies repeated). Unlike the teachers, however, the children were also *more* likely to repeat a teacher's spoken strategy when it was accompanied by a matching gesture than when it was accompanied by no gesture at all (.40 vs. .28). In addition (and like the teachers), the children were able to glean substantive information from gesture. They repeated the strategy conveyed in the *gestural* component of a mismatch as often as they repeated the strategy conveyed in the *spoken* component of a mismatch (.14 vs. .14). These patterns replicate in a completely different sample those found in a previous study of child reactions to teacher gesture (Goldin-Meadow, Kim, & Singer, 1999), and confirm that gesture can substantively affect the information children and teachers take from their partners' communications.

GESTURE AND COGNITIVE CHANGE

To summarize thus far, gesture, when interpreted in relation to the speech it accompanies, provides a useful index of who will, and who will not, profit from instruction on a particular task. As a result, gesture has the potential to play an important role in the learning process itself.

Gesture signals to others that the learner is in a relatively unstable cognitive state, and offers insight into the areas that the learner is currently working on. What I have argued here is that adults, even those who have not been trained to attend to and interpret gesture, are able to glean information from the spontaneous gestures that children produce and then use that information to alter the way they interact with those children. Thus, children can have an effect on the type of input they receive from their communication partners simply by gesturing while they talk.

The Listener's Role in Effecting Cognitive Change

What is remarkable about the phenomenon I have been describing is the teachers—they notice a child's gestures, make inferences about the child's knowledge as a function of those gestures, and then provide the child with instruction that may be just right for learning. Two further questions need to be asked about the teachers.

First, why might a teacher present one strategy in one modality and a different strategy in the other modality when instructing a child? In other words, why might a *teacher* produce a gesture-speech mismatch? I have argued that children produce a large number of gesture-speech mismatches on a task when they are in transition with respect to that task—that is, when they are "ready" to profit from instruction and improve their performance on the task. Children who produce many mismatches are in a state of cognitive uncertainty, possessing knowledge about the task that they cannot quite organize into a coherent whole.

The teachers conducting the math tutorials were obviously not at all uncertain about the principle of mathematical equivalence that underlies the problems they taught. However, they may have been uncertain about how best to teach this principle, particularly in light of all of the incorrect strategies their pupils were espousing. They may have been unsure about how to integrate into a single lesson strategies that lead to incorrect solutions with strategies that lead to correct solutions. It is this uncertainty that may then have been reflected in their mismatches. In general, a mismatch reflects the fact that the speaker is holding two ideas in mind—two ideas that that speaker has not yet integrated into a single story. This way of describing mismatch is as applicable to the teachers and other adults as it is to children.

Second, do the teachers know what they're doing when they respond to the children? Would it help if they did? We really have no idea whether the teachers knew they were responding to the children's gestures, or knew that variability might be a good type of instruction for some of the children. And I can easily imagine that the teachers responded to the children's gestures without being aware of what they were doing. Consider an actual example from one of our studies.

On the problem 5 + 3 + 4 = __ + 4, the child pointed simultaneously at the left 4 with his left hand and the right 4 with his right hand while expressing an incorrect strategy in his speech. The teacher did not reiterate the notion conveyed in the child's gestures—that there are "equal addends" on each side of the equation. Indeed, the teacher may not have been consciously aware of the fact that the child had conveyed an equal addends strategy with his hands. Nevertheless, the teacher behaved as though she had processed the child's gestures. She expressed the grouping strategy in both speech and gesture—"you can solve the problem by adding the 5 and the 3 and putting the sum in the blank," accompanied by a V-shaped point at the 5 and 3. Note that the grouping strategy works in this problem because there are equal addends, one on each side of the equation, that can be canceled. The fact that the child demonstrated some awareness of equal addends in gesture seemed to give the teacher license to introduce grouping, a procedure that the child then picked up on in his next turn and continued to use throughout the interaction. This was the right moment to introduce grouping to the child and, whether or not she was aware of it, the teacher seemed to have learned that this was the right moment from the child's gestures.

Thus, adults need not be aware of the fact that have been influenced by a child's gestures in order to act on the information they get from those gestures. Indeed, the adult may get it just wrong and still be able to provide useful input to the child. Consider, for example, the following case described by Alibali et al. (1997). The child said he solved the problem 5 + 6 + 7 = __ + 7 by adding the 5, 6, and 7 (an add-to-equal-sign strategy), while pointing only at the 5 and 6 (a grouping strategy). After observing this child, the teacher said that the child did *not* understand the grouping strategy: "What I'm picking up now is [the child's] inability to realize that these (indicates 5 and 6) are meant to represent the same number ... there isn't a connection being made by the fact that the 7 on this side of the equal sign (indicates left sign) is supposed to also be the same as this 7 on this side of the equal side (indicates right side), which would, you know, once you made that connection it should be fairly clear that the 5 and 6 belong in the box."

Note that, at some level the teacher was incorrect—the child *did* indeed have an understanding, however implicit, of the grouping strategy, an understanding which he expressed only in gesture. I think it is very likely that the teacher chose the grouping strategy to highlight as the one the child *did not* know because she detected the strategy in the child's gestures. The fact that the teacher did not explicitly recognize the child's grasp of this strategy may not matter if, in instructing the child, the teacher focuses on what she thinks the child needs most—input about the grouping strategy. Instruction about grouping might be especially effective at this moment for this particular child because it might help him to transform or "redescribe" his emerging knowledge into a problem-solving strategy that he could apply and articulate in speech (cf. Karmiloff-Smith, 1992).

As a final example, an adult in a study in which we taught people how to read gesture (Kelly, Singer, Hicks, & Goldin-Meadow, 2002) paraphrased the child's spoken add-to-equal-sign strategy in speech, while at the same time reiterating the child's gestured add-all-numbers strategy in gesture—and only in gesture. It is likely that the adult was aware of repeating the child's correct spoken strategy, but not aware of repeating the child's incorrect gestured strategy. Nonetheless, adult actions of this sort could have an impact on the child simply because children do pay attention to the gestures their teachers produce (see the earlier discussion, Goldin-Meadow et al., 1999, and Singer & Goldin-Meadow, 2005). When an adult "seconds" a child's gestures, it may serve to reinforce the meaning of those gestures for the child—be that meaning correct or, as in this case, incorrect.

Thus, adults can respond to the gesture component of a child's mismatch by "seconding" it in their own gestures, translating it into their own speech, or acting on it without articulating the information at all. In all three cases, the adults might—but they also might not—be aware of the fact that they are responding to gesture. Nevertheless, those responses can have an impact on child learning

Gesture Can Bring About Change Directly and Indirectly

I have been emphasizing here the *indirect* role that gesture plays in cognitive change—the speaker gestures; the listener takes note and behaves differently; the speaker's understanding of the task improves as a result of this changed behavior. Gesture's effect on learning is mediated by the communication partner, thus making gesture an important social tool in cognitive change.

But gesture may also play a more *direct* role in cognitive change. For example, gesturing can aid thinking by reducing cognitive effort (Goldin-Meadow, Nusbaum, Kelly, & Wagner, 2001; Wagner, Nusbaum, & Goldin-Meadow, 2004). The effort saved by gesturing can then be used on some other task, one that would have been performed less well had the speaker not gestured on the first task. Gesturing thus allows speakers to do more with what they've got and, in this way, can also lead to cognitive change.

Another way gesturing could contribute to cognitive change is by influencing the particular ideas that a learner entertains. Gesture offers a route, and a unique one, through which new information can be considered. Because the representational formats underlying gesture are mimetic and analog rather than discrete, gesture permits speakers to represent ideas that lend themselves to these formats (e.g., shapes, sizes, spatial relationships)—ideas that, for whatever reason, may not be encoded in speech (Alibali, Kita, & Young, 2000; Goldin-Meadow, 2003). Gesture provides a format that makes it easy for the child to entertain certain ideas, and thus allows these novel ideas to be considered earlier than they might have been without gesture. Once considered, the new ideas can then serve as a catalyst for change.

The suggestion here is that gesture doesn't just reflect the incipient ideas that a learner has but actually helps the learner formulate and therefore develop these new ideas. In other words, the course of cognitive change may be different by virtue of the fact that the learner gestured (see, e.g., Wagner & Goldin-Meadow, in press). Of course, because gesture is available for all the world to see, it may be the *listener* who first discovers that a child is on the brink of a new insight. And, as we have seen in this chapter, the listener could act on this information and provide just the right input to help the child solidify and further develop that insight. Thus, it may not always be easy to separate the direct and indirect roles gesture can play in cognitive change. The important point, however, is that gesture can cause cognitive change and not just reflect it.

The Breadth of the Phenomenon

The challenge at this juncture is to determine how widespread this phenomenon is. We know that gesture crops up whenever people talk, and that people frequently express different information in their gestures than they express in their words—that is, they produce gesture-speech mismatches. Thus, for example, mismatches have been found in toddlers going through a vocabulary spurt (Gershkoff-Stowe & Smith, 1997); preschoolers explaining a game (Evans & Rubin, 1979) or counting a set of objects (Alibali & DiRusso, 1999; Graham, 1999); elementary school children explaining Piagetian conservation problems (Church & Goldin-Meadow, 1986), mathematical equations (Perry et al., 1988), and seasonal change (Crowder & Newman, 1993); children and adults discussing moral dilemmas (Church et al., 1995); children and adults explaining how they solved Tower of Hanoi puzzles (Garber & Goldin-Meadow, 2002); adolescents explaining when rods of different materials and thicknesses will bend (Stone, Webb, & Mahootian, 1992);

adults explaining how gears work (Perry & Elder, 1997; Schwartz & Black, 1996); adults describing pictures of landscapes, abstract art, buildings, people, machines, etc. (Morrel-Samuels & Krauss, 1992); adults describing problems involving constant change (Alibali et al., 1999); adults narrating cartoon stories (Beattie & Shovelton, 1999b; McNeill, 1992; Rauscher, Krauss, & Chen, 1996). Assuming that the relation between gesture and speech can serve as an index of cognitive stability for all ages and tasks (which is not at all unlikely), the signal is there for the taking, even when adults interact with other adults.

The question then is whether gesture-speech mismatch routinely elicits variable input from listeners. It's very possible that it does simply because listener mismatch could be a direct result of speaker mismatch. Listeners who are attempting to be responsive to the speaker may recognize, at least implicitly, the multiple messages the speaker is conveying. The listeners may respond by incorporating some of the information that the speaker presents into their own speech and incorporating other information into their own gesture. The within-response variability that the listener then displays may be a reaction to the within-response variability the speaker displays.

Consider, for example, the young children we observed making the transition from one- to two-word speech (Goldin-Meadow & Butcher, 2003). Perhaps parents present children who produce one-proposition sentences across modalities (e.g., point at dad's hat + "dada") with more different kinds of utterances than they present to children who don't produce these gesture-speech combinations. And perhaps this variable input is one reason the children who produce mismatches progress seamlessly toward two-word speech. We are currently investigating this hypothesis with respect to the transition to two-word speech and, of course, the question can profitably be asked with respect to any transition.

In summary, gesture is a gold mine for those who pay attention. It can signal when the speaker is ready for change and what new, unacknowledged thoughts the speaker may be having. What I have suggested here is that people pay attention—they alter the way they react to a speaker as a function of the speaker's gestures. Gesture can thus play a pivotal role in the learning process simply because it is an integral part of social interaction.

REFERENCES

Alibali, M. W. (1999). How children change their minds: Strategy change can be gradual or abrupt. *Developmental Psychology, 35*, 127–145.

Alibali, M. W., Bassok, M., Olseth, K. L., Syc, S. E., & Goldin-Meadow, S. (1999). Illuminating mental representations through speech and gesture. *Psychological Sciences, 10,* 327–333.

Alibali, M. W., & DiRusso, A. A. (1999). The function of gesture in learning to count: More than keeping track. *Cognitive Development, 14,* 37–56.

Alibali, M. W., Flevares, L., & Goldin-Meadow, S. (1997). Assessing knowledge conveyed in gesture: Do teachers have the upper hand? *Journal of Educational Psychology, 89,* 183–193.

Alibali, M. W., Kita, S., & Young, A. J. (2000). Gesture and the process of speech production: We think, therefore we gesture. *Language and Cognitive Processes, 15,* 593–613.

Ames, G. J., & Murray, F. B. (1982). When two wrongs make a right: Promoting cognitive change by social conflict. *Developmental Psychology, 18*(6), 894–897.

Beattie, G., & Shovelton, H. (1999a). Mapping the range of information contained in the iconic hand gestures that accompany spontaneous speech. *Journal of Language and Social Psychology, 18,* 438–462.

Beattie, G., & Shovelton, H. (1999b). Do iconic hand gestures really contribute anything to the semantic information conveyed by speech? An experimental investigation. *Semiotica, 123,* 1–30.

Behr, M., Erlwanger, S., & Nichols, E. (1980). How children view the equal sign. *Mathematics Teaching, 92,* 13–15.

Capirci, , O., Montanari, S., & Volterra, V. (1998). Gestures, signs, and words in early language development. In J. M. Iverson & S. Goldin-Meadow (Eds.), *The nature and functions of gesture in children's communications* (pp. 45–60). San Francisco: Jossey-Bass.

Church, R. B., & Goldin-Meadow, S. (1986). The mismatch between gesture and speech as an index of transitional knowledge. *Cognition, 23,* 43–71.

Church, R. B., Schonert-Reichl, K., Goodman, N., Kelly, S. D., & Ayman-Nolley, S. (1995). The role of gesture and speech communication as reflections of cognitive understanding. *Journal of Contemporary Legal Issues, 6,* 123–154.

Crowder, E. M., & Newman, D. (1993). Telling what they know: The role of gesture and language in children's science explanations. *Pragmatics and Cognition, 1,* 341–376.

de Laguna, G. (1927). *Speech: Its function and development.* Bloomington: Indiana University Press.

Doise, W. (1985). Social regulations in cognitive development. In R. A. Hinde, A.-N. Perret-Clermont, & J. Stevenson-Hinde (Eds.), *Social relationships and cognitive development* (pp. 294–308). Oxford: Clarendon Press.

Evans, M. A., & Rubin, K. H. (1979). Hand gestures as a communicative mode in school-aged children. *The Journal of Genetic Psychology, 135,* 189–196.

Flavell, J. H., Speer, J. R., Green, F. L., & August, D. L. (1981). The development of comprehension monitoring and knowledge about communication. *Monographs of the Society for Research in Child Development, 46*(5, Serial No. 192).

Garber, P., & Goldin-Meadow, S. (2002). Gesture offers insight into problem-solving in children and adults. *Cognitive Science, 26,* 817–831.

Gershkoff-Stowe, L., & Smith, L. B. (1997). A curvilinear trend in naming errors as a function of early vocabulary growth. *Cognitive Psychology, 34,* 37–71.

Ginsburg, H. (1977). *Children's arithmetic.* New York: Van Nostrand.

Goldin-Meadow, S. (2003). *Hearing gesture: How our hands help us think.* Cambridge, MA: Harvard University Press.

Goldin-Meadow, S., & Alibali, M. W. (2002). Looking at the hands through time: A microgenetic perspective on learning and instruction. In N. Granott & J. Parziale (Eds.), *Microdevelopment: Transition processes in development and learning* (pp. 80–105). New York: Cambridge University Press.

Goldin-Meadow, S., & Butcher, C. (2003). Pointing toward two-word speech in young children. In S. Kita (Ed.), *Pointing: Where language, culture, and cognition meet.* Mahwah, NJ: Lawrence Erlbaum Associates.

Goldin-Meadow, S., Kim, S., & Singer, M. (1999). What the teacher's hands tell the student's mind about math. *Journal of Educational Psychology, 91,* 720–730.

Goldin-Meadow, S., & Morford, M. (1985). Gesture in early child language: Studies of deaf and hearing children. *Merrill-Palmer Quarterly, 31,* 145–76.

Goldin-Meadow, S., Nusbaum, H., Kelly, S. D., & Wagner, S. (2001). Explaining math: Gesturing lightens the load. *Psychological Science, 12,* 516–522.

Goldin-Meadow, S. & Sandhofer, C. M. (1999). Gesture conveys substantive information about a child's thoughts to ordinary listeners. *Developmental Science, 2,* 67–74.

Goldin-Meadow, S., & Singer, M. A. (2003). From children's hands to adults' ears: Gesture's role in teaching and learning. *Developmental Psychology, 39,* 509–520.

Goldin-Meadow, S., Wein, D., & Chang, C. (1992). Assessing knowledge through gesture: Using children's hands to read their minds. *Cognition and Instruction, 9,* 201–219.

Goodwyn, S. W., & Acredolo, L. P. (1998). Encouraging symbolic gestures: A new perspective on the relationship between gesture and speech. In J. M. Iverson & S. Goldin-Meadow (Eds.), *The nature and functions of gesture in children's communications* (pp. 61–73). San Francisco: Jossey-Bass.

Graham, T. A. (1999). The role of gesture in children's learning to count. *Journal of Experimental Child Psychology, 74,* 333–355.

Greenfield, P., & Smith, J. (1976). *The structure of communication in early language development.* New York: Academic Press.

Guillaume, P. (1927). Les debuts de la phrase dans le langage de l'enfant. *Journal de Psychologie, 24,* 1–25.

Iverson, J. M., & Goldin-Meadow, S. (in press). Gesture paves the way for language development. *Psychological Science.*

Jancovic, M. A., Devoe, S., & Wiener, M. (1975). Age-related changes in hand and arm movements as nonverbal communication: Some conceptualizations and an empirical exploration. *Child Development, 46,* 922–928.

Karmiloff-Smith, A. (1992). *Beyond modularity: A developmental perspective on cognitive science.* Cambridge, MA: MIT Press.

Kelly, S. D., & Church, R. B. (1997). Can children detect conceptual information conveyed through other children's nonverbal behaviors? *Cognition and Instruction, 15,* 107–134.

Kelly, S. D., & Church, R. B. (1998). A comparison between children's and adults' ability to detect conceptual information conveyed through representational gestures. *Child Development, 69,* 85–93.

Kelly, S. D., Singer, M., Hicks, _., & Goldin-Meadow, S. (2002). A helping hand in assessing children's knowledge: Instructing adults to attend to gesture. *Cognition and Instruction, 20,* 1–26.

Kendon, A. (1980). Gesticulation and speech: Two aspects of the process of utterance. In M. R. Key (Ed.), *Relationship of verbal and nonverbal communication* (pp. 207–228). The Hague: Mouton.

Kieran, C. (1980). The interpretation of the equal sign: Symbol for an equivalence relation vs. an operator symbol. *Proceedings of the Fourth International Conference for the Psychology of Mathematics Education,* 163–169.

Kuhn, D. (1972). Mechanisms of change in the development of cognitive structures. *Child Development, 43,* 833–844.

Leopold, W. (1949). *Speech development of a bilingual child: A linguist's record, Volume 3.* Evanston: Northwestern University Press.

Machida, S. (1986). Teacher accuracy in decoding non-verbal indicants of comprehension and noncomprehension in Anglo- and Mexican-American children. *Journal of Educational Psychology, 6,* 454–464.

Masur, E. F. (1982). Mothers' responses to infants' object-related gestures: Influences on lexical development. *Journal of Child Language, 9,* 23–30.

Masur, E. F. (1983). Gestural development, dual-directional signaling, and the transition to words. *Journal of Psycholinguistic Research, 12,* 93–109.

McNeill, D. (1992). *Hand and mind: What gestures reveal about thought.* Chicago: University of Chicago Press.

McNeill, D., Cassell, J., & McCullough, K.-E. (1994). Communicative effects of speech-mismatched gestures. *Research on Language and Social Interaction, 27,* 223–237.

Morford, M., & Goldin-Meadow, S. (1992). Comprehension and production of gesture in combination with speech in one-word speakers. *Journal of Child Language, 19,* 559–580.

Morrel-Samuels, P., & Krauss, R. M. (1992). Word familiarity predicts temporal asynchrony of hand gestures and speech. *Journal of Experimental Psychology: Learning, Memory, and Cognition, 18,* 615–622.

Patterson, C. J., Cosgrove, J. M., & O'Brien, R. G. (1980). Nonverbal indicants of comprehension and noncomprehension in children. *Developmental Psychology, 16,* 38–48.

Perret-Clermont, A.-N., & Brossard, A. (1985). On the interdigitation of social and cognitive processes. In R. A. Hinde, A.-N. Perret-Clermont, & J. Stevenson-Hinde (Eds.), *Social Relationships and Cognitive Development* (pp. 309–327). Oxford: Clarendon Press.

Perry, M., Church, R. B., & Goldin-Meadow, S. (1988). Transitional knowledge in the acquisition of concepts. *Cognitive Development, 3,* 359–400.

Perry, M., Church, R. B., & Goldin-Meadow, S. (1992). Is gesture-speech mismatch a general index of transitional knowledge? *Cognitive Development, 7,* 109–122.

Perry, M., & Elder, A. D. (1997). Knowledge in transition: Adults' developing understanding of a principle of physical causality. *Cognitive Development, 12,* 131–157.

Rauscher, F. H., Krauss, R. M., & Chen, Y. (1996). Gesture, speech, and lexical access: The role of lexical movements in speech production. *Psychological Science, 7,* 226–231.

Schwartz, D. L. & Black, J. B. (1996). Shuttling between depictive models and abstract rules: Induction and fallback. *Cognitive Science, 20,* 457–497.

Singer, M. A. (2004). *Gesture-speech mismatches during instruction and learning: Handing out more information*. Unpublished doctoral dissertation, University of Chicago.

Singer, M. A., & Goldin-Meadow, S. (2005). Children learn when their teachers' gestures and speech differ. *Psychological Science, 16,* 85–89.

Stone, A., Webb, R., & Mahootian, S. (1992). The generality of gesture-speech mismatch as an index of transitional knowledge: Evidence from a control-of-variables task. *Cognitive Development, 6,* 301–313.

Thompson, L., & Massaro, D. (1986). Evaluation and integration of speech and pointing gestures during referential understanding. *Journal of Experimental Child Psychology, 57,* 327–354.

Turiel, E. (1969). Developmental processes in the child's moral thinking. In P. Mussen, J. Langer, & M. Covington (Eds.), *Trends and issues in developmental psychology* (pp. 92–133). New York: Holt, Rinehart & Winston.

Vygotsky, L. S. (1978). *Mind in society: The development of higher psychological processes.* Cambridge, MA: Harvard University Press.

Wagner, S., & Goldin-Meadow, S. (in press). The role of gesture in learning: Do children use their hands to change their minds? *Journal of Cognition and Development.*

Wagner, S., Nusbaum, H., & Goldin-Meadow, S. (2004). Probing the mental representation of gesture: Is hand waving spatial? *Journal of Memory and Language, 50,* 395–407.

Zinober, B., & Martlew, M. (1985). Developmental changes in four types of gesture in relation to acts and vocalizations from 10 to 21 months. *British Journal of Developmental Psychology, 3,* 293–306.

Part IV

Narrative and Autobiographical Memory

The three chapters in this section offer contextualized portrayals of children's earliest stories—stories shared with parents during reminiscing about the past, as well as fantasy stories borne of children's imaginations. Brockmeier opens with a theoretical analysis of a story told by a young child named Hannah. He interprets Hannah's narrative through different philosophical lenses, providing a fitting framework for the book's final section. Fivush next describes variation in parent–child reminiscing about the past, and shows how social categories such as gender are communicated in the earliest dialogues between parents and children. Leichtman and Wang end the section with an intriguing description of cultural differences in the prevalence and quality of shared memories in India, China, and the United States. They contrast distinct styles of parent-child talk, and demonstrate how conversations about the past are both shaped by broader cultural ideologies and come to shape children's developing sense of self.

EXPLORING NARRATIVE MEANINGS

In his chapter entitled *Pathways of narrative meaning construction,* Brockmeier describes narratives as a form of discourse that connects several distinct elements to create a meaningful whole. How might scholars characterize the nature of the connection that binds together the elements of a narrative? Brockmeier's comparative essay is motivated by the quest to understand the conceptual gestalts of children's earliest stories.

As Brockmeier points out, scholars have traditionally emphasized the temporal organization of narratives. For example, a mother and child might talk about a past trip to the zoo, describing the activities of getting dressed and packing lunch in the morning, arriving at their destination, visiting the different animal exhibits, and culminating with their reluctant departure. For a traditionalist, this temporal chronology of events is what makes a narrative cohesive.

However, Brockmeier challenges this traditional definition of narrative cohesion. The temporal alignment of events is only one of several features that can give narratives structure; thematic, spatial and historical elements are other possible organizing themes. Moreover, Brockmeier asserts that a narrative might be analyzed for its conversational and performative coherence. Conversational coherence refers to the transactional, socially dynamic quality of narratives. Narratives unfold in real time, and participants each offer their unique perspectives to the shared story. Consequently, the course of a narrative can change through the very process of narration. Performative coherence refers to the physical enactments that occur during oral narrations, such as when a child incorporates gestures in a story in ways that enhance its meaning. Symbolic play exemplifies a context that affords children opportunities to "act out" narratives.

To illustrate the many "coherences" that could characterize a single narrative, Brockmeier presents a brief narrative told by Hannah, a young girl he observed during a train ride in Western Europe. As Hannah poked at a hole in a train seat, she tells a story about the popular bear Pooh, who becomes separated and then reunited with his mother. Brockmeier examines Hannah's story through the lenses of Russian formalists, sociolinguists, structuralists, deconstructionists and discourse theorists. Brockmeier's many readings of Hannah's story illustrate the rich complexity of what at first glance appears to be a simple narrative. He closes by stating that narratives are co-constructed in the broader context of culture, a point that provides a timely segue into the chapters that follow.

TALKING ABOUT THE PAST

In their chapter, *Parent–child reminiscing and the construction of a subjective self*, Fivush and Haden offer a rich portrayal of both developmental change and individual differences in parent–child reminiscing. The authors note that children develop a personal perspective of their past, or subjective self, through participation in joint reminiscing with others. Through the process of recollecting the past, children come to recognize that individuals hold varying psychological perspectives on past events. This personalized orientation toward past experiences is what comes to define a unique self. The chapter is founded on the authors' programmatic research on parents' conversations with children aged 30 to 70 months.

The first theme of the chapter focuses on developmental change. Over the course of the preschool years, children's reminiscing becomes increasingly sophisticated, and parents' talk about the past changes in ways that parallel the changes observed in their children. In particular, parent–child shared memories gradually shift from being adult-driven to child-initiated. Midway through the second year, most toddlers understand a substantial number of words and simple sentences, and most have experienced a vocabulary spurt in their productive language. Nonetheless, it is rare for toddlers to take the lead in recounting past experiences. Rather, parents provide the bulk of direction in shared conversations with their 16- to 20-month-olds. By 36 months, children play a more active role in shared conversations, and by about 4 years they are able to narrate past experiences surprisingly well. By 8 years, dialogues about the past have progressed to stories that are truly co-constructed.

What emerging capacities enable children to improve in their verbal reminiscing about past experiences? In addition to the obvious contenders of language and cognitive development, the authors suggest that children's growing abilities to organize and evaluate past experiences support advances in narrative skills. More specifically, with development, children display an increasing number of evaluative devices (i.e., words that emphasize subjective reactions to events), mental state terms (i.e., words that refer explicitly to internal thoughts or feelings), and emotion talk (i.e., explicit references to emotions, such as happy, joy, scared) when talking about the past.

The second theme of the chapter speaks to the substantial individual differences that characterize parent–child shared memories. Parents and children vary in how they talk about the past, and the content of parents' talk relates to the content of children's talk in highly specific ways. As three examples, mothers' use of narrative evaluations predicts children's development of an evaluative stance about the past; mothers' mental state talk is associated with children's use of mental state terms; and, both mothers' and fathers' use of emotion language relates to the use of emotion language in their daughters and sons.

Moreover, parent and child gender affect the content of shared memories. The research of Fivush and Haden reveals that mothers refer to emotions more than fathers and both mothers and fathers use more emotion talk with their daughters than sons. Excerpts of shared parent–child dialogues illustrate the contrast between conversations that are rich in subjective reminiscing versus those that are more fact-based. According to Fivush and Haden, conversations that are rich in thoughts and emotions emphasize the "internal landscape of experience." The authors speculate that gender differences in parent–child talk about the past might cause girls to focus more on the internal landscape of experience, thereby leading girls to develop a more elaborated perspective on the past than boys.

MEMORIES IN CULTURAL PERSPECTIVE

The final chapter of the book builds on Fivush and Haden's observations of individual differences in shared talk about the past by extending the study of reminiscing to different cultural groups. In their chapter entitled *Autobiographical memory in the developmental niche: A cross-cultural perspective*, Leichtman and Wang document the variation that exists across societies in the frequency and content of parent–child shared memories.

Leichtman and Wang begin their chapter by noting that the study of episodic memory (i.e., memory for events) has only gained the attention of scholars in recent years. Historically, researchers have explored people's memories for facts, or semantic aspects of memory and have documented the central role of context in the processes of encoding, representation and retrieval. Context is equally important, if not more so, to the study of autobiographical memories. The essence of autobiographical memories are bound to and reflective of the cultural context of experience, and memories about the past are beholden to the cultural dictates of whether and how those experiences are verbally shared by participants.

Leichtman and Wang offer a descriptive account of individual differences in the form and content of adults' and children's memories and interpret these differences in terms of cultural beliefs about memory. They posit that cultural ideologies influence the ways that parents reminisce with their children, and these parenting styles come to shape the content and depth of children's autobiographical memories. For example, parents from cultures that value autonomy and independence might be more likely to reflect upon and discuss personal experiences with their children. In turn, the extent to which parents engage in such detailed conversations about children's past experiences will play a formative role in children's development of self concepts.

Leichtman and Wang's programmatic research on parent–child talk about the past lends empirical support to their predictions. Importantly, the authors took a multi-method approach to the study of memories by conducting interviews with college students and adults, gathering written accounts of autobiographical memories from adults, and observing parents and children talking about the past. Participants were drawn from diverse income strata and cultures, including adults and children from Korea, China, rural and urban India, England, and the United States. Findings revealed provocative cultural variation in how adults shared memories with their children, both within and across the cultures studied. For example, preschool children differed in how much they elaborated on their roles, preferences and feelings, attitudes, beliefs and traits in line with the broader cultural orientations of independence versus interdependence. Children from China offered skeletal accounts of past experiences, whereas U.S. children offered more embellished accounts that centered on highly personalized experiences. Studies of parent–child discourse showed that parents in the different cultures varied in how they socialized thematic and linguistic features of children's discussions about the past. Parents displayed distinct styles of prompting and elaborating and they channeled their children's attention toward specific aspects of experiences through the topics and details they chose to discuss. In response, the number and types of details that children recalled about their personal pasts varied with their parents' socialization styles.

SUMMARY

The complementary chapters by Brockmeier, Fivush and Haden, and Leichtman and Wang reveal the social embeddedness of children's stories specifically, and cognition more broadly. As the authors consistently demonstrate, even the most individualized of thoughts and experiences—reflections on the self and one's personal past—are shaped by nested social contexts, including but not limited to the family, social constructions of gender, and culture. Moreover, this social molding of children's stories occurs across multiple time frames. Personal experiences are reflected upon, constructed and shared during the moment-to-moment real-time frame of co-performed conversations, and personal experiences are integrated into a sense of subjective self that is continually changing across the entirety of one's lifespan. Indeed, the points raised in this closing section reflect a theme that lies at the core of this book: cognition is a socially embedded, transactional process between the internal and external worlds of the child.

Chapter 12

Pathways of Narrative Meaning Construction

Jens Brockmeier
New School University/Free University Berlin

In this chapter I am going to make the case that narrative is a central category of understanding human social cognition. I shall argue that narrative, in particular, gives coherence and intelligibility to complex forms of communication and cognition. Furthermore, I shall show that it even does so at an early stage in children's linguistic, cognitive, and social development—even at a time when children are usually not viewed as active creators and narrators of fully blown stories.

To flesh out this argument, I need first to specify what I mean by narrative and narrative coherence. The literature offers a variety of concepts and ideas of narrative which imply not only different concepts of communication and cognition but also of coherence. The following is a working definition of narrative which I unpack in this chapter; it focuses on what I believe to be the three essential features that make narrative discourse such a powerful form of communication and cognition. First, narrative brings a perspective to our experience, knowledge, thought, and much of our emotional life, a perspective that organizes how we face the world in which we live and how we position ourselves and others in this world. Second, it connects (through this perspective) several distinct elements to each other as to constitute a whole; that is, it creates a synthesis of meaning, a gestalt that is more than the sum of its isolated elements. Coherence, in this view, emerges as the connective force of a meaning structure or, put differently, it is a side effect of narrative meaning construction. And third, narrative is a way to do things. It is discourse in a strong sense, that is, a mode of action and performance inextricably entangled with the cultural grammar of a community of action and interpretation. In this sense, narrative is what Wittgenstein described as a form of life. In short, in my understanding, narrative is a perspective, a synthesis, and a form of life.

Admittedly, at this point this definition sounds quite elementary and, what is worse, dry. Moreover, it misses one aspect of narrative which, despite the variety of concepts and views in the literature, is almost unanimously agreed on (at least, among nonliterary theorists and empirical researchers of narrative): This is that narrative is a form of temporal sequencing. Closely connected to this idea, coherence is usually conceived of as an issue of temporal organization, as a way of ordering narrative in time. In fact, temporal ordering (and often this is meant to be chronological ordering) is commonly considered to be essential for making a narrative coherent.

Now, my definition of both narrative and coherence has left out time and temporal sequencing as a constitutive feature of narrative; and it has done so for a good reason. In what follows, I explain why the focus on time, so dominant in psychological, linguistic, and narratological theorizing of narrative, is misleading. It is misleading, I shall point out, because it fails to capture more fundamental qualities of narrative. These qualities only come into sight if narrative is viewed not primarily as a form of temporal sequencing or ordering in time but as a particular way of meaning construction. In offering a perspective, creating a synthesis, and organizing an action, narrative discourse is a way of meaning-making that follows pathways which, as I would like to show, often go beyond traditional linguistic and psychological categories both of narration and meaning.

NARRATIVE COHERENCE: TEMPORAL SEQUENCING OR MEANING CONSTRUCTION

One might date the beginning of the narrative turn in psychology to 1986. In that year, some influential books were published, among them Bruner's *Actual Minds, Possible Worlds*. In this book, Bruner suggested that there are two modes of thought, the paradigmatic mode, dominant in the domain of scientific, logical, and propositional reasoning, and the narrative mode, dominant in social and interpretive domains of human meaning construction. This juxtaposition has often been quoted and used as an argument in debates about narrative and the mind. But it also has faced several objections which have repudiated the claim of a clear-cut borderline between narrative and paradigmatic modes of thought and discourse. In fact, Bruner (1996, 2002) himself later suggested a more differentiated version of this view.

Still, there is one area where this distinction may enable us to understand things better. This is the study of time, more precisely, of the temporal dimension of our lives and thoughts. The notion of time and temporality in psychology is almost entirely determined by "paradigmatic" concepts. From Piaget and classical general, cognitive, and neurocognitive psychology to narrative and discursive psychology, time is conceived of after the model of clock and calendar time: It is homogeneous, continuous, linear, and directed; it is subject to, and standard of, objective reckoning and measurement, as well as logical reflection. The overarching conception here, as in most technical and practical forms of "time management," is the Newtonian model of absolute time. It represents time either as a homogeneous time-space or as an linear and endless line, the "arrow of time," on which all events can be marked in infinitely small and large sections.

The problem I am driving at arises from the fact that the Newtonian model is not only used to "paradigmatically" project quantifiable and measurable events and processes onto a homogeneous matrix of time or time-space. It also serves to give order and coherence to psychological processes and cultural meaning systems, to phenomena, that is, which pertain to the domain of the narrative or interpretive mode. What is more, narrative itself is often conceived of as a primary form and practice to organize events and experiences along the lines of a sequential temporal order. In developmental, educational, and clinical psychology, narrative tests typically associate the ability of children and people with psychiatric and neurological disorders to chronologically tell or retell a sequence of events with their cognitive and linguistic abilities. What is offered in this way is a sort of narratological translation of traditional views of normal cognitive development—as, for example, in Piaget's model of development, according to which the concept of time emerges as a result of children's growing logico-intellectual competence.[1]

My argument is that temporal ordering is but one feature of narrative, and this feature might not even be an essential one. There are many forms and practices of narrative that are characterized by qualities more

[1]I have described this "narratological translation" of the paradigmatic mode of thought in some more detail in another work (see Brockmeier, 2004).

fundamental than a specific temporal organization. Moreover, the time order of many narratives—especially, life- and self-narratives—is all but that of chronological sequentiality (Brockmeier, 2000). That is to say, if we want to understand what makes narrative coherent we cannot just "paradigmatically" impose a Newtonian time grid on a seemingly inchoate array of narrative raw material. Instead, we must investigate the particular narrative registers of meaning construction—which is, as we will see, quite a different business.

What, then, are the registers and devices of meaning construction that make a narrative coherent?

FORMS OF NARRATIVE COHERENCE

To tell a story chronologically, that is, to align events or actions in a linear temporal sequence—"one after the other"—is one possibility to give events or actions the coherence of a whole. Yet there are a number of others. Coherence can also be based on the linguistic composition of a narrative (how is it "internally" organized?), on its paratexts (how is it "externally" framed and distinguished from other speech acts, types of discourse, and different social activities?), and on the discursive context of the narrative event (who tells it to whom, why, and in which cultural setting?). Each of these, as well as any combination among them, can give coherence to narrative discourse.

Let me point out a few forms of coherence, different from that of temporal sequentiality, that are created in this way. I shall call them narrative coherence, conversational coherence, performative coherence, and multiple coherence.

Narrative Coherence

The linguistic composition of an account can be organized according to several narrative criteria (in this context I understand "narrative" in a narrow linguistic sense; in a moment, I also discuss the term in a broader sense). One important criteria of narrative coherence is *thematic* or *topical*: What is the story about, what happens, and why does it happen? Another one is *spatial*: What happens at a particular location? A third one is *historical*: What happens at a particular time or time period? These compositional features typically correlate with particular *genres* and other culturally established *narrative models*, for example, models of stories that are considered to be funny or comic, provocative, morally didactic, or historically instructive. There also are several *poetic and rhetorical forms*—metaphors, metonymies, parables, and other tropes—contributing to the coherence of a story and, in fact, often defining the very character of a narrative as, for example, in fables and fairy tales. The protagonists in many fairytales or fable-like children's stories are animals who take the parts of adults but act, think, and feel like children. Although human adults who act like children are, at best, childish, it makes perfect sense within these genres when adult animals speak to human children. Finally, there are *stylistic* features that bring a defining point of view to a narrative—as when a story is told from the vantage point of a child (who may be represented by a little bear), or from a genderized perspective (as Robyn Fivush points out in her chapter in this book). Defining point of view and perspective are terms that can also be used to describe the overall effect of all the aspects of narrative mentioned here: They bring a perspective to our experience, knowledge, and intentions, a perspective that organizes how we face the world in which we live.

In such perspective individual and cultural orientations overlap and fuse. I just referred to gender, which is per definition a cultural perspective, that can shape a narrative, as it is itself shaped by numberless narratives. Yet there are many more forms in which culture impacts on narrative and, in particular, on what counts as narrative coherence. Ultimately, there is no such thing as narrative discourse or narrative practice isolated from its living cultural and historical milieu, and it is here where we have to search for criteria of coherence. Consider the *storylines* of mythical narratives of origin which typically unfold along patterns of genealogy or kinship. Such accounts are only temporally sequenced in as far as they place events in an unspecified "mythical time," a temporality without any chronological marking in terms of clock and calendar time. In many religious narratives, episodes appear to be coherently connected because they all belong to a special sphere of being, a world of transcendence and wonder in which our everyday plausibilities are suspended.

In all these cases, narratives are distinguishable forms of discourse, oral or written, not because they are governed by the principle of time but because of the particular perspective they bring to our experience and thought. This perspective emerges from their particular linguistic composition, their external framework or paratext, and the discursive situation—the narrative event—in which they take place.

But not all narratives have such a clear-cut frame that separates them from other activities, linguistic or not. Narratives can also be open events, embedded in all kinds of other linguistic and nonlinguistic activities; they can be try-outs, incomplete and enigmatic, told in passing as element of a conversation, as excuse, or joke.

Conversational Coherence

Indeed, what makes many narratives coherent is that they are part of an ongoing social interaction. Narratives are communicative events, integrated in interpersonal exchange. Narrative acts are extended speech acts. In everyday life, stories typically are not told in isolation but intermingled with all kinds of communicative practices. Still, communicating events, experiences, and ideas often take the form of narrative. But this "form" is not necessarily that of closed and well-ordered stories. In conversational narratives, stories usually are not told "as such" but as part of an extended social dynamic. Integrated in the flow of talk, they are subordinated to rhetorical strategies that may or may not underlie participants' discursive behavior. Their "logic" is not determined by narratological considerations but by the dynamic of talk-in-interaction. As a consequence, conversational narratives mostly are interrupted and fragmentary; often it is hard to identify them as real stories at all (as we see in some detail when we study an example of a "fuzzy story"). Overlapping with and varying stories (or elements of stories) of others, their organization and, indeed, their entire plot can change in the very process of being narrated. Sometimes, there might not even be a proper plot at all. Everyday conversational narratives, as Ochs and Capps (2001) put it, can be regarded the "country cousins of well-wrought narratives" (p. 3). The narrators we meet and become in one of the many social encounters of our everyday life, "are not renowned storytellers, and their narratives [usually] are not entertaining anecdotes, well-known tales, or definitive accounts of a situation. Rather ... the narrators often are bewildered, surprised, or distressed by some unexpected events and begin recounting so that they may draw conversational partners into discerning the significance of their experiences" (p. 2).

In contrast with the traditional idea of narrative as organized by a cognitive or linguistic story scheme, a normative script, or an organized plot—an idea that can be traced back to the Aristotelian conception of drama—there recently has been a tendency to understand narrative as a more fleeting form of discourse, as a form of talk-in-interaction.[2] In this post-Aristotelian view, narrative is primarily understood not as a textual result and a given genre but as a discursive activity. That is, it is as much a process, the activity of telling, as it is an outcome of this process, a product, the story. The general idea here is that the organization of narrative discourse emerges as a function of what the talk (as a site and practice of

---

[2]See, for example, Bamberg, 2000; Brockmeier & Harré, 2001; Edwards, 1997; Miller, 1994; Norrick, 2000; Ochs & Capps, 2001; Schegloff, 1992.

social interaction) does, or what participants want to do in and through talk. One thing that they want to do and, in fact, unavoidably do is *to position* themselves with regard to others and others with regard to themselves (Bamberg, 1997; Harré & Langenhove, 1999). Positioning is to take over a role or a position in a field of social interaction. "With positioning," Harré and van Langenhove (1999, p. 17) write, "the focus is on the way in which the discursive practices constitute the speakers and the hearers in certain ways and yet at the same time, they are a resource through which speakers and hearers can negotiate new positions."

In contrast to viewing the temporal order of what is told as something that is "re-presented," "depicted," or "reflected" by narrative, the conversational and discursive approach suggests that the temporal ordering of a story is an interactional accomplishment. It is used as a communicative resource. However, this resource is not a given but emerges in the process of communication itself; thus, often it becomes only visible in a microgenetic reconstruction. In other words, the frame of reference at stake here is not an order that exists outside of the discursive dynamics (like, say, a grammatical rule), but rather it is these dynamics that creates the reference. This leads to and overlaps with a third form of coherence, which I call performative coherence.

Performative Coherence

Stories, as already mentioned, are narrative speech acts. They are told in order "to do things," to use Austin's (1962) famous expression. On the discursive account, stories are strategic interventions into ongoing activities. In this sense, Edwards (1998) speaks of an "action-performing, rhetorically potent notion of discourse"—a notion that might help us to view forms of communicative action as forms of narrative coherence. At the same time, this notion also suggests that narratives are not only told but also performed and enacted. They are not only part of and intermingled with actions, but often set the stage for actions. A case in point is children's symbolic play. In symbolic play, it is typically narrative to set up the scene and trigger the symbolic imagination: It is a story to connect a chair to a racing car and make one turn into a princess by putting on mom's high-heeled shoes. More extended stories from books, television, or video often serve not just as starting points, but also as scripts for the entire symbolic performance. In the course of such "narrative play-acting," as Nicolopoulou (1997) has called it, various interpretations of the script may be acted out. It is a well established result from research in theory of mind that by about four years of age children understand others' minds and can predict the actions of others, regardless whether these are real-life actions or actions within the contexts of a story that has been told to them.[3]

Bruner (1990, 2002), Nelson (1996, 2003) and others have argued that children's performative understanding and enacting of narrative begins even earlier, namely, at the onset of their cognitive and communicative development. Children's first narratives are told in nonverbal forms: in playful interactions with a parent, in mime, and through pictures, dolls, and other toys. Drawing on Donald's (1991) thesis that mimesis preceded language as a symbolic form in anthropogenesis, Nelson proposes the priority of these forms of narrative also in ontogeny. Even if narrative can be seen as natural product of language, in fact, as the very embodiment of language, this does not exclude, as Nelson (1996, p. 191) goes on to argue, that "the existence of narrative in nonverbal forms suggests the possibility that as a form it may develop independently of language, or at least that there may be other contributions to its development. Children not only hear stories read from books but also watch narrations on televisions and in films, and construct narratives in play." It might be added that all of these activities—watching television and videos and playing narrative scenarios—are, in one form or another, closely intertwined with language. In fact, children's games are arenas of language. Particularly in pretend games, as has often pointed out (e.g., Garvey, 1984), the saying is the playing. Fantasy and pretend games, writes Cook-Gumperz (1984), "are social projects where children are spontaneously involved in self-organized settings and where speech is a naturally occurring part of the context" (p. 341). That is to say, games (as well as watching television and videos) are discursive activities which defy the idea of a clear borderline between nonverbal and verbal forms of narrative (Brockmeier, 1998).

Other authors (e.g., Miller, 1982, 1994; Engel, 1995; Zentella, 1998) have emphasized that children are virtually immersed in narratives. Growing up in a world densely populated by stories, they continuously engage in narrative practices that involve fictive and personal stories as well as stories about other people. These stories are told by adults to children and children to adults, among adults in the presence of children, and among children; they are presented and performed in a variety of media: oral, literal, musical, iconic, filmic, and other. In short, children grow up in a multimodal symbolic space of narrative.

---

[3]See Astington, Harris, & Olson, 1988; Astington & Jenkins, 1995; Brockmeier, 1995/1997. Nelson (2003) has suggested that the development of children's theory of mind is closely intertwined with the development of their ability to engage in narrative discourse. She argues that shared narratives which are based on personal experience are the "symbolic vehicles" through which children develop an understanding of different perspectives on the world of experience. "The claim here is that shared experiential narratives are the symbolic vehicles, available only to humans, through which such insights are gained, including the important insight that the other has a past and a present that differ from one's own, as well as the accompanying insight that one's own past is unique to oneself" (p. 29).

Multiple Coherences

Furthermore—and to make things even more complicated—one can do several things at the same time. In fact, usually we do. We are simultaneously entangled in various ongoing activities and events that are intermingled with language. In talk we combine multiple orders of activity and meaning construction. More technically put, language is multifunctional and polysemic; it can realize different actions and meanings simultaneously. Moreover, narrative discourse is not the only form of talk, talk is not the only form of communication, and communication is not the only form of human activity. Each of these forms and formats of action and interaction sets up its own pragmatic and pragmatist criteria of coherence—be it narrative, conversational, performative, or simultaneously on several levels of action and communication. To be sure, this is a rather complicated scenario. To explain how it works in detail, I therefore would like to have a look at an unspectacular little narrative, a simple story; at least that's what the story of Hanna looks like at first sight.

HANNA'S STORY

Hanna's story is an example of a natural or spontaneous everyday narrative, taken from a collection of "train stories" from and about children traveling on railway trains in several Western European countries.[4] Hanna, a girl of 31 months of age, is traveling with her mother and father (who is reading and uninvolved in the narrative event); in the same compartment there is another passenger (who recorded the scene).[5]

---

[4]Several authors (e.g, Dunn, 1999; Miller, 1994; Nicolopoulou, 1996; Ochs & Capps, 2001) have emphasized the necessity of studying children's natural or spontaneous narratives in the social context of everyday life because experimental elicitation techniques, artificial monological settings, and adult-oriented contexts exclude important resources, motivations, and "extra-linguistic" aspects of children's narrative activities.

[5]Transcription conventions:

> <	Speed-up talk
[ ]	Start and end of overlapping speech
(3)	Pauses in seconds
(.)	Micropause
(:)	Prolongation of preceding vowel
((Text))	Transcriber's comment
{Text}	Added by transcriber
Underlining	Emphasis
CAPITALS	Speech that is louder than surrounding speech.
—	Utterance interrupted

1. Mother: >DON'T PUT YOUR FINGER IN THAT HOLE<: it's sharp. You'll get hurt.
2. Hanna: What here?
3. M: It's broken.
(3)
4. H: Who lives here?
5. M: Little Pooh.
(6)
6. H: ((pointing at the hole)): Mommy?
7. M: Yes, his Mommy also lives there.
(10) ((H continues to investigate the broken armrest))
8. H: She gone?
9. M: Yes, she's gone out.
10. H: Gone [out?]
11. M: [WATCH OUT] (.) It's very sharp. Don't touch that.
(3)
12. H: Alo(:)ne?
13. M: Yes, Pooh now is alone at home.
(5)
14. H: ((turns to another passenger sitting across from them)): Mommy back {in a} whi:le (.) Pooh alone.
15. Passenger: I'm sure she will be back soon to look after Pooh.
16. H: Soon back.

Admittedly, this is a simple story, so simple that we might wonder if it is a story at all. Does this sequence live up to a level of narrativity that meets the criteria of meaning coherence outlined earlier? This question brings us back to the issue of how to define narrative and coherence. As already mentioned, there is no commonly shared concept of narrative. In my working definition I suggested three essentials of a narrative: It brings a perspective to our experience and thought; it constitutes a whole, a synthesis or gestalt of meaning that is more than the sum of its isolated elements; and it is a mode of action. Now what is the narrative whole, the gestalt of meaning emerging in this sequence of utterances? What kind of coherence—narrative, conversational, performative, or multiple—is created in those few minutes in Hanna's train compartment that are captured by this transcription?

To better understand what this sequence is all about, I reread it a few times, each time through the lenses of a different narratological master doctrine—a different *grand narrative* of narrative, so to speak—using in this way the rich analytical knowledge provided by a long and multidisciplinary tradition of narrative investigation. As a consequence, we have to deal not just with one but with several stories.

HOW MANY STORIES DID HANNA TELL?

The Classic Story

Let me begin with literary theory, and here with one of the most venerable notions of narrative, that of Aristotle, which was already mentioned. The classic Aristotelian criterion to determine narrativity is that a story is a structured and closed whole: It has a beginning, a middle, and an end (Aristotle, 1967). We do not have much difficulty to recognize Hanna's story as a dramatic narrative in the Aristotelian sense: It is the story of little Pooh and his Mommy (beginning in line 4) who live together at their home. The "rising action" begins, and with it what Aristotle called "complication," when Mommy goes out (or when it is discovered that she went out) and Pooh remains alone at home. This is the middle part of the story (8–13). The end begins with the turning point that leads to a reversal—in Aristotelian terms—the *peripeteia* or peripety, in the protagonist's (that is, we may assume, Pooh's) fortunes: the recognition or anticipation that Mommy will come back soon (14-16). Hanna's story is not quite an antique tragedy but it shows the elementary form of a classic dramatic action; an ancient Greek probably would not have any difficulty in recognizing it as a meaningful plot.

Some further literary features of Hanna's narrative come into view if we take a Burkean stance. For Burke (1945), a modern Aristotelian, stories are based on an imbalance in the "ratio" of what he considers to be their five constitutive elements: protagonist, action, scene, goal or intention, and means. To be sure, in Hanna's story there is serious trouble. After the *scene* is set (in 1–5), we learn that the *protagonist*, Pooh, has been left alone by his Mommy, which is the *action*. As a consequence, Hanna suggests, he feels lonely and afraid, his obvious *goal* or *intention* being to have his Mommy back. Now to identify the *means* in the sense of Burke, we might need a little interpretive effort. For example, as I would propose, we might bring into the picture the storyteller herself, that is, Hanna, and her clear sympathy for the hero, which finds additional support in the sympathy of the other passenger (15). Viewed in this manner, the story not only unfolds an imbalance in the ratio of its five Burkean elements but also suggests a perspective to resolve the tension and reestablish the proper balance which has at its core the unity between Mommy and Pooh.

A Structural Story

One of the most influential approaches to language and literature in the twentieth century was structuralism. It all began, early in the century, with Russian Formalism which set the scene for a new way to look at common "structural" qualities of stories. If faced with Hanna's story, a Russian formalist would have been quick to point out that Hanna's story shows an archetypal "deep structure" or, in Proppian terms, an universal "basic theme" (Erlich, 1981). This is about mother–child separation and separation anxiety. In the process of narration this theme is instantiated in a particular plot, the *sjuzet*. As with every sjuzet, its very composition has transformed the underlying story, the *fabula*, which consists of the simple sequence of events—in this case, the fabula is that mother and child are separated and reunified. In the process of this transformation, the fabula is turned into a narrative proper. This precisely is what happens in Hanna's narration. Rather than presenting a simple sequence of events, which just recapitulates the fabula, the order is reversed. The plot starts in a retrospective mode with the gradual discovery of what happened before the actual narrative event: It unveils that, at some point in the past, mother and child were separated. Together with the narrator we, the listeners, only learn in 8–10 about the drama that must have unfolded in the past, even if all details are invitingly left to our imagination. Technically speaking, this is a flashback toward an earlier time plane, which is followed (in 14 and 15) by a flashforward to an indefinite future. Looking at it through this formalist lens, Hanna's story then is about to lose its narratological innocence.

The structuralists of the next generation also would have no difficulty identifying Hanna's account as a proper narrative. For sociolinguists like Labov and Waletzky (1967) all narrative is temporally sequential and organized around a high point. More precisely, it is sequential in so far as it connects at least two distinct events in time. In Hanna's story we easily recognize not only two but at least three such events: the separation, its discovery, and the prospective reunion. In a view a bit broader but still in line with Labov and Waletzky's basic idea we also might count Hanna's sympathetic intervention in 14 as a further event. As far as the second criterion is concerned, the centrally situated high point of the story—the discovery that little Pooh is alone at home (8–13)—is all the more foregrounded by the unexpected interruption "Watch out" of Hanna's mother. This foregrounding, as linguists call it, signals a "relevant now" by bringing it into the highest prominence, making sure it becomes the dominant focus of our perception.

Note that the development of the narrated event culminating in this dramatic high point takes place in a "landscape of consciousness": in

Hanna's—and our—imagination. In this sense, we might view Hanna's story more as a "psychological" narrative than an action story. But we must carefully qualify terms such as *consciousness* and *psychological* in this context. Structuralist theory of literature introduced the distinction of "landscape of consciousness" and "landscape of action" to identify a particular quality of literature. Bruner (1986) took up these concepts to characterize the specific way in which humans interpret actions in terms of intentions, goals, beliefs, and emotions. More precisely, they make sense of the landscape of action by implementing it into a landscape of consciousness, that is, a landscape of intentionality. Investigating the extended monologues of little Emily, a girl more or less the age of Hanna's, Bruner and Lucariello (1989) argued that with the beginning of children's narrative soliloquies the dual worlds of action and consciousness emerge. However, as we can see both in Hanna's and in many of Emily's narratives (Nelson, 1989), these two worlds or "landscapes" are as inextricably entangled as are children's consciousness and action.

Examining, in comparison, fictional storytelling among 5- and 6-year-olds, we find that the ability and the inclination to integrate these two dimensions increases with age and experience, but also varies considerably from child to child (Brockmeier, 2004). Such findings support Nelson's (1996, p. 186) suggestion that "from the developmental point of view, we may inquire as to whether and when children incorporate the landscape of consciousness in the landscape of action. Are they ever separate in ontogeny, or do they constitute from the beginning a single 'flow'?" We will see that in Hanna's story and in the landscape of action in which it is embedded this distinction is indeed difficult to maintain.

For Structuralists in the area of semiotic narratology (as proposed by Greimas and his school), narrativity is defined as a mode of transformation in which a central "narrative kernel" (the deep structure) serves to produce a variety of meanings and values. These transformational derivatives from the relatively simple kernel narrative exist both objectively in the text and subjectively in the mind of the reader. For a Greimasian narratologist, a typical narrative kernel, for instance, would be the dichotomy between absence and presence in Hanna's story. The story begins with a first transformation of Pooh's position from negative (it is unclear who lives "here," at the scene of action) to positive (Pooh lives here). It continues in several transformations of the position of Pooh's mother (who also lives there, even if she is not there right now, but will again be there). Both transformational lines finally intersect (Pooh is present when his mother is absent), which, according to the structuralist, creates the resulting "surface structure" of the narrative.

An Open Story

Following the path of the history of ideas, we encounter several waves of criticism not only of structuralism but of all conceptions that privilege the isolated individual and his or her mind (or brain) as the center of linguistic analysis, rather than examining the social and cultural dynamics of linguistic forms of life. For example, a post-structuralist or deconstructionist reading of Hanna's story would not deny that it is a narrative but would question that it is *Hanna's* narrative in the first place. For theorists like Derrida and Kristeva not only is the idea of an individual narrator or author creating his or her text independently from any narrative or textual context a highly problematic abstraction, but also the entire notion of an autonomous text is untenable. Instead, the deconstructionist concept of intertextuality aims to signify the multiple ways in which any literary or natural text is inseparably intermingled with other texts. Every spoken or written text—even every spoken and written word, as Bakhtin (1981) would add—is the site of an intersection of numberless other texts and words: an ongoing dialogue, in fact, a polyphonic conversation which also includes those words and texts that have been produced in the past and will be produced in the future.

In this view, Hanna's story, like any text, is part of a meandering and open intertext. The meaning of this story, as simple as it may appear and as spontaneously as it might have been told, cannot be determined within its own limits—limits which, by the way, only seem to be its own but in reality are set by the observer and transcriber of the narrative. The meaning of Hanna's narrative only results from its connection to a much larger world of texts and meanings. Note that there are several open and covert citations and allusions; most evidently, of course the reference to Winnie the Pooh, the hero of many books, films, cartoons, and play scenarios. In fact, one of the picture books Hanna and her mother read and watched briefly before the narrative event in question took place was a book about Winnie the Pooh.

So why then would we want to view Hanna's story as a case of intertextuality? Intertextuality has been defined in a restricted way as the relation(s) between one text and other texts which are in some way or another present in it. In a more general and radical way it also has been conceived as the relation(s) between "any text (in the broad sense of signifying matter) and the sum of knowledge, the potentially infinite network of codes and signifying practices that allows it to have meaning" (Prince, 1987, p. 46). Finally, the term intertextuality has been used to capture references both to texts and to experiences of the extra-textual world, bringing the life worlds of authors, readers, and speakers to the text, while situating the interpretation of the text within the life worlds of everyday culture. This perspective seems to be particularly appropriate to explore children's construction and understanding of stories because it requires "linking [their] meaning-making through texts to life experiences and vice versa" (Eriksson, 2002, p. 16).

A Reader's Story

A similar picture emerges if we look at Hanna's narrative from the point of view of reader-response criticism and reception theory. In contrast with earlier theories of literature and text that focus on the author or are primarily interested in the text as an autonomous construct, in many recent studies the attention has shifted to the reader and his or her constructions of meaning. The basic assumption of all reception-oriented research is that the reader is the co-creator of the text or, perhaps more precisely, the meaning of the text. To understand this multilayered co-construction, we need to take into account not only the history of the text (and, possibly, the author) and its cultural semantics but also the history of the reader. Viewing in this light Hanna as a reader of a story about Winnie the Pooh suggests examining her own narrative as the account of a very personal interpretation of the story, an interpretation oscillating between fiction and life. This, of course, is all but unusual. Developmental psychologists from Piaget (1951) and Vygotsky (1987) to Donaldson (1978) and Harris (2000) have pointed out that neither in the minds nor in life worlds of preschool children is there a borderline between what adults call the realm of reality and the realm of imagination, fantasy, play, and dream. We also can add here the realm of narrative fiction. Each story told to a child is an invitation to blur this borderline—which, as anthropologists tell us, is anyway a highly cultural configuration. Offering scenarios of real and possible worlds, stories draw the mind of the child into an open universe of meanings and, in doing so, bind the meanings of a culture into the child's mind.

Yet Hanna's story does not simply use elements from a Winnie the Pooh plot to interpret them from the point of view of her immediate life world. Her interpretation has already assimilated formal and substantive features of many earlier narrative texts, including fictional or narrativized real life experiences. The mother-child-separation theme is a case in point. And it unavoidably has done so because Hanna's story draws upon the common stock of linguistic conventions and narrative models that are always already in place, constituting the symbolic space of cultural discourses in which she grows up. At this point, another distinction becomes blurred: that between cultural and personal narratives.[6] Gee (1991) has pointed out that a personal narrative would be meaningless apart from a surrounding narrative context and its manifold cultural traditions. For Carrithers (1991), these traditions also include knowledge of a culture's social life, institutions, and history. Personal narratives only have meaning and can be shared, understood, and responded to because they interact with what Gee called "the resources of a system of themes that can create (what counts in a given group as) coherent (satisfying) pattern" (p. 13). Gee went on to argue that "narrative is fundamentally a perspective that human beings take on the way in which certain themes fall into a satisfying pattern, a perspective stemming from their social identity and the resources their social group(s) make available to them ..." To my mind, the idea of intertextuality is one way to capture this interface between personal and cultural narrative, reception-oriented research is another.

A Joint Story

Discourse analysis, to which I turn now, shares the assumption with its post-structuralist cousins deconstructionism and reader-response theory that there is no such thing as a fixed and autonomous meaning created, represented, or conveyed in narrative. A discourse theorist—be it a discursive psychologist or a conversation analyst—would point out that Hanna's story obviously is a co-production told by three narrators. Both Hanna's mother and the other passenger play important roles as co-narrators. The narrative dynamic is triggered by a social interaction that starts when the mother picks up Hanna's "offer" of a joint narrative—"Who lives here?" (4)—by introducing "little Pooh" (5). These two words are momentous, for they outline not only a protagonist and a genre but also a particular storyline: The mother says "*little* Pooh." Accordingly, Hanna now further develops the plot by introducing Pooh's mother which is a detail worth noting because in the original story version Winnie the Pooh does not have a mother.

Besides the design of the storyline, there are several other discursive activities going on. The joint storytelling is enmeshed with other concerns. For the mother, co-narrating stories with Hanna also serves the purpose to pass time, which always is a challenge on long train rides with children. For the other passenger in the compartment who, as it happens, is interested in the cultural study of narrative discourse, the unfolding conversation is a most welcome occasion. He therefore is most attentive and supportive, as to be able to immediately participate

[6] I have discussed this "blurring" of personal and cultural narratives in more detail in Brockmeier (2001).

in the storytelling when he is invited (14). Of course it has not escaped Hanna's attention that all the time there has been a potential co-narrator, in contrast with her father who has been deeply immersed into his book (thereby illustrating another possible way of giving oneself up to narrative). Everyone here seems to know about the others and about what the others know. They share not only the three-dimensional space of a train compartment, but also a multidimensional social and symbolic space.

An Enacted Story

Finally, from a performance-theoretical point of view it is interesting to note that the narrative develops out of and continues to be entangled with very practical and material activities. Hanna, as we remember, is probing the broken armrest. During her investigation she shifts back and forth from material practices to narrative practices, from a technical world to the world of imagination. Moreover, she also enacts, or acts out, the narrative from within this world of imagination. I already mentioned the aspect of enacted narrative play—call it playacting or storyacting—and now it appears again. In telling Pooh's story, Hanna takes over his point of view and his voice. Quite obviously, her sympathetic narrative performance demonstrates that she is sharing the shock and anxiety of Pooh in discovering that his mother is gone out. In a word, Hanna *is* Pooh.

But she is not only protagonist. She also contributes to the joint narrative by asking questions—technically speaking, she orchestrates the story—whereas her co-narrators give answers. However, note one exception. It is Hanna who overcomes the dramatic "complication" by assertively suggesting to the passenger (and not to her mother) an answer to the open question of how the story may end: There will be a happy end. Pooh's mother will come back because Pooh feels alone (14). And apparently, she rightly assessed the stance of the passenger: He confirms her tentative flashforward—which sounds almost like a question—and she seems relieved (16).

Although Hanna appears to be the main narrator and initiator of the storytelling, analytically speaking, she represents only one voice, whereas her mother and the other passenger represent the omniscient narrator's perspective. Again, there is one exception. When the tension gets too high (in 13), Hanna's perspective shifts from that of Pooh to that of the (almost) omniscient narrator: Now it is her turn to be in charge of suggesting a solution to Pooh's trouble. And so she does.

Vivian Paley (1990) pointed out that children's stories often are tryouts, attempts to play through difficult situations and uncertainties.

The imaginative worlds of narrative fantasy allow for serious plays about loneliness, fear, and confusion, as they allow for establishing comfortable relationships with people and situations that make it possible to stage these plays, risky as they are. Paley (1990) reports a story which a boy called Joseph, putting aside his usual Batman or snake stories, told the day after his baby sister was born:

> Once upon a time there was a forest. And there was a husband came. And a wife to the husband. And a baby was there. And the baby had a gun. And when the baby grew up the baby went hunting with the father. (pp. 10–11)

Paley wonders where such stories originate and she sets out to imagine possible meanings. The forest could represent the unknown; calling mother and father a "wife" and a "husband" might show Joseph's feeling of distance and estrangement; and because babies never have guns, a baby with a gun may ensure its separation from the mother. Yet Paley (1990) emphasizes that ultimately there are no answers and certainties. In fact, the story is not told to give answers and to present certainties: "Joseph has envisioned a story in which to place his confusion. Having told his story and acted it out, he knows something he did not know before, and he will use the new information as the need arises" (p. 11). Although Joseph is a bit older than Hanna (his is a story told in the classroom), for both children storytelling provides performative formats of problem solving, to use Fleisher Feldman's (1989) formulation. From the very beginning, narrative is experienced as an enormously flexible format to simulate and elaborate problems, uncertainties, confusions, whether they are real or imagined or both.

Finally, there is at least one more practical concern that is relevant for Hanna's mother and which keeps her involved in the common storytelling. She carefully watches Hanna's narrative performance because she wants to make sure that her daughter does not get physically hurt during her physical explorations (11).

CONCLUSIONS: EMBEDDED COHERENCE

Each of the six readings I have presented unfold a specific concept of narrative; each frame narrative within different contexts of action and interaction; each bring to the fore different pathways of meaning construction. My first readings—from the theoretical points of view of Aristotle, Burke, Russian Formalism, sociolinguistic and narratological structuralism—identified Hanna's narrative as a classic story and as structured (or perhaps more precisely, structural) story. Underlying these readings was a closed and autonomous model of the narrative text, a text understood in an exclusively linguistic sense. In contrast, the latter four post-structuralist conceptions of narrative—deconstructionism, reader-response criticism and reception theory, discourse analysis, and performance theory—have suggested a view of narrative as a context-embedded, dynamic, and social event. Accordingly, Hanna's story turned into an open story, a reader's story, a jointly constructed story, and an enacted story.

In my account I have used these approaches not only to make Hanna's story the subject of a variety of interpretations but also to propose a number of possible, even contradictory, ways of meaning construction. In doing so, I wanted to bring into prominence the polysemic quality of narrative, its multifunctional and multimodal nature. These qualities have often made it difficult for psychologists to see narrative as subject of scientific investigation, which, as a consequence, has led them to redefine the narrative mode in terms of the paradigmatic mode of thought. The reduction of narrative coherence to temporal sequentiality is a case in point.

I suspect that the polysemic and open character of narrative would be less puzzling if the story under examination would have been unambiguously labeled a fantasy story or, simply, literary fiction. It is, however, precisely one of my arguments that the sharp distinction between the fictional and real worlds of narrative, between narrative fantasy and reality is grounded in the same precarious assumption as the distinction between a narrative-interpretive mind and a paradigmatic-explanative mind (Brockmeier, 1996). Historically and ontogenetically, this distinction is the outcome of a very specific cultural-historical development in the West, a development that can be traced back to the emerging split between humanist and discursive modes of thought, on the one hand, and scientific and technological modes of thought, on the other, in the late Renaissance and early Modern Times (Toulmin, 1990). At any rate, this distinction does not help us to understand what took place in those minutes in Hanna's train compartment.

What makes a narrative coherent is not the degree to which it is ordered in a chronological or any other temporal sequence. Rather, its coherence and, thus, intelligibility depends on the specific context of practice and the cultural fabric of meaning within which the narrative event takes place. As we have seen, this context can consist of several overlapping contexts of practice and meaning. We might call this *embedded coherence*. I have pointed out four forms of such embedded coherence—narrative, conversational, performative, and multiple coherence—all of which are based on practices and principles of meaning construction. (In the six readings of Hanna's stories, only the literary-theory and structuralist approaches focus almost entirely on narrative coherence; all other perspectives include at least aspects of conversational coherence, with the performance-theoretical point of view particularly aiming at performative and multiple forms of coherence.) All of these forms and modes of coherence differ from temporal sequencing.

Thus, I have offered a definition of narrative which is not based on a paradigmatic model of time. Rather, I have proposed a concept of narrative as a discursive practice: a context-embedded practice of communication and cognition which, in forming a perspective on experience, connects several distinct elements to each other as to constitute a whole. Narrative, in this view, is an operation that creates a synthesis of meaning, an intelligible gestalt that is more than the sum of its isolated elements. I could also have used the term *emplotment* in this context, but I would have had to redefine it in the sense just described, because the concept of emplotment, in the wake of Paul Ricoeur's (1984–1991) momentous studies, designates narrative in the first place as a temporal order. In contrast, I have suggested understanding narrative coherence as the emerging connective force of a meaning structure.

Applying a number of different readings, of *master narratives* of narrative, to Hanna's story, I have tried to elaborate this concept of narrative as discursive practice embedded in multiple contexts of action and interpretation. One upshot of this comparative reading was that we have as many stories as we have interpretive frameworks, because it is the interpretive framework put into operation that sets the scene for what counts as a story, its protagonists, and tellers. Accordingly, we deal with *Hanna's* story or with a narrative co-production, with an exclusively linguistic event or with a narrative performance, with a narrative text (the story of Pooh and his mother) or with an intertext that includes previous reading events, literate and oral, as well as many other stories about Pooh and other protagonists of the cultural world in which Hanna lives.

I believe that from the point of view of a cultural psychology Hanna's story is a compelling example of what I take to be an essential premise of this perspective: that human beings—children and adults—create meanings in cultural contexts of action and interpretation. It demonstrates that the coherence of these meanings is primarily a function of what persons are doing or trying to do in that particular cultural context.

REFERENCES

Aristotle. (1967). *Poetics.* (G. F. Else, Ed.). Ann Arbor, MI: University of Michigan Press.

Astington, J. W., & Jenkins, J. M. (1995). Theory of mind development and social understanding. *Cognition and Emotion, 9,* 151–165.

Astington, J. W., Olson, D. R., & Harris, P. (Eds.). (1988). *Developing theories of mind.* Cambridge, UK: Cambridge University Press.

Austin, J. (1962). *How to do things with words.* Oxford: Clarendon.

Bakhtin, M. (1981). *The dialogic imagination.* Austin: University of Texas Press.

Bamberg, M. (1997). Positioning between structure and performance. *Journal of Narrative and Life History, 7,* 335–342.

Bamberg, M. (2000). Language and communication—What develops? Determining the role of language practices for a theory of development. In N. Budwig, I. Uzgiris, & J. Wertsch (Eds.), *Communication: Arenas of development* (pp. 55–77). Norwood, NJ: Ablex.

Brockmeier, J. (1995/1997). What are we reading when we are "mind-reading"? Paper presented at the conference *Children's theories of mind grow up: Theoretical issues in children's understanding of the mind.* Centre for Applied Cognitive Science, University of Toronto (1995). Italian version "Che cosa leggiamo quando "leggiamo la mente"? In *Archivio di Psicologia, Neurologia e Psichiatria (1997), 58,* 118–132.

Brockmeier, J. (1996). Explaining the interpretive mind. *Human Development, 39,* 287–295.

Brockmeier, J. (1998). *Literales Bewusstsein. Schriftlichkeit und das Verhältnis von Sprache und Kultur* [*The literate mind: Literacy and the relationship between language and culture*]. Munich: Fink.

Brockmeier, J. (2000). Autobiographical time. *Narrative Inquiry 10*(1), 51–73.

Brockmeier, J. (2001). Texts and other symbolic spaces. *Mind, Culture, and Activity, 8*(3), 215–231.

Brockmeier, J. (2004). What makes a story coherent? In A. Uchoa Branco & J. Valsiner (Eds.), *Communication and metacommunication in human development* (pp. 285–306). Greenwich, CT: Information Age.

Brockmeier, J., & Harré, R. (2001). Narrative: Problems and promises of an alternative paradigm. In J. Brockmeier & D. Carbaugh (Eds.), *Narrative and identity: Studies in autobiography, self and culture* (pp. 39–58). Amsterdam: John Benjamins.

Bruner, J. S. (1986). *Actual minds, possible worlds.* Cambridge, MA: Harvard University Press.

Bruner, J. S. (1990). *Acts of meaning.* Cambridge, MA: Harvard University Press.

Bruner, J. S. (1996). Frames for thinking: Ways of making meaning. In D. R. Olson & N. Torrance (Eds.), *Modes of thought: Explorations in culture and cognition* (pp. 93–105). Cambridge, UK: Cambridge University Press.

Bruner, J. S. (2002). Narrative distancing: A foundation of literacy. In J. Brockmeier, M. Wang, & D. R. Olson (Eds.), *Literacy, narrative and culture.* Richmond, UK: Curzon Press.

Bruner, J. S., & Lucariello, J. (1989). Monologue as narrative recreation of the world. In K. Nelson (Ed.), *Narratives from the crib* (pp. 73–97). Cambridge, MA: Harvard University Press.

Burke, K. (1945). *A grammar of motives.* New York: Prentice-Hall.

Carrithers, M. (1991). Narrativity: Mindreading and making societies. In A. Whiten (Ed.), *Natural theories of mind: Evolution, development and simulation of everyday mindreading* (pp. 305–318). Oxford: Blackwell.

Cook-Gumperz, J. (1984). Keeping it together: Text and context in children's language socialization. In D. Tannen (Ed.), Coherence in spoken and written discourse (pp. 337–356). Norwood, NJ: Ablex.

Donald, M. (1991). *Origins of the modern mind.* Cambridge, MA: Harvard University Press.

Donaldson, M. (1978). *Children's minds.* Glasgow: Fontana/Collins.

Dunn, J. (1999). Making sense of the social world: Mindreading, emotion, and relationships. In Zelazo, P. D., Astington, J. W., & Olson, D. R. (Eds.), *Developing theories of intention: Social understanding and self-control* (pp. 229–242). Mahwah, NJ: Lawrence Erlbaum Associates.

Edwards, D. (1997). *Discourse and cognition.* London: Sage.

Edwards, D. (1998). Discourse and information. Review article on W. Chafe's "Discourse, consciousness, and time: The flow and displacement of conscious experience in speaking and writing." *Culture & Psychology, 4*(1), 91–105.

Engel, S. (1995). *The stories children tell: Making sense of the narratives of childhood.* New York: Freeman.

Eriksson, K. (2002). *Life and fiction: On intertextuality in children's booktalk.* Linkoping, Sweden: Linkoping UniTryck.

Erlich, V. (1981). *Russian Formalism.* Revised Edition. New Haven: Yale University Press.

Fleisher Feldman, C. (1989). Monologue as problem-solving narrative. In K. Nelson (Ed.), *Narratives from the crib* (pp. 98–119). Cambridge MA: Harvard University Press.

Garvey, C. (1984). *Children's talk.* Cambridge, MA: Harvard University Press.

Gee, J. P. (1991). Memory and myth: A perspective on narrative. In A. McCabe & C. Peterson (Eds.), *Developing narrative structure* (pp. 1–25). Mahwah, NJ: Lawrence Erlbaum Associates.

Harré, R., & Van Langenhove, L. (Eds.). (1999). *Positioning theory: Moral contexts of intentional action.* Malden, MA: Blackwell.

Harris, P. L. (2000). *The work of the imagination.* Oxford: Blackwell.

Labov, W., & Waletzky, J. (1967). Narrative analysis: Oral versions of personal experience. In J. Helm (Ed.), *Essays on the verbal and visual Arts* (pp. 12–44). Seattle: University of Washington Press.

Miller, P. (1982) *Amy, Wendy, and Beth: Learning language in South Baltimore.* Austin: University of Texas Press.

Miller, P. J. (1994). Narrative practices: Their role in socialization and self-construction. In U. Neisser & R. Fivush (Eds.), *The remembering self: Construction and accuracy in the self-narrative* (pp. 158–179). Cambridge, UK: Cambridge University Press.

Nelson, K. (1996). *Language in cognitive development: The emergence of the mediated mind.* New York: Cambridge University Press.

Nelson, K. (2003). Narrative and the emergence of a consciousness of self. In G. Fireman, T. McVay, & O. Flanagan (Eds.), *Narrative and consciousness: Literature, psychology, and the brain* (pp. 17–36). New York: Oxford University Press.

Nelson, N. (Ed.). (1989). *Narratives from the crib.* Cambridge, MA: Harvard University Press.

Nicolopoulou, A. (1996). Narrative development in social context. In D. I. Slobin, J. Gerhardt, J. Guo, & A. Kyratzis (Eds.), *Social interaction, social context, and language* (pp. 369–390). Mahwah, NJ: Lawrence Erlbaum Associates.

Nicolopoulou, A. (1997). Worldmaking and identity formation in children's narative play-acting. In B. D. Cox & C. Lightfoot (Eds.), *Sociogenetic perspectives on internalization* (pp. 157–187). Mahwah, NJ: Lawrence Erlbaum Associates.

Norrick, N. R. (2000). *Conversational narrative: Storytelling in everyday talk.* Amsterdam: John Benjamins.

Ochs, E., & Capps, L. (2001). *Living narrative: Creating lives in everyday storytelling.* Cambridge, MA: Harvard University Press.

Paley, V. G. (1990). *The boy who would be a helicopter: The uses of storytelling in the classroom.* Cambridge, MA: Harvard University Press.

Piaget, J. (1951). *The child's conception of the world.* London: Routledge & Kegan Paul.

Prince, G. (1987). *A dictionary of narratology.* Lincoln: University of Nebraska Press.

Ricoeur, P. (1984–1991). *Narrative and time, Vols. 1–3.* Chicago: University of Chicago Press.

Schegloff, E. A. (1992). In another context. In A. Duranti & C. Goodwin (Eds.), *Rethinking context: Language as an interactive phenomenon* (pp. 193–227). Cambridge, UK: Cambridge University Press.

Toulmin, S. (1990). *Cosmopolis. The hidden agenda of Modernity.* New York: The Free Press.

Vygotsky, L. S. (1987). *Thinking and speech.* New York: Plenum.

Zentella, A. C. (1998). Multiple codes, multiple identities: Puerto Rican children in New York City. In S. M. Hoyle & C. T. Adger (Eds.), *Kids talk: Strategic language use in later childhood* (pp. 95–112). New York: Oxford University Press.

Chapter 13

Parent–Child Reminiscing and the Construction of a Subjective Self

Robyn Fivush
Emory University

Catherine A. Haden
Loyola University Chicago

When we talk about the past, we are talking about our selves. More specifically, we are linking our past activities, thoughts, and emotions to our current self, and in this way we are constructing an autobiographical life narrative. As William James (1890) argued, we do not wonder whose thoughts are in our head, whose dreams we awake from. But how do we learn to connect our past thoughts and emotions to our current self?

In this chapter, we argue that through participating in joint reminiscing with parents, young children develop a sense of subjective perspective on their personal past. Reminiscing is not just about what happened, but what happened *to me*, and this necessitates distinguishing what happened *to me* from what happened *to you*. Personal memories are autobiographical in the sense that one has a unique perspective on one's own past experiences (Fivush, 2001; Nelson, 2001). My thoughts, my feelings, my evaluations of the past are separate and possibly different from your thoughts, your feelings, and your evaluations of what happened, and it is this unique perspective based on my subjective experiences that makes the past relevant for self-understanding. I am who I am not just because I have had these experiences but because of what these experiences mean to me.

In order to develop the idea of a subjective self, we first review research on joint reminiscing. We then turn to a more focused discussion of the ways in which joint reminiscing facilities children's developing awareness of their own unique perspective on the past. We focus on three related aspects of the content of parent–child reminiscing that are instrumental in this development: the inclusion of narrative evaluations, the inclusion of mental state talk more generally, and the specific inclusion of emotion talk. Inclusion of information about inner mental life moves narrative reminiscing beyond simply reporting what happened to marking individual reactions and perspectives on external events. We argue that through participating in adult-guided conversations about their past that are replete with information about their inner mental life, children develop a subjective sense of self.

JOINT REMINISCING

Parents and children begin to discus shared past experiences virtually as soon as children begin to talk (Eisenberg, 1985; Sachs, 1983). However, at first, when children are 16- to 20-months of age, parents provide much of the content and structure of these conversations, and children participate minimally, most often by confirming or repeating what the parent says. Between 20- and 36-months of age, children become more active participants in these conversations, responding to specific questions and offering new bits of information into the ongoing conversations (Harley & Reese, 1999). By 3-years of age, children begin to introduce personally experienced events as topics of conversation and are able to engage in more extended discussions of events that happened in the more remote past. By the end of the preschool years, children are surprisingly competent in narrating their own past experiences, both in joint reminiscing with others who shared those experiences with them, and in independent narratives, in which the listener did not share the experiences and therefore is less able to co-construct the narrative with the child (see Fivush & Haden, 1997; Fivush, Haden, & Reese, 1996, for reviews). Following from Vygotsky's theoretical framework (1978), we argue that children are learning the forms and functions for talking about the past in these early parent-guided conversations. More specifically, children are learning the conventional narrative forms for reporting past experiences, as well as learning the social and emotional functions of sharing the past with others (Fivush & Reese, 2002; Fivush & Vasudeva, 2002). There is now a substantial body of research demonstrating that the ways in which parents reminisce with their preschool children has an enduring influence on children's developing autobiographical memory skills. Although using somewhat different terminology, multiple studies have documented individual differences in parental reminiscing that fall along a dimension of elaborativeness (Fivush & Fromhoff, 1988; Hudson, 1990; Peterson & McCabe, 1992; Reese, Haden, & Fivush, 1996). Some parents demonstrate a highly elaborative style, talking in great detail about the past, including more embellished information in each conversational turn. In contrast, some parents appear less elaborative, asking fewer and more redundant questions about past events. Importantly, longitudinal research across the preschool years suggests that parents with a more elaborative style facilitate children's ability to tell richly detailed stories of their own lives (Harley & Reese, 1999; Reese, Haden, & Fivush, 1993).

We argue that children are not simply learning more sophisticated ways of verbalizing what they remember in these conversations; they are learning how to organize and evaluate their past experiences. Language provides both the context and the medium for learning how to talk about and think about the past (Nelson, 1996). It is only through language that we are able to share our past experiences with others, and it is through sharing the past that we come to reevaluate and reinterpret these experiences for ourselves (Fivush, 2001; Nelson, 2001). Moreover, there is growing evidence that culture and class differences in the ways in which parents and children reminisce together play a fundamental role in children's developing autobiographical memories and concepts of self (see Fivush & Haden, 2003, for a review). It is through language, and more specifically, through the use of particular language forms that children learn culturally appropriate ways of evaluating their past and themselves. It is through reminiscing not just about what happened but how one thought and felt about the event, that parents are helping their children to develop a clearer understanding of the relations between the event in the world and the event as experienced in the individual's mind. As children talk about the past in more subjective ways, they come to understand the past and themselves in more subjective ways. There are three related ways in which the subjective inner landscape is expressed in reminiscing: through narrative evaluation, through mental state language, and most specifically, through talk about emotion.

NARRATIVE EVALUATION

Narrative reminiscing moves beyond reporting what happened, beyond providing referential information about the external actions, objects and people involved in the event. Narratives include evaluative devices that provide the listener and the self with a perspective on the inner landscape including ones thoughts, emotions, and reactions to the event (Bruner, 1987, 1990; Labov, 1982). Evaluative devices involve explicit comments on one's internal states, such as an individual's thoughts, emotions and desires, as well as linguistic devices for implicitly marking one's subjective reactions to an event (Labov, 1982; Peterson & McCabe, 1982). These devices include the use of intensifiers (e.g., "It was a *huge* bowl." and "It was *very* cold.") affective modifiers (e.g., "She was *ugly.*" and "Mommy was *wrong.*") and the use of emphasis (e.g., "It *never* stopped." and "I ran *and ran and ran.*"), all of which serve to note the individual's subjective or emotional perspective on an action, object or person (Peterson & McCabe, 1982). As children begin to tell more coherent narratives, they also begin to incorporate a larger number and a greater variety of these types of evaluations into their narratives (Fivush, Haden, & Adam, 1995; Peterson & McCabe, 1982). But how do children learn to include these kinds of narrative evaluative devices? In particular, are children learning these devices through participating in joint reminiscing with their parents?

In a preliminary study examining relations between mothers' and children's use of narrative evaluations, Fivush (1991) examined mother-child reminiscing when children were between 30- and 35-months of age, and then children's independent narratives with an unfamiliar adult 14 months later. Mothers who used more evaluative devices when reminiscing with their young children had children who were using more evaluative devices when independently recounting their past experiences more than a year later, supporting the thesis that children are learning to evaluate their past in early parent-guided reminiscing.

In order to examine this possibility in more depth, we conducted a longitudinal study across the preschool years (Haden, Haine, & Fivush, 1997). Families were visited in their homes when children were 40-months of age and again at 70-months of age, and during two separate home visits at each time point, the mothers and the fathers independently reminisced with their children. In addition, children were interviewed about past experiences by a relatively unfamiliar adult. We included fathers in this study for several reasons. First, there is some indication in the adult literature that females report more detailed, vivid and emotional autobiographical narratives than males (see Fivush & Buckner, 2003, for a review). Thus we were interested in whether mothers and fathers would differ from each other in the amount or type of evaluative devices they used when reminiscing with their preschoolers. Second, previous research has found that parents are more elaborative when reminiscing with daughters than with sons (Reese, et al., 1996), so we were interested in examining whether this difference would extend to evaluative devices as well.

Overall, there were no differences between mothers and fathers or daughters and sons in the types of evaluative devices used. There were also no differences between mothers and fathers in the number of evaluations they included in their narratives with their children. However, both mothers and fathers increased in their use of evaluations over time, from a mean of about 6 evaluative utterances per narrative when children were 40-months-old to a mean of just over 12 evaluative devices per narrative when children were 70-months-old. Children used very few evaluations in reminiscing with their parents when they were 40-months-old (a mean of just over 2 per narrative), but increased in their inclusion of evaluative information by 70-months of age (a mean of just over 7 per narrative). Further, at 70-months of age, girls used significantly more evaluations (a mean of almost 10 per narrative) than did boys (a mean of just over 5 per narrative). Thus, not surprisingly, all conversational participants increased in their use of evaluations as children grew older; however, although mothers and fathers did not differ from each other, girls did begin to use more evaluative devices than boys by the end of the preschool years.

The longitudinal design of this study also allowed us to examine the relative influence of mothers', fathers', and children's early use of evaluative devices in predicting children's later use of evaluative devices in their independent narratives with an unfamiliar interviewer. More specifically, in a regression analysis, children's use of evaluations with the experimenter when they were 40 months old was entered first, followed by fathers' evaluations when the children were 40 months, with mothers' evaluations when the children were 40 months entered last. The overall model was significant, $R = .78$, $F(3, 11) = 5.60$, $p < .01$, accounting for half the variance in children's evaluations in the experimenter-elicited narratives at 70 months of age. In this model, the children's use of evaluations with the experimenter at 40 months, and the mothers' use of narrative evaluations with their children at 40 months each contributed uniquely to the prediction of the children's evaluations at 70 months. Thus, it appears that children are learning to evaluate their past in reminiscing with their parents, and perhaps specifically with their mothers, and girls seem to be learning to evaluate their past to a greater extent than boys. Importantly, children's use of narrative evaluations was not related to other measures of language (e.g., mean length of utterance or vocabulary measures). Thus, children's increasing use of narrative evaluation is not a simple function of increasing linguistic sophistication. Rather, as the regression analyses clearly indicate, maternal use of narrative evaluation uniquely predicts children's developing evaluative stance on their own personal past.

MENTAL STATE LANGUAGE

Narrative evaluations are a heterogeneous group of linguistic devices that include both implicit (e.g., intensifiers, affective modifiers, and emphasis) and explicit (i.e., internal state language) markers of subjective perspective. Although all of these devices offer evidence of a particular perspective on an event, perhaps the clearest indication of subjective perspective is the use of internal state language. By specifically reporting one's own thoughts, emotions, and desires narrators are highlighting their individual perspective on what occurred. Moreover, by including thoughts, emotions, and desires of others, narrators are explicitly noting that individual perspectives can differ, and in this way, one's own perspective is unique.

We know based on observations of naturally-occurring linguistic interactions (Bartsch & Wellman, 1995; Bretherton & Beeghly, 1982; Shatz, Wellman, & Silber, 1983) that children begin using mental terms almost as soon as they begin combining words. And although their first uses of mental terms are often "conversational" (e.g., "*You know what?*"; "*I don't know.*"), by 2," years of age, an increasing number of mental term uses by children to "genuinely" reference internal states in such a way that indicates a reasonable understanding of thoughts, beliefs, or desires (e.g., "I didn't know that she was going to be there." "I thought he was going to be coming back."). Several studies have documented linkages between parental and sibling uses of mental state language in daily activities and children's subsequent uses of these terms when talking about present events (e.g., Dunn, Brown, Slomkowski, Tesla, & Youngblade, 1991; Furrow, Moore, Davidge, & Chiasson, 1992; Moore, Furrow, Chiasson, & Patriquin, 1994). For example, Furrow et al. (1992) found that the frequency of mothers' uses of mental terms in mealtime, story reading, and playtime conversations with their 2-year-olds was positively associated with the children's use of these terms in these contexts at age 3. And in a similar analysis, Bartsch and Wellman (1995) observed that children who were exposed to frequent parental talk about desires made references to beliefs earlier than those who were exposed to less desire talk. Moreover, a number of theorists (e.g., Nelson, 1996; Olson, 1988) have implicated the acquisition of internal state language in the development of children's theory of mind. And a growing body of research provides support for the view that mothers' talk about mental states in discourse with young children is of critical importance to this process (Dunn, Brown, & Beardsall, 1991; Ruffman, Slade, & Crowe, 2002).

Recently, Rudek and Haden (2002) explored mothers' use and children's use of mental state language in conversations about the past. We reasoned that just as the style mothers' display in reminiscing with their young children can facilitate children's skills for telling richly embellished personal stories, the use of mental state language in these discussions of past events may be instrumental in the development of children's understanding of their own and others' mental lives. In this short-term longitudinal investigation, we examined how frequently mothers and children discussed internal states during conversations about previously experienced events that were recorded when the children were 30- and 42-months-old.

Not surprisingly given the nature of these conversations, the mental terms most commonly used by mothers and children were *remember, know,* and *think*. Excluding formulaic mental term uses that seemed to serve a conversational or objective reference function (see Shatz et al., 1983; Wellman & Estes, 1987), on average, mothers' included 21 "genuine" mental term uses—that could be attributed to mental states—when reminiscing with their 30-month-olds, and 19 mental terms when the children were 42 months, which translated to about 17% of the mothers' memory-related utterances at the two age points. Although mothers' mean-level use of mental terms did not change significantly over time, the children's mental term language increased during this period. To be sure, the children were not referring to mental states very often in these memory conversations at either time point, but they did include more genuine mental terms uses in their talk about the past at 42 months (a mean of just less than 3) than they had a 30 months of age (a mean of just less than 1). Mothers and children most often referred to the children's mental states. But at 42 months, mothers were commenting more about their own mental states, and children were commenting more about their own mental states than at the 30 month time point.

Importantly, mothers' reports of the children's vocabulary (as indicated on the MacArthur Communicative Development Inventory) at 30 months, and measures of the children's mean length of utterance (MLU) obtained from observations of mother-child free-play at each age point, were not associated with mothers' and children's mental term use. Thus, increases in children's mental state language use during reminiscing are not simply related to increases in their language skills. As such, mothers' use of mental terms when discussing past events appear to reflect stylistic differences and not merely their knowledge or beliefs about their children's linguistic capabilities.

A critical next question concerned the potential concurrent and longitudinal linkages between mothers' and children's use of mental terms when talking about previously experienced events. Correlations were computed between mothers' and children's total use of mental terms at each time point. As illustrated in Fig. 13.1, there was an impressive amount of consistency in the mothers' and children's mental term use over time. Mothers' and children's use of mental terms at 30 months was highly correlated with their respective uses of mental terms at 42 months. Further, concurrent correlations between mothers and children's use of mental terms within each time point suggested that mothers who used more mental terms had children who used more mental terms within the memory conversations. Most interestingly, the cross lagged correlations indicated that mothers' mental term use at 30 months was positively associated with the children's total use at 42 months. However, bidirectionality was apparent as well, such that with children's total use of mental state terms at 30 months was related to mothers' later use when children were 42 months. Regression analyses (which should be considered exploratory given our sample size of 21) conducted to examine these links did not reveal a unique contribution of mothers' term use at 30 months, over and above children's mental term use at 30 months, in predicting children's mental term use one year later. Nevertheless, the concurrent and longitudinal relations here are consistent with previous work concerning parent–child mental state language in other settings (e.g., Dunn, et al., 1991; Furrow, et al., 1992; Moore, et al., 1994). To be sure, further studies are necessary to elucidate the processes by which children learn about their own and others mental worlds, but conversations about past events may be an important context in which mental state language and an understanding of internal states is fostered.

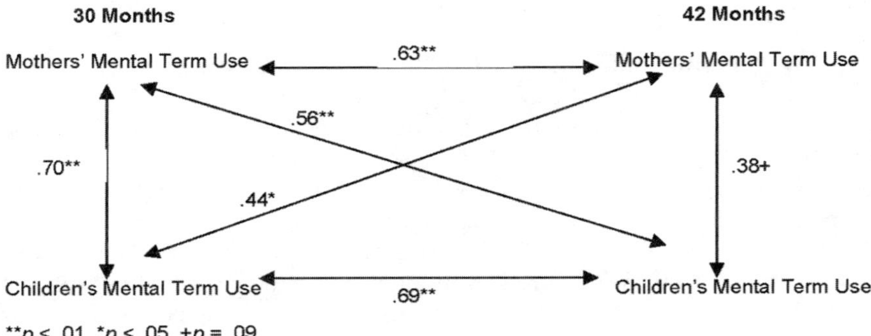

FIG. 13.1. Relations Between Mothers' and Children's Mental Term Use in Memory Conversations Concurrently and over Time.

EMOTION TALK

Perhaps the most direct link between our past and our present is emotional. When we recall the past, we not only recall how we felt at that time, we often feel the same emotion in the present. Although events certainly lose some of their emotional power over time, there is no doubt that they retain their emotional resonance. In sharing our past emotional experiences with others, we have an opportunity to reflect on and introspect about our emotional life (Lewis & Michealson, 1983). Perhaps more important for the arguments presented here, reminiscing about emotions allows parents and children to engage in a re-evaluation and reinterpretation of emotional experience and what it means (Dunn, Brown, & Beardsall, 1991; Fivush, 1993). Again, the previous sections have already provided some evidence of the ways in which inclusion of emotion in parent–child reminiscing influences children's developing understanding of their own subjective mental life, but here we focus explicitly on how emotion is incorporated into joint reminiscing and what specific effects this kind of talk has on children's developing autobiographical narratives.

Children begin talking about their emotions as early as 13 months of age and by 2 years children are referring to both their own and others' emotions in everyday conversation (Bretherton, Fritz, Zahn-Waxler, & Munn, 1987). In accord with the arguments presented here, mothers who talk more about emotion have children who come to talk more about emotion (Denham, Zoller, & Couchoud, 1994; Dunn, Bretherton, & Munn, 1987), and there is also some suggestion that mothers talk about emotion more overall with daughters than with sons (Dunn et al., 1987; Zahn-Waxler, Cole, & Barrett, 1991). However, reminiscing about past emotions may differ in important ways from talking about emotions experienced in the here-and-now. More specifically, parents can focus on particular types of emotional experiences over other's when reminiscing. For example, parents can choose to talk about emotionally positive or negative experiences. In this way, parents may be informing their children which emotions are deemed appropriate to experience. Further, when reminiscing, children have some distance from the immediacy of the emotion and may be better able to reflect on and evaluate the experience. Importantly, reminiscing conversations can focus only on the child's emotional reactions, or can also highlight other's emotions, thus explicitly expressing multiple perspectives on the same event. Finally, in reminiscing, parents can chose how to verbally describe the emotional experience; are children mad, or are they angry, upset and frustrated? Are children sacred or are they frightened, squeamish and trembling? The kind of emotional vocabulary that parents provide for their children's emotional experiences may influence how nuanced children's memories of their past emotions become.

In a longitudinal study examining mother–child emotion talk during reminiscing across the preschool years (Kuebli, Butler, & Fivush, 1995), mothers discussed shared past experiences with their children at 40-, 58- and 70-months of age.[1] We examined both the total number of emotion words used by mothers and children (i.e., all emotion words used during the conversations including repetitions of the same word) as well as the number of unique words used (i.e., the number of different emotion words within the conversation). We also coded whether the emotion was attributed to the child or to another person, and whether the emotion expressed was positive (e.g., happy, joy, love) or negative (e.g., sad, angry, scared).

Looking first at relations over time, cross-lagged correlations were computed between the number of emotions words used by mothers and children, as shown in Fig. 13.2.

Both mothers and children were consistent in how much they mentioned emotion between the last two time points, but not earlier in development. And mothers who used more emotion words had children who used more emotion words at 40- and 70-months of age. Interestingly, mothers who used more emotions words at the earliest time point, had children who were using more emotion words 1.5 years later, but this was the only longitudinal relation obtained. Thus there is some lim-

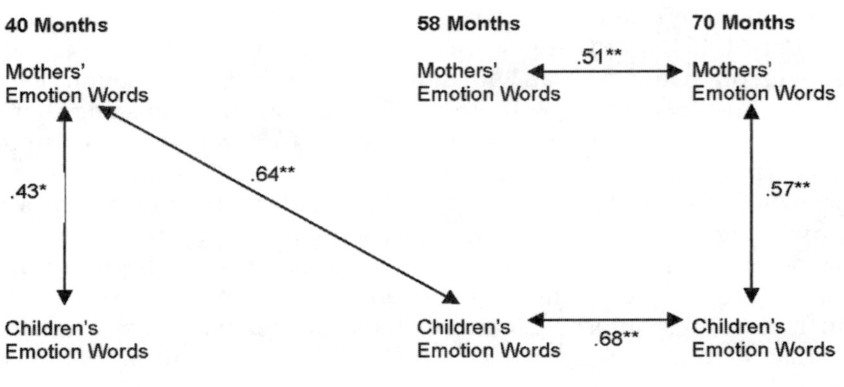

FIG. 13.2. Relations Between Mothers' and Children's Use of Emotion Words over Time.

[1]These data come from the same longitudinal sample as the Haden, et al. (1997) study on narrative evaluation discussed earlier.

ited suggestion that children are learning to incorporate emotion into their reminiscing through participating in early adult-guided conversations about past emotional experience.

Mothers also talked more about other people's emotions over time, increasing from 31% of all emotions discussed being attributed to others at 40 months to 57% attributed to others at 70 months. Finally, mothers varied in their emotion talk depending on the gender of the child. They used more emotion words and a greater variety of emotion words with daughters (a mean total of 11.5 words and 7.3 different emotion words during each event discussed over time) than with sons (a mean total of 6.8 and a mean of 4.1 different emotion words), and girls used more emotion words (a mean of 3.7) and a greater variety of emotion words (a mean of 2.6) than boys (a mean total of 1.4 and a mean of 1.3 different emotion words) at all time points. In addition, girls increased in the number and variety of emotion words used over time, whereas boys did not. Mothers also talked more about other people's emotions over time, increasing from 31% of all emotions discussed being attributed to others at 40 moths to 57% attributed to others at 70 months. Mother–son conversations had a higher proportion of positive affect (85%) than mother–daughter conversations (68%), and more of the emotions attributed to the child were positive in mother–son conversations (86%) than in mother–daughter conversations (57%). These findings indicate that mother–daughter reminiscing is more emotion laden, including a greater number, a greater variety, and a more balanced valence of past emotional experiences discussed than in mother–son reminiscing.

The gender differences obtained in this study were particularly intriguing. As adults, females report experiencing and expressing emotions to a greater extent than males (Fischer, 2000), and females include more emotional content in their autobiographical narratives than do males (Bauer, Stennes, & Haight, 2003; Davis, 1990). Our findings suggest that girls may be socialized into these patterns of emotional expression very early in development. It also raises the question of how mothers and fathers might differ in how they reminisce about emotions with their young children. In order to explore this in more detail, we asked mothers and fathers to independently reminisce about 4 specific types of emotional experiences with their 4-year-old children, a time the child was happy, scared, angry, and sad (Fivush, Brotman, Buckner, & Goodman, 2000). Overall, mothers talked more about emotion (a mean of 5.23 emotion words per event discussed) than fathers (a mean of 3.99 emotion word), but both mothers and fathers talked about sadness, and especially the causes of sadness, more with daughters (a mean of 4.05 mentions) than with sons (1.95 mentions). In this study, girls talked more about being scared than did boys, but there were no differences in conversations about feeling happy, sad or angry.

In order to examine relations between parents' use of emotion language and children's use of emotion language, correlations were computed for mothers and fathers with daughters and sons for three variables: number of attributions of an emotion (e.g., "You were sad" and "I was angry"), number of causes of emotional experience mentioned (e.g., "What made you so scared?" and "You were mad when Mommy wouldn't let you stay up late."), and number of emotion words used throughout the conversation. These correlations are displayed in Table 13.1.[2] Although a few of these correlations did not reach statistical significance, the overall pattern clearly suggests that both mothers' and fathers' use of emotion language is related to their daughters and their sons use of emotion language.

Together, these studies suggest that parents who talk more about emotion, and more about attributions and causes of emotions, have children who include more information about emotion in their own reminiscing. Further, emotion talk may be more gendered than other types of subjective perspective language. Both mothers and fathers and daughters and sons differ in emotional reminiscing. Mothers' reminiscing is more emotionally laden than fathers, and both mothers and fathers reminisce more about emotion with daughters than with sons. Similarly, there is some suggestion that girls include more emotion in their reminiscing than do boys.

DEVELOPING SUBJECTIVE PERSPECTIVE

The three lines of research reviewed here on narrative evaluations, mental state, and emotion language in parent–child reminiscing converge

TABLE 13.1 Correlations Between Mothers and Fathers Emotion Language With Daughters and Sons

Emotion Language	*Mothers*		*Fathers*	
	With Daughters	*With Sons*	*With Daughters*	*With Sons*
Emotion Attributions	.67*	.31	.64*	.84**
Emotion Causes	.82**	.90**	.93**	.83**
Emotion Words	.14	.46+	.27	.84**

***p* < .01; **p* < .05; +*p* = .09.

[2]These correlations were not presented in the published report.

on four conclusions. First, and not surprisingly, children are reminiscing in more sophisticated ways over time, including more evaluative and internal state information in their narratives of personal experience as they grow older. Second, although mothers do not seem to be increasing in their use of mental state terms early in development, across the preschool years, we do see an increase in both mothers and fathers use of narrative evaluations and emotion language during reminiscing. It is also interesting to note that mothers are referring to other people's mental states and especially other people's emotions more as children get older. Third, and most provocative, there are clear linkages between parental use of these various narrative contents and children's developing inclusion of this content in their own reminiscing. More specifically, there are substantial correlations over time between maternal use of narrative evaluations and mental state language and children's developing use of these devices, and less substantial but still provocative evidence of associations between parents' and children's use of emotion language in reminiscing. Finally, there are also indications of gender differences in narrative content. Mothers talk about emotion more than fathers, and both mothers and fathers talk more about emotion with girls than with boys. Similarly, girls talk more about emotion than do boys, at least by the end of the preschool years. Girls also use a greater number of narrative evaluations than boys, although there are no differences between mothers and fathers in the use of evaluations and there do not appear to be gender differences in mental state talk more generally. Brought together, findings from these three lines of research indicate that children are learning to incorporate subjective perspective in their own personal narratives through participating in parent-guided reminiscing.

Before returning to a discussion of the development of a subjective self, we present excerpts from two mother–child dyads reminiscing at two points in time, first when the child is 46-months-old and again when the child is 8-years-old.[3] The first dyad illustrates a mother and daughter who engage in richly subjective reminiscing. When the child is younger the mother provides a great deal of scaffolding to help the child think about the event in more subjective ways; by the time the child is 8, we see a truly co-constructed narrative of a past event in which each member contributes a unique perspective (in these examples, M stands for Mother, C for Child and "..." represents some missing dialogue). In this excerpt, the mother and child are talking about a family trip to the lake:

[3]The conversational excerpts are part of the longitudinal data set analyzed in Haden, et al. (1997) and Kuebli, et al. (1995), but the data from the last time point, when then children were 8 years old, have never been published.

M: ... Did you like Lauren?
C: Yes.
M: Oh, remember when we got in Lauren's little float?
C: Yes
M: and what happened?
C: (whispers)
M: You did? (laughs) Was that scary?
C: Yes, and I didn't (like it).
M: Yeah, I know you didn't. What did you do?
C: I said boo hoo
M: No, you said "cry cry", that's what you said. You were crying. Remember and then you wanted to get out of the water?
C: I almost drowned.
M: You didn't almost drown. You didn't almost drown ... I was right there. Remember, I got you out of the water. Right away.

Several things are notable in this example. First, the mother focuses her child not just on what happened but on how the child thought and felt about it ("Did you like Lauren?", "Was that scary?" and "... you wanted to get out of the water"). The mother also confirms her child's reaction ("I didn't like it") and affirms the mother's internal understanding of that reaction ("I know you didn't"). In addition, the mother uses several evaluative devices, including the use of modifiers and emphasis. Thus in this quite short excerpt, we see the way in which some mothers highlight the internal landscape of an event for their child. Four years later, this same dyad are discussing a family bike ride:

M: And we were all goin' on a bike and you didn't wanna go on a bike and so you were going to jog but then you got so tired—
C: NOT TIRED (shouting)
M: (laughing) you didn't get tired. Ok. You didn't get tired—
C: (giggles)
M: —but you wanted to sit on the bike seat I was peddling,... What do you remember about that?
C: Wanting you to go really really slow. My legs were hurting.
M: (laughs) Why were your legs hurting?
C: Cuz I was like this (spreads legs apart) all the time.
M: Cuz your legs were spread apart like that ...
C: yeah, but if you went slowly I could relax.
M: uh huh
C: And you went too fast
M: But you had fun, though, didn't you?

C: ... it was great.
M: What was that, a half-mile or something?
C: I was afraid I might, uh, you might go flying off the edge (both mother and child are laughing), edge of the bridge and , umm, I just wanted to jog.
M: And you were afraid of riding on the bike with me across the bridge, huh?
C: uh huh, uh huh, uh huh
M: Uh huh, but you liked it when we went fast after a while, didn't you?
C: yeah.

Obviously, the child is now capable of participating more fully in the co-construction of the narrative. But more importantly, we see both mother and child explicitly sharing their own perspective on the event. Although they are clearly agreeing on what happened, they are not always agreeing on their interpretation (whether or not the child was tired, whether the child liked going fast, what the child was afraid of, wanted to do, etc.). All of these aspects of the event are explicitly discussed and negotiated, each participant bringing her own point of view to the conversation. Notice also, that the child is now using many evaluative devices in her contributions as well, including modifiers and emphasis, as well as prosadic intonation. The mother and daughter are clearly engaged and enjoying reminiscing and together they construct a clear narrative of what happened woven through with their individual perspectives. In contrast, here is a mother–son dyad discussing an airplane trip when the child is 40-months of age:

M: How did we get there?
C: um, we flew on a airplane
M: Yeah, what kind of airplane?
C: Delta
M: uh huh. Did we eat on the airplane?
C: Yep
M: Do you remember what we ate?
C: ... nut cake
M: uh huh
C: and beans
M: uh huh
C: And I don't know what else.
M: some chicken?
C: yep
M: Did you have something to drink?
C: ... Sprite

M: That's right. Did we eat both times or just one time?
C: one time.
M: Going up or coming back?
C: um, going up there.
M: Yeah, you remember that.

Unlike the first mother, this mother focuses her child on the facts of what happened. Together, the mother and child recall a great deal of specific information about their airplane trip, but at no point do they discuss anything about internal states or reactions. The conversation is a simple listing of the facts. Four years later, this dyad is discussing a family trip to Charleston:

M: When did we go?
C: December
M: Yeah, yeah. Who all went?
C: Me, and you and Ellen (sister)
M: And we saw, who did we see there?
C: Aunt Joan and Uncle Bud.
M: Right. Did we take the van?
C: Nope, we took a rental car.
M: I don't remember what color it was, do you?
C: I think it was gray.
M: ... Where did we stay, hmmm?
C: Hilton? Hotel?
M: In a hotel ... Do you remember what we had for breakfast?
C: I think I had orange juice.
M: yeah, and it seems like a lot of muffins and things like that.

This conversation is quite similar to the earlier one; the mother essentially asks for pieces of factual information and the child provides them. There is only one point where the mother asks a "real" question ("I don't remember what color it was, do you?") and this is about a factual piece of information as well. In juxtaposition to the first dyad, it is clear that this dyad is not sharing the event in a personally meaningful way, discussing what made the event interesting or fun, or sharing anything about their own personal take on what happened. They are simply giving a factual account.

These excerpts illustrate the empirical data. There are individual differences in the extent to which parent–child reminiscing highlights the subjective as well as objective facts of personal experience. Some parent–child dyads engage in reminiscing rich in evaluative detail, focusing on each individual's thoughts and emotions, creating a tension between the ways in which each individual makes sense of the past. Parents who focus their children on the internal landscape of experience have children who come to include more of this kind of information in their own personal reminiscing as they develop more sophisticated memory and narrative skills. Other parent–child dyads focus on the objective facts of the past event, the people, places and objects involved, without discussing reactions to these facts. Parents who spend little time drawing their children's attention to the more subjective aspects of experience have children who do not incorporate this kind of information into their own reminiscing later in development. All children develop the skills to narrate their personal past; our data indicate that for some children, this skill involves a more nuanced understanding of perspective than for other children.

THE SUBJECTIVE SELF: CONCLUSIONS AND IMPLICATIONS

It is through our past that we see ourselves in the present. Although self-concept cannot be reduced to memories of past events, there is little doubt that part of our current understanding of self relies on memories of our past experiences. But more than what has happened in our past, the way in which we understand, interpret, and evaluate our experiences is critical to current understanding of self. In this chapter, we have demonstrated three ways in which parents help guide children's developing understanding and evaluation of their past, through narrative evaluations, mental state, and emotion language. Although these three domains have been studied somewhat independently, the conversational excerpts underscore that all three are interrelated in reminiscing, and together contribute to a more nuanced subjective perspective on the past. Through sharing their past with others, children are learning how to evaluate their past, and simultaneously, how to evaluate themselves. Subjective perspective can be contested, negotiated, or ultimately agreed on; through discussing one's thoughts and emotions about past events, children come to understand that they stand in a unique position to view their own experience, and thus they have a unique perspective on who they are. Self comes to be defined not simply through objective facts but through subjective evaluations and interpretations.

Intriguingly, not all children participate in richly subjective joint reminiscing to the same extent. Even within the white middle-class population discussed in this chapter, there are substantial individual differences in the social context within which children are developing a subjective sense of self. One factor that has emerged from the research that may help explain some of this variability is gender. Moreover, gender differences in parent–child reminiscing may be explained by some of the same factors that explain cultural differences in parent–child reminiscing. More specifically, we know that the ways in which parents talk about the past with their young children varies by culture (see Leicthman, Wang, & Pillemer, 2003, for a review). The amount and the content of parent–child reminiscing will be a function of the values and goals inherent in any given cultural context. Cultures that value an independent sense of self will focus on self as an active agent when reminiscing whereas cultures that value an interdependent self will focus on others, community, and moral imperatives when reminiscing.

Just as culturally-related values and goals help shape cultural differences in reminiscing, gender-related values and goals may help shape gender differences in reminiscing. In this culture, females report valuing reminiscing to a greater extent than males, engaging in reminiscing more so than males, and engage in more emotionally laden reminiscing than do males (see Fivush & Buckner, in press, for a review). The obtained gender differences in parent–child reminiscing discussed here suggests that parents are already engaged in facilitating certain forms of reminiscing with daughters versus sons very early in development, and these differences may lead girls to have a more elaborated and nuanced subjective perspective on the past and on themselves than do boys.

Regardless of the ultimate interpretation of gender differences, the data presented in this chapter underscore that parent–child reminiscing is not simply about recalling what happened in the past; parents and children co-construct narratives rich in subjective perspective and evaluation. Through participating in adult-guided reminiscing, children develop a sense of self in the past based on how they thought, felt, and reacted to these events. Individual differences in this process suggest that some children develop a more embellished and nuanced subjective self. What this might mean for an understanding of self and others in the present is an intriguing question for the future.

REFERENCES

Bartsch, K., & Wellman, H. M. (1995). *Children talk about the mind*. New York: Oxford University Press.

Bauer, P. J., Stennes, L., & Haight, J. (2003). Representation of the inner self in autobiography: Women's and men's use of internal state language in personal narratives. *Memory, 11*, 27–42.

Bretherton, I., & Beeghly, M. (1982). Talking about internal states: The acquisition of an explicit theory of mind. *Developmental Psychology, 18*, 906–921.

Bretherton, I., Fritz, J., Zahn-Waxler, C., & Ridgeway, D. (1986). Learning to talk about emotions: A functionalist perspective. *Child Development, 57*, 529–548.

Bruner, J. (1987). Life as narrative. *Social Research, 54*, 11–32.

Bruner, J. S. (1990). *Acts of meaning.* Cambridge, MA: Harvard University Press.

Davis, P. J. (1990). Gender differences in autobiographical memories for childhood emotional experiences. *Journal of Personality and Social Psychology, 76*, 498–510.

Denham, S. A., Zoller, D., & Couchoud, E. A. (1994). Socialization of preschoolers' emotion understanding. *Developmental Psychology, 30*, 928–936.

Dunn, J., Bretherton, I., & Munn, P. (1987). Conversations about feeling states between mothers and their young children. *Developmental Psychology, 23*, 132–139.

Dunn, J., Brown, J., & Beardsall, L. (1991). Family talk about feeling states and children's later understanding of others' emotions. *Developmental Psychology, 27*, 448–455.

Dunn, J., Brown, J., Slomkowski, C., Tesla, C., & Youngblade, L. (1991). Young children's understanding of other people's feelings and beliefs: Individual differences and their antecedents. *Child Development, 62*, 1352–1366.

Eisenberg, A. (1985). Learning to describe past experience in conversation. *Discourse Processes, 8*, 177–204.

Fischer, A.H. (2000). *Gender and emotion: Social psychological perspectives.* New York: Cambridge University Press.

Fivush, R. (1991). The social construction of personal narratives. *Merrill-Palmer Quarterly, 37*, 59–82.

Fivush, R. (1993). Emotional content of parent-child conversations about the past. In C. A. Nelson (Ed.), *The Minnesota Symposium on Child Psychology: Memory and affect in development* (pp. 39–77). Mahwah, NJ: Lawrence Erlbaum Associates.

Fivush, R. (2001). Owning experience: The development of subjective perspective in autobiographical memory. In C. Moore & K. Lemmon (Eds.), *The self in time: Developmental perspectives* (pp. 35–52). Mahwah, NJ: Lawrence Erlbaum Associates.

Fivush, R., Brotman, M., Buckner, J. P., & Goodman, S. (2000). Gender differences in parent-child emotion narratives. *Sex Roles, 42*, 233–254.

Fivush, R., & Buckner, J.P. (2003). Constructing gender and identity through autobiographical narratives. In R. Fivush & C. Haden (Eds.), *Autobiographical memory and the construction of a narrative self: Developmental and cultural perspectives.* Mahwah, NJ: Lawrence Erlbaum Associates.

Fivush, R., & Fromhoff, F. (1988). Style and structure in mother-child conversations about the past. *Discourse Processes, 11*, 337–355.

Fivush, R., & Haden, C. A. (1997). Narrating and representing experience: Preschoolers' developing autobiographical recounts. In P. van den Broek, P. A. Bauer, & T. Bourg (Eds.), *Developmental spans in event comprehension and representation: Bridging fictional and actual events.* Mahwah, NJ: Lawrence Erlbaum Associates.

Fivush, R., & Haden, C. A. (Eds.). (2003). *Autobiographical memory and the construction of a narrative self: Developmental and cultural perspectives.* Mahwah, NJ: Lawrence Erlbaum Associates.

Fivush, R., Haden, C. A., & Adam, S. (1995). Structure and coherence of preschoolers' personal narratives over time: Implications for childhood amnesia. *Journal of Experimental Child Psychology, 60*, 32–56.

Fivush, R., Haden, C. A., & Reese, E. (1996). Remembering, recounting and reminiscing: The development of autobiographical memory in social context. In D. Rubin (Ed.), *Reconstructing our past: An overview of autobiographical memory* (pp. 341–359). New York: Cambridge University Press.

Fivush, R., & Reese, E. (2002). Origins of reminiscing. In J. Webster & B. Haight (Eds.), *Critical advances in reminiscence work* (pp. 109–122). New York: Springer.

Fivush, R., & Vasudeva, A. (2002). Remembering to relate: Maternal reminiscing style and attachment. *Journal of Cognition and Development, 3,* 73–90.

Furrow, D., Moore, C., Davidge, J., & Chiasson, L. (1992). Mental terms in mothers' and children's speech: similarities and relationships. *Journal of Child Language, 19,* 617–631.

Haden, C. A., Haine, R. A., & Fivush, R. (1997). Developing narrative structure in parent-child conversations about the past. *Developmental Psychology, 33,* 295–307.

Harley, K., & Reese, E. (1999). Origins of autobiographical memory. *Developmental Psychology, 35,* 1338–1348.

Hudson, J. A. (1990). The emergence of autobiographic memory in mother–child conversation. In R. Fivush & J. A. Hudson (Eds.), *Knowing and remembering in young children* (pp. 166–196). New York: Cambridge University Press.

James, W. (1890). *The principles of psychology.* New York: Dover.

Kuebli, J., Butler, S., & Fivush, R., (1995). Mother–child talk about past events: Relations of maternal language and child gender over time. *Cognition and Emotion, 9,* 265–293.

Labov, W. (1982). Speech actions and reaction in personal narrative. In D. Tannen (Ed.) *Analyzing discourse: Text and talk.* Washington, DC: Georgetown University Press.

Leichtman, M., Wang, Q., & Pillemer, D. P. (2003). In R. Fivush & C. A. Haden (Eds.), *Autobiographical memory and the construction of a narrative self: Developmental and cultural perspectives.* Mahwah, NJ: Lawrence Erlbaum Associates.

Lewis, M., & Michealson, L. (1983). *Children's emotions and moods.* New York: Plenum.

Moore, C., Furrow, D., Chiasson, L., & Patriquin, M. (1994). Developmental relationships between production and comprehension of mental terms. *First Language, 14,* 1–17.

Nelson, K. (1996). *Language in cognitive development: Emergence of the mediated mind.* New York: Cambridge University Press.

Nelson, K. (2001). From the experiencing I to the continuing me. In C. Moore & K. Skene (Eds.), *The self in time: Developmental perspectives.* Mahwah, NJ: Lawrence Erlbaum Associates.

Olson, D. R. (1988). On the origins of beliefs and other intentional states in children. In J. W. Astington, P. L. Harris, & D. R. Olson (Eds.), *Developing theories of mind.* Cambridge, UK: Cambridge University Press.

Peterson, C., & McCabe, A. (1982). *Developmental psycholinguistics: Three ways of looking at a narrative.* New York: Plenum.

Peterson, C., & McCabe, A. (1992). Parental styles of narrative elicitation: Effect on children's narrative structure and content. *First Language, 12,* 299–321.

Reese, E., Haden, C. A., & Fivush, R. (1993). Mother-child conversations about the past: Relationships of style and memory over time. *Cognitive Development, 8,* 403–430.

Reese, E., Haden, C. A., & Fivush, R. (1996). Mothers, father, daughters sons: Gender differences in reminiscing. *Research on Language and Social Interaction, 29,* 27–56.

Rudek, D. J., & Haden, C. A. (2002). *Mothers' and preschoolers' mental state language during reminiscing over time.* Manuscript under review.

Ruffman, T., Slade, L., & Crowe, E. (2002). The relation between children's and mothers' mental state language and theory-of-mind understanding. *Child Development, 73,* 734–751.

Sachs, J. (1983). Talking about the there and then: The emergence of displaced reference in parent-child discourse. In K. Nelson (Ed.), *Children's language* (Vol. 4, pp. 1– 28). Hillsdale, NJ: Lawrence Erlbaum Associates.

Shatz, M., Wellman, H. M., & Silber, S. (1983). The acquisition of mental verbs: A systematic investigation of the first reference to mental state. *Cognition, 14,* 301–321.

Vygotsky, L. S. (1978). *Mind in society: The development of higher psychological processes.* Cambridge, MA: Harvard University Press.

Wellman, J. M., & Estes, D. (1987). Children's early use of mental verbs and what they mean. *Discourse Processes, 10,* 141–156.

Zahn-Waxler, C., Cole, P., & Barrett, K. (1991). Guilt and empathy: Sex differences and implications for the development of depression. In J. Garber & K. Dodge (Eds.), *The development of emotion regulation and deregulation: Cambridge studies in social and emotional development* (pp. 243–272). New York: Cambridge University Press.

Chapter 14

Autobiographical Memory in the Developmental Niche: A Cross-cultural Perspective

Michelle D. Leichtman
University of New Hampshire

Qi Wang
Cornell University

As ecological and cultural theorists have noted, developmental processes are best studied as a function of the rich, synergistic and interactive contextual factors that constitute children's physical and social environments (e.g., Bronfenbrenner, 1979; Super & Harkness, 1986). The myriad processes involved in memory are a case in point. Despite a formidable history of memory research in psychology (e.g., Bartlett, 1932; Ebbinghaus, 1885), the specific parameters that determine encoding, retention and retrieval performance are still being explored across a variety of paradigms (e.g., Schacter, 1996; Wright & Loftus, 1998). A developmental perspective highlights the inherent complexity of these processes. In particular, considering how memory develops in the natural world underscores its essential relationship with a complex set of environmental features. As Ceci and Leichtman

(1992) noted, "to think about memory without considering the contexts that lead children to remember is akin to thinking about smiles independently of the faces on which they appear" (p. 223).

This analogy is particularly apt when applied to the case of autobiographical memory, or memory for personally experienced past events. Autobiographical memories are by definition memories related to the self, and as such their contents are infused with the particulars of the physical, cognitive, social, and emotional contexts in which they are experienced. In addition to these encoding based influences, contextual factors may also influence autobiographical processes at storage and retrieval (e.g., Han, Leichtman, & Wang, 1998; Nelson, 2003). Relative to other areas of memory, episodic memory—including autobiographical processes—has traditionally received less research attention (Martin, 1993; Pillemer, 1998). Thus, the profound influence of context at every stage of autobiographical remembering has been brought to light with force only recently, as research has begun to focus on the development of autobiographical memory across cultures. The present chapter focuses on this research.

The "developmental niche" model developed by Super and Harkness (1986, 1999, 2002) has proven to be a useful framework for describing the relevant contexts of children's development. This model underscores the contribution of three main subsystems, or elements of the environment, to developmental processes (Super and Harkness, 1986). These elements include the psychology of those who care for children, the customs and practices of child rearing and the physical and social settings in which children live. Although these elements have certainly been incorporated into earlier thinking about context, one advantage of the "developmental niche" model is the view it affords of "cultural thematicity." As Super and Harkness (2002) describe, focusing on these three subsystems of children's environments brings into relief the regularities that exist in terms of the "core messages" or themes that any given culture delivers. Such messages can vary widely across cultures, and they presumably reflect cultural differences in beliefs, preoccupations, and adaptive behavioral strategies (Leichtman, Wang, & Pillemer, 2003; Super & Harkness, 1986; Wang, Ceci, Williams, & Kopko, in press). The repeated themes that children experience from different aspects of the environment can have profound effects on developmental processes, and in this way the developmental niche perspective reveals that "culture structures the environment for development" (Super & Harkness, 2002, p. 270).

Importantly, as we speak about culture throughout this chapter, we consider the definition that follows. Culture is "the system and the process of symbolic mediation—a mode of configuration.... Manifesting itself in social institutions as well as in the actions, thoughts, emotions, beliefs, and moral values of individuals, culture regulates both intra-personal and inter-personal psychological functions" (Wang & Brockmeier, 2002, pp. 45–46).

Given the complexity of this definition, we do not assume that individuals from a single country or region necessarily share the same cultural environment. We acknowledge that variations at the level of subculture are certain to exist, and in many cases environmental variations at the subcultural level may be marked (Fiske, 2002; Oyserman, Coon, & Kemmelmeier, 2002). We also acknowledge that for any psychological variable, there may be extensive within-group variation within a single cultural context. Recognizing that findings are unlikely to extend to all potential subgroups within a region or country, and recognizing individual differences within-groups, we nonetheless find it useful to consider group-level data throughout the world.

In this chapter, we focus on the following question: "How does culture structure the environment relevant to the development of autobiographical memory?" A number of recent studies, from our laboratories and others, have begun to provide insight into this question. To frame our discussion of these studies, we consider the environmental subsystems that the developmental niche model suggests are most prominent in shaping developmental processes.

We begin by discussing the end products of development, such as differences in the form and content of memories expressed by adults, when reflecting on recent or long-past events. We then turn to a number of research issues that map onto Super and Harkness's (2002) triarchy of essential subsystems within the developmental niche. First, we treat differences in cultural beliefs about memory, underscoring their relationship with cultural beliefs about the role of the self. We argue that this aspect of adult caregiver's psychology has implications for children's memory development. Second, we turn to data on parental practices in memory sharing. Third, in close connection with parental practices we consider the larger social and narrative environments in which children live, and how these impact autobiographical memory over the long term. Finally, we examine data suggesting that children's memory narratives differ across cultures, early in development when the environment is just beginning to have an impact.

DIFFERENCES IN LONG TERM RECOLLECTIONS AMONG ADULTS

A number of cross-cultural studies have focused on the age and nature of the earliest memories that adults are able to recall. These studies offer an intriguing point of departure, because they underscore the potential for normative differences in long term event memories. Within culture, researchers have long recognized that adults typically exhibit a dearth of recollections for the first few years of life, a phenomenon termed *childhood amnesia* (Freud, 1920/1953; Pillemer & White, 1989). Freud (1920/1953), for example, noted that patients had trouble retrieving memories from earlier than ages 6 to 8 years. Research in the United States has substantiated similar difficulties recalling events from before the age of 3 to 4 years (e.g., Kihlstrom & Harackiewicz, 1982; Wetzler & Sweeney, 1986).

Systematic contemporary research has also revealed substantial individual variation among participants within the United States, even when the populations questioned are relatively homogenous. Individual variation within culture is certainly connected theoretically with potential explanations for childhood amnesia, and these have abounded in recent years. Such explanations have focused on ontological changes at the level of the memory system and also on diverse maturational, social, and linguistic advances that permit children to lay down increasingly accessible and enduring event memories as they grow (e.g., Howe, 2003; Pillemer & White, 1989).

At the level of the population these theories help explain the factors involved in childhood amnesia, and by extension they contribute to speculations about why the timing of the earliest memory differs from one person to the next (e.g., Howe, 2003; Kihlstrom & Harackiewicz, 1982; Wetzler & Sweeney, 1986). The source of such differences in timing, like the source of childhood amnesia itself, is likely to be multicausal and may also be linked with esoteric differences in the specific events individuals have experienced during childhood (e.g., Usher & Neisser, 1993). However, research within single North American populations has not fully evaluated variations in the environment that may contribute to differences in the timing of earliest memories. Cross-cultural work is helpful to consider in this connection because the range of individual differences in data sets that include several cultures is large, and environmental differences that may affect the timing of earliest memory can be more marked—and thus more easily ascertained—than in studies involving a single culture. Normative differences in environmental factors and autobiographical memory performance provide insights that can be applied to thinking about individual differences within culture.

Comparing across cultures, Mullen (1994) considered how early autobiographical memories differed for Korean and American adults. Using a questionnaire method, she documented that a mixed group of Asian and Asian-American adults reported earliest memories that took place 6 months later than a similar group of Caucasian-American adults. When only the native Korean participants' memories were included in the analyses, the data revealed that Koreans' memories were a full 16.7 months later than the Caucasian Americans'. In addition to these differences in the timing of earliest memories, American adults tended to report memories that were more detailed and more self focused than the memories of their Korean counterparts.

To explore the relation between memory and cultural self-construct (which we discuss in a later section), Wang (2001a) asked college students in major cities in China and the United States to write down and date their earliest memories. The findings indicated that, on average, Caucasian American participants' earliest memories took place when they were 3 years, 3 months old. In contrast, Chinese participants' earliest memories took place an average of 6 months later. As in Mullen's (1994) study, not only the timing but also the content of these earliest memories differed across cultures. Wang used a coding scheme developed by Pillemer, Rhinehart & White (1986) to code memories as specific, one-point-in-time events (e.g., "the day I got an A on my English exam") as opposed to routines or scripted activities (e.g., "writing at school"). When evaluated according to this scheme, American participants provided more detailed memories of distinct, one-point-in-time events. Chinese participants provided briefer, more skeletal memories focusing on routine or general occurrences. In addition, American participants' memories often focused on the rememberer and were emotionally expressive, whereas Chinese participants' memories often centered on group activities and significant others and were emotionally unexpressive.

In another recent study, Wang, Conway, and Hou (2003) investigated in three culture groups two components of childhood amnesia: 1) the accessibility of memory events occurring in the childhood amnesia period (birth to 5 years), and 2) the offset (earliest age of recall). Participants ($N = 349$) from the United States, England, and China were asked to recall within a 5-minute period as many memories as they could about events that occurred before age 5. Compared with the two Western groups, particularly the U.S. group, Chinese participants recalled fewer childhood memories (China $M = 5.68$; England $M = 9.83$; US $M = 12.24$), showed slower age-linked increase in memory accessibility, and had their earliest memory a few months later. These findings suggest that childhood amnesia differs in degree across cultures, with Chinese showing the strongest effect and Caucasian Americans the weakest. The British group fell in between.

Investigating cultural differences between two distinct populations in New Zealand, Hayne & McDonald (2003) also examined the timing and other characteristics of earliest memories. The researchers focused on Maori, or indigenous adults and their Pakeha, or Caucasian counterparts. They reasoned that adults from Maori culture, which places significant evidence on oral traditions, might produce earlier autobiographical memories. In response to a written instrument that elicited memory reports, the 16 Maori adults in their sample provided earliest memories from a mean age of around 33 months, whereas Pakeha adults provided significantly later earliest memories from a mean age of around 43 months. Other aspects of the memory reports, such as length and specific content, varied more significantly along gender lines than across cultures in this study (Hayne & McDonald, 2003).

In a related vein, Leichtman, Bhogle, Sankaranarayanan, & Hobeika (2003) conducted an interview study of rural and urban Indian adults of low socio-economic status, all from the southern region of India near Bangalore. These two Indian populations were contrasted with a sample of upper middle class European-American adults living in the Boston, Massachusetts region of the United States, for a total sample size of 111. All participants were interviewed in their own homes or workplaces by trained native interviewers who came from the same socio-economic background as the participants. The interviewers asked a series of questions about autobiographical memory, beginning with an open-ended question about whether participants remembered any event from childhood. Notably, participants were not asked for their earliest childhood memory, but for any memory of childhood. We chose this broader manner of questioning because pilot testing in the Indian sample indicated that prompting for earliest memory resulted in little in the way of narrative memory reports.

Ninety-seven percent of American participants reported recalling a childhood memory, and 69% of these provided a one-point-in time, datable episode, whereas 28% provided a more general memory. Participants were not prompted to provide the date of their childhood memories, but more than half of American participants spontaneously dated their memories from ages 3 to 12 years. In contrast, 57% of rural Indian participants and 26% of urban Indian participants reported having no recollection of childhood. Only 14 % of participants in the rural sample provided a specific, datable episode while 29% provided a general memory. In the urban sample, 22% of participants provided a specific memory, while 52% provided a general memory. Most Indian participants were unsure of their own birthdates, potentially complicating the dating of their memories. In the Indian sample, only 6 participants, all in the urban sample, provided their ages at the time of their childhood memories. Their estimates ranged from 6 to 11 years of age. The specific timing of the recollections is perhaps less noteworthy than the marked differences in reported accessibility to event memories from childhood across these cultural groups.

Further analyses revealed differences in the qualitative nature of the childhood memories that Indian and American participants provided. Childhood memories were randomly selected from the sets of Indian and American memories. Each memory selected was typed on a separate index card with culture-specific terms disguised. (For example, the Indian food *uppitu* was changed to "peanut butter" in the memory typed on the card.) Ten college students came into the lab individually to serve as raters. Raters were blind to the experimental methods and hypotheses and were unaware that the memories came from individuals from two different countries. A researcher told raters, "people differ in the ease and richness with which they can recall autobiographical memories. By richness, we mean how vivid, detailed and accessible. We would like you to evaluate memories people provided when they were interviewed about autobiographical memories." The researcher asked raters to read all of the memories, and to sort them into two equal piles, with the first pile representing "the richest memories" and the second pile representing "the least rich memories." The results indicated that 69% of American memories were sorted into the "richest" pile, while only 32% of the Indian memories were sorted into the "richest" pile. Thus, using this crude method, untrained raters distinguished qualitatively between the style of childhood memories from the two cultures.

In summary, recent investigations suggest normative cultural differences among adults in the timing of the earliest childhood memory, the content and specificity of childhood and more recent memories, and the ease of access to specific autobiographical memories. But when do these differences in memory emerge developmentally, and in what ways does culture give rise to them? To consider this question, we turn to an evaluation of those elements of the developmental niche that Super & Harkness (2002) have suggested have the most profound influence on developmental processes.

BELIEFS ABOUT MEMORIES AND THE SELF

One particularly critical aspect of the environment for children growing up is the psychology of their caregivers (Super & Harkness, 2002). This is most obviously true if one considers the explicit beliefs that caregivers hold about the optimal environments and practices involved in raising children. As Super and Harkness (2002) describe, such beliefs are reflected in "ethnotheories," or articulated and socially shared perspectives on raising children.

Closely linked with beliefs about child-rearing practices are caregivers' more general values and beliefs about optimal human thought and behavior patterns. These beliefs vary across individuals and also vary substantially at the cultural level (e.g., Bronfenbrenner, 1979; Fiske, Kitayama, Markus, & Nisbett, 1998). They include conscious, articulated thoughts or attitudes and implicit beliefs that may be outside of awareness but influence behavior nonetheless (e.g., Greenwald & Banaji, 1995). Beliefs at both levels of awareness are likely to direct adults' practices in their own lives and also child-rearing practices.

Relevant to autobiographical memory, adults belonging to different cultural groups may hold different explicit beliefs about the importance of the personal past, and these may coincide with different memory practices (Wang & Brockmeier, 2002). Studies of autobiographical memory typically have not probed directly participants' attitudes towards sharing and reflecting on personal event memories. An example of cultural differences in such attitudes emerged in Leichtman, et. al.'s (2003) study contrasting Indian and American adults. The researchers asked all participants "Do you talk about the past in your daily life?" In response, 90% of American participants responded "yes," and the qualitative nature of their answers was revealing. Many participants made comments such as "of course, what would I be without my personal memories of my life?" In contrast, only 12% of rural Indian participants said that they talked about the past in their daily lives. The remaining 88% said that they did not talk about the past, and their qualitative answers were equally noteworthy. Many rural Indian participants made comments such as, "why would I do such a thing? It's nonsense." Urban Indian participants' answers fell between—and were significantly different from—both of the other groups': 71% of urban Indian participants said that they talked about the past in their daily lives, while 29% said that they did not. These contrasting responses among the groups suggest that normative cultural and subcultural differences may exist in the meaning of thinking about and talking about personally experienced past events.

To understand why personal event memories may be more valued in some cultures than others, it is useful to consider research on normative differences in social orientation. Speaking broadly, societies such as those in the United States and some European countries embrace a set of values in which autonomy, self-expression and unique characteristics of the person are highly valued. In short, such societies represent a social orientation towards independence of the individual, sometimes at the expense of the larger community. In contrast, Asian societies, such as those found in China, Korea, and India, place a premium on harmony in interpersonal relationships and emphasize common goals and shared identities among people, consistent with an interdependent social orientation (Markus & Kitayama, 1991; Wang & Leichtman, 2000). Such dichotomous categories in social orientation may be misleading, in that they may not reflect a cohesive picture of all aspects of social cognition (Oyserman, et al., 2002). Similarly, the potential exists for over-generalizing the degree to which such concepts extend to all social groups within a given country (Fiske, 2002). Nonetheless, they help make sense of the kinds of autobiographical memory differences we might expect between groups.

In connection with autobiographical memory, how might global differences in social orientation affect beliefs and practices? Part of what it means to live in an independently oriented society is to focus on and communicate what is special about the self. Hence, keeping a detailed mental record of personal event memories, thinking of past events in evaluative terms and sharing memories with others makes good sense (Leichtman, Wang, & Pillemer, 2003; Pillemer, 1998; Wang, 2003). In independently oriented cultures, a rich store of autobiographical memories may serve to define and affirm the self, to enhance social status and to enhance bonding with other people. In contrast, the same extensive, explicit focus on the personal past is largely inconsistent with the values espoused in such societies. Where overarching cultural values dictate a subjugation of personal interests to the larger dictates of the group, the role of personal event memories is diminished. In fact, within such a context extensive discussion about the details of one's own past experiences may appear selfish and inappropriate.

Thus, there is a clear theoretical connection between the extent to which various cultures embrace an independent versus interdependent social orientation and the likely value of personal event memory. In daily life, social values may dictate that individuals engage in very little or very frequent and extensive talk and reflection on personally experienced past events. Such differences in memory practices are not only interesting in their own right; they are likely to affect how easily individuals can access specific events in memory, how much and what details they remember and the manner in which they describe events. Differences we noted earlier between some Asian and American populations in the timing, accessibility and style of reporting personal event memories make sense from this perspective.

If differences in social orientation are truly connected with differences in autobiographical event memories, then such a connection should be apparent at both the individual and cultural group levels. To evaluate this empirically, we conducted several studies targeted at the association between memory narratives and measures of social orientation, indexed by self-description tasks presumed to reflect the accessibility and organization of self-related information.

Beginning with a within-culture sample, Wang, Leichtman, and White (1998) studied Chinese only- and sibling-children who were now of high school and college age. Since the one-child policy came into effect in China in 1979, commentators have scrutinized the effects on children of growing up without the siblings who were traditionally present in Chinese homes. Some have noted that the new, smaller family size creates a very different environment for children than collectivist values would dictate. The notion of a "4-2-1 syndrome," in which four grandparents and two parents focus on a single child, is indicative of this (Lee, 1992). Chinese observers have noted that the only-child family structure may place excessive, unhealthy attention on the child, producing "little emperors." Some reports have described only-children as self-centered, willful, egocentric, and undisciplined in comparison with their sibling counterparts (Fan, 1994; Jiao, Ji, & Jing, 1986). This situation offered a premier opportunity to evaluate differences in social orientation associated with only child status, and to see whether these were related to differences in autobiographical memory reports.

The study was conducted in Beijing, where a sample of 99 only-child participants and 156 participants with siblings filled out two questionnaires in Chinese. The first questionnaire asked participants to describe and date their earliest autobiographical memory, and then to do the same for 3 other childhood memories. The results paralleled cultural differences described earlier in the age of earliest childhood memory across independently-oriented and interdependently-oriented societies. Only-child participants reported earliest memories that dated from the time they were 39 months old, on average, while siblings reported earliest memories from almost 9 months later. Other aspects of the memories also differed between groups: only-child participants reported fewer memories focusing on social interactions, fewer memories focusing on family, more memories focusing on personal experiences and feelings, and more memories focusing solely on themselves. Only-child participants also reported a greater number of specific memories, referring to one-point-in-time events, than their sibling counterparts. Finally, only- child participants' memories contained a lower ratio of other/self mentions, indicating a relatively greater focus on their own past thoughts and activities.

The second questionnaire was a version of Kuhn and McPartland's (1954) Twenty Statements Test (TST), which elicited self-descriptions. Participants filled in the blank after 10 statements phrased "I am __."

TST responses fell into two primary scoring categories: private versus collective self-descriptions. *Private* self-descriptions focus on personal traits, states, or behaviors (e.g., "I am intelligent") whereas *collective* self-descriptions focus on group membership (e.g., "I am a Buddhist") (Greenwald & Pratkanis, 1984; Triandis, 1989). In other studies, participants from independently-oriented cultures have provided a predominance of private self-descriptions, while participants from interdependently-oriented cultures have provided more collective self-descriptions (Bochner, 1994; Trafimow, Triandis, & Goto, 1991). Such results accord with the idea that members of independently-oriented cultures have highly-organized and readily accessible sets of information about the private self in memory, whereas members of interdependently-oriented cultures have disproportionately more information available about the collective self (Markus & Kitayama, 1991; Triandis, 1989). Consistent with predicted differences in their social orientations, only-child participants reported relatively more private self-descriptions than their sibling-child counterparts, who reported relatively more collective self-descriptions.

Across the entire sample, participants' scores on the self-description questionnaire were related to several autobiographical memory variables. Private self-description scores were positively related to narrative length, mentions of the self, and memory specificity, while collective self-description scores were negatively related to each of these memory measures.

Wang (2001a) also examined autobiographical memories and self-description scores, this time in a large sample of Caucasian-American and Chinese college students. Significant effects of culture were obtained on both sets of variables, in the direction predicted by differences in social orientation. The TST scores of Americans indicated proportionately more "private" and fewer "collective" self-descriptions than those of Chinese, and Americans' autobiographical memories were earlier, more autonomously oriented and more likely to be specific. Partial correlations with group factors (i.e., culture, gender) controlled for showed that individuals who described themselves in more self-focused and positive terms provided more specific and self-focused memories.

Strikingly, such a connection between autobiographical memory and social orientation as indexed by one's self-concept appears to become established in children even before the age of formal schooling. In a recent study, Wang (2004) examined autobiographical memory and self-description in European-American and Chinese children in preschool through second grade ($N = 180$). Native female researchers interviewed children individually at school. During a "question-and-answer game," children recounted four autobiographical events and described themselves in response to open-ended questions. American children tended to provide lengthy, detailed, and emotionally elaborate memories and to focus on their own roles, preferences, and feelings in telling the story; they also frequently described themselves in terms of personal attitudes, beliefs, and dispositional traits, in a positive light. In comparison, Chinese children provided relatively skeletal accounts of past experiences that often centered on social interactions and daily routines; they were also more likely to describe themselves in terms of social roles, relationships, and context-specific behaviors in a neutral or modest tone. These cultural differences became larger and more stable among older children. In addition, at the individual level, children who focused more on their private aspects of the self gave lengthier memory accounts and placed more emphasis on personal roles and predilections.

Thus, taken together, the literature suggests that different beliefs—as reflected in different social orientations and views of the importance of retaining and sharing personal event memories—may be intimately linked with adults' daily memory practices and with the timing, availability and content of event memories during adulthood. Such beliefs may also be associated with different views and practices during child rearing. A large body of work attests to significant variations from culture to culture in both explicit and implicit beliefs about appropriate child rearing practices more generally (e.g., DeLoache & Gottlieb, 2000). We do not know of empirical data directly assessing cultural differences in parents views of the role autobiographical memory should play in the child rearing process. However, we do know that caregivers' actual practices reflect very different notions of how the autobiographical past should be treated, and that these are consistent with differences in the caregivers' own social orientations and memory practices. We turn next to the literature documenting these practices, and the closely related issue of relevant differences in the settings of childhood.

PARENTAL MEMORY PRACTICES AND THE SOCIAL SETTINGS OF CHILDHOOD

The following discussion was recently recorded in the home of a 3-year-old European-American child, Samantha. Samantha and her mother sat at the kitchen table, talking about a splinter that Samantha had received in her foot earlier that morning.

M: Well honey it might tickle for just a minute. But if I don't take it out it's really going to hurt you later on. Do you remember the story that I told you about when I was a little girl and I fell off my bicycle? And what happened?
C: You had to go to Aunt Maryland's because Mama wasn't there.
M: And what did my Aunt Maryland do?
C: She took the boo-boo off.
M: Right, and then what did she do?
C: She put Band-Aid on it.

M: Did she take all the dirt out of it?
C: Yeah.
M: She put a Band-Aid on it?
C: And she took off the rocks.
M: And did I cry?
C: No.
M: Did I cry just a little bit or was I okay?
C: Yeah.
M: And then what did I do right afterwards?
C: You ride outside on your bike because you were riding on sand.
M: And did I go back and ride again?
C: Yeah.
M: Because I was being a little brave and even though it hurt I was o.k.?
C: Yeah.
M: Do you think that you can do that? Be brave about things?
C: Maybe ... when I'm a grown-up.

This discussion represents the kind of talk about past events that many American parents and their children engage in (Haden, Haine, & Fivush, 1997; Leichtman, Pillemer, Wang, Koreishi, & Han, 2000). The discussion focused on an event from the past that served social purposes in the present; in this case the purposes of persuasion and the facilitation of mother–child bonding. In this example, Samantha's mother shared an event from her own childhood at which Samantha was not present. In other conversations on the same day, she talked about events that she and Samantha had both participated in and events that Samantha had experienced without her. It would be equally plausible to find each kind of conversation about the personal past in middle-class European-American homes.

A significant literature on mother-child conversation in the United States has distinguished between two predominant styles of talking about the personal past (Fivush & Fromhoff, 1988; Pillemer, 1998; Reese, Haden, & Fivush, 1993). A number of different names have referred to similar conceptual dichotomies (e.g., elaborative/high-elaborative vs. pragmatic/repetitive/low-elaborative). At one end of the spectrum are high-elaborative mothers, who frequently speak with their children about the past. During their discussions, they tend to give extensive descriptive information about experiences, and regularly prompt children to provide similarly embellished past-event narratives. On the other end of the spectrum are low-elaborative mothers, who talk less frequently about past events. Low elaborative mothers tend to provide fewer details about past events, and tend to pose pointed questions with single correct and incorrect answers when questioning their children (Fivush & Fromhoff, 1988; Reese, Haden & Fivush, 1993).

Nelson (1996) has pointed out that conversations about the personal past between parents and their children represent a kind of "co-construction." Through such conversations, parents teach children implicitly how to speak about and think about their own past experiences and what the social meaning of such experiences should be. In connection with the developmental niche model, variations in just this kind of parental practice are assumed to have important developmental outcomes for children (Super & Harkness, 2002).

One of the major organizational aspects of the environment that Super and Harkness (2002) have discussed is "thematic elaboration." Thematic elaboration refers to "the repetition and cultivation over time of core symbols and systems of meaning" (p. 272). The sharing of autobiographical memories can be construed as such a system of meaning that operates within the framework of a particular set of shared values. Like the acquisition of discourse styles more generally or the regulation of emotion (Super & Harkness, 2002), at the level of culture the rules that regulate the sharing of autobiographical memories are likely to emerge and be refined in connection with other systems in the environment. In terms of development, Super & Harkness (2002) assert that "children appear effortlessly to detect, abstract and internalize culturally based rules of performance and systems of meaning" (p. 272).

This notion of talk about the personal past as a culture-specific practice that children internalize is consistent with the findings of recent cross-cultural studies. A number of researchers have documented cultural differences in the nature of past event talk between parents and their children. Further, evidence is beginning to mount that children themselves absorb these different ways of talking about the past at an early age.

To evaluate differences in mother–child conversations about the past, Choi (1992) recorded the conversations of Canadian and Korean mothers and children. Choi (1992) reported that during conversations about past events, Korean mothers infrequently sought new information from their children, but instead prompted children to confirm that they understood information the mothers had introduced. Korean mothers generally expected children to follow their conversational leads. They often made statements unrelated to what their child had just said and did not encourage children to introduce their own ideas into the conversation. Canadian mothers more often extended the discussion of what their child had just said, encouraged their child to contribute unique ideas, and took the role of conversational partner, rather than director.

Mullen and Yi (1995) also examined naturally occurring conversation, in this case between Korean or American mothers and their preschool-aged children. The researchers obtained tape recordings of one full day of ongoing mother–child dialogue and transcribed and analyzed only talk about past events . During each hour mothers and children spent together, American mothers referred to an average of 3 times more past events than their Korean counterparts. It is uncertain from these results whether American children were exposed to more conversation in total than Korean children, but it is clear that they were exposed to more conversation about the past. Analyses of the contents of past-event talk indicated that American mothers talked more than Koreans about the child's feelings and thoughts, other people's feelings and thoughts, and the child's personal attributes, while Korean mothers talked more about norms of social behavior.

Using a different method, Wang, Leichtman, & Davies (2000) asked American and Chinese mothers to talk with their 3-year-old children at home about two past events and a story. American mothers demonstrated a more elaborative style in both kinds of conversation, more often posing open-ended "wh" questions and elaborating on children's responses. American mothers also focused significantly more often on children's opinions and desires. In contrast, Chinese mothers often dominated the conversation. They used a low-elaborative conversational style, frequently posing and repeating factual questions, and rarely allowing children's statements to change the direction of the conversation. They also used memory conversations as a forum to instill proper behavioral conduct in the child and to emphasize the role of significant others in the child's life. The same pattern of cultural differences in the style and content of mother–child reminiscing is further observed in conversations of emotionally salient events in U.S. and Chinese families (Wang, 2001b), which has important implications for children's remembering of significant personal experiences and developing coping strategies.

The characteristics of memory sharing in Asian families are illustrated in the following conversation between a Chinese mother and her 3-year-old daughter, Yangyang (Wang, Leichtman, & Davies, 2000).

M: The other day, mom took you to the zoo. What did you play? What did you play at the zoo? You played on the slide. Whom did you play with?
C: With the ... little sister.
M: You played with the little sister, right?
C: um.
M: You played with the little sister the whole time.
C: um.

M: You were in the front, she was behind you, right?
C: um.
M: What else did you play at the zoo besides the slide?
C: I also played with a big dragon.
M: A big dragon?
C: um.
M: Which big dragon?
C: That big dragon.
M: oh, right, the one that you went through, right?
C: um.
M: Then it got dark. And mom took you home, right?
C: um.

The aforementioned studies provide evidence of cultural differences in the caretaker practices that Super & Harkness (2002) have emphasized are important to development. At the same time, one could also view these studies as attesting to differences in children's social environments, to the extent that memory sharing is part of the child's larger social world. In a study of rural Indian and American children, Leichtman, et al. (2003) adopted this latter perspective, and sought to evaluate cultural differences in the entirety of children's memory-relevant narrative environments at home.

Leichtman, et. al. (2003) made naturalistic observations of fourteen 3- to 4-year-old rural Indian children and 14 suburban European American children of the same age. The researchers filmed children and their families in their homes. They told participants that they were simply interested in looking at the lifestyle and activities of young children and that everyone should go about their business as usual. The only stipulation was that the mother in the family be present in the home with the child during the filming. The researchers recorded all speech over the course of one hour in the home of each child and the Indian data was translated from the native language Kannada into English for coding purposes. The researchers were interested in potential differences between children's total environments, and thus in the analyses mother's speech was combined with the speech of all other adults who were present in the home ("mothers and others"). The results indicated that American children heard an average of 474 sentences from mothers and others; 3 times the number of sentences that their Indian counterparts heard. Even taking this difference in amount of talk into account, there were some very significant differences between the two environments in terms of memory talk in particular.

One major set of analyses concerned where in time the sentences that children heard were "located." In an analysis that amounted to a kind of temporal mapping, each sentence was coded, depending on the time frame it referenced, as belonging to one of the following mutually-exclusive categories: the present, the proximal past (i.e., just occurred), the distant past (i.e., occurred before the proximal past), the proximal future (i.e., about to occur) or the distant future (i.e., to occur after the proximal future). The data indicated strikingly different patterns. Commands constituted 50% of all sentences Indian children heard, and 5% of all sentences American children heard. References to the present constituted 35% of all sentences Indian children heard and 69% of all sentences American children heard. References to the proximal future constituted 8% of all sentences Indian children heard and 15% of all sentences that American children heard. References to the proximal past constituted 5% of all sentences for both groups.

Most central to the present discussion, the distant past constituted 4% of all sentences American children heard and less than 1% of all sentences Indian children heard. Because of the difference between groups in the total number of sentences, this small difference in percentages amounted to a discernable difference in actual exposure to past event talk. Over the course of an hour, American children heard an average of 20 sentences referring to the distant past, whereas Indian children heard an average of less than 2. This difference remained significant in analyses controlling for the total number of sentences children heard, which was not the case for the between-group differences in any other category except references to the proximal future.

Consistent with the findings of previous observational studies incorporating Asian and North American cultural groups (e.g., Choi, 1992; Mullen & Yi, 1995), there were also stylistic differences in the observed conversations. For example, in comparison with Indian mothers and others, American mothers and others used more open-ended questions, more descriptives and evaluatives (i.e., references to preferences and judgements) and more references to cognitive states. This kind of naturalistic data provides a sense that caretakers' practices of modeling and encouraging talk about the personal past can differ considerably across cultures. In conjunction with other factors, such differences play a role in shaping what amounts to distinct social environments for children.

CHILDREN'S AUTOBIOGRAPHICAL MEMORY TALK

In line with data on other kinds of cultural meaning systems (Super & Harkness, 2002), evidence suggests that children naturally learn to use and appreciate talk about past events in ways that accord with the values of their caretakers and other adults in the societies in which they live. Just as Super and Harkness (2002) have described, children appear to intuit the rules that govern the sharing of autobiographical events in their particular culture. At the level of the individual, several studies have shown that children of high-elaborative mothers have themselves provided longer, more detailed and more descriptive memory narratives than children of low-elaborative mothers (Haden, Haine, & Fivush, 1997; McCabe & Peterson, 1991; Reese, Haden, & Fivush, 1993). At the level of culture, studies have indicated that children's autobiographical narratives vary from an early age.

Han, Leichtman, and Wang (1998) studied fifty 4- and 6-year-old children from upper middle class, urban backgrounds in each of three countries: Korea, China, and the United States. Investigators interviewed 50 children in each country in their native languages, asking each child the same series of free-recall questions about recent events in the children's lives (e.g., questions about the children's last birthday and what they had done at bedtime the day before). Measured in number of words, American and Chinese children provided relatively long reports about past events, whereas Korean children provided only brief reports. On most other variables, the American sample stood apart from the two Asian groups. American participants used more words per proposition (defined as any subject-verb construction) than both Korean and Chinese children. This indicated that as a group, American children had a relatively detailed, descriptive style of talking about their memories. Supporting this notion, when compared with both Asian groups, American children's narratives contained more descriptives (i.e., adjectives, adverbs, modifiers), more personal preferences, more judgments and opinions and more references to thoughts or cognitive states. American children also made comparatively more self references, as opposed to references to others, than children from either Asian group. American children gave many more memories that referred to specific one-point-in-time episodes as opposed to repeated or routine events. American children tended to give long, detailed and evaluative descriptions of one or two single activities (e.g., taking a bath) whereas Korean and Chinese children tended to give skeletal descriptions of multiple events (e.g., "watched television, took a bath, brushed my teeth"). Korean and Chinese children's narratives were similar to each other in style, but Chinese children talked about more activities within a single narrative than their Korean peers.

From a developmental perspective, for children from the United States, Korea, and China, age was associated with longer narratives, more elaboration, and more description of personal preferences and cognitive states. However, although American children's narratives were specific and quite elaborated by the age of 4, Korean and Chinese children's narratives at the same age were relatively general and sparse. By the age of 6, Korean and Chinese children provided narratives that were characterized by a degree of specificity similar to American 4-year-olds.

Wang, Leichtman, and Davies (2000) looked more directly at the relationship between parent's conversational styles and children's autobiographical memories in China and the United States. The researchers asked Chinese and European-American mother–child dyads to discuss memories of shared past events in their own natural style, and also requested that they make up stories together to go along with a picture book. In this study, American mothers were more high-elaborative and child-focused, and the data indicated that this affected their children. In comparison with Chinese children, American children provided more information when talking about past events and tended to provide elaborative, detailed descriptions of the past in response to their mothers' questions. The researchers employed contingency analyses to evaluate the relationship between mothers' and children's narrative styles, and these documented a close correspondence between the two. Mothers within each culture who were relatively more elaborative had children who provided more embellished memory and story narratives.

In their study with New Zealand Maori and Pakeha populations, Hayne and MacDonald (2003) also documented differences in children's narratives that corresponded with those of their parents. The researchers reported that Maori mothers used a more repetitive style than Pakeha mothers. Similarly, Maori children used more elaborations than Pakeha children, whereas Pakeha children used more elaborations and evaluations than Maori children.

Some studies have focused on the content of memory sharing from a cultural perspective. Miller and colleagues, for example, demonstrated that Chinese parents tend to discuss their children's past experiences in terms of rule violations to a larger extent than do American parents (Miller, Wiley, Fung, & Liang, 1997). Accordingly, Wang and Leichtman (2000) were interested in how the thematic content of children's personal memories might differ across cultures. They asked Chinese and European-American 6-year-olds to tell stories prompted by pictures and standard verbal leads, and then prompted children to recount seven emotional memories. Memory prompts took the following form: "Now tell me one time when you felt really disgusted (ashamed, scared, angry, guilty, happy, sad)." Content analyses focused on the social, emotional and cognitive characteristics of the stories and memories children provided. In the case of both stories and memories, the findings showed differences between samples from the two countries. For example, compared with American children's stories and memories, those of Chinese children showed a greater orientation toward social engagement. This was indicated by the following: the number of characters present in the stories, incidents of group action and cooperation, instances of the protagonist (or child herself, in the memories) helping or being helped by others, and instances in which a relationship continued after a disruption. Chinese children's stories and memories also showed a greater concern with moral correctness, indicated by didactic statements and references to proper behavior and moral character. Chinese children's stories and memories showed a greater concern with authority, referring to a larger number of authority figures, instances of conformity to authority, instances of authority approval and punishment. Chinese children showed a less autonomous orientation, indexed by mentions of personal needs and preferences, dislikes and avoidance, evaluations and judgements and instances in which a character retained personal control in the face of authority.

In summary, the styles with which children talk about the past and the themes that predominate their autobiographical reports are closely connected with similar characteristics in the memory conversations of their caregivers. Both the linguistic and thematic features of adults' discussions of the personal past help convey social information to children, and children pick up on this information early in the process of learning to construct their own memories, during the preschool years.

IN CONCLUSION: THE IMPLICATIONS FOR WHAT CHILDREN REMEMBER

A number of studies have suggested that parent–child talk about events both during and after they occur affects not only children's reporting styles, but what children can actually recall. In striking research on this point, Tessler and Nelson (1994) tape-recorded dialogues between mothers and children walking together through a museum. During probing interviews one week later, children could only recall museum exhibits they had talked about with their mothers. Supporting these findings, Haden, Didow, Ornstein, and Eckerman (1997) interviewed preschool children about a series of planned events they had experienced with their parents. The children showed excellent recall of information that was discussed during the events, and poor recall of information that was not discussed.

Leichtman, Pillemer, Wang, Koreishi, & Han (2000) focused on post-event parent–child conversations using a sample of preschoolers. The children experienced a surprise event in their preschool classroom, during which a series of scripted activities occurred. On the same day, mothers interviewed their own children individually about the event. Mothers had not been present during the event and had no details about it; they were told to question their children in whatever way was natural to them. Three weeks later, children were interviewed by a researcher who had not been present during the event and who had no information about the content of the parent–child interviews. The researcher asked each child the same set of open-ended and direct questions about the event.

The results showed that children whose mothers conducted more elaborative interviews, and who in turn provided their mothers with richer answers, remembered more details regarding the event after the 3-week delay. For example, mother–child conversations influenced children's recall of the specific objects present during the event. Eighty-three percent of the items that children recalled during the researcher-child interview had also been discussed with their mothers. Thus, at least under some circumstances, talking about events with parents seems to directly affect the number and type of details that children are likely to remember.

A contextualist perspective on children's event memories makes clear that many aspects of the environment are likely to influence their event reports and actual autobiographical memories. Children absorb the rules and meanings of sharing memories that are particular to their own cultural environments, and these emerge across time in connection with other elements of the environment. Beliefs among adults about the self, the personal past, and the best way to raise children combine with other elements of children's physical and social contexts to shape how memory sharing takes place. For example, factors such as whether children typically co-sleep with their parents, whether they endure long daily separations from their parents, and the degree to which their relationships are hierarchical may all affect the normative characteristics of talking and thinking about the past (Pillemer, 1998; Leichtman, Wang & Pillemer, 2003).

Super & Harkness (2002) have introduced the concept of *chaining*, asserting that no one element of the environment is likely to produce a particular developmental outcome. Instead, a confluence of factors at various levels combines to produce a qualitatively new phenomenon. Although parent–child talk is a perceptible mode through which particular autobiographical styles are transmitted, it is likely that children's event memories themselves are directly influenced by many other elements of the societies in which they live (Wang, 2003). To complicate the picture, such contextual elements meet with the individual biologies and life experiences of each young child to determine what and how they remember personal events.

REFERENCES

Bartlett, F.C. (1932). *Remembering*. Cambridge, UK: Cambridge University Press.

Bochner, S. (1994). Cross-cultural differences in the self concept. *Journal of Cross-Cultural Psychology, 25*, 2, 273–283.

Bronfenbrenner, U. (1979). *The ecology of human development.* Cambridge, MA: Harvard University Press.
Ceci, S. J., & Leichtman, M. D. (1992). Memory, cognition and learning. In S. Segalowitz & I. Rapin (Eds.), *Handbook of neuropsychology* (pp. 223–240). Amsterdam: Elsevier.
Choi, S. H. (1992). Communicative socialization processes: Korea and Canada. In S. Iwasaki, Y. Kashima, & K. Leung (Eds.), *Innovations in cross-cultural psychology* (pp. 103–122). Amsterdam: Swets & Zeitlinger.
DeLoache, J., & Gottlieb, A. (2000). *A world of babies.* Cambridge: Cambridge University Press.
Ebbinghaus, H. (1885). *Memory: A contribution to experimental psychology* (H. A. Ruger & C. E. Bussenius, Trans). New York: Dover.
Fan, C. (1994). A comparative study of personality characteristics between only and nononly children in primary schools in Xian. *Psychological Science, 17,* 2, 70–74 (in Chinese).
Fiske, A. P. (2002). Using individualism and collectivism to compare cultures—A critique of the validity and measurement of the constructs: Comment on Oyserman et al. (2002). *Psychological Bulletin, 128,* 1, 78–88.
Fiske, A. P., Kitayama, S., Markus, H. R., & Nisbett, R. E. (1998). The cultural matrix of social psychology. In D. T. Gilbert, S. T. Fiske, & G. Lindzey (Eds.), *The handbook of social psychology* (pp. 915–981). New York, NY: McGraw-Hill.
Fivush, R., & Fromhoff, F. A. (1988). Style and structure in mother-child conversations about the past. *Discourse Processes, 11,* 337–355.
Freud, S. (1920/1953). *A general introduction to psychoanalysis.* New York: Simon & Schuster.
Greenwald, A. G., & Banaji, M. (1995). Implicit social cognition: Attitudes, self-esteem and stereotypes. *Psychological Review, 102,* 4–27.
Greenwald, A. G., & Pratkanis, A. R. (1984). The self. In R. S. Wyer & T. K. Srull (Eds.), Handbook of social cognition (vol. 3, pp. 129–178). Hillsdale, NJ: Lawrence Erlbaum Associates.
Haden, C. A., Haine, R. A., & Fivush, R. (1997). Developing narrative structure in parent-child reminiscing across the preschool years. *Developmental Psychology, 33,* 295–307.
Haden, C. A., Didow, S. M., Ornstein, P. A., & Eckerman, C. O. (1997, April). Mother-child talk about the here and now: Linkages to subsequent remembering. In E. Reese (Chair), *Adult-child talk about the past: Theory and Practice.* Symposium conducted at The Biennial Meeting of the Society for Research in Child Development, Washington, DC.
Han, J. J., Leichtman, M. D., & Wang, Q. (1998). Autobiographical memory in Korean, Chinese and American children. *Developmental Psychology, 34,* 4, 701–713.
Hayne, H., & McDonald, S. (2003). The socialization of autobiographical memory in children and adults: The roles of culture and gender. In R. Fivush & C. Haden (Eds.), *Autobiographical memory and the construction of a narrative self.* Mahwah, NJ: Lawrence Erlbaum Associates.
Howe, M. (2003). Memories from the cradle. *Current Directions in Psychological Science, 12,* 2, 62–65.
Jiao, S., Ji, G., & Jing, Q. (1986). Comparative study of behavior qualities of only children and sibling children. *Child Development, 57,* 357–361.
Kihlstrom, J. F., & Harackiewicz, J. M. (1982). The earliest recollection: A new survey. *Journal of Personality, 50,* 134–148.

Kuhn, M. H., & McPartland, T. S. (1954). An empirical investigation of self-attitudes. *American Sociological Review, 19,* 68–76.

Lee, L. C. (1992). Day care in the People's Republic of China. In M. E. Lamb & K. Sternberg (Eds.), *Child care in context: Cross cultural perspectives* (pp. 355–392). Hillsdale, NJ: Lawrence Erlbaum Associates.

Leichtman, M. D., Bhogle, S., Sankaranarayanan, A., & Hobeika, D. (2003). *Autobiographical memory and children's narrative environments in Southern India and the Northern United States.* Unpublished manuscript.

Leichtman, M. D., Pillemer, D. B., Wang, Q., Koreishi, A., & Han, J. J. (2000). When Baby Maisy came to school: Mother's interview styles and preschoolers' event memories. *Cognitive Development, 15,* 1–16.

Leichtman, M. D., Wang, Q., & Pillemer, D. B. (2003.) Cultural variations in interdependence and autobiographical memory: Lessons from Korea, China, India, and the United States. In R. Fivush & C. Haden (Eds.), *Autobiographical memory and the construction of a narrative self.* Mahwah, NJ: Lawrence Erlbaum Associates.

Markus, H. R., & Kitayama, S. (1991). Culture and the self: Implications for cognition, emotion & motivation. *Psychological Review, 98,* 2, 224–253.

Martin, J. (1993). Episodic memory: A neglected phenomenon in the psychology of education. *Educational Psychologist, 28,* 2, 169–183.

McCabe, A., & Peterson, C. (1991). Getting the story: A longitudinal study of parenting styles in eliciting narratives and developing narrative skill.

Miller, P. J., Wiley, A. R., Fung, H., & Liang, C. (1997). Personal storytelling as a medium of socialisation in Chinese and American families. *Child Development, 68,* 557–568.

Mullen, M. K. (1994). Earliest recollections of childhood: A demographic analysis. *Cognition, 52,* 1, 55–79.

Mullen, M. K., & Yi, S. (1995). The cultural context of talk about the past: Implications for the development of autobiographical memory. *Cognitive Development, 10,* 407–419.

Nelson, K. (1996). *Language in cognitive development: The emergence of the mediated mind.* New York: Cambridge University Press.

Nelson, K. (2003). Selfa nd social functions: Individual autobiographical memory and collective narrative. *Memory, 11,* 125–136.

Oyserman, D., Coon, H. M., & Kemmelmeier, M. (2002). Rethinking individualism and collectivism: Evaluation of theoretical assumptions and meta-analysis. *Psychological Bulletin, 128,* 3–72.

Pillemer, D. B. (1998). *Momentous events, vivid memories.* Cambridge, MA: Harvard University Press.

Pillemer, D. B., Rhinehart, E. D., & White, S. H. (1986). Memories of life transitions: The first year in college. *Human Learning, 5,* 109–123.

Pillemer, D. B., & White, S. H. (1989). Childhood events recalled by children and adults. In H. W. Reese (Ed.) *Advances in child development and behavior* (Vol. 21, pp. 297–340). Orlando, FL: Academic Press.

Reese, E., Haden, C., & Fivush, R. (1993). Mother-child conversations about the past: Relationships of style and memory over time. *Cognitive Development, 8,* 403–430.

Schacter, D. L. (1996). *Searching for memory: The brain, the mind and the past.* New York: Basic Books.

Super, C. M., & Harkness, S. (1986). The developmental niche: A conceptualization at the interface of child and culture. *International Journal of Behavioral Development, 9,* 545–569.

Super, C. M., & Harkness, S. (1999). The environment as culture in developmental research. In T. Wachs & S. Friedman (Eds.), *Measurement of the environment in developmental research* (pp. 279–323). Washington, DC: American Psychological Association.

Super, C. M., & Harkness, S. (2002). Culture structures the environment for development. *Human Development, 45,* 4, 270–274.

Tessler, M., & Nelson, K. (1994). Making memories: the influence of joint encoding on later recall by young children. *Consciousness and Cognition, 3,* 307–326.

Trafimow, D. Triandis, H. C., & Goto, S. G. (1991). Some tests of the distinction between private and collective self. *Journal of Personality and Social Psychology, 60,* 5, 649–655.

Triandis, H. C. (1989). The self and social behavior in differing cultural contexts. *Psychological Review, 96,* 506–520.

Usher, J. A,. & Neisser, U. (1993). Childhood amnesia and the beginnings of memory for four early life events. *Journal of Experimental Psychology: General, 122,* 155–165.

Wang, Q. (2001a). Cultural effects on adults' earliest childhood recollection and self-description: Implications for the relation between memory and the self. *Journal of Personality and Social Psychology, 81,* 2, 220–233.

Wang, Q. (2001b). "Did you have fun?": American and Chinese mother-child conversations about shared emotional experiences. *Cognitive Development, 16,* 693–715.

Wang, Q. (2003). Infantile amnesia reconsidered: A cross-cultural analysis. *Memory, 11,* 1, 65–80.

Wang, Q. (2004). The emergence of cultural self-constructs: Autobiographical memory and self-description in European American and Chinese children. *Developmental Psychology, 40,* 1, 3–15.

Wang, Q., & Brockmeier, J. (2002). Autobiographical remembering as cultural practice: Understanding the interplay between memory, self and culture. *Culture & Psychology, 8,* 45–64.

Wang, Q., Ceci, S. J., Williams, W. M., & Kopko, K. A. (in press). Culturally situated cognitive competence: A functional framework. In R. Sternberg (Ed.), *Culture and competence.*

Wang, Q., Conway, M. A., & Hou, Y. (2003). *Infantile amnesia and (cultural) self-construct: A cross-cultural investigation.* Manuscript submitted for publication.

Wang, Q., & Leichtman, M. D. (2000). Same Beginnings, different stories: A comparison of American and Chinese children's narratives. *Child Development, 71,* 5.

Wang, Q., Leichtman, M. D., & Davies, K. I. (2000). Sharing memories and telling stories: American and Chinese mothers and their 3-year-olds. *Memory, 8,* 3, 159–177.

Wang, Q., Leichtman, M. D., & White. S. H. (1998). Childhood memory and self-description: The impact of growing up an only child. *Cognition, 69,* 1, 73–103.

Wetzler, S. E., & Sweeney, J. A. (1986). Childhood amnesia: An empirical demonstration. In D. C. Rubin (Ed.), *Autobiographical memory* (pp. 191–221). New York: Cambridge University Press.

Wright, D. B., & Loftus, E. F. (1998). How misinformation alters memories. *Journal of Experimental Child Psychology, 71,* 155–164.

Author Index

Note: Page numbers followed by *f* indicate a figure; *n* indicates a note; *t* indicates a table.

C

D

E

F

G

H

I

J

K

N

O

S

X

Y

Z

Subject Index

Note: Page numbers followed by *f* indicate a figure; *n* indicates a note; *t* indicates a table.

D

E